Empirical Knowledge

EMPIRICAL KNOWLEDGE

Readings in
Contemporary Epistemology

EDITED BY
PAUL K. MOSER
Loyola University of Chicago

Rowman & Littlefield Publishers, Inc.

Rowman & Littlefield Publishers, Inc.

Published in the United States of America in 1986
by Rowman & Littlefield, Publishers
(a division of Littlefield, Adams & Company)

Reprinted in 1989 by Rowman & Littlefield Publishers, Inc.

Copyright © 1986 by Rowman & Littlefield

Library of Congress Cataloging-in-Publication Data

Moser, Paul K., 1957–
  Empirical knowledge.

  Bibliography: p. 271
  Includes index.
    1. Knowledge, theory of—Addresses, essays,
lectures. 2. Empiricism—Addresses, essays, lectures.
3. Justification (Theory of knowledge)—Addresses,
essays, lectures. I. Title.
  BD161.M845   1986   121   86-3197
  ISBN 0-8476-7492-4
  ISBN 0-8476-7493-2 (pbk.)

Printed in the United States of America

Contents

Preface

This book makes available some of the most important contemporary essays on the nature of empirical knowledge and provides a comprehensive and nontechnical overview of the central issues of contemporary epistemology. Part I contains ten substantial essays focusing on the justification-condition for empirical knowledge, while Part II contains five essays concerned with what has come to be called "the Gettier Problem," the problem of identifying the logically sufficient conditions for one's having empirical knowledge.

All the essays in this book are accessible, at least for the most part, to middle- and upper-level undergraduate philosophy students. (None of the essays will be incomprehensible because of elaborate symbolism or logical notation.) Yet each essay is sufficiently substantial to be beneficial reading for graduate-level philosophy students also. The introduction draws some general distinctions of central importance to the theory of empirical knowledge and summarizes the major themes of the following essays; it thus can serve as a beginning orientation for students who are not specialists in epistemology. The concluding bibliography lists in topical arrangement, many of the most important contemporary books and articles on empirical knowledge. It also contains complete data for the incomplete references in the essays.

With much appreciation, I want to thank William Alston for very helpful comments on the initial proposal for this book, and Richard Baluck for indispensable assistance in the preparation of the book's manuscript. Also I would like to thank Janet Johnston for her thorough copyediting of the book.

Paul K. Moser
Chicago, Illinois

INTRODUCTION

Empirical Knowledge

PAUL K. MOSER

I. Some Preliminary Distinctions

Contemporary philosophers working on the analysis of empirical knowledge, or what may be called "perceptual knowledge," have been motivated largely by a single question: What is empirical knowledge? Typically, an answer to this question sets forth logically necessary and sufficient conditions for empirical knowledge, i.e., conditions that are required by and are adequate for a person's having empirical knowledge. For instance, an answer called "the traditional analysis of empirical knowledge" claims that a person has empirical knowledge of a proposition, p, if and only if that person has empirically justified true belief that p. This analysis is suggested in the writings of Locke, Hume, Kant, and Russell, but is nowadays in disrepute because of counterexamples like Edmund Gettier's presented in Chapter 11. Specifically, Gettier-style counterexamples are now widely received as having shown that empirically justified true belief is insufficient for empirical knowledge; that something more is needed. Yet philosophers still commonly assume that empirically justified true belief is necessary for empirical knowledge. Unfortunately, as Chapters 12–15 indicate, philosophers are nowhere near agreement on the logically sufficient conditions of empirical knowledge.[1]

The major question occupying contemporary epistemologists concerns the nature of the justification condition for empirical knowledge. Specifically, the question is: What are the necessary and sufficient conditions for empirical justification, the kind of justification appropriate to empirical knowledge? Chapters 1–10 of this book are largely concerned with this basic question. Chapters 11–15 also bear on the question, but their main focus is, in light of Gettier-style counterexamples, on the logically sufficient conditions of empirical knowledge. It should be emphasized that the relevant kind of empirical justification is *epistemic* justification, the kind of justification appropriate to knowledge. There are other kinds of justification, such as prudential justification, but it is epistemic justification that is distinctively related to knowledge, specifically the truth condition of knowledge. One straightforward way to portray this relation is to specify that a belief is epistemically justified for a person only if that belief is more likely to be true, on that person's total evidence, than is the denial of that belief. (The notion of likelihood presupposed by this requirement can be understood in a number of ways, but we can safely overlook this matter for present purposes.)[2] We can proceed now with the notion of likelihood as *confirmation*. Thus, if a proposition, *p*, is more likely to be true than its denial, not-*p*, then the truth of *p* is more confirmed than the truth of not-*p*. The issue of just what provides confirming grounds for the truth of an empirical proposition is one of the major topics of dispute in the following chapters.

Let us keep in mind a general distinction between two kinds of epistemic justification: *propositional* justification and *doxastic* justification.[3] Propositional justification obtains when a person's total evidence makes a proposition likely to be true (i.e., more likely to be true than its denial) on that person's total evidence (even if the person in question does not believe that proposition or believes it for the wrong reason). Doxastic justification obtains when a proposition has propositional justification for a person, and when that person believes that proposition *on the basis of* the justifying evidence. Thus, doxastic justification requires that one's justified belief be "appropriately related" to one's evidence. The relevant basing relation between belief and evidence provides a topic of controversy for contemporary epistemologists and so is discussed in some of the following essays (e.g., Chapters 1 and 7). One key question is whether the basing relation can be analyzed as a causal relation. Also, some philosophers have suggested that if one's belief that *p* is based on evidence, *e*, then if one were to try to justify (i.e., provide a justificatory argument for) the belief that *p*, one would invoke *e* as support for *p*.[4] Perhaps this subjunctive conditional will be part of a plausible analysis of the basing relation, but we should not be led to think that one's *having* justified belief requires one's *showing* that one has justified belief. One's showing that one has justified belief requires that arguments be set forth in support of a belief, but it is doubtful that one's merely having justified belief requires this. Let us then avoid any confusion between the having and the showing of justification.

A particular question about empirical justification recurs throughout this book: Does empirical knowledge have foundations and, if so, in what sense? Many philosophers have construed this question as asking whether empirical knowledge is based on beliefs that are indubitable (not subject to doubt), incorrigible (not subject to falsity), or irrevisable (not subject to revision). But this construal will involve only one species of the view that knowledge has foundations: so-called *radical* foundationalism. Radical foundationalism is endorsed in Descartes's *Meditations* and is developed at length in C. I. Lewis's *An Analysis of Knowledge and Valuation*, but no longer meets with much favor.[5] For, first, it is highly questionable whether any of our empirical beliefs enjoys the immunity of indubitability, incorrigibility, or irrevisability; and second, whatever beliefs qualify as candidates for having such immunities evidently fail to be sufficiently informative to provide foundations for our knowledge of physical objects. For instance, perhaps my belief that I am now thinking is a candidate for having one or more of the above immunities, but it is not clear how such a minimal belief can support my present belief that there is a blue book on the desk before me.

A less controversial way to construe the question about foundations is to ask whether our empirical knowledge depends ultimately on *noninferentially*, or *immediately*, justified beliefs, i.e., justified beliefs whose justification does not depend on the justification of further beliefs. A "yes" answer to this question commits one at most to what is called *modest foundationalism*, the view that empirical knowledge rests on foundational beliefs that need not be indubitable, incorrigible, or irrevisable, but need only have sufficient noninferential justification to satisfy the justification condition for knowledge. At least three sorts of noninferential justification are available to modest foundationalism: (a) self-justification, (b) justification via nonbelief experiences, and (c) justification due to the reliable origin of a belief. According to proponents of self-justification, such as R. M. Chisholm, foundational beliefs justify themselves, with no evidential support from anything (see Chapter 2 below). According to proponents of noninferential justification via nonbelief experiences, foundational beliefs are justified by means of sensory and perceptual experiences that make those beliefs true, such as one's feeling pain or one's seeming to see a blue book.[6] And according to proponents of noninferential justification via reliable origins, foundational beliefs are noninferentially justified due to their being reliably produced by truth-conducive mechanisms or processes, such as memory and perception.[7] Roughly speaking, a belief-producing mechanism is reliable, or truth-conducive, only if it tends to produce more true beliefs than false beliefs in the relevant situations. (The issue of what situations are "relevant" is disputed by proponents.) This latter view bases noninferential justification on the *reliability* of a belief's causal origin; the previous view appeals not to reliability, but to particular sensory and perceptual experiences that make the beliefs in question true. (See Chapters 7 and 8 for discussion of the relevant notion of reliability.) Despite the diversity of views here, proponents of modest foundationalism usually agree that noninferential justification is *defeasible*, that is, can be defeated or overridden, by an expansion of one's set of justified beliefs. One simple instance of such defeasibility is the case where one's justification for the belief that there is a blue book on the table is overridden by the introduction of new evidence that there is a blue light shining on the book.

Given the disagreements over the exact character of noninferential justification, we should state the minimal foundational thesis as a claim about the *structure* of justification. Let us say that minimal foundationalism is the view that empirical knowledge requires noninferentially justified beliefs that provide the justification for all justified beliefs not among the foundations of knowledge. On this view knowledge has a two-tier structure, which consists of the set of basic, foundational beliefs and the set of nonbasic, nonfoundational beliefs. The rejection of such a two-tier structure entails the rejection of epistemic foundationalism.

Traditionally, the motivation for epistemic foundationalism has been provided by a regress argument found in embryonic form in Aristotle's *Posterior Analytics*. (Compare Chapters 3 and 4 below.) The argument purports to show that inferential justification, i.e., one belief's being justified by means of another belief, must come to an end with a belief (or set of beliefs) whose justification does not depend on the justification of some other belief. Before considering the alternatives to this view, we should be clear about what inferential justification is. Suppose that while walking along the lake I decide that although a swim would be very enjoyable, the present dangers of swimming are too great. My belief that swimming is dangerous is justified for me because it is supported by other justified beliefs of mine. For instance, I am justified in believing that (a) the local meteorologists have predicted heavy lightning for today, (b) there are cumulonimbus clouds in the sky, and (c) the reports of the meteorologists and the presence of cumulonimbus clouds are reliable signs of impending lightning. It is therefore plausible to suppose that my belief that swimming is dangerous today is inferentially justified for me by means of my beliefs (a), (b), and (c). But what justifies (a), (b), and (c)? Presumably other beliefs of mine will play a central role in this justification, and so the justification in question will be inferential insofar as it will be due to connections between beliefs. For instance, part of my justification for (a) might be my justified belief that (d) I heard a radio report from the local meteorologists. And part of my inferential justification for (b) might be my justified belief that (e) I see dark, foreboding thunderclouds in the sky. Further, the justification of (d) and (e) might be similarly inferential and so depend on the justification of further justified beliefs of mine. But according to foundationalism, such a regress of inferential justification cannot continue indefinitely, but must terminate in noninferentially justified beliefs of some sort. These terminal beliefs are among the foundations of justification.

Yet we should also be clear about the three available alternatives to the foundational view of inferential justification, for the regress argument in question proceeds by eliminating those alternatives. The first alternative proposes that regresses of inferential justification are infinite, that they extend endlessly. Thus, on this view, my belief that swimming is dangerous today would be justified by belief (a) above, belief (a) would be justified by belief (d) above, belief (d) would be justified by a further belief, and so on ad infinitum. This view, which may be called *epistemic infinitism,* has had few proponents but receives some support from Charles Peirce, the founder of pragmatism.[8] To be clear about infinitism, we should notice that it does not require that one *set forth* an infinite number of justifying beliefs in order to have a justified belief. But the view does seem to require that one *have* an infinity of justifying beliefs, for lacking such an infinity, one will also lack the required justification for an inferentially justified belief. For a similar reason, it seems inadequate, given infinitism, for one to be merely *disposed to believe* an infinite number of supporting propositions.

The second alternative to foundationalism proposes that all beliefs are justified by means of other justified beliefs, but that inferential justification is not linear in the manner suggested by the idea of infinite, or endless, regresses of justification. On this view, which may be called *epistemic coherentism,* all justification is in a sense inferential, since all justification derives from what are called "coherence relations" among beliefs. Proponents of coherentism do not share a uniform account of the relevant coherence relations. But there are three prominent notions of coherence in circulation: coherence as logical consistency, coherence as logical implication, and coherence as explanation.[9] According to the notion of coherence as logical consistency, two beliefs are coherent, or cohere, with each other, if and only if it is logically possible that both of those beliefs are true. According to the notion of coherence as logical implication, two beliefs are coherent if and only if the truth of one logically guarantees the truth of the other. And according to the notion of coherence as explanation, two beliefs are coherent if one explains (the truth or the falsity of) the other. But whatever notion of coherence is preferred, one of the central themes of coherentism is that empirical knowledge does not have a two-tier structure but is essentially non-axiomatic in its systematic, network-like structure. Thus, on this view, empirical knowledge does not have noninferentially justified foundations.

The third alternative to foundationalism, which may be called *epistemic contextualism,* proposes that inferential justification terminates ultimately in beliefs not in need of any justification. These latter beliefs are said to be "contextually basic" insofar as in some context or other they serve as justifying reasons for other beliefs, but do not find evidential support from anything, including themselves. Some proponents of contextualism hold that a belief qualifies as contextually basic as long as one's peers allow one to hold the belief without any reasons. But the main emphasis of contextualism is that empirical knowledge requires unjustified basic beliefs that themselves need no evidential support of any kind, and that contextually basic basic beliefs can vary from context to context.[10] Thus, while contextualism, like foundationalism, endorses a two-tier structure of knowledge, contextualism clearly differs from foundationalism insofar as it does not require that the foundations of knowledge be justified in any of the ways suggested above.

The eliminative regress argument for foundationalism typically proceeds as follows: First, epistemic infinitism must be rejected, because no matter how far back we go in an infinite regress of inferential justification, we find beliefs that are justified only inferentially, i.e., justified on the basis of some further belief(s). But this means that no beliefs in such a regress are actually justified; at most they are *conditionally* justified, justified *if* their predecessors are. Yet the predecessors themselves are, similarly, at most conditionally justified and not actually justified. The main problem with this first step of the argument is that it appears to *assume* that actual inferential justification depends on noninferential justification. But this assumption is the purported *conclusion* of the regress argument, so it cannot be used as a premise. The foundationalist, therefore, needs to explain how the regress argument can avoid the threatening circularity. Notice that it might be argued that human empirical knowledge cannot depend on infinite regresses of justification, because our having an infinity of justifying beliefs would take an infinite amount of time, and we mortals, of course, do not exist for an infinite amount of time. But two points should be emphasized about such an argument. First, it is not obvious that our having an infinite number of justifying beliefs would take an infinite amount of time; and, second, even if such an argument based on temporal considerations were sound, we would not be able to infer the *conceptual* impossibility of infinite regresses of justification, for at most such an argument would show that infinite regresses of justification are unavailable *to humans*.[11]

The second step of the traditional regress argument for foundationalism opposes coherentism by stating that coherentism either commits one to circular justification or divorces justification from the empirical world. On one very simplistic version of coherentism, we have the claim that part of the inferential justification for my belief that swimming is dangerous today is this belief itself. The idea here, roughly, is that this belief is supported by another belief—call it B1—which, in turn, is supported by another belief, B2, which is supported by a still further belief, B3; but B3 is supported by my original belief that swimming is dangerous today. Inferential justification thus forms a circle. And if we assume that justification is transitive through coherence relations, we are left with the controversial view that a belief can justify itself. But the prominent contemporary versions of epistemic coherentism deny that justification is transitive and reject the above simplistic linear conception of inferential justification. Thus, they are not committed either to self-justification or to straightforward circular justification. (See Chapters 5 and 12 below.) But the second objection to coherentism, which may be called *the isolation objection,* is more serious. The challenge here is for the proponent of coherentism to explain how coherence relations among beliefs can provide a high probability of truth, or a reliable indication of how things are in the empirical world. And we can apply this challenge to the above notions of coherence by asking why one should think that merely the belief-relations of either logical consistency, logical implication, or explanation indicate that the relevant beliefs are likely to be true. Given any of those prominent notions of coherence, we apparently can imagine any number of extremely coherent belief-systems that consist of *obviously* false beliefs. (This isolation objection to coherentism is discussed below in Chapters 5 and 6.)

The third step of the regress argument objects to epistemic contextualism, the view that inferential justification terminates in unjustified contextually basic beliefs that are not in need of any justification. The challenge for the contextualist is to explain how a belief that is itself unjustified can provide justification for other beliefs. Surely not just *any* unjustified belief can terminate a regress of inferential justification; and it is not clear how a belief can derive any epistemic support, or any likelihood, from the simple fact that one's peers allow one to hold that belief with no supporting reasons. In any case, the contextualist owes us an explanation of how contextualism can avoid the implausible implication that just any belief, including self-contradictory beliefs, can be justified for a person. To put the objection differently, the contextualist needs to explain how contextual justification preserves the distinctive relationship between epistemic justification and the truth condition for knowledge, how contextual justification guarantees the likely truth of a belief. (In Chapter 9, David Annis discusses this type of worry.)

It might seem that if the foundationalist could substantiate the three above-mentioned steps of the eliminative regress argument, epistemic foundationalism then could be justified. But more argument, of course, is needed before we can conclude that we possess empirical knowledge based on noninferentially justified foundations. For the latter conclusion presupposes that a skeptical account of inferential justification has been eliminated. According to such skepticism, we are not inferentially justified in believing anything, whether by foundational beliefs, infinite regresses, coherence relations, or contextually basic beliefs.[12] But nothing in the above regress argument counts against skepticism concerning inferential justification. Furthermore, we cannot reasonably infer that foundationalism is justified just because the alternative accounts for inferential justification have serious defects. For foundationalism may have equally serious defects and thus may be on a par with its troubled, nonskeptical competitors.

Let us consider, in this connection, two serious problems facing a foundationalist account of inferential justification: a problem concerning the nature of noninferential justification, and a problem concerning inferential justification via foundational beliefs. The first problem is sketched in some epistemological writings by Wilfrid Sellars and receives a clear formulation in Chapter 4, below, by Bonjour.[13] The problem is illustrated in what may be called an *epistemic ascent argument* against foundationalism. According to this argument, one cannot be *noninferentially* justified in holding any beliefs, since one is epistemically justified in holding a belief only if one has good reason to think the belief is true. But according to the present argument, this means that the justification of a foundational belief will depend on an argument such as the following:

(I)   (a)   My foundational belief that *p* has feature *F*.
       (b)   Beliefs having feature *F* are likely to be true.
       (c)   Hence, my foundational belief that *p* is likely to be true.

Yet if the justification of one's foundational beliefs depends on such an argument, those beliefs will not be foundational after all: their justification will depend on the justification of further beliefs, viz., the beliefs represented by the premises of argument (I).

Some foundationalists reply that although the justification of the noninferentially justified belief that *p* requires the truth of the premises of (I), that justification does not depend on one's justified belief that those premises are true. Those premises need only *be* true. The foundationalists in question endorse, at least in the case of noninferential justification, what is called *epistemic externalism*—the view that one need not have any cognitive awareness of the justifying conditions of one's justified beliefs. On this view, those justifying conditions can be quite external to anything one is aware of. (Such externalism is criticized by Bonjour in Chapter 4.)[14] One of the major problems with externalism is that it conflicts with what appears to be the primary sense of "justified belief," according to which if one is justified in believing a proposition, *p*, then one has cognitive possession, in some sense, of justifying evidence for *p*, and one is capable of invoking that evidence in support of *p*. Given externalism, one can be justified in believing that *p*, even though one is incapable of adducing (even to oneself) any evidence in support of the truth of *p* against skeptical doubts. But this implication of externalism seems to neglect the connection between justified belief and probable truth *from an individual believer's perspective*.

The simplest alternative to externalism is also troublesome, insofar as it commits us to endless regresses of required justified beliefs. Consider the straightforward view that the required cognitive possession of one's justifying evidence is *justified belief*. (Such a view is at least suggested in Chapter 4 below by Bonjour.) On this view, a person will be justified in believing a proposition, *p*, only if his belief that *p* has a truth-conducive feature, *F*, and he is justified in believing that his belief that *p* has *F*. But, given this requirement, the person in question will be justified in believing that (i) his belief that *p* has *F* only if he is justified in believing a further proposition, viz. (ii) his belief that (i) has *F*. And there evidently is no nonarbitrary way to avoid the troublesome implication that a similar requirement applies not only to this latter proposition, viz. (ii), but also to the ensuing infinity of required justified beliefs. Since it is quite doubtful that any of us has an infinity of justified beliefs, we should be most hesitant to endorse the present alternative to epistemic externalism.

What the proponent of foundationalism apparently needs, then, is an alternative both to externalism and to the above simple reaction to externalism. Lacking such an alternative, the foundationalist either will be open to the objection that he has divorced justification from its distinctive relation to the truth condition for knowledge, or will be hard put to avoid the threat of an infinite regress of required justified beliefs. This dilemma illustrates the first major problem facing foundationalism.

The second major problem facing foundationalism concerns those versions of foundationalism that restrict noninferential justification to sensory and perceptual beliefs about what one *seems* to see, hear, feel, smell, and taste. The problem for those versions is to explain how such subjective beliefs can provide justification for beliefs about physical objects like chairs, tables, and cars. It is clear that those subjective beliefs do not logically entail the truth of any physical-object beliefs. Given the ever-present possibility of extensive hallucination, it will always be possible that one's subjective beliefs are true while the relevant physical-object beliefs are false. This possibility undercuts the strategy of those foundationalists who endorse a version of the phenomenalism made famous by the writings of A. J. Ayer.[15] Perhaps the foundationalist could appeal to a set of nondeductive principles to explain how physical-object beliefs can be justified on the basis of subjective beliefs.[16] But this remains as a challenge for the foundationalist, since no attempt at such an appeal has met with widespread acceptance. And until the foundationalist can meet the present challenge, foundationalism of the sort under consideration cannot be superior to the forementioned alternatives to foundationalism. Yet it should be noted that some versions of foundationalism do allow for the noninferential justification of physical-object beliefs, and so do not face quite the same problem mentioned here.

Still the general point remains: until the foundationalist can show his account of justification to be superior to the nonfoundationalist alternatives, he cannot use the traditional eliminative regress argument to justify foundationalism. At most, the regress argument indicates the defects of the straightforward alternatives to foundationalism; it does not show that foundationalism is the superior theory of epistemic empirical justification.

The majority of the following chapters bear, at least indirectly, on the issue of whether, and if so in what sense, empirical knowledge actually has foundations.

II. A Summary of the Essays

In Chapter 1 William Alston provides an original critical overview of current prominent notions of epistemic justification. While drawing numerous important distinctions concerning concepts of epistemic justification, Alston distinguishes in general between a deontological and a nondeontological evaluative notion of justification. According to the deontological notion, one is justified in believing a proposition, *p*, if and only if no intellectual obligations concerning belief-formation or belief-sustenance are violated in one's believing that *p*. According to the nondeontological evaluative notion, one is justified in believing a proposition, *p*, if and only if one's believing that *p*, as one now does, is a good thing from the epistemic point of view. This latter notion presupposes that there is a way of being good from the epistemic point of view that is not identical to one's being blameless regarding the violation of an intellectual obligation. Alston defines the epistemic point of view in terms of the aim to maximize truth and minimize falsity. Further, he proposes that goodness relative to this aim is to be understood as a belief's being true *as far as the believer can tell from what is available to him*. Such epistemic goodness thus requires *adequate evidence* for a belief, where adequate evidence is warrant that is sufficiently indicative of the truth of the belief in question. Alston elaborates on this notion and argues that this notion, and not the former deontological notion, is essential to our concept of empirical knowledge.

In Chapter 2 Roderick Chisholm presents an account of his influential foundationalist version of empirical knowledge. He begins by clarifying the controversial doctrine of the "epistemological given" as a thesis about the two-tier structure of knowledge and about the self-justifying foundations of knowledge. Further, Chisholm uses an eliminative regress argument to support the claim that empirical knowledge has self-justified foundations. But he opposes the view that our empirical knowledge is an edifice supported by sense-impressions alone; he argues that we need to recognize the central role of certain "rules of evidence" in the derivation of empirical knowledge.

In Chapter 3 William Alston presents the doctrine of epistemic foundationalism and draws an important distinction between simple and iterative foundationalism. Simple foundationalism is the view that for any person who has knowledge there are some beliefs which that person is immediately justified in holding, i.e., beliefs which are justified for that person,

I need to answer this ,

but which are justified by something other than their relation to other justified beliefs. Iterative foundationalism, in contrast, is the view that for any person who has knowledge there are some beliefs which that person is immediately justified in holding, and that person is immediately justified in believing that he is immediately justified in holding those beliefs. Alston lays out the traditional regress argument for foundationalism, and he argues that this argument *at most* supports simple foundationalism and does not support iterative foundationalism. In addition, Alston raises doubts about the defensibility of iterative foundationalism and about the sort of regress argument employed in the previous chapter by Chisholm.

In Chapter 4 Laurence Bonjour sets forth what is perhaps the most threatening available challenge to foundationalism. The gist of the argument is that foundationalist accounts of empirical knowledge, such as those discussed in the previous chapters by Chisholm and Alston, face a serious dilemma: they commit one either to an implausible sort of "epistemic externalism" (like that mentioned above) or to a dubious doctrine of "the given." Bonjour argues forcefully against both epistemic externalism and the relevant doctrine of the given. In light of the forementioned dilemma, Bonjour concludes further that foundationalism provides at best an ad hoc evasion of the epistemic regress problem, the problem of explaining the nature of inferential justification. If Bonjour's argument is sound, the traditional regress argument, as characterized above, is incapable of justifying epistemic foundationalism.

In Chapter 5 Bonjour develops and defends a coherentist alternative to foundationalism. Specifically, he defends the coherence theory of empirical knowledge against its biggest threat: the isolation objection. His major aim is to show how the coherence theory of empirical knowledge can provide a significant epistemic role for observation. Bonjour takes this aim to be equivalent to the task of showing how coherentism can afford a central epistemic role to "cognitively spontaneous" observation beliefs, i.e., beliefs about the perceptual world that have a noninferential, spontaneous origin. But Bonjour emphasizes that an account of *empirical* knowledge must not merely allow, but *require* observational input from the perceptual world into one's belief-system. Consequently, he finds that the coherence theory of empirical knowledge is committed to the following *observation requirement:* for a belief-system to be a candidate for the status of empirical knowledge, it must include laws attributing high reliability to a variety of kinds of cognitively spontaneous beliefs. As Bonjour sees it, coherentism is committed to this requirement as an *a priori* truth. Further, Bonjour argues that the observation requirement enables coherentism to avoid the notorious isolation objection.

In Chapter 6 Ernest Sosa sums up clearly the key differences between foundationalist and coherentist approaches to empirical knowledge and argues that neither foundationalism nor coherentism is ultimately adequate. Furthermore, he takes issue with the sort of antifoundationalist dilemma proposed by Bonjour in Chapter 4, and with the traditional regress argument for foundationalism that aims to rule out the very possibility of infinite regresses of justification. On the constructive side, Sosa distinguishes between formal and substantive foundationalism and proposes a novel "intellectual virtues" approach to empirical knowledge. In general, formal foundationalism with respect to a normative feature like justification is the view that the conditions under which that feature obtains can be specified in a general way. Substantive foundationalism is simply the above-described alternative to coherentism that is committed to noninferential justification and the two-tier structure of empirical knowledge. But both substantive foundationalism and coherentism are species of formal foundationalism. According to Sosa's alternative to substantive foundationalism and coherentism, primary justification applies to "intellectual virtues," which are dispositions for belief-acquisition that contribute toward our acquiring truth; and secondary justification applies to particular beliefs that have their origins in intellectual virtues. Such a view has definite affinities to the reliabilism found in Chapter 7.

In Chapter 7 Alvin Goldman develops an account of empirical justification in terms of causal-reliability factors. The basis of this account is the idea that the justificational status of a belief is a function of the reliability of the process that causes it, where reliability consists in a process's tendency to produce beliefs that are true rather than false. Goldman calls his account *Historical Reliabilism* and contrasts it with *Current Time-Slice* theories of justification. According to Current Time-Slice theories, the justificational status of a belief is a function of what is true of a believer at the time of the belief. But according to an historical theory, the justificational status of a belief is a function of the belief's prior causal history. Goldman's historical theory emphasizes the reliability of the relevant belief-producing processes. Further, since standard foundationalist and coherentist theories are Current Time-Slice theories, Goldman's reliabilism differs significantly from these theories. In conclusion Goldman relates his historical reliabilism to the topic of epistemic externalism and to the above-mentioned distinction between propositional and doxastic justification.

In Chapter 8 John Pollock forcefully attacks the sort of epistemic reliabilism endorsed by Goldman in Chapter 7. One of Pollock's anti-reliabilist arguments is that since the notion of justification is normative, reliability cannot play any direct role in justification. Pollock holds that reliability cannot be a necessary condition for epistemic justification, because one can have overwhelming reasons to hold that one's beliefs are reliable when actually they are not. And he holds that reliability cannot be a sufficient condition for epistemic justification, because of the cases in which, although one's beliefs arise from a reliable process, one has no right to take those beliefs to be true. In addition, Pollock argues that reliabilism neglects the essential role of reasoning in justified belief and that it presupposes a troublesome notion of single-case probability. Finally, Pollock concludes by proposing that the connection between justification and reliability is to be found in the fact that justification is undercut by defeaters, which are reasons for thinking that our prima facie (i.e., defeasible) justifying reasons are unreliable.

In Essay 9 David Annis develops a theory of justification that purports to differ from foundationalism, coherentism, and reliabilism. The theory emphasizes the pragmatic and social (i.e., contextual) factors in the acquisition of empirical knowledge. Specifically, Annis bases his contextualism on the notions of an *issue-context* and an appropriate *objector-group*. The issue-context concerning a belief is merely the specific issue someone raises about the belief; and the appropriate objector-group is simply the group of people qualified to raise objections about the belief. According to Annis, a belief is *contextually basic* for a person at a particular time, relative to an appropriate objector-group, if and only if at that time the objector-group does not require the person in question to have any reasons for the belief. But if some member of the objector-group raises an objection to a belief, one will have to provide an appropriate response to support the belief. And given such a reason, the belief in question will not be contextually basic. On Annis's contextualism, however, a belief is epistemically justified if and only if it is itself contextually basic or is supported by reasons that are contextually basic beliefs. One of the key implications of Annis's account is that epistemology must be *naturalized;* for given contextualism, we cannot neglect the *actual* social practices and standards of justification of a group of inquirers.

In Chapter 10 W. V. Quine provides additional support for the proposal to naturalize epistemology. Basically, Quine's argument is that since we cannot justify our knowledge-claims in any foundational way, we should give up traditional epistemology and settle for empirical psychology instead. The argument relies on considerations germane to Quine's notorious argument for the so-called "indeterminacy of translation." Quine maintains that a belief about the empirical world does not typically have a separable set of empirical consequences peculiar to it. But if this is so, we will not be able to provide, in the spirit of Rudolf Carnap and some other earlier foundationalists, a reduction of the sort where every justified belief is equated with a set of beliefs whose members are constituted by observational and logical terms. As Quine sees it, the impossibility of such a reduction removes the major advantage that traditional foundationalist epistemology appeared to have over empirical psychology. In conclusion, Quine provides an account of observation sentences which aims to avoid the "epistemological nihilism" suggested, for instance, in the writings of Michael Polanyi, Thomas Kuhn, and N. R. Hanson.

In Chapter 11 Edmund Gettier presents two widely discussed counterexamples to the traditional analysis of knowledge, specifically to the thesis that justified true belief is sufficient for one's having knowledge. Although Gettier does not defend a way to block the counterexamples, over the past twenty years his essay has generated a highly diversified literature on the conditions for knowing. (A comprehensive critical survey of this literature can be found in Robert Shope, *The Analysis of Knowing*.) Shope has provided the following useful abstract description of Gettier-style counterexamples:

(G) In a Gettier-style counterexample concerning a person, *S*, and a proposition, *p:*
   (a) the truth condition holds regarding *p;*
   (b) the belief condition holds regarding *p;*
   (c) the justification condition holds regarding *p;*
   (d) some proposition, *q*, is false;
   (e) either the justification condition holds regarding *q* or at least *S* would be justified in believing *q;*
   (f) *S* does not know *p*.

The notorious Gettier problem is simply the problem of finding an alternative to, or modification of, the traditional justified-true-belief analysis that avoids counterexamples of form (G). Chapters 12–15 provide several nontechnical samples of the proposed solutions.[17]

In Chapter 12 Gilbert Harman provides a straightforward attempt to undercut Gettier's counterexamples to the traditional analysis of knowledge. The following principle is central to Harman's attempt:

(P) Reasoning that essentially involves false conclusions, whether intermediate or final, cannot give one knowledge.

Although some of the examples in Chapter 15 raise problems for Harman's reliance on (P), Harman argues persuasively that (P) enables us to account for some Gettier-style counterexamples. In addition, Harman argues that we must recognize the prominence of the role of "inference to the best explanation" in empirical knowledge. Yet it should be emphasized that Harman's main aim is not to defend the traditional analysis of knowledge, but is rather to examine our notion of knowledge in order to learn about reasoning and justification.

In Chapter 13 Roderick Chisholm provides an introduction to, diagnosis of, and straightforward solution for the Gettier problem. Chisholm's solution relies on the notion of "nondefective evidence," evidence which does not rest on basic propositions that justify a false proposition.

Chisholm's main proposal is that we can undercut Gettier-style counterexamples by construing knowledge as nondefectively justified true belief.

In Chapter 14 Richard Feldman argues that, contrary to some philosophers, we cannot take Gettier-style counterexamples to be defective on the ground that they rely on the false principle that false propositions can justify one's belief in other propositions. Feldman shows that there are examples much like Gettier's that do not depend on this allegedly false principle. In doing so, Feldman sets forth one of the most difficult Gettier-style counterexamples. An important question is whether the proposals of Chapters 12 and 13 can handle counterexamples such as Feldman's.

In Essay 15 Robert Shope concisely assesses a prominent controversy over Gettier-style counterexamples by focusing on the issue whether those examples are vitiated because of the way in which they ascribe false beliefs to a knower. Shope argues that what is crucial to avoiding Gettier-style counterexamples is the issue whether falsehoods play certain roles in relation to a person's justification for his beliefs. He characterizes these roles by relating them to justification-explanations of the person's justified beliefs and of various justified unaccepted propositions relevant to the person's situation. Roughly speaking, a justification-explanation is a set of propositions explaining why some other proposition is justified. In Gettier-style counterexamples, according to Shope, some justification-explanations contain false propositions; and in cases of factual knowledge, one's belief must be justified through its connection with a sequence of justification-explanations that do not involve falsehoods. Shope calls a sequence of justification-explanations a *justification-explaining chain,* and he holds that the members of such a chain must themselves be justified. Shope's proposed solution to the Gettier-problem is arguably one of the most promising available.

The concluding bibliography focuses on twentieth-century works on empirical knowledge.

Notes

1. The best evidence for this observation is provided in Robert Shope, *The Analysis of Knowing.* (All shortened references appear in full in the bibliography at the end of the book.)

2. For a nice overview of some prominent notions of likelihood, see Henry E. Kyburg, *Probability and Inductive Logic* (New York: Macmillan, 1970); and Kyburg, "Epistemological Probability," in *Epistemology and Inference* (Minneapolis: University of Minnesota Press, 1983), pp. 204–16.

3. Here I borrow the terminology from Roderick Firth, "Are Epistemic Concepts Reducible to Ethical Concepts?" in *Values and Morals,* ed. A. I. Goldman and J. Kim (Dordrecht: D. Reidel, 1978), pp. 217–18. See also Chapter 7 below.

4. There is some helpful discussion of the basing relation in George S. Pappas, "Basing Relations," in *Justification and Knowledge*, pp. 51–63. See also Robert Audi, "The Causal Structure of Indirect Justification," *The Journal of Philosophy* 80 (1983): 398–415. For an important discussion of subjunctive conditionals, which bears on an analysis of the basing relation, see Robert Shope, "The Conditional Fallacy in Contemporary Philosophy," *The Journal of Philosophy* 75 (1978): 397–413; and Shope, *The Analysis of Knowing*, chapter 2.

5. For relevant discussion see, for example, Mark Pastin, "Lewis' Radical Foundationalism"; William Alston, "Varieties of Privileged Access"; and Keith Lehrer, *Knowledge*, chap. 4.

6. Arguments in favor of this view can be found in Paul K. Moser, *Empirical Justification*, especially chap. 5. For critical discussion of the view, see Chapter 4 below by Bonjour. See also Keith Lehrer, "Knowledge, Truth, and Ontology," pp. 208–9.

7. Some arguments in favor of this view can be found in William Alston, "Self-Warrant: A Neglected Form of Privileged Access"; Marshall Swain, *Reasons and Knowledge*, chap. 4; and George Pappas, "Non-Inferential Knowledge." For some critical discussion of Pappas's arguments, see Paul K. Moser, "Knowledge Without Evidence."

8. See, for instance, Charles Peirce, "Questions Concerning Certain Faculties Claimed for Man," *Collected Papers* (Cambridge: Harvard University Press, 1935), Vol. 5, pp. 135–55.

9. A leading proponent of coherence as consistency is Nicholas Rescher, *The Coherence Theory of Truth;* a leading proponent of coherence as logical implication is Brand Blanshard, *The Nature of Thought;* and a leading proponent of coherence as explanation is Gilbert Harman, *Thought;* see Chapter 12 below. For still another approach to coherence, based on subjective probability estimates, see Keith Lehrer, *Knowledge*, chapters 7 and 8. See also Chapter 5 below.

10. Some leading proponents of epistemic contextualism are David B. Annis, in Chapter 9 below; Richard Rorty, *Philosophy and the Mirror of Nature;* and Michael Williams, "Coherence, Justification, and Truth." Contextualism is inspired largely by Ludwig Wittgenstein, *On Certainty;* but cf. Roger Shiner, "Wittgenstein and the Foundations of Knowledge."

11. For further discussion of the conceptual possibility of infinite regresses of justification, see Chapter 6 below by Sosa. Cf. James Cornman, *Skepticism, Justification, and Explanation*, pp. 135–37; John Post, "Infinite Regresses of Justification and of Explanation," *Philosophical Studies* 38 (1980): 32–37; and Paul K. Moser, "Whither Infinite Regresses of Justification?"

12. This kind of skepticism receives some forceful support in I. T. Oakley, "An Argument for Scepticism Concerning Justified Belief." For a detailed challenge to skepticism, see Peter Klein, *Certainty: A Refutation of Scepticism.*

13. For Sellars's statement of the problem, see his "Epistemic Principles." Bonjour's further discussion of the problem can be found in "Externalist Theories of Empirical Knowledge." For critical reaction in support of foundationalism, see Chapter 6 below by Sosa; William Alston, "What's Wrong With Immediate Knowledge?"; and Paul K. Moser, "A Defense of Epistemic Intuitionism."

14. For additional criticisms, see Bonjour, "Externalist Theories of Empirical Knowledge"; and Chapter IV and the Appendix of Moser, *Empirical Justification.*

15. See A. J. Ayer, "Phenomenalism," in *Philosophical Essays* (London:

Macmillan, 1954), pp. 134–39; and cf. Ayer, *The Problem of Knowledge,* pp. 125–26. For a more recent defense of phenomenalism, see Georges Dicker, *Perceptual Knowledge,* pp. 193–209. For criticisms of Ayer and Dicker, see Richard Fumerton, *Metaphysical and Epistemological Problems of Perception,* chapters 5 and 6; and Paul K. Moser, "Ascending from Empirical Foundations."

16. See, in this connection, R. M. Chisholm, "On the Nature of Empirical Evidence"; and James Cornman, "On Justifying Non-Basic Statements by Basic-Reports." But see also Moser, "Ascending from Empirical Foundations."

17. The reader interested in the widely discussed defeasibility approach to the Gettier problem should consult the following works: Peter Klein, "Knowledge, Causality, and Defeasibility"; Stewart Cohen, "Defeasibility and Background Beliefs"; and Robert Shope, *The Analysis of Knowing,* chap. 2.

PART I
JUSTIFIED BELIEF

1   Concepts of Epistemic Justification

WILLIAM P. ALSTON

I

Justification, or at least "justification," bulks large in recent epistemology. The view that knowledge consists of true-justified-belief (+ . . .) has been prominent in this century, and the justification of belief has attracted considerable attention in its own right. But it is usually not at all clear just what an epistemologist means by "justified," just what concept the term is used to express. An enormous amount of energy has gone into the attempt to specify conditions under which beliefs of one or another sort are justified; but relatively little has been done to explain *what it is* for a belief to be justified, what that is for which conditions are being sought.[1] The most common procedure has been to proceed on the basis of a number of (supposedly) obvious cases of justified belief, without pausing to determine what property it is of which these cases are instances. Now even if there were some single determinate concept that all these theorists have implicitly in mind, this procedure would be less than wholly satisfactory. For in the absence of an explicit account of the concept being applied, we lack the most fundamental basis for deciding between supposed intuitions and for evaluating proposed conditions of justification. And in any event, as philosophers we do not seek merely to speak the truth, but also to gain an explicit, reflective understanding of the matters with which we deal. We want to know not only when our beliefs are justified, but also what it is to enjoy that status. True, not every fundamental concept can be explicated, but we shall find that much can be done with this one.

And since, as we shall see in this essay, there are several distinct concepts that are plausibly termed "concepts of epistemic justification," the need for analysis is even greater. By simply using "justified" in an unexamined, intuitive fashion the epistemologist is covering up differences that make important differences to the shape of a theory of justification. We cannot fully understand the stresses and strains in

---

Reprinted from *The Monist* 68 (1985): 57–89, by permission of the author and the publisher. Copyright 1985, *The Monist*.

thought about justification until we uncover the most crucial differences between concepts of epistemic justification.

Not all contemporary theorists of justification fall under these strictures. Some have undertaken to give an account of the concept of justification they are using.[2] But none of them provides a map of this entire conceptual territory.

In this essay I am going to elaborate and interrelate several distinct concepts of epistemic justification, bringing out some crucial issues involved in choosing between them. I shall give reasons for disqualifying some of the contenders, and I shall explain my choice of a winner. Finally I shall vouchsafe a glimpse of the enterprise for which this essay is a propadeutic, that of showing how the differences between these concepts make a difference in what it takes for the justification of belief, and other fundamental issues in epistemology.

Before launching this enterprise we must clear out of the way a confusion between one's *being* justified in believing that p, and one's *justifying* one's belief that p, where the latter involves one's *doing* something to show that p, or to show that one's belief was justified, or to exhibit one's justification. The first side of this distinction, on the other hand, is a state or condition one is in, not anything one does or any upshot thereof. I might *be* justified in believing that there is milk on the table because I see it there, even though I have done nothing to show that there is milk on the table or to show that I am justified in believing there to be. It is amazing how often these matters are confused in the literature. We will be concentrating on the "be justified" side of this distinction, since that is of more fundamental epistemological interest. If epistemic justification were restricted to those cases in which the subject carries out a "justification," it would *obviously* not be a necessary condition of knowledge or even of being in a strong position to acquire knowledge. Most cases of perceptual knowledge, for example, involve no such activity.[3]

II

Let's begin our exploration of this stretch of conceptual territory by listing a few basic features of the concept that would seem to be common ground.

1. It applies to beliefs, or alternatively to a cognitive subject's having a belief. I shall speak indifferently of S's belief that p being justified and of S's being justified in believing that p. This is the common philosophical concept of belief, in which S's believing that p entails neither that S knows that p nor that S does not know that p. It is not restricted to conscious or occurrent beliefs.

2. It is an evaluative concept, in a broad sense in which this is

contrasted with "factual." To say that S is justified in believing that *p* is to imply that there is something all right, satisfactory, in accord with the way things should be, about the fact that S believes that *p*. It is to accord S's believing a positive evaluative status.

3. It has to do with a specifically *epistemic* dimension of evaluation. Beliefs can be evaluated in different ways. One may be more or less prudent, fortunate, or faithful in holding a certain belief. Epistemic justification is different from all that. Epistemic evaluation is undertaken from what we might call the "epistemic point of view." That point of view is defined by the aim at maximizing truth and minimizing falsity in a large body of beliefs. The qualification "in a large body of beliefs" is needed because otherwise one could best achieve the aim by restricting one's belief to those that are obviously true. That is a rough formulation. How large a body of beliefs should we aim at? Is any body of beliefs of a given size, with the same truth-falsity ratio, equally desirable, or is it more important, epistemically, to form beliefs on some matters than others? And what relative weights should be assigned to the two aims at maximizing truth and minimizing falsity? We can't go into all that here; in any event, however these issues are settled it remains true that our central cognitive aim is to amass a large body of beliefs with a favorable truth-falsity ratio. For a belief to be epistemically justified is for it, somehow, to be awarded high marks relative to that aim.

4. It is a matter of degree. One can be more or less justified in believing that *p*. If, e.g., what justifies one is some evidence one has, one will be more or less justified depending on the amount and strength of the evidence. However, in this essay I shall, for the sake of simplicity, treat justification as absolute. You may, if you like, think of this as the degree of justification required for some standard of acceptability.

III

Since any concept of epistemic justification is a concept of some condition that is desirable or commendable from the standpoint of the aim at maximizing truth and minimizing falsity, in distinguishing different concepts of justification we will be distinguishing different ways in which conditions can be desirable from this standpoint. As I see it, the major divide in this terrain has to do with whether believing and refraining from believing are subject to obligation, duty, and the like. If they are, we can think of the favorable evaluative status of a certain belief as consisting in the fact that in holding that belief one has fulfilled one's obligations, or refrained from violating one's obligations, to achieve the fundamental aim in question. If they are not so subject, the favorable status will have to be thought of in some other way.

I shall first explore concepts of the first sort, which I shall term "deontological,"[4] since they have to do with how one stands in believing that p, vis-à-vis duties or obligations. Most epistemologists who have attempted to explicate justification have set out a concept of this sort.[5] It is natural to set out a deontological concept on the model of the justification of behavior. Something I *did* was justified just in case it was *not in violation* of any relevant duties, obligations, rules, or regulations, and hence was not something for which I could rightfully be blamed. To say that my expenditures on the trip were justified is not to say that I was obliged to make those expenditures (e.g., for taxis), but only that it was all right for me to do so, that in doing so I was not in violation of any relevant rules or regulations. And to say that I was justified in making that decision on my own, without consulting the executive committee, is not to say that I was required to do it on my own (though that *may* also be true); it is only to say that the departmental by-laws permit the chairman to use his own discretion in matters of this kind. Similarly, to say that a belief was deontologically justified is not to say that the subject was obligated to believe this, but only that he was permitted to do so, that believing this did not involve any violation of relevant obligations. To say that I am justified in believing that salt is composed of sodium and chlorine, since I have been assured of this by an expert, is not to say that I am obligated to believe this, though this might also be true. It is to say that I am permitted to believe it, that believing it would not be a violation of any relevant obligation, e.g., the obligation to refrain from believing that p in the absence of adequate reasons for doing so. As Carl Ginet puts it, "One is *justified* in being confident that p if and only if it is not the case that one ought not to be confident that p; one could not be justly reproached for being confident that p."[6]

Since we are concerned specifically with the *epistemic* justification of belief, the concept in which we are interested is not that of *not violating obligations of any sort in believing,* but rather the more specific concept of *not violating "epistemic," "cognitive,"* or *"intellectual" obligations in believing.* Where are such obligations to be found? If we follow out our earlier specification of the "epistemic point of view," we will think of our basic epistemic obligation as that of doing what we can to achieve the aim at maximizing truth and minimizing falsity within a large body of beliefs. There will then be numerous more specific obligations that owe their status to the fact that fulfilling them will tend to the achievement of that central aim. Such obligations might include *to refrain from believing that p in the absence of sufficient evidence* and *to accept whatever one sees to be clearly implied by something one already believes (or, perhaps, is already justified in believing).*[7] Of course other positions might be taken on this point.[8] One might suppose that there are a number of ultimate, irreducible intellectual duties that cannot be derived from any basic goal of our cognitive life. Or alternative versions of the central aim might be proposed. Here we shall think of terms of the basic aim we have specified, with more specific obligations derived from that.

Against this background we can set out our first concept of epistemic justification as follows, using "d" for "deontological":

    I. S is J_d in believing that *p iff* in believing that *p* S is not violating any epistemic obligations.

There are important distinctions between what we may call "modes" of obligation, justification, and other normative statuses. These distinctions are by no means confined to the epistemic realm. Let's introduce them in connection with moral norms for behavior. Begin with a statement of obligation in "objective" terms, a statement of the objective state of affairs I might be said to be obliged to bring about. For example, it is my obligation as a host to make *my guest, G, feel welcome*. Call that underlined state of affairs "A." We may think of this as an *objective* conception of my obligation as a host. I have fulfilled that obligation *iff* G feels welcome.[9] But suppose I did what I sincerely believed would bring about A? In that case surely no one could blame me for dereliction of duty. That suggests a more *subjective* conception of my obligation as *doing what I believed was likely to bring about A*.[10] But perhaps I should not be let off so easily as that. "You should have realized that what you did was not calculated to make G feel welcome." This retort suggests a somewhat more stringent formulation of my obligation than the very permissive subjective conception just specified. It suggests that I can't fulfill my obligation by doing just anything I happen to believe will bring about A. I am not off the hook unless *I did what the facts available to me indicate will have a good chance of leading to A*. This is still a subjective conception in that what it takes to fulfill my obligation is specified from my point of view; but it takes my point of view to range over not all my beliefs, but only my justified beliefs. This we might call a *cognitive* conception of my obligation.[11] Finally, suppose that I did what I had adequate reason to suppose would produce A, and I did produce A, but I didn't do it for that reason. I was just amusing myself, and I would have done what I did even if I had known it would not make G feel welcome. In that case I might be faulted for moral irresponsibility, however well I rate in the other modes. This suggests what we may call a motivational conception of my obligation as *doing what I believed (or was justified in believing) would bring about A, in order to bring about A*.

We may sum up these distinctions as follows:

    II. S has fulfilled his *objective* obligation *iff* S has brought about A.

    III. S has fulfilled his *subjective* obligation *iff* S has done what he believed to be most likely to bring about A.

IV. S has fulfilled his *cognitive* obligation *iff* S did what he was justified in believing to be most likely to bring about A.

V. S has fulfilled his *motivational* obligation *iff* S has done what he did because he supposed it would be most likely to bring about A.

We can make analogous distinctions with respect to the justification of behavior or belief, construed as the absence of any violation of obligations.[12] Let's indicate how this works out for the justification of belief.

VI. S is *objectively* justified in believing that *p iff* S is not violating any objective obligation in believing that *p*.

VII. S is *subjectively* justified in believing that *p iff* S is not violating any subjective obligation in believing that *p*.

VIII. S is *cognitively* justified in believing that *p iff* S is not violating any cognitive obligation in believing that *p*.

IX. S is *motivationally* justified in believing that *p iff* S is not violating any motivational obligation in believing that *p*.

If we assume that only one intellectual obligation is relevant to the belief in question, viz., the obligation to believe that *p* only if one has adequate evidence for *p*, we can be a bit more concrete about this.

X. S is objectively justified in believing that *p iff* S has adequate evidence for *p*.[13]

XI. S is subjectively justified in believing that *p iff* S believes that he possesses adequate evidence for *p*.

XII. S is cognitively justified in believing that *p iff* S is justified in believing that he possesses adequate evidence for *p*.[14]

XIII. S is motivationally justified in believing that *p iff* S believes that *p* on the basis of adequate evidence, or, alternatively, on the basis of what he believed, or was justified in believing, was adequate evidence.

I believe that we can safely neglect XI. To explain why, I will need to make explicit what it is to have adequate evidence for *p*. First a proposition, *q*, is adequate evidence for *p* provided they are related in such a way that if *q* is true then *p* is at least probably true. But I *have* that evidence only if I believe that *q*. Furthermore I don't "have" it in such a way as to thereby render my belief that *p* justified unless I know or am justified in believing that *q*. An unjustified belief that *q* wouldn't do it. If I believe that Begin has told the cabinet that he will resign, but only because I credited an unsubstantiated rumor, then even if Begin's having told the cabinet that he would resign is an adequate indication that he will resign, I will not thereby be justified in believing that he will resign.

Now I might very well *believe* that I have adequate evidence for *q* even though one or more of these conditions is not satisfied. This is an especially live possibility with respect to the first and third conditions. I might mistakenly believe that my evidence is adequate support, and I might mistakenly suppose that I am justified in accepting it. But, as we have just seen, if I am not justified in accepting the evidence for p, then my believing it cannot render me justified in believing that p, however adequate that evidence. I would also hold, though this is perhaps more controversial, that if the evidence is not in fact adequate, my having that evidence cannot justify me in believing that p. Thus, since my believing that I have adequate evidence is compatible with these non-justifying states of affairs, we cannot take subjective justification, as defined in XI, to constitute epistemic justification.

That leaves us with three contenders. Here I will confine myself to pointing out that there is a strong tendency for J_d to be used in a cognitive rather than a purely objective form. J_d is, most centrally, a concept of freedom from blameworthiness, a concept of being "in the clear" so far as one's intellectual obligations are concerned. But even if I don't have adequate evidence for p, I could hardly be blamed for believing that p (even assuming, as we are in this discussion, that there is something wrong with believing in the absence of adequate evidence), provided I am justified in supposing that I have adequate evidence. So long as that condition holds I have done the right thing, or refrained from dong the wrong thing, so far as I am able to tell; and what more could be required of me? But this means that it is XII, rather than X, that brings out what it takes for freedom from blame, and so brings out what it takes for being J_d.[15]

What about the motivational form? We can have J_d in any of the first three forms with or without the motivational form. I can have adequate evidence for p, and believe that p (XI), whether or not my belief is based on that evidence; and so for the other two. But the motivational mode is parasitic on the other modes, in that the precise form taken by the motivational mode depends on the status of the (supposed) evidence on which the belief is based. This "unsaturated" character of the motivational mode is reflected in the threefold alternative that appears in our formulation of XIII. If S bases his belief that p on actually possessed adequate evidence, then XIII combines with X. If the evidence on which it is based is only believed to be adequate evidence, or only justifiably believed to be adequate evidence, then XIII combines with XI or XII. Of course, it may be based on actually possessed adequate evidence, which is justifiably believed to be such; in which case S is justified in all four modes. Thus the remaining question concerning J_d is whether a "motivational rider" should be put on XII. Is it enough for J_d that S be justified in believing that he has adequate evidence for p, or should it also be required that S's belief that p be based on that evidence? We will address this question in section V in the form it assumes for a quite different concept of justification.[16]

IV

We have explained *being* J_d *in believing that p as not violating any intellectual obligations in believing that p*. And, in parallel fashion, being J_d in refraining from believing that p would consist in not having violated any intellectual obligations in so doing. But if it is possible for me to violate an obligation in refraining from believing that p, it must be that I can be obliged, under certain conditions, to believe that p. And, by the same token, if I can violate obligations in believing that p, then I can be obliged to refrain from believing that p. And this is the way we have been thinking of it. Our example of an intellectual obligation has been the obligation to refrain from believing that p in the absence of adequate evidence. On the other side, we might think of a person as being obliged to believe that p if confronted with conclusive evidence that p (where that includes the absence of sufficient overriding evidence to the contrary).

Now it certainly looks as if I can be obliged to believe or to refrain from believing, only if this is in my direct voluntary control; only if I can, here and now, believe that p or no just by willing (deciding, choosing . . .). And that is the way many epistemologists seem to construe the matter. At least many formulations are most naturally interpreted in this way. Think back, e.g., on Chisholm's formulation of our intellectual obligation (1977, p. 14), cited in n16. Chisholm envisages a person thinking of a certain proposition as a candidate for belief, and then effectively choosing belief or abstention on the basis of those considerations.[17] Let's call the version of J_d that presupposes direct voluntary control over belief (and thus thinks of an obligation to believe as an obligation to bring about belief here and now) "J_{dv}" ("v" for "voluntary").

I find this assumption of direct voluntary control over belief quite unrealistic. There are strong reasons for doubting that belief is usually, or perhaps ever, under direct voluntary control. First, think of the beliefs I acquire about myself and the world about me through experience—through perception, self-consciousness, testimony, and simple reasoning based on these data. When I see a car coming down the street I am not capable of believing or disbelieving this at will. In such familiar situations the belief-acquisition mechanism is isolated from the direct influence of the will and under the control of more purely cognitive factors.

Partisans of a voluntary control thesis will counter by calling attention to cases in which things don't appear to be so cut and dried: cases of radical underdetermination by evidence, as when a general has to dispose his forces in the absence of sufficient information about the position of enemy forces; or cases of the acceptance of a religious or philosophical position where there seem to be a number of equally viable alternatives. In such cases it can appear that one makes a decision as to what to believe and what not to believe. My view on these matters is that insofar as something is chosen voluntarily it is something other than a belief or abstention from belief. The general chooses to proceed on the working assumption that the enemy forces are disposed in such-and-such a way. The religious convert to whom it is not clear that the beliefs are correct has chosen to live a certain kind of life, or to selectively subject himself to certain influences. And so on. But even if I am mistaken about these kinds of cases, it is clear that for the vast majority of beliefs nothing like direct voluntary control is involved. And so J_{dv} could not possibly be a generally applicable concept of epistemic justification.

If I am right in rejecting the view that belief is, in general or ever, under direct voluntary control, are we foreclosed from construing epistemic justification as freedom from blameworthiness? Not necessarily. We aren't even prevented from construing epistemic justification as the absence of obligation-violations. We *will* have to avoid thinking of the relevant obligations as obligations to believe or refrain from believing, on the model of obligations to answer a question or to open a door, or to do anything else over which we have immediate voluntary control.[18] If we are to continue to think of intellectual obligations as having to do with believing, it will have to be more on the model of the way in which obligations bear on various other conditions over which one lacks direct voluntary control but which one can influence by voluntary actions, such conditions as being overweight, being irritable, being in poor health, or having friends. I can't institute, nullify, or alter any of those conditions here and now just by deciding to do so. But I can do things at will that will influence those conditions, and in that way they may be to some extent under my indirect control. One might speak of my being obliged to be in good health or to have a good disposition, meaning that I am obliged to do what I can (or as much as could reasonably be expected of me) to institute and preserve those states of affairs. However, since I think it less misleading to say exactly what I mean, I will not speak of our being obliged to weigh a certain amount or to have a good disposition, or to believe a proposition; I will rather speak of our having obligations to do what we can, or as much as can reasonably be expected of us, to influence those conditions.[19]

The things we can do to affect our believings can be divided into (a) activities that bring influences to bear, or withhold influences from, a particular situation, and (b) activities that affect our belief-forming habits. (a) includes such activities as checking to see whether I have considered all the relevant evidence, getting a second opinion, searching my memory for analogous cases, and looking into the question of whether there is anything markedly abnormal about my current perceptual situation. (b) includes training myself to be more critical of gossip, talking myself into being either more or less subservient to authority, and practicing greater sensitivity to the condition of other people. Moreover, it is plausible to think of these belief-influencing activities as being subject to intellectual obligations. We might, e.g., think of ourselves as being under an obligation to do what we can (or what could reasonably be expected of us) to make our belief-forming processes as reliable as possible.

All this suggests that we might frame a deontological conception of being epistemically justified in believing that *p*, in the sense that one's believing that *p* is not the result of one's failure to fulfill one's intellectual obligations vis-à-vis one's belief-forming and -maintaining activities. It would, again, be like the way in which one is or isn't to blame for other conditions that are not under direct voluntary control but which one can influence by one's voluntary activities. I am to blame for being over-weight (being irritable, being in poor health, being without friends) only if that condition is in some way due to my own past failures to do what I should to limit my intake or to exercise or whatever. If I would still be overweight even if I had done everything I could and should have done about it, then I can hardly be blamed for it. Similarly, we may say that I am subject to reproach for believing that *p*, provided that I am to blame for being in the doxastic condition, in the sense that there are things I could and should have done, such that if I had done them I would not be believing that *p*. If that is the case I am unjustified in that belief. And if it is *not* the case, if there are no unfulfilled obligations the fulfilling of which would have inhibited that belief-formation, then I am justified in the belief.

Thus we have arrived at a deontological concept of epistemic justification that does not require belief to be under direct voluntary control. We may label this concept "J_{di}" ("i" for "involuntary"). It may be more formally defined as follows:

XIV. S is J_{di} in believing that *p* at *t iff* there are no intellectual obligations that (a) have to do with the kind of belief-forming or -sustaining habit the activation of which resulted in S's believing that *p* at *t*, or with the particular process of belief-formation or -sustenance that was involved in S's believing that *p* at *t*, and which (b) are such that:

A. S had those obligations prior to *t*.
B. S did not fulfill those obligations.
C. If S had fulfilled those obligations, S would not have believed that *p* at *t*.[20]

As it stands, this account will brand too many beliefs as unjustified, just because it is too undiscriminating in the counter-factual condition C.

There are ways in which the non-fulfillment of intellectual obligations can contribute to a belief-acquisition without rendering the belief unjustified. Suppose that I fail to carry out my obligation to spend a certain period in training myself to observe things more carefully. I use the time thus freed up to take a walk around the neighborhood. In the course of this stroll I see two dogs fighting, thereby acquiring the belief that they are fighting. There was a relevant intellectual obligation I didn't fulfill, which is such that if I had fulfilled it I wouldn't have acquired that belief. But if that is a perfectly normal perceptual belief, it is surely not thereby rendered unjustified.

Here the dereliction of duty contributed to belief-formation simply by facilitating access to the data. That's not the kind of contribution we had in mind. The sorts of cases we were thinking of were those most directly suggested by the two sorts of intellectual obligations we distinguished: (a) cases in which the belief was acquired by the activation of a habit that we would not have possessed had we fulfilled our intellectual obligations; (b) cases in which we acquire, or retain, the belief only because we are sheltered from adverse considerations in a way we wouldn't be if we had done what we should have done. Thus we can avoid counterexamples like the above by reformulating C as follows:

> C. If S had fulfilled those obligations, then S's belief-forming habits would have changed, or S's access to relevant adverse considerations would have changed, in such a way that S would not have believed that *p* at *t*.

But even with this refinement J_{di} does not give us what we expect of epistemic justification. The most serious defect is that it does not hook up in the right way with an adequate, truth-conducive ground. I may have done what could reasonably be expected of me in the management and cultivation of my doxastic life, and still hold a belief on outrageously inadequate grounds. There are several possible sources of such a discrepancy. First there is what we might call "cultural isolation." If I have grown up in an isolated community in which everyone unhesitatingly accepts the traditions of the tribe as authoritative, then if I have never encountered anything that seems to cast doubt on the traditions and have never thought to question them, I can hardly be blamed for taking them as authoritative. There is nothing I could reasonably be expected to do that would alter that belief-forming tendency. And there is nothing I could be expected to do that would render me more exposed to counterevidence. (We can suppose that the traditions all have to do with events distant in time and/or space, matters on which I could not be expected to gather evidence on my own.) I am J_{di} in believing these things. And yet the fact that it is the tradition of the tribe that *p* may be a very poor reason for believing that *p*.

Then there is deficiency in cognitive powers. Rather than looking at the extremer forms of this, let's consider a college student who just doesn't have what it takes to follow abstract philosophical reasoning, or exposition for that matter. Having read Bk. IV of Locke's *Essay,* he believes that it is Locke's view that everything is a matter of opinion, that one person's opinion is just as good as another's, and that what is true for me may not be true for you. And it's not just that he didn't work hard enough on this particular point, or on the general abilities involved. There is nothing that he could and should have done such that had he done so, he would have gotten this straight. He is simply incapable of appreciating the distinction between "One's knowledge is restricted to one's own ideas" and "Everything is a matter of opinion." No doubt teachers of philosophy tend to assume too quickly that this description applies to some of their students, but surely there can be such cases—cases in which either no amount of time and effort would enable the student to get straight on the matter, or it would be unreasonable to expect the person to expend that amount of time or effort. And yet we would hardly wish to say that the student is justified in believing what he does about Locke.

Other possible sources of a discrepancy between J_{di} and epistemic justification are poor training that the person lacks the time or resources to overcome, and an incorrigible doxastic incontinence. ("When he talks like that I just can't help believing what he says.") What this spread of cases brings out is that J_{di} is not sufficient for epistemic justification; we may have done the best we can, or at least the best that could reasonably be expected of us, and still be in a very poor epistemic position in believing that $p;$ we could, blamelessly, be believing p for outrageously bad reasons. Even though J_{di} is the closest we can come to a deontological concept of epistemic justification, if belief is not under direct voluntary control, it still does not give us what we are looking for.

V

Thus neither version of J_d is satisfactory. Perhaps it was misguided all along to think of epistemic justification as freedom from blameworthiness. Is there any alternative, given the non-negotiable point that we are looking for a concept of epistemic evaluation? Of course there is. By no means all evaluation, even all evaluation of activities, states, and aspects of human beings, involves the circle of terms that includes "obligation," "permission," "right," "wrong," and "blame." We can evaluate a person's abilities, personal appearance, temperament, or state of health as more or less desirable, favorable, or worthwhile, without taking these to be within the person's direct voluntary control and so subject to obligation in a direct fashion (as with J_{dv}, and without making the evaluation depend on whether the person has done what she should to influence these states (as with J_{di}). Obligation and blame need not come into it at all. This is most obvious when we are dealing with matters that are not even under indirect voluntary control, like one's basic capacities or bodily build. Here when we use positively evaluative terms like "gifted" or "superb," we are clearly not saying that the person has done all she could to foster or encourage the condition in question. But even where the condition is at least partly under indirect voluntary control, as with personal appearance or state of health, we need not be thinking in those terms when we take someone to present a pleasing appearance or to be in splendid health. Moreover, we can carry out these evaluations from a certain point of view. We can judge that someone has a fine bodily constitution from an athletic or from an aesthetic point of view, or that someone's manner is a good one from a professional or from a social point of view.

In like fashion one can evaluate S's believing that *p* as a good, favorable, desirable, or appropriate thing, without thinking of it as fulfilling or not violating an obligation, and without making this evaluation depend on whether the person has done what she could to carry out belief-influencing activities. As in the other cases, it could simply be a matter of the possession of certain good-making characteristics. Furthermore, believings can be evaluated from various points of view, including the epistemic, which, as we have noted, is defined by the aim of maximizing truth and minimizing falsity. It may be a good thing that S believes that *p* for his peace of mind, or from the standpoint of loyalty to the cause, or as an encouragement to the redoubling of his efforts. But none of this would render it a good thing for S to believe that *p* from the epistemic point of view. To believe that *p* because it gives peace of mind or because it stimulates effort may not be conducive to the attainment of truth and the avoidance of error.

All of this suggests that we can frame a concept of epistemic justification that is "evaluative," in a narrow sense of that term in which it contrasts with "deontological," with the assessment of conduct in terms of obligation, blame, right, and wrong. Let's specify an "evaluative" sense of epistemic justification as follows:

XV. S is J_e in believing that *p* iff S's believing that *p*, as S does, is a good thing from the epistemic point of view.

This is a way of being commendable from the epistemic point of view that is quite different from the subject's not being to blame for any violation of intellectual obligations.[21] The qualification "as S does" is inserted to make it explicit that in order for S to be J_e in believing that *p*, it need not be the case that any believing of *p* by S would be a good thing epistemically, much less any believing of *p* by anyone. It is rather that there are aspects of *this* believing of *p* by S that make it a good thing epistemically.

There could conceivably be person-proposition pairs such that any belief in that proposition by that person would be a good thing epistemically, but this would be a limiting case and not typical of our epistemic condition.

Is there anything further to be said about this concept? Of course we should avoid building anything very substantive into the constitution of the concept. After all, it is possible for epistemologists to differ radically as to the conditions under which one or another sort of belief is justified. When this happens they are at least sometimes using the same concept of justification; otherwise they wouldn't be disagreeing over what is required for justification, though they could still disagree over which concept of justification is most fundamental or most useful. Both our versions of J_d are quite neutral in this way. Both leave it completely open as to what intellectual obligations we have, and hence as to what obligations must not be violated if one is to be justified. But while maintaining due regard for the importance of neutrality, I believe that we can go beyond XV in fleshing out the concept.

We can get a start on this by considering the following question. If goodness from an epistemic point of view is what we are interested in, why shouldn't we identify justification with truth, at least extensionally? What could be better from that point of view than truth? If the name of the game is the maximization of truth and the minimization of falsity in our beliefs, then plain unvarnished truth is hard to beat. However, this consideration has not moved epistemologists to identify justification with truth, or even to take truth as a necessary and sufficient condition for justification. The logical independence of truth and justification is a staple of the epistemological literature. But why should this be? It is obvious that a belief might be J_d without being true and vice versa, but what reason is there for taking J_e to be independent of truth?

I think the answer to this has to be in terms of the "internalist" character of justification. When we ask whether S is justified in believing that p, we are, as we have repeatedly been insisting, asking a question from the standpoint of an aim at truth; but we are not asking whether things are in fact as S believes. We are getting at something more "internal" to S's "perspective on the world." This internalist feature of justification made itself felt in our discussion of J_d when we pointed out that to be J_{dv} is to fail to violate any relevant intellectual obligations, *so far as one can tell*, to be J_{dv} in what we call the "cognitive" mode. With respect to J_e the analogous point is that although this is goodness vis-à-vis the aim at truth, it consists not in the beliefs fitting the way the facts actually are, but something more like the belief's being true "so far as the subject can tell from what is available to the subject." In asking whether S is J_e in believing that p, we are asking whether the truth of p is strongly indicated by what S has to go on; whether, given what S had to go on, it is at least quite likely that p is true. We want to know whether S had *adequate* grounds for believing that *p*, where *adequate* grounds are those sufficiently indicative to the truth of *p*.

If we are to make the notion of *adequate grounds* central for J_e we must say more about it. A belief has a certain ground, G, when it is "based on" G. What is it for a belief, B, to be *based on* G? That is a difficult question. So far as I know, there is no fully satisfactory general account in the literature, nor am I able to supply one. But we are not wholly at a loss. We do have a variety of paradigm cases; the difficulty concerns just how to generalize from them and just where to draw the line. When one infers *p* from *q* and *thereby* comes to accept *p*, this is a clear case of basing one belief on another. Again, when I come to believe that that is a tree because this visually appears to me to be the case, that is another paradigm; here my belief that that is a tree is based on my visual experience, or, if you prefer, on certain aspects of that experience. The main difficulties arise with respect to cases in which no conscious inference takes place but in which we are still inclined to say that one belief is based on another. Consider, e.g., my forming the belief that you are angry on seeing you look and act in a certain way. I perform no conscious inference from a proposition about your demeanor and behavior to a proposition about your emotional state. Nevertheless it seems plausible to hold that I did learn about your demeanor and behavior through seeing it, and that the beliefs I thereby formed played a crucial role in my coming to believe that you are angry. More specifically it seems that the former beliefs gave rise to the latter belief; that if I hadn't acquired the former I would not have acquired the latter; and, finally, that if I am asked why I suppose that you are angry I would cite the behavior and demeanor as my reason (perhaps only as "the way he looked and acted"). How can we get this kind of case together with the conscious-inference cases into a general account? We might claim that they are all cases of inference, some of them being unconscious. But there are problems as to when we are justified in imputing unconscious inferences. We might take it that what lets in our problem cases is the subject's disposition to cite the one belief(s) as his reason for the other belief, and then make our general condition a disjunction of conscious inference from *q* and a tendency to cite *q* as the reason. But then what about subjects (small children and lower animals) that are too unsophisticated to be able to answer questions as to what their reasons are? Can't their beliefs be based on something when no conscious inference is performed? Moreover this disjunctive criterion will not include cases in which a belief is based on an experience, rather than on other beliefs. A third suggestion concerns causality. In all cases mentioned thus far it is plausible to suppose that the belief that *q* was among the causes of the belief that *p*. This suggests that we might try to cut the Gordian knot by boldly identifying "based on" with "caused by." But this runs into the usual difficulties of simple causal theories. Many items enter into the causation of a belief, e.g., various neuro-physiological happenings, that clearly don't qualify as even part of what the belief is based on. To make a causal account work we would have to beef it up into "caused by q in a certain way." And what way is that? Some way that is paradigmatically exemplified by our paradigms? But how are we to state this way in such a fashion that it applies equally to the non-paradigmatic cases?[22]

In the face of these perplexities our only recourse is to keep a firm hold on our paradigms, and work with a less than ideally determinate concept of a relationship that holds in cases that are "sufficiently like" the paradigms. That will be sufficient to do the job over most of the territory.[23]

Let's return to "grounds." What a belief is based on we may term the ground of the belief. A ground, in a more dispositional sense of the term, is the sort of item on which a belief can be based. We have already cited beliefs and experiences as possible grounds, and these would seem to exhaust the possibilities. Indeed, some epistemologists would find this too generous already, maintaining that beliefs can be based only on other beliefs. They would treat perceptual cases by holding that the belief that a tree is over there is based on the *belief that* there visually appears to me to be a tree over there, rather than, as we are suggesting, on the visual appearance itself. I can't accept that, largely because I doubt that all perceptual believers have such beliefs about their visual experience,[24] but I can't pause to argue the point. Suffice it to say that since my opponents' position is, to be as generous as possible, controversial, we do not want to build a position on this issue into the *concept* of epistemic justification. We want to leave open at least the *conceptual* possibility of *direct* or *immediate* justification by experience (and perhaps in other ways also), as well as *indirect* or *mediate* justification by relation to other beliefs (inferentially in the most explicit cases). Finally, to say that a subject *has adequate* grounds for her belief that p is to say that she has other justified beliefs, or experiences, on which the belief could be based and which are strongly indicative of the truth of the belief. The reason for the restriction to *justified* beliefs is that a ground shouldn't be termed adequate unless it can confer justification on the belief it grounds. But we noted earlier that if I infer my belief that p, by even impeccable logic, from an *unjustified* belief that q, the former belief is not thereby justified.[25]

To return to the main thread of the discussion, we are thinking of S's being J_e in believing that p as involving S's having adequate grounds for that belief. That is, we are thinking of the possession of those adequate grounds as constituting the goodness of the belief from the epistemic point of view. The next thing to note is that the various "modes" of J_d apply here as well.

Let's begin by noting an objective-subjective distinction. To be sure, in thinking of J_e as *having truth-indicative grounds within one's "perspec-*

tive on the world," we are already thinking of it as more subjective than flat-out truth. But within that perspectival conception we can set the requirements as more objective or more subjective. There is more than one respect in which the possession of adequate grounds could be "subjectivized." First, there is the distinction between the existence of the ground and its adequacy. S is *objectively* J_e in believing that p if S does in fact have grounds that are in fact adequate grounds for that belief. A subjective version would require only that S *believe* one or the other part of this, or both; either (a) that there are (possible) grounds that are in fact adequate and he believes of those grounds that he has them; or (b) that he has grounds that he believes to be adequate; or the combination, (c), that he believes himself to have adequate grounds. Moreover, there are two ways in which the possession-of-grounds belief could go wrong. Confining ourselves to beliefs, one could mistakenly suppose oneself to believe that p, or one could mistakenly suppose one's belief that p to be justified. Lacking time to go into all these variations, I shall confine this discussion to the subjectivization of adequacy. So our first two modes will be:

XVI. Objective—S does have adequate grounds for believing that p.

XVII. Subjective—S has grounds for believing that p and he believes them to be adequate.

And here too we have a "justified belief," or "cognitive" variant on the subjective version.

XVIII. Cognitive—S has grounds for believing that p and he is justified in believing them to be adequate.

We can dismiss XVII by the same arguments we brought against the subjective version of J_d. The mere fact that I believe, however unjustifiably or irresponsibly, that my grounds for believing that p are adequate could scarcely render me justified in believing that p. If I believe them to be adequate just because I have an egotistical penchant to overestimate my powers, that could hardly make it rational for me to believe that p. But here we will not find the same reason to favor XVIII over XVI. With J_d the cognitive version won out because of what it takes for blameworthiness. But whether one is J_e in believing that p has nothing to do with whether he is subject to blame. It depends rather on whether his believing that p is a *good thing* from the epistemic point of view. And however justifiably S believes that his grounds are adequate, if they are not then his believing that p on those grounds is not a good move in the truth-seeking game. Even if he isn't to blame for making that move it is a bad move nonetheless. Thus J_e is properly construed in the objective mode.

We are also confronted with the question of whether J_e should be construed "motivationally." Since we have already opted for an objective reading, the motivational version will take the following form:

XIX. Motivational—S's belief that p is based on adequate grounds.

So our question is whether it is enough for justification that S *have* adequate grounds for his belief, whether used or not, or whether it is also required that the belief be based on those grounds. We cannot settle this question on the grounds that were available for J_{dv}, since with J_e we are not thinking of the subject as being obliged to take relevant considerations into account in *choosing* whether to believe that p.

There is something to be said on both sides of this issue. In support of the first, source-irrelevant position (XVI without XIX), it can be pointed out that S's *having a justification* for believing that p is independent of whether S does believe that p; I can have adequate grounds for believing that p, and so *have* a justification, even though I do not in fact believe that p. Hence it can hardly be a requirement for having a justification for p that my non-existent belief have a certain kind of basis. Likewise my having adequate grounds for believing that p is sufficient for this being *a rational thing for me to believe*. But, says the opponent, suppose that S does believe that p. If simply having adequate grounds were sufficient for this belief to be justified, then, provided S does have the grounds, her belief that p would be justified however frivolous the source. But surely a belief that stems from wishful thinking would not be justified, however strong one's (unutilized) grounds for it.[26]

Now the first thing to say about this controversy is that both antagonists win, at least to the extent that each of them is putting forward a viable concept, and one that is actually used in epistemic assessment. There certainly is the concept of *having* adequate grounds for the belief that p, whether or not one does believe that p, and there equally certainly is the concept of one's belief being based on adequate grounds. Both concepts represent favorable epistemic statuses. *Ceteris paribus*, one is better off believing something for which one has adequate grounds than believing something for which one doesn't. And the same can be said for the contrast between having a belief that is based on adequate grounds and having one that isn't. Hence I will recognize that these are both concepts of epistemic justification, and I will resist the pressure to decide which is *the* concept.

Nevertheless we can seek to determine which concept is more fundamental to epistemology. On this issue it seems clear that the motivational concept is the richer one and thereby embodies a more complete account of a belief's being a good thing from the epistemic point of view. Surely there is something epistemically undesirable about a belief that is generated in an intellectually disreputable way, however adequate the unutilized grounds possessed by the subject. If, possessing excellent reasons for supposing that you are trying to discredit me professionally, I nevertheless believe this, not for those reasons but out of paranoia, in such a way that even if I didn't have those reasons I would have believed this just as firmly, it was undesirable from the point of view of the aim at truth for me to form that belief as I did. So if we are seeking the most inclusive concept of what makes a belief a good thing epistemically, we will want to include a consideration of what the belief is based on. Hence I will take XIX as the favored formulation of what makes a belief a good thing from the epistemic point of view.

I may add that XVI can be seen as derivative from XIX. To simply *have* adequate grounds is to be in such a position that *if* I make use of that position as a basis for believing that *p* I will thereby be justified in that belief. Thus XVI gives us a concept of a potential for XIX; it is a concept of having resources that are sufficient for believing justifiably, leaving open the question of whether those resources are used.

The next point to be noted is that XIX guarantees only *prima facie* justification. As often noted, it is quite possible for my belief that *p* to have been formed on the basis of evidence that in itself adequately supports *p,* even though the totality of the evidence at my disposal does not. Thus the evidence on which I came to believe that the butler committed the murder might strongly support that hypothesis, but when arriving at that belief I was ignoring other things I know or justifiably believe that tend to exculpate the butler; the total evidence at my disposal is not sufficient support for my belief. In that case we will not want to count my belief as justified all things considered, even though the grounds *on the basis of which* it was formed were themselves adequate. Their adequacy is, so to say, *overridden* by the larger perspectival context in which they are set. Thus XIX gives us *prima facie* justification, what will be justification provided it is not cancelled by further relevant factors. Unqualified justification requires an additional condition to the effect that S does not also have reasons that suffice to override the justification provided by the grounds on which the belief is based. Building that into XIX we get:

XX. Motivational—S's belief that *p* is based on adequate grounds, and S lacks overriding reasons to the contrary.

Even though XX requires us to bring in the unused portions of the perspective, we cannot simplify the condition by ignoring the distinction between what provides the basis and what doesn't, and make the crucial condition something like "The totality of S's perspective provides adequate support." For then we would run up against the considerations that led us to prefer XIX to XVI.

We have distinguished two aspects of our evaluative concept of justification, the strictly evaluative portion—goodness from the epistemic point of view—and the very general statement of the relevant good-making characteristic, *based on adequate grounds in the absence of overriding reasons to the contrary.* In taking the concept to include this second component we are opting for the view that this concept, though unmistakably evaluative rather than "purely factual" in character, is not so purely evaluative as to leave completely open the basis on which this evaluative status supervenes. I do not see how to justify this judgment by reference to any more fundamental considerations. It is just that in reflecting on epistemic justification, thought of in evaluative (as contrasted with deontological) terms, it seems clear to me that the range of possible bases for epistemic goodness is not left completely open by the concept, that it is part of what we mean in terming a belief justified, that the belief was based on adequate grounds (or, at least, that the subject had adequate grounds for it).[27] Though this means that J_e is not maximally neutral on the question of what it takes for justification, it is still quite close to that. It still leaves open whether there is immediate justification and if so on the basis of what, how strong a ground is needed for justification, what dimensions of strength there are for various kinds of grounds, and so on.

Let's codify our evaluative concept of justification as follows:

> XXI. S is J_{eg} in believing that p *iff* S's believing that p, as S did, was a good thing from the epistemic point of view, in that S's belief that p was based on adequate grounds and S lacked sufficient overriding reasons to the contrary.

In the subscript "g" stands for "grounds."

My supposition that all justification of belief involves adequate grounds may be contested. This does seem incontrovertible for beliefs based on other beliefs and for perceptual beliefs based on experience. But what about beliefs in self-evident propositions where the self-evidence is what justifies me in the belief.[28] On considering the proposition that two quantities equal to the same quantity are equal to each other, this seems obviously true to me; and I shall suppose, though this is hardly uncontroversial, that in those circumstances I am justified in believing it. But where are the adequate grounds on which my belief is based? It is not that there are grounds here about whose adequacy we might well have doubts; it is rather that there seems to be nothing identifiable as grounds. There is nothing here that is distinguishable from my belief and the proposition believed, in the way evidence or reasons are distinct from that for which they are evidence or reasons, or in the way my sensory experience is distinct from the beliefs about the physical world that are based on it. Here I simply consider the proposition and straightaway accept it. A similar problem can be raised for normal beliefs about one's own conscious states. What is the ground for a typical belief that one feels sleepy?[29] If one replies "One's being conscious of one's feeling of sleepiness," then it may be insisted, with some show of plausibility, that where one is consciously feeling sleepy there is no difference between one's feeling sleepy and one's being conscious that one is feeling sleepy.

This is a very large issue that I will not have time to consider properly. Suffice it to say that one may treat these as limiting cases in which the ground, though real enough, is minimally distinguishable either from the belief it is grounding or from the fact that makes the belief true. In the first person belief about one's own conscious state, the ground coincides with the fact that makes the belief true. Since the fact believed is itself an experience of the subject, there need be nothing "between" the subject and the fact that serves as an indication of the latter's presence. The fact "reveals itself" directly. Self-evident propositions require separate treatment. Here I think that we can take the *way* the proposition appears to one, variously described as "obviously true," "self-evident," and "clear and distinct," as the ground on which the belief is based. I accept the proposition because it *seems* to me so obviously true. This is less distinct from the belief than an inferential or sensory experiential ground, since it has to do with how I am aware of the proposition. Nevertheless there is at least a minimal distinctness. I can form an intelligible conception of someone's failing to believe that *p,* where *p* seems obviously true. Perhaps this person has been rendered unduly sceptical by over-exposure to the logical paradoxes.

VI

Let's go back to the idea that the "based on adequate grounds" part of J_{eg} is there because of the "internalist" character of justification. Contrasts between internalism and externalism have been popular in epistemology lately, but the contrast is not always drawn in the same way. There are two popular ways, both of which are distinct from what I have in mind. First there is the idea that justification is internal in that it depends on what support is available for the belief from "within the subject's perspective," in the sense of what the subject knows or justifiably believes about the world.[30] This kind of internalism restricts justification to mediate or discursive justification, justification by reasons. Another version takes "the subject's perspective" to include whatever is "directly accessible" to the subject, accessible just on the basis of reflection; internalism on this version restricts justifiers to what is directly accessible to the subject.[31] This, unlike the first version, does not limit us to mediate justification, since experience can be taken to be at least as directly accessible as beliefs and knowledge.

In contrast to both these ways of drawing the distinction, what I take to be internal about justification is that whether a belief is justified depends on what it is based on (grounds), and grounds must be other psychological state(s) of the same subject. I am not absolutely certain that grounds are confined to beliefs and experiences, even if experiences are not confined to sensations and feelings but also include, e.g., the way a proposition seems obvious to one, and religious and aesthetic experiences; but these are the prime candidates, and any other examples must belong to some kind of which these are the paradigms. So in taking it to be conceptually true that one is justified in believing that *p iff* one's belief that *p* is based on an adequate ground, I take justification to be "internal" in that it depends on the way in which the belief stems from the believer's psychological states, which are "internal" to the subject in an obvious sense. What would be an externalist contrast with this kind of internalism? We shall see one such contrast in a moment, in discussing the relation of J_{eg} to reliabilism. Moreover, it contrasts with the idea that one can be justified in a certain belief just because of the status of the proposition believed (necessary, infallible). My sort of internalism is different from the first one mentioned above, in that experiences as well as beliefs can figure as grounds. And it is different from the second if, as I believe, what a belief is based on may not be directly accessible. This will be the case if, as seems plausible, much belief-formation goes on below the conscious level. It would seem, e.g., that, as we move about the environment, we are constantly forming short-term perceptual beliefs without any conscious monitoring of this activity.

The most prominent exponents of an explicitly non-deontological conception of epistemic justification have been reliabilists, who have either identified justification with reliability[32] or have taken reliability to be an adequate criterion of justification.[33] The reliability that is in question here is the reliability of belief-formation and -sustenance.[34] To say that a belief was formed in a reliable way is, roughly, to say that it was formed in a way that can be depended on generally to form true rather than false beliefs, at least from inputs like the present one, and at least in the sorts of circumstances in which we normally find ourselves.[35] Thus if my visual system, when functioning as it is at present in yielding my belief that there is a tree in front of me, generally yields true beliefs about objects that are fairly close to me and directly in front of me, then my present belief that there is a tree in front of me was formed in a reliable manner.

Now it may be supposed that J_{eg}, as we have explained it, is just reliability of belief-formation with an evaluative frosting. For where a belief is based on adequate grounds, that belief has been formed in a reliable fashion. In fact, it is plausible to take reliability as a *criterion* for adequacy of grounds. If my grounds for believing that *p* are not such that it is generally true that beliefs like that formed on grounds like that are true, they cannot be termed "adequate." Why do we think that wanting State to win the game is not an adequate reason for supposing that it has won, whereas the fact that a victory has been reported by several newspapers is an adequate reason? Surely it has something to do with the fact that beliefs like that when formed on the first sort of grounds are not *generally* true, while they are *generally* true when formed on grounds of the second sort. Considerations like this may lead us to suppose that J_{eg}, in effect, identifies justification with reliability.[36]

Nevertheless the internalist character of justification prevents it from being identified with reliability, and even blocks an extensional equivalence. Unlike justification, reliability of belief-formation is not limited to cases in which a belief is based on adequate grounds within the subject's psychological states. A reliable mode of belief-formation *may* work through the subject's own knowledge and experience. Indeed, it is plausible to suppose that all of the reliable modes of belief-formation available to human beings are of this sort. But it is quite conceivable that there should be others. I might be so constituted that beliefs about the weather tomorrow which apparently just "pop into my mind" out of nowhere are in fact reliably produced by a mechanism of which we know nothing, and which does not involve the belief being based on anything. Here we would have reliably formed beliefs that are not based on adequate grounds from within my perspective, and so are not J_{eg}.

Moreover, even within the sphere of beliefs based on grounds, reliability and justification do not necessarily go together. The possibility of divergence here stems from another feature of justification embodied in our account, the way in which unqualified justification requires not only an adequate ground but also the absence of sufficient overriding reasons. This opens up the possibility of a case in which a belief is formed on the basis of grounds in a way that is in fact highly reliable, even though the subject has strong reasons for supposing the way to be unreliable. These reasons will (or may) override the *prima facie* justification provided by the grounds on which the belief was based. And so S will not be justified in the belief, even though it was reliably generated.

Consider, in this connection, a case presented by Alvin Goldman.[37]

> Suppose that Jones is told on fully reliable authority that a certain class of his memory beliefs are almost all mistaken. His parents fabricate a wholly false story that Jones suffered from amnesia when he was seven but later developed *pseudo*-memories of that period. Though Jones listens to what his parents say and has excellent reasons to trust them, he persists in believing the ostensible memories from his seven-year-old past.

Suppose that Jones, upon recalling his fifth birthday party, believes that he was given an electric train for his fifth birthday because, as it seems to him, he remembers being given it.[38] By hypothesis, his memory mechanism is highly reliable, and so his belief about his fifth birthday was reliably formed. But this belief is not adequately supported by the *totality* of what he justifiably believes. His justifiable belief that he has no real memory of his first seven years overrides the support from his ostensible memory. Thus Jones is not J_{eg} in his memory belief, because the "lack of overriding reasons to the contrary" requirement is not satisfied. But reliability is subject to no such constraint. Just as reliable mechanisms are not restricted to those that work through the subject's perspective, so it is not a requirement on the reliability of belief-formation that the belief be adequately supported by the totality of the subject's perspective. However many and however strong the reasons Jones has for distrusting his memory, the fact remains that his memory beliefs are still reliably formed. Here is another way in which the class of beliefs that are J_{eg} and the class of reliably formed beliefs can fail to coincide.[39]

I would suggest that, of our candidates, J_{eg} most fully embodies what we are looking for under the heading of "epistemic justification." (a) Like its deontological competitors it is an evaluative concept, in a broad sense, a concept of a favorable status from an epistemic point of view. (b) Unlike J_{dy} it does not presuppose that belief is under direct voluntary control. (c) Unlike J_{di}, it implies that the believer is in a strong epistemic position in believing that p, i.e., that there is something about the way in which he believes that p that renders it at least likely that the belief is true. Thus it renders it intelligible that justification is something we should prize from an epistemic point of view. (d) Unlike the concept of a reliable mode of belief-formation, it represents this "truth-conducivity" as a matter of the belief's being based on an adequate ground within the subject's own cognitive states. Thus it recognizes the "internalist" character of justification; it recognizes that in asking whether a belief is justified we are interested in the prospects for the truth of the belief, given what the subject "has to go on." (e) Thus the concept provides broad guidelines for the specification of conditions of justification, but within those guidelines there is ample room for disagreement over the precise conditions for one or another type of belief. The concept does not leave us totally at a loss as to what to look for. But in adopting J_{eg} we are not building answers to substantive epistemological questions into the concept. As the only candidate to exhibit all these desiderata, J_{eg} is clearly the winner.

VII

It may be useful to bring together the lessons we have learned from this conceptual exploration.

1. Justifying, an activity of showing or establishing something, is much less central for epistemology than is "being justified," as a state or condition.

2. It is central to epistemic justification that *what justifies* is restricted to the subject's "perspective," to the subject's knowledge, justified belief, or experience.

3. Deontological concepts of justification are either saddled with an indefensible assumption of the voluntariness of belief (J_{dv}) or allow for cases in which one believes that p without having any adequate ground for the belief (J_{di}).

4. The notion of one's belief being based on adequate grounds incorporates more of what we are looking for in a concept of epistemic justification than the weaker notion of having adequate grounds for belief.

5. Justification is closely related to reliability, but because of the perspectival character noted in 2, they do not completely coincide; much less can they be identified.

6. The notion of believing that p in a way that is good from an epistemic point of view in that the belief is based on adequate grounds (J_{eg}) satisfies the chief desiderata for a concept of epistemic justification.

VIII

The ultimate payoff of this conceptual exploration is the increased sophistication it gives us in dealing with substantive epistemological issues. Putting our scheme to work is a very large enterprise, spanning a large part of epistemology. In conclusion I will give one illustration of the ways in which our distinctions can be of help in the trenches. For this purpose I will restrict myself to the broad contrast between J_{dv} and J_{eg}.

First, consider what we might term "higher-level requirements" for S's being justified in believing that p. I include under that heading all requirements that S know or justifiably believe something *about* the epistemic status of p, or about the strength of S's grounds for p. This would include requirements that S be justified in believing that:

1. R is an adequate reason for p (where R is alleged to justify S's belief that p).[40]
2. Experience e is an adequate indication that p (where e is alleged to justify S's belief that p).[41]

On J_{eg} there is no temptation to impose such requirements. If R *is* an adequate reason (e *is* an adequate indication), then if one believes that p on that basis, one is *thereby* in a strong position, epistemically; and the further knowledge, or justified belief, that the reason is adequate (the experience is an adequate indication), though no doubt quite important and valuable for other purposes, will do nothing to improve the truth-conduciveness of one's believing that p. But on J_{dv} we get a different story. If it's a question of being blameless in believing that p, it can be persuasively argued that this requires not only forming the belief on what is in fact an adequate ground, but doing so in the light of the realization that the ground is an adequate one. If I decide to believe that p without knowing whether the ground is adequate, am I not subject to blame for proceeding irresponsibly in my doxastic behavior, whatever the actual strength of the ground? If the higher-level requirements are plausible only if we are using J_{dv}, then the dubiousness of that concept will extend to those requirements.[42]

In the above paragraph we were considering whether S's being justified in believing that his ground is adequate is a *necessary* condition of justification. We can also consider whether it is sufficient. Provided that S is justified in believing that his belief that *p* is based on an adequate ground, G, does it make any difference, for his being justified in believing that *p*, whether the ground *is* adequate? Our two contenders will line up here as they did on the previous issue. For J_{eg} the mere fact that S is justified in supposing that G is adequate will cut no ice. What J_{eg} requires is that S *actually be* in an epistemically favorable position; and although S's being justified in supposing G to be adequate is certainly good evidence for that, it doesn't *constitute* being in such a position. Hence J_{eg} requires that the ground of the belief actually be an adequate one. As for J_{dv}, where it is a question of whether S is blameworthy in believing that *p*, what is decisive is how S's epistemic position appears within S's perspective on the world. If, so far as S could tell, G is an adequate ground, then S is blameless, i.e., J_{dv}, in believing that *p* on G. Nothing else could be required for justification in that sense. If S has chosen his doxastic state by applying the appropriate principles in the light of all his relevant knowledge and justified belief, then he is totally in the clear. Again the superior viability of J_{eg}, as over against J_{dv}, should tip the scales in favor of the more objective requirement of adequacy.[43]

Notes

1. Of late a number of theorists have been driving a wedge between what it is to *be* P or what *property* P is, on the one hand, and what belongs to the *concept* of P or what is the meaning of "P" on the other. Thus it has been claimed (Kripke, 1972) that *what heat is* is determined by the physical investigation into the nature of heat, whether or not the results of that investigation are embodied in our *concept* of heat or in the meaning of "heat." I shall take it that no such distinction is applicable to epistemic justification, that here the only reasonable interpretation to be given to "what it is" is "what is involved in the concept" or "what the term means." If someone disagrees with this, that need not be a problem. Such a person can simply read "what concept of justification is being employed" for "what justification is taken to be."

2. I think especially of Chisholm (1977), chap. 1; Ginet (1975), chap. 3; Goldman (1979, 1980); Wolterstorff (1983).

3. It may be claimed that the activity concept is fundamental in another way viz., by virtue of the fact that one is justified in believing that *p* only if one is *capable* of carrying out a justification of the belief. But if that were so we would be justified in far fewer beliefs than we suppose. Most human subjects are quite incapable of carrying out a justification of any perceptual or introspective beliefs.

4. I am indebted to Alvin Plantinga for helping me to see that this term is more suitable than the term "normative" that I had been using in earlier versions of this paper. The reader should be cautioned that "deontological" as used here does not carry the contrast with "teleological" that is common in ethical theory. According to that distinction, a deontological ethical theory, like that of Kant's, does not regard principles of duty or obligation as owing their status to the fact that acting in the way they prescribe tends to realize certain desirable states of affairs. Whereas a teleological theory, like Utilitarianism, holds that this is what renders a principle of obligation acceptable. The fact that we are not using "deontological" with this force is shown by the fact that we are thinking of epistemic obligations as owing their validity to the fact that fulfilling them would tend to lead to the realization of a desirable state of affairs; viz., a large body of beliefs with a favorable truth-falsity ratio.

5. See Chisholm (1977), chap. 1; Ginet (1975), chap. 3; Wolterstorff (1983). An extended development of a deontological concept of epistemic justification is to be found in Naylor (1978). In my development of deontological concepts in this essay I have profited from the writing of all these people and from discussions with them.

6. (1975), p. 28. See also Ayer (1956), pp. 31–34; Chisholm (1977), p. 14; Naylor (1978), p. 8.

7. These examples are meant to be illustrative only; they do not necessarily carry the endorsement of the management.

8. Here I am indebted to Alvin Plantinga.

9. A weaker objective conception would be this. My obligation is to do what in fact is *likely* to bring out A. On this weaker conception I could be said to have fulfilled my obligation in (some) cases in which A is not forthcoming.

10. We could also subjectivize the aimed-at result, instead of or in addition to subjectivizing what it takes to arrive at that result. In this way one would have subjectively fulfilled one's obligation if one had done what one believed to be one's obligation. Or, to combine the two moves to the subjective, one would have subjectively fulfilled one's obligation if one had done what one believed would lead to the fulfillment of what one believed to be one's obligation. But sufficient unto the day is the distinction thereof.

11. I would call this "epistemic obligation," except that I want to make these same distinctions with respect to epistemic justification, and so I don't want to repeat the generic term for one of the species.

12. Since we are tacitly restricting this to epistemic justification, we will also be, tacitly, restricting ourselves to intellectual obligations.

13. Since this is all on the assumption that S does believe that *p*, we need not add that to the right hand side in order to get a sufficient condition.

14. Note that XI, XII, and some forms of XIII are in terms of higher-level beliefs about one's epistemic status *vis-à-vis p.* There are less sophisticated sorts of subjectivization. For example: S is subjectively justified in believing that *p iff* S believes that *q,* and *q* is evidence for *p.* (For the reason this does not count as having adequate evidence see the next paragraph in the text.) Or even more subjectively: S is subjectively justified in believing that *p iff* S believes that *q* and bases his belief that *p* on his belief that *q.* The definitions presented in the text do not dictate what we should say in the case in which S does not have the higher level belief specified in XI and XII, but satisfies either of the above conditions. A thorough treatment of modes of normative status would have to go into all of this.

15. We have been taking it that to be, e.g., subjectively or cognitively justified

in believing that p is to not be violating any subjective or cognitive obligations in believing that p. That means that if we opt for cognitive justification we are committed to giving a correspondingly cognitive formulation of what intellectual obligations one has. But that isn't the only way to do it. We could leave all the obligations in a purely objective form, and vary the function that goes from obligation to justification. That is, we could say that one is subjectively justified if one believes that one has not violated an (objective) obligation (or perhaps believes something that is such that, given one's objective obligations, it implies that none of those obligations have been violated). And a similar move could be made for the other modes.

16. Here are a couple of examples of the attraction of XII for J_d. Chisholm (1977) presents an informal explanation of his basic term of epistemic evaluation, "more reasonable than" in terms of an "intellectual requirement." The explanation runs as follows:

> One way, then, of re-expressing the locution "p is more reasonable than q for S at t" is to say this: S is so situated at t that his intellectual requirement, his responsibility as an intellectual being, is better fulfilled by p than by q [p. 14].

The point that is relevant to our present discussion is that Chisholm states our basic intellectual requirement in what I have called "cognitive" rather than "objective" terms; and with a motivational rider.

> We may assume that every person is subject to a purely intellectual requirement—that of trying his best to bring it about that, for every proposition h that he considers, he accepts h if and only if h is true [p. 14].

The "requirement" is that one *try one's best* to bring this about, rather than that one does bring it about. I take it that to try my best to bring about a result, R, is to do what, so far as I can tell, will bring about R, insofar as that is within my power. (It might be claimed that so long as I do what I believe will bring about R I am trying my best, however irresponsible the belief. But it seems to me that so long as I am not acting on the best of the indications available to me I am not "trying my best.") The motivational rider comes in too, since unless I do what I do *because* I am taking it to (have a good chance to) lead to R, I am not trying at all to bring about R.

Of course, Chisholm is speaking in terms of fulfilling an intellectual obligation rather than, as we have been doing, in terms of not violating intellectual obligations. But we are faced with the same choice between our "modes" in either case.

For a second example I turn to Wolterstorff (1983). Wolterstorff's initial formulation of a necessary and sufficient condition of justification (or, as he says, "rationality") for an "eluctable" belief of S that P is: *S lacks adequate reasons for ceasing from believing that p* (p. 164). But then by considerations similar to those we have just adduced, he recognizes that even if S does not in fact have adequate reason for ceasing to believe that p, he would still be unjustified in continuing to hold the belief if he were "rationally obliged" to believe that he does have adequate reason to cease to believe that p. Moreover Wolterstorff recognizes that S would be justified in believing that p if, even though he does have adequate reason to cease from believing that p, he is rationally justified in supposing that he doesn't. Both these qualifications amount to recognizing that what is crucial is not what reasons S has in fact, but what reasons S is justified in supposing himself to have. The final formulation, embodying these and other qualifications, runs as follows:

A person is rational in his eluctable and innocently produced belief *Bp* if and only if S does believe *p* and either:
  (i) S neither has nor ought to have adequate reason to cease from believing *p*, and is not rationally obliged to believe that he *does* have adequate reason to cease; or
  (ii) S does have adequate reason to cease from believing *p* but does not realize that he does, and is rationally justified in that [p. 168].

17. See also Ginet (1975), p. 36.

18. Note that I am not restricting the category of what is within my immediate voluntary control to "basic actions." Neither of the actions just mentioned would qualify for that title. The category includes both basic actions and actions that involve other conditions, where I can satisfy those other conditions, when I choose, just at the moment of choice. Thus my point about believing is not just that it is not a basic action, but that it is not even a non-basic action that is under my effective immediate control. Whatever is required for my believing that there will never be a nuclear war, it is not something that I can bring about immediately by choosing to do so; though, as I am about to point out, I can affect my believings and abstentions in a more long-range fashion.

19. For other accounts of the indirect voluntary control of beliefs see Naylor (1978), pp. 19–20; Wolterstorff (1983), pp. 153–55.

20. Our four "modes" can also be applied to J_{di}. Indeed, the possibilities for variation are even more numerous. For example, with respect to the *subjective* mode we can switch from the objective fact to the subject's belief with respect to (a) the circumstances of a putative violation, (b) whether there was a violation, and (c) whether the violation was causally related to the belief-formation in question. We will leave all this as an exercise for the reader.

21. I must confess that I do not find "justified" an apt term for a favorable or desirable state or condition, when what makes it desirable is cut loose from considerations of obligation and blame. Nevertheless, since the term is firmly ensconced in the literature as the term to use for any concept that satisfies the four conditions set out in section II, I will stifle my linguistic scruples and employ it for a non-deontological concept.

22. There are also problems as to where to draw the line. What about the unconscious "use" of perceptual cues for the depth of an object in the visual field or for "size constancy"? And however we answer that particular question, just where do we draw the line as we move farther and farther from our initial paradigms?

23. For some recent discussion of "based on" see Swain (1981), chap. 3, and Pappas (1979). One additional point I do need to make explicit is this. I mean "based on" to range over both what initially gave rise to the belief, and what sustains it while it continues to be held. To be precise one should speak of *what the belief is based on at time t*. If *t* is the time of acquisition, one is speaking of what gave rise to the belief; if *t* later than that, one is speaking of what sustains it.

24. For an interesting discussion of this point see Quinton (1973), chap. 7. My opponent will be even more hard pressed to make out that beliefs about one's own conscious experience are based on other beliefs. His best move here would be

either to deny that there are such beliefs or to deny that they are based on anything.

25. No such restriction would be required just for having grounds (of some sort). Though even here the word "ground" by itself carries a strong suggestion that what is grounded is, to some extent, supported. We need a term for anything a belief might be based on, however vainly. "Ground" carries too much positive evaluative force to be ideally suitable for this role.

26. For some recent discussion of this issue see Harman (1973), chap. 2; Lehrer (1974), chap. 6; Firth (1978); Swain (1981), chap. 3; Foley (1984).

27. Even though we have opted for the "based on" formulation as giving us the more fundamental concept of epistemic justification, we have also recognized the "has adequate grounds" formulation as giving us a concept of epistemic justification. Either of these will introduce a "basis of evaluative status" component into the concept.

28. This latter qualification is needed, because I might accept a self-evident proposition on authority. In that case I was not, so to say, taking advantage of its self-evidence.

29. We are not speaking here of a belief that one *is* sleepy. There a ground is readily identifiable—one's feeling of sleepiness.

30. See Bonjour (1980); Kornblith (1984); Bach (1985).

31. See Goldman (1980); Chisholm (1977), chap. 4, pp. 63–64; Ginet (1975), pp. 34–37.

32. Swain (1981), chap. 4.

33. Goldman (1979).

34. For simplicity I shall couch the ensuing formulations solely in terms of belief-formation, but the qualification "or sustenance" is to be understood throughout.

35. These two qualifications testify to the difficulty of getting the concept of reliability in satisfactory shape; and there are other problems to be dealt with, e.g., how to identify the general procedure of which the present belief-formation is an instance.

36. An alternative to explicating "adequate" in terms of reliability would be to use the notion of conditional probability. G is an adequate ground for a belief that *p* just in case the probability of *p* on G is high. And since adequacy is closely related both to reliability and to conditional probability, they are presumably closely related to each other. Swain (1981), chap. 4, exploits this connection to explicate reliability in terms of conditional probability, though in a more complex fashion than is indicated by these brief remarks.

37. (1979), p. 18. (See Chapter 7 below.)

38. If you have trouble envisaging his trusting his memory in the face of his parents's story, you may imagine that he is not thinking of that story at the moment he forms the memory belief.

39. In the article in which he introduces this example, Goldman modifies the "reliability is a criterion of justification" view so that it will accommodate the example. The modified formulation runs as follows:

> If S's belief in *p* at *t* results from a reliable cognitive process, and there is no reliable or conditionally reliable process available to S which had it been used by S in addition to the process actually used, would have resulted in S's not believing *p* at *t*, then S's belief in *p* at *t* is justified [p. 20].

On this revised formulation, being formed by a reliable process is sufficient for justification only if there is no other reliable process that the subject could have used and such that if he had used it he would not have come to believe that *p*. In the case cited there is such a reliable process, viz., taking account of the strong reasons for believing one's memory of pre-seven-years-old events to be unreliable. The revised reliability criterion yields the correct result in this case. However, this move leaves unshaken the point that in this case Jones's belief *is* reliably formed but unjustified. That remains true, whatever is to be said about the revised criterion.

40. See, e.g., Armstrong (1973), p. 151; Skyrms (1967), p. 374.

41. See, e.g., Sellars (1963), pp. 168–69; Bonjour (1978), pp. 5–6; Lehrer (1974), pp. 103–5.

42. In my paper "What's Wrong with Immediate Knowledge?" *Synthese* 55, no. 2 [May 1983]: pp. 73–95, I develop at much greater length this kind of diagnosis of Bonjour's deployment of a higher-level requirement in his argument against immediate knowledge (Bonjour, 1978).

43. Ancestors of this essay were presented at SUNY at Albany, SUNY at Buffalo, Calvin College, Cornell University, University of California at Irvin, Lehigh University, University of Michigan, University of Nebraska, Syracuse University, and the University of Western Ontario. I wish to thank members of the audience in all these institutions for their helpful comments. I would like to express special appreciation to Robert Audi, Carl Ginet, George Mavrodes, Alvin Plantinga, Fred Schmitt, and Nicholas Wolterstorff for their penetrating comments on earlier versions.

References

Armstrong, D.M. 1973. *Belief, Truth, and Knowledge*. Cambridge: Cambridge University Press.

Ayer, A. J. 1956. *The Problem of Knowledge*. London: Macmillian.

Bach, K. 1985. "A Rationale for Reliabilism." *The Monist* 68.

Bonjour, L. 1978. "Can Empirical Knowledge Have a Foundation?" *American Philosophical Quarterly* 15: 1–13. (Chapter 4 below.)

Chisholm, R. M. 1977. *Theory of Knowledge*, 2nd ed. Englewood Cliffs, N.J.: Prentice-Hall.

Dretske, F. 1981. *Knowledge and the Flow of Information*. Cambridge: MIT Press.

Firth, R. 1978. "Are Epistemic Concepts Reducible to Ethical Concepts?" In A. I. Goldman and J. Kim, eds., *Values and Morals*. Dordrecht: D. Reidel.

Foley, R. 1984. "Epistemic Luck and the Purely Epistemic." *American Philosophical Quarterly*.

Ginet, C. 1975. *Knowledge, Perception, and Memory*. Dordrecht.: D. Reidel.

Goldman, A. I. 1979. "What Is Justified Belief?" In G. S. Pappas, ed., *Justification and Knowledge*. Dordrecht: D. Reidel. (Chapter 7 below.)

———. 1980. "The Internalist Conception of Justification." *Midwest Studies in Philosophy*, vol. 5. Pp. 27–51.

Harman, G. 1973. *Thought*. Princeton: Princeton University Press.

Kornblith, H. 1985. "Ever Since Descartes." *The Monist* 68, no. 2.

Kripke, S. A. 1972. "Naming and Necessity." In D. Davidson and G. Harman, eds., *Semantics of Natural Language*. Dordrecht: D. Reidel.

Lehrer, K. 1974. *Knowledge*. New York: Oxford University Press.

Naylor, M. B. 1978. "Epistemic Justification." Unpublished.

Pappas, G. S. 1979. "Basing Relations." In G. S. Pappas, ed., *Justification and Knowledge*. Dordrecht: D. Reidel.

Pollock, J. 1975. *Knowledge and Justification*. Princeton: Princeton University Press.

Quinton, A. 1973. *The Nature of Things*. London: Routledge & Kegan Paul.

Sellars, W. 1963. *Science, Perception, and Reality*. London: Routledge & Kegan Paul.

Skyrms, B. 1967. "The Explication of 'X Knows that P.' " *Journal of Philosophy* 64: 373–89.

Swain, M. 1981. *Reasons and Knowledge*. Ithaca: Cornell University Press.

Wolterstorff, N. 1983. "Can Belief in God Be Rational if It Has No Foundations?" In A. Plantinga and N. Wolterstorff, eds. *Faith and Rationality*. Notre Dame: University of Notre Dame Press.

2   The Myth of the Given

RODERICK CHISHOLM

1. The doctrine of "the given" involved two theses about our knowledge. We may introduce them by means of a traditional metaphor:

> (A) The knowledge which a person has at any time is a structure or edifice, many parts and stages of which help to support each other, but which as a whole is supported by its own foundation.

The second thesis is a specification of the first:

> (B) The foundation of one's knowledge consists (at least in part) of the apprehension of what have been called, variously, "sensations," "sense-impressions," "appearances," "sensa," "sense-qualia," and "phenomena."

These phenomenal entities, said to be at the base of the structure of knowledge, are what was called "the given." A third thesis is sometimes associated with the doctrine of the given, but the first two theses do not imply it. We may formulate it in the terms of the same metaphor:

> (C) The *only* apprehension which is thus basic to the structure of knowledge is our apprehension of "appearances" (etc.)—our apprehension of the given.

Theses (A) and (B) constitute the "doctrine of the given"; thesis (C), if a label were necessary, might be called "the phenomenalistic version" of the doctrine. The first two theses are essential to the empirical tradition in Western philosophy. The third is problematic for traditional empiricism and depends in part, but only in part, upon the way in which the metaphor of the edifice and its foundation is spelled out.

I believe it is accurate to say that, at the time at which our study begins, most American epistemologists accepted the first two theses and thus accepted the doctrine of the given. The expression "the given"

---

became a term of contemporary philosophical vocabulary partly because of its use by C. I. Lewis in his *Mind and the World-Order* (1929). Many of the philosophers who accepted the doctrine avoided the expression because of its association with other more controversial parts of Lewis's book—a book which might be taken (though mistakenly, I think) also to endorse thesis (C), the "phenomenalistic version" of the doctrine. The doctrine itself—theses (A) and (B)—became a matter of general controversy during the period of our survey (1930–1960).

Thesis (A) was criticized as being "absolute" and thesis (B) as being overly "subjective." Both criticisms may be found in some of the "instrumentalistic" writings of John Dewey and philosophers associated with him. They may also be found in the writings of those philosophers of science ("logical empiricists") writing in the tradition of the Vienna Circle. (At an early stage of this tradition, however, some of these same philosophers seem to have accepted all three theses.) Discussion became entangled in verbal confusions—especially in connection with the uses of such terms as "doubt," "certainty," "appearance," and "immediate experience." Philosophers, influenced by the work that Ludwig Wittgenstein had been doing in the 1930s, noted such confusions in detail, and some of them seem to have taken the existence of such confusions to indicate that (A) and (B) are false.[1] Many have rejected both theses as being inconsistent with a certain theory of thought and reference; among them, in addition to some of the critics just referred to, we find philosophers in the tradition of nineteenth-century "idealism."

Philosophers of widely diverging schools now believe that "the myth of the given" has finally been dispelled.[2] I suggest, however, that, although thesis (C), "the phenomenalistic version," is false, the two theses (A) and (B), which constitute the doctrine of the given, are true.

The doctrine is not merely the consequence of a metaphor. We are led to it when we attempt to answer certain questions about *justification*—our justification for supposing, in connection with any one of the things that we know to be true, that it is something that we know to be true.

2. To the question "What justification do I have for thinking I know that *a* is true?" one may reply: "I know that *b* is true, and if I know that *b* is true then I also know that *a* is true. And to the question "What justification do I have for thinking I know that *b* is true?" one may reply: "I know that *c* is true, and if I know that *c* is true then I also know that *b* is true." Are we thus led, sooner or later, to something *n* of which one may say: "What justifies me in thinking I know that *n* is true is simply the fact that *n* is true"? If there is such an *n*, then the belief or statement that *n* is true may be thought of either as a belief or statement which "justifies itself" or as a belief or statement which is itself "neither justified nor unjustified." The distinction—unlike that between a Prime Mover which moves itself and a

Prime Mover which is neither in motion nor at rest—is largely a verbal one; the essential thing, if there is such an *n,* is that it provides a stopping place in the process, or dialectic, of justification.

We may now re-express, somewhat less metaphorically, the two theses which I have called the "doctrine of the given." The first thesis, that our knowledge is an edifice or structure having its own foundation, becomes (A) "every statement, which we are justified in thinking that we know, is justified in part by some statement which justifies itself." The second thesis, that there are appearances ("the given") at the foundation of our knowledge, becomes (B) "there are statements about appearances which thus justify themselves." (The third thesis—the "phenomenalistic version" of the doctrine of the given—becomes (C) "there are no self-justifying statements which are not statements about appearances.")

Let us now turn to the first of the two theses constituting the doctrine of the given.

3. "Every justified statement is justified in part by some statement which justifies itself." Could it be that the question which this thesis is supposed to answer is a question which arises only because of some mistaken assumption? If not, what are the alternative ways of answering it? And did any of the philosophers with whom we are concerned actually accept any of these alternatives? The first two questions are less difficult to answer than the third.

There are the following points of view to be considered, each of which *seems* to have been taken by some of the philosophers in the period of our survey.

(1) One may believe that the questions about justification which give rise to our problem are based upon false assumptions and hence that they *should not be asked* at all.

(2) One may believe that no statement or claim is justified unless it is justified, at least in part, by some other justified statement or claim which it does not justify; this belief may suggest that one should continue the process of justifying *ad indefinitum,* justifying each claim by reference to some additional claim.

(3) One may believe that no statement or claim *a* is justified unless it is justified by some other justified statement or claim *b,* and that *b* is not justified unless it in turn is justified by *a;* this would suggest that the process of justifying is, or should be, *circular.*

(4) One may believe that there are some particular claims *n* at which the process of justifying should stop, and one may then hold of any such claim *n* either: (a) *n* is justified by something—viz., *experience* or *observation*—which is not itself a claim and which therefore cannot be said itself either to be justified or unjustified; (b) *n* is itself *unjustified;* (c) *n* justifies itself; or (d) *n* is *neither justified nor unjustified.*

These possibilities, I think, exhaust the significant points of view; let us now consider them in turn.

4. "The questions about justification which give rise to the problem are based upon false assumptions and therefore should not be asked at all."

The questions are *not* based upon false assumptions, but most of the philosophers who discussed the questions put them in such a misleading way that one is very easily misled into supposing that they *are* based upon false assumptions.

Many philosophers, following Descartes, Russell, and Husserl, formulated the questions about justification by means of such terms as "doubt," "certainty," and "incorrigibility," and they used, or misused, these terms in such a way that, when their questions were taken in the way in which one would ordinarily take them, they could be shown to be based upon false assumptions. One may note, for example, that the statement "There is a clock on the mantelpiece" is not self-justifying—for to the question "What is your justification for thinking you know that there is a clock on the mantelpiece?" the proper reply would be to make some other statement (e.g., "I saw it there this morning and no one would have taken it away")—and one may then go on to ask "But are there any statements which can be said to justify themselves?" If we express these facts, as many philosophers did, by saying that the statement "There is a clock on the mantelpiece" is one which is not "certain," or one which may be "doubted," and if we then go on to ask "Does this doubtful statement rest upon other statements which are certain and incorrigible?" then we are using terms in an extraordinarily misleading way. The question "Does this doubtful statement rest upon statements which are certain and incorrigible?"—if taken as one would ordinarily take it—does rest upon a false assumption, for (we may assume) the statement that there is a clock on the mantelpiece is one which is not doubtful at all.

John Dewey, and some of the philosophers whose views were very similar to his, tended to suppose, mistakenly, that the philosophers who asked themselves "What justification do I have for thinking I know this?" were asking the quite different question "What more can I do to verify or confirm that this is so?" and they rejected answers to the first question on the ground that they were unsatisfactory answers to the second.[3] Philosophers influenced by Wittgenstein tended to suppose, also mistakenly, but quite understandably, that the question "What justification do I have for thinking I know this?" contains an implicit challenge and presupposes that one does not have the knowledge concerned. They then pointed out, correctly, that in most of the cases where the question was raised (e.g., "What justifies me in thinking I know that this is a table?") there is no ground for challenging the claim to knowledge and that questions presupposing that the claim is false should not arise. But the question "What justifies me in thinking I know that this is a table?" does not challenge the claim to know that this is a table, much less presuppose that the claim is false.

The "critique of cogency," as Lewis described this concern of epistemology, presupposes that we *are* justified in thinking we know most of the things that we do think we know, and what it seeks to elicit is the nature of this justification. The enterprise is like that of ethics, logic, and aesthetics:

> The nature of the good can be learned from experience only if the content of experience be first classified into good and bad, or grades of better and worse. Such classification or grading already involves the legislative application of the same principle which is sought. In logic, principles can be elicited by generalization from examples only if cases of valid reasoning have first been segregated by some criterion. In esthetics, the laws of the beautiful may be derived from experience only if the criteria of beauty have first been correctly applied.[4]

When Aristotle considered an invalid mood of the syllogism and asked himself "What is wrong with this?" he was not suggesting to himself that perhaps nothing was wrong; he presupposed that the mood *was* invalid, just as he presupposed that others were not, and he attempted, successfully, to formulate criteria which would enable us to distinguish the two types of mood.

When we have answered the question "What justification do I have for thinking I know this?" what we learn, as Socrates taught, is something about ourselves. We learn, of course, what the justification happens to be for the particular claim with which the question is concerned. But we also learn, more generally, what the criteria are, if any, in terms of which we believe ourselves justified in counting one thing as an instance of knowing and another thing not. The truth which the philosopher seeks, when he asks about justification, is "already implicit in the mind which seeks it, and needs only to be elicited and brought to clear expression."[5]

Let us turn, then, to the other approaches to the problem of "the given."

5. "No statement or claim would be justified unless it were justified, at least in part, by some other justified claim or statement which it does not justify."

This regress principle might be suggested by the figure of the building and its support: no stage supports another unless it is itself supported by some other stage beneath it—a truth which holds not only of the upper portions of the building but also of what we call its foundation. And the principle follows if, as some of the philosophers in the tradition of logical empiricism seemed to believe, we should combine a frequency theory of probability with a probability theory of justification.

In *Experience and Prediction* (1938) and in other writings, Hans Reichenbach defended a "probability theory of knowledge" which seemed to involve the following contentions:

(I) To justify accepting a statement, it is necessary to show that the statement is probable.

(2) To say of a statement that it is probable is to say something about statistical frequencies. Somewhat more accurately, a statement of the form "It is *probable* that any particular *a* is a *b*" may be explicated as saying "Most *a's* are *b's*." Or, still more accurately, to say "The probability is *n* that a particular *a* is a *b*" is to say "The limit of the relative frequency with which the property of being a *b* occurs in the class of things having the property *a* is *n*."

(3) Hence, by (2), to show that a proposition is probable it is necessary to show that a certain statistical frequency obtains; and, by (I), to show that a certain statistical frequency obtains it is necessary to show that it is probable that the statistical frequency obtains; and therefore, by (2), to show that it is probable that a certain statistical frequency obtains, it is necessary to show that a certain frequency of frequencies obtains . . .

(4) And therefore "there is no Archimedean point of absolute certainty left to which to attach our knowledge of the world; all we have is an elastic net of probability connections floating in open space (Reichenbach, p. 192).

This reasoning suggests that an infinite number of steps must be taken in order to justify acceptance of any statement. For, according to the reasoning, we cannot determine the probability of one statement until we have determined that of a second, and we cannot determine that of the second until we have determined that of a third, and so on. Reichenbach does not leave the matter here, however. He suggests that there is a way of "descending" from this "open space" of probability connections, but, if I am not mistaken, we can make the descent only by letting go of the concept of justification.

He says that, if we are to avoid the regress of probabilities of probabilities of probabilities . . ., we must be willing at some point merely to make a guess; "there will always be some blind posits on which the whole concatenation is based" (p. 367). The view that knowledge is to be identified with certainty and that probable knowledge must be "imbedded in a framework of certainty" is "a remnant of rationalism. An empiricist theory of probability can be constructed only if we are willing to regard knowledge as a system of posits."[6]

But if we begin by assuming, as we do, that there is a distinction between knowledge, on the one hand, and a lucky guess, on the other, then we must reject at least one of the premises of an argument purporting to demonstrate that knowledge is a system of "blind posits." The unacceptable conclusion of Reichenbach's argument may be so construed as to follow from premises (1) and (2); and premise (2) may be accepted as a kind of definition (though there are many who believe that this definition is not adequate to all of the uses of the term "probable" in science and everyday life). Premise (1), therefore, is the one we should reject, and there are good reasons, I think, for rejecting (1), the thesis that "to justify accepting a proposition it is necessary to show that the proposition is probable." In fairness to Reichenbach, it should be added that he never explicitly affirms premise (1); but some such premise is essential to his argument.

6. "No statement or claim *a* would be justified unless it were justified by some other justified statement or claim *b* which would not be justified unless it were justified in turn by *a*."

The "coherence theory of truth," to which some philosophers committed themselves, is sometimes taken to imply that justification may thus be circular; I believe, however, that the theory does not have this implication. It does define "truth" as a kind of systematic consistency of beliefs or propositions. The truth of a proposition is said to consist not in the fact that the proposition "corresponds" with something which is not itself a proposition, but in the fact that it fits consistently into a certain more general system of propositions. This view may even be suggested by the figure of the building and its foundations. There is no difference in principle between the way in which the upper stories are supported by the lower, and that in which the cellar is supported by the earth just below it, or the way in which that stratum of earth is supported by various substrata farther below; a good building appears to be a part of the terrain on which it stands, and a good system of propositions is a part of the wider system which gives it its truth. But these metaphors do not solve philosophical problems.

The coherence theory did in fact appeal to something other than logical consistency; its proponents conceded that a system of false propositions may be internally consistent and hence that logical consistency alone is no guarantee of truth. Brand Blanshard, who defended the coherence theory in *The Nature of Thought,* said that a proposition is true provided it is a member of an internally consistent system of propositions and *provided further* this system is "the system in which everything real and possible is coherently included."[7] In one phase of the development of "logical empiricism" its proponents seem to have held a similar view: a proposition—or, in this case, a statement—is true provided it is a member of an internally consistent system of statements and *provided further* this system is "the system which is actually adopted by mankind, and especially by the scientists in our culture circle."[8]

A theory of truth is not, as such, a theory of justification. To say that a proposition is true is not to say that we are justified in accepting it as true, and to say that we are justified in accepting it as true is not to say that it is true. Whatever merits the coherence theory may have as an answer to certain questions about truth, it throws no light upon our present epistemological question. If we accept the coherence theory, we may still ask, concerning any proposition *a* which we think we know to be true, "What is my justification for thinking I know that *a* is a member of the system of propositions in which everything real and possible is coherently included, or that *a* is a member of the system of propositions which is actually adopted by mankind and by the scientists of our culture circle?" And when we ask such a question, we are confronted, once again, with our original alternatives.

7. If our questions about justification do have a proper stopping place, then, as I have said, there are still four significant possibilities to consider. We may stop with some particular claim and say of it that either:

(a) it is justified by something—by experience, or by observation—which is not itself a claim and which, therefore, cannot be said either to be justified or to be unjustified;

(b) it is justified by some claim which refers to our experience or observation, and the claim referring to our experience or observation has *no* justification;

(c) it justifies itself; or

(d) it is itself neither justified nor unjustified.

The first of these alternatives leads readily to the second, and the second to the third or to the fourth. The third and the fourth—which differ only verbally, I think—involve the doctrine of "the given."

Carnap wrote, in 1936, that the procedure of scientific testing involves two operations: the "confrontation of a statement with observation" and the "confrontation of a statement with previously accepted statements." He suggested that those logical empiricists who were attracted to the coherence theory of truth tended to lose sight of the first of these operations—the confrontation of a statement with observation. He proposed a way of formulating simple "acceptance rules" for such confrontation, and he seemed to believe that, merely by applying such rules, we could avoid the epistemological questions with which the adherents of "the given" had become involved.

Carnap said this about his acceptance rules: "If no foreign language or introduction of new terms is involved, the rules are trivial. For example: 'If one is hungry, the statement "I am hungry" may be accepted'; or: 'If one sees a key one may accept the statement "there lies a key." '" As we shall note later, the first of these rules differs in an important way from the second. Confining ourselves for the moment to rules of the second sort—"If one sees a key one may accept the statement 'there lies a key' "—let us ask ourselves whether the appeal to such rules enables us to solve our problem of the stopping place.

When we have made the statement "There lies a key," we can, of course, raise the question "What is my justification for thinking I know, or for believing, that there lies a key?" The answer would be "I see the key." We cannot ask "What is my justification for seeing a key?" But we *can* ask "What is my justification for thinking that it is a *key* that I see?" and, if we *do* see that the thing is a key, the question will have an answer. The answer might be "I see that it's shaped like a key and that it's in the lock, and I remember that a key is usually here." The possibility of this question, and its answer, indicates that we cannot stop our questions about justification merely by appealing to observation or experience. For, of the statement "I observe that this is an A," we can ask, and answer, the question "What is my justification for thinking that I observe that there is an A?"

It is relevant to note, moreover, that there may be conditions under which seeing a key does *not* justify one in accepting the statement "There is a key" or in believing that one sees a key. If the key were so disguised or concealed that the man who saw it did not recognize it to be a key, then he might not be justified in accepting the statement "There is a key." Just as, if Mr. Jones unknown to anyone but himself is a thief, then the people who see him may be said to see a thief—but none of those who thus sees a thief is justified in accepting the statement "There is a thief."[10]

Some of the writings of logical empiricists suggest that, although some statements may be justified by reference to other statements, those statements which involve "confrontation with observation" are not justified at all. C. G. Hempel, for example, wrote that "the acknowledgement of an experiential statement as true is psychologically motivated by certain experiences; but within the system of statements which express scientific knowledge or one's beliefs at a given time, they function in the manner of postulates for which no grounds are offered."[11] Hempel conceded, however, that this use of the term "postulate" is misleading, and he added the following note of clarification: "When an experiential sentence is accepted 'on the basis of direct experiential evidence,' it is indeed not asserted arbitrarily; but to describe the evidence in question would simply mean to repeat the experiential statement itself. Hence, in the context of cognitive justification, the statement functions in the manner of a primitive sentence."[12]

When we reach a statement having the property just referred to—an experiential statement such that to describe its evidence "would simply mean to repeat the experiential statement itself"—we have reached a proper stopping place in the process of justification.

8. We are thus led to the concept of a belief, statement, claim, proposition, or hypothesis, which justifies itself. To be clear about the concept, let us note the way in which we would justify the statement that we have a certain belief. It is essential, of course, that we distinguish justifying the statement *that* we have a certain belief from justifying the belief itself.

Suppose, then, a man is led to say "I believe that Socrates is mortal" and we ask him "What is your justification for thinking that you believe, or for thinking that you know that you believe, that Socrates is mortal?" To this strange question, the only appropriate reply would be "My justification for thinking I believe, or for thinking that I know that I believe, that Socrates is mortal is simply the fact that I *do* believe that Socrates is mortal." One justifies the statement simply by reiterating it; the statement's justification is what the statement says. Here, then, we have a case which satisfies Hempel's remark quoted above; we describe the evidence for a statement merely by repeating the statement. We could say, as C. J. Ducasse did, that "the occurrence of belief is its own evidence."[13]

Normally, as I have suggested, one cannot justify a statement merely by reiterating it. To the question "What justification do you have for thinking you know that there can be no life on the moon?" it would be inappropriate, and impertinent, to reply by saying simply "There *can* be life on the moon," thus reiterating the fact at issue. An appropriate answer would be one referring to certain *other* facts—for example, the fact that we know there is insufficient oxygen on the moon to support any kind of life. But to the question "What is your justification for thinking you know that you believe so and so?" there is nothing to say other than "I *do* believe so and so."

We may say, then, that there are some statements which are self-justifying, or which justify themselves. And we may say, analogously, that there are certain beliefs, claims, propositions, or hypotheses which are self-justifying, or which justify themselves. A statement, belief, claim, proposition, or hypothesis may be said to be self-justifying for a person, if the person's justification for thinking he knows it to be true is simply the fact that it *is* true.

Paradoxically, these things I have described by saying that they "justify themselves" may *also* be described by saying they are "neither justified nor unjustified." The two modes of description are two different ways of saying the same thing.

If we are sensitive to ordinary usage, we may note that the expression "I believe that I believe" is ordinarily used not to refer to a second-order belief about the speaker's own beliefs, but to indicate that the speaker has not yet made up his mind. "I *believe that* I *believe* that Johnson is a good president" might properly be taken to indicate that, if the speaker *does* believe that Johnson is a good president, he is not yet firm in that belief.

Hence there is a temptation to infer that, if we say of a man who is firm in his belief that Socrates is mortal, that he is "justified in believing that he believes that Socrates is mortal," our statement "makes no sense." And there is also a temptation to go on and say that it "makes no sense" even to say of such a man, that his *statement* "I believe that Socrates is mortal" is one which is "justified" for him.[14] After all, what would it mean to say of a man's statement about his own belief, that he is *not* justified in accepting it?[15]

The questions about what does or does not "make any sense" need not, however, be argued. We *may* say, if we prefer, that the statements about the beliefs in question are "neither justified nor unjustified." Whatever mode of description we use, the essential points are two. First, we may appeal to such statements in the process of justifying some *other* statement or belief. If they *have* no justification they may yet *be* a justification—for something other than themselves. ("What justifies me in thinking that he and I are not likely to agree? The fact that I believe that Socrates is mortal and he does not.") Second, the making of such a statement does provide what I have been calling a "stopping place" in the dialectic of justification; but now, instead of signalizing the stopping place by reiterating the questioned statement, we do it by saying that the question of its justification is one which "should not arise."

It does not matter, then, whether we speak of certain statements which "justify themselves" or of certain statements which are "neither justified nor unjustified," for in either case we will be referring to the same set of statements. I shall continue to use the former phrase.

There are, then, statements about one's own beliefs ("I believe that Socrates is mortal")—and statements about many other psychological attitudes—which are self-justifying. "What justifies me in believing, or in thinking I know, that I *hope* to come tomorrow? Simply the fact that I *do* hope to come tomorrow." Thinking, desiring, wondering, loving, hating, and other such attitudes are similar. Some, but by no means all, of the statements we can make about such attitudes, when the attitudes are our own, are self-justifying—as are statements containing such phrases as "I think I remember" or "I seem to remember" (as distinguished from "I remember"), and "I think that I see" and "I think that I perceive" (as distinguished from "I see" and "I perceive"). Thus, of the two examples which Carnap introduced in connection with his "acceptance rules" discussed above, viz., "I am hungry" and "I see a key," we may say that the first is self-justifying and the second not.

The "doctrine of the given," it will be recalled, tells us (A) that every justified statement, about what we think we know, is justified in part by some statement which justifies itself and (B) that there are statements about appearances which thus justify themselves. The "phenomenalistic version" of the theory adds (C) that statements about appearances are the *only* statements which justify themselves. What we have been saying is that the first thesis, (A), of the doctrine of the given is true and that the "phenomenalistic version," (C), is false; let us turn now to thesis (B).

9. In addition to the self-justifying statements about psychological attitudes, are there self-justifying statements about "appearances"? Now we encounter difficulties involving the word "appearance" and its cognates.

Sometimes such words as "appears," "looks," and "seems" are used to convey what one might also convey by such terms as "believe." For example, if I say "It appears to me that General de Gaulle was successful," or "General de Gaulle seems to have been successful," I am likely to mean only that I believe, or incline to believe, that he has been successful; the words "appears" and "seems" serve as useful hedges, giving me an out, should I find out later that de Gaulle was not successful. When "appear"-words are used in this way, the statements in which they occur add nothing significant to the class of "self-justifying" statements we have just provided. Philosophers have traditionally assumed, however, that such terms as "appear" may also be used in a quite different way. If this assumption is correct, as I believe it is, then this additional use does lead us to another type of self-justifying statement.

Later we shall have occasion to note some of the confusion to which the substantival expression "appearance" gave rise. The philosophers who exposed these confusions were sometimes inclined to forget, I think, that things do appear to us in various ways.[16] We can alter the appearance of anything we like merely by doing something which will affect our sense organs or the conditions of observation. One of the important epistemological questions about appearances is "Are there self-justifying statements about the ways in which things appear?"

Augustine, refuting the skeptics of the late Platonic Academy, wrote: "I do not see how the Academician can refute him who says: 'I know that this appears white to me, I know that my hearing is delighted with this, I know this has an agreeable odor, I know this tastes sweet to me, I know that this feels cold to me.' . . . When a person tastes something, he can honestly swear that he knows it is sweet to his palate or the contrary, and that no trickery of the Greeks can dispossess him of that knowledge."[17] Suppose, now, one were to ask "What justification do you have for believing, or thinking you know, that this appears white to you, or that that tastes bitter to you?" Here, too, we can only reiterate the statement: "What justifies me in believing, or in thinking I know, that this appears white to me and that that tastes bitter to me is the fact that this *does* appear white to me and that *does* taste bitter."

An advantage of the misleading substantive "appearance," as distinguished from the verb "appears," is that the former may be applied to those sensuous experiences which, though capable of being appearances of things, are actually not appearances of anything. Feelings, imagery, and the sensuous content of dreams and hallucination are very much like the appearances of things and they are such that, under some circumstances, they could be appearances of things. But if we do not wish to say that they are experiences wherein some external physical thing *appears* to us, we must use some expression other than "appear." For "appear," in its active voice, requires a grammatical subject and thus requires a term which refers, not merely to a way of appearing, but also to something *which* appears.

But we may avoid *both* the objective *"Something* appears blue to me," and the substantival "I sense a blue *appearance."* We may use another verb, say "sense," in a technical way, as many philosophers did, and equate it in meaning with the passive voice of "appear," thus saying simply "I *sense* blue," or the like. Or better still, it seems to me, and at the expense only of a little awkwardness, we can use "appear" in its passive voice and say "I am *appeared to* blue."

Summing up, in our new vocabulary, we may say that the philosophers who talked of the "empirically given" were referring, not to "self-justifying" statements and beliefs generally, but only to those pertaining to certain "ways of being appeared to." And the philosophers who objected to the doctrine of the given, or some of them, argued that no statement about "a way of being appeared to" can be "self-justifying."

10. Why would one suppose that "This appears white" (or, more exactly, "I am now appeared white to") is not self-justifying? The most convincing argument was this: If I say "This appears white," then, as Reichenbach put it, I am making a "comparison between a present object and a formerly seen object."[18] What I am saying *could* have been expressed by "The present way of appearing is the way in which white objects, or objects which I believe to be white, ordinarily appear." And this new statement, clearly, is not self-justifying; to justify it, as Reichenbach intimated, I must go on and say something further—something about the way in which I remember white objects to have appeared.

"Appears white" *may* thus be used to abbreviate "appears the way in which white things normally appear." Or "white thing," on the other hand, *may* be used to abbreviate "thing having the color of things which ordinarily appear white." The phrase "appear white" as it is used in the second quoted expression cannot be spelled out in the manner of the first; for the point of the second can hardly be put by saying that "white thing" may be used to abbreviate "thing having the color of things which ordinarily appear the way in which *white things* normally appear." In the second expression, the point of "appears white" is not to *compare* a way of appearing with something else; the point is to say something about the way of appearing itself. It is in terms of this second sense of "appears white"—that in which one may say significantly and without redundancy "Things that are white may normally be expected to appear white"—that we are to interpret the quotation from Augustine above. And, more generally, when it was said that "appear"-statements constitute the foundation of the edifice of knowledge, it was not intended that the "appear"-statements be interpreted as statements asserting a comparison between a present object and any other object or set of objects.

The question now becomes "Can we formulate any significant "appear"-statements *without* thus comparing the way in which some object appears with the way in which some other object appears, or with the way in which the object in question has appeared at some other time? Can we interpret "This appears white" in such a way that it may be understood to refer to a present way of appearing *without* relating that way of appearing to any other object?" In *Experience and Prediction*, Reichenbach defended his own view (and that of a good many others) in this way:

> The objection may be raised that a comparison with formerly seen physical objects should be avoided, and that a basic statement is to concern the present fact only, as it is. But such a reduction would make the basic statement empty. Its content is just that there is a similarity between the present object and one formerly seen; it is by means of this relation that the present object is described. Otherwise the basic statement would consist in attaching an individual symbol, say a number, to the present object; but the introduction of such a symbol would help us in no way, since we could not make use of it to construct a comparison with other things. Only in attaching the same symbols to different objects, do we arrive at the possibility of constructing relations between the objects [pp. 176–77].

It is true that, if an "appear"-statement is to be used successfully in communication, it must assert some comparison of objects. Clearly, if I wish *you* to know the way things are now appearing to me, I must relate these ways of appearing to something that is familiar to you. But our present question is not "Can you understand me if I predicate something of the way in which something now appears to me without relating that way of appearing to something that is familiar to you?" The question is, more simply, "Can I predicate anything of the way in which something now appears to me without thereby comparing that way of appearing with something else?" From the fact that the first of these two questions must be answered in the negative it does not follow that the second must also be answered in the negative.[19]

The issue is not one about communication, nor is it, strictly speaking, an issue about language; it concerns, rather, the nature of thought itself. Common to both "pragmatism" and "idealism," as traditions in American philosophy, is the view that to *think* about a thing, or to *interpret* or *conceptualize* it, and hence to have a *belief* about it, is essentially to relate the thing to *other* things, actual or possible, and therefore to "refer

beyond it." It is this view—and not any view about language or communication—that we must oppose if we are to say of some statements about
appearing, or of any other statements, that they "justify themselves."

To think about the way in which something is now appearing, according to the view in question, is to relate that way of appearing to something
else, possibly to certain future experiences, possibly to the way in which
things of a certain sort may be commonly expected to appear. According
to the "conceptualistic pragmatism" of C. I. Lewis's *Mind and the World-
Order* (1929), we grasp the present experience, any present way of
appearing only to the extent to which we relate it to some future
experience.[20] According to one interpretation of John Dewey's "instrumentalistic" version of pragmatism, the present experience may be used
to present or disclose something else, but it does not present or disclose
itself. And according to the idealistic view defended in Brand Blanshard's
The Nature of Thought, we grasp our present experience only to the
extent that we are able to include it in the one "intelligible system of
universals" (vol. 1, p. 632).

This theory of reference, it should be noted, applies not only to
statements and beliefs about "ways of being appeared to" but also to
those other statements and beliefs which I have called "self-justifying." If
"This appears white," or "I am appeared white to," compares the present
experience with something else, and thus depends for its justification
upon what we are justified in believing about the something else, then so,
too, does "I believe that Socrates is mortal" and "I hope that the peace
will continue." This general conception of thought, therefore, would
seem to imply that no belief or statement can be said to justify itself. But
according to what we have been saying, if there is no belief or statement
which justifies itself, then it is problematic whether any belief or statement is justified at all. And therefore, as we might expect, this conception
of thought and reference has been associated with skepticism.

Blanshard conceded that his theory of thought "does involve a degree
of scepticism regarding our present knowledge and probably all future
knowledge. In all likelihood there will never be a proposition of which we
can say, 'This that I am asserting, with precisely the meaning I now attach
to it, is absolutely true.'"[21] On Dewey's theory, or on one common
interpretation of Dewey's theory, it is problematic whether anyone can
now be said to *know* that Mr. Jones is working in his garden. A. O.
Lovejoy is reported to have said that, for Dewey, "I am about to have
known" is as close as we ever get to "I know."[22] C. I. Lewis, in his *An
Analysis of Knowledge and Valuation* (1946) conceded in effect that the
conception of thought suggested by his earlier *Mind and the World-Order*
does lead to a kind of skepticism; according to the later work there *are*
"apprehensions of the given" (cf. pp. 182–83)—and thus beliefs which
justify themselves.

What is the plausibility of a theory of thought and reference which seems to imply that no one knows anything?

Perhaps it is correct to say that when we think about a thing we think about it as having certain properties. But why should one go on to say that to think about a thing must always involve thinking about some *other* thing as well? Does thinking about the other thing then involve thinking about some third thing? Or can we think about one thing in relation to a second thing without thereby thinking of a third thing? And if we can, then why can we not think of one thing—of one thing as having certain properties—without thereby relating it to another thing?

The linguistic analogue of this view of thought is similar. Why should one suppose—as Reichenbach supposed in the passage cited above and as many others have also supposed—that to *refer* to a thing, in this instance to refer to a way of appearing, is necessarily to relate the thing to some *other* thing?

Some philosophers seem to have been led to such a view of reference as a result of such considerations as the following: We have imagined a man saying, in agreement with Augustine, "It just does appear white—and that is the end of the matter." Let us consider now the possible reply "That it is not the end of the matter. You are making certain assumptions about the language you are using; you are assuming, for example, that you are using the word 'white,' or the phrase 'appears white,' in the way in which you have formerly used it, or in the way in which it is ordinarily used, or in the way in which it would ordinarily be understood. And if you state your justification for this assumption, you *will* refer to certain other things—to yourself and to other people, to the word 'white,' or to the phrase 'appears white,' and to what the word or phrase has referred to or might refer to on other occasions. And therefore, when you say 'This appears white' you are saying something, not only about your present experience, but also about all of these other things as well."

The conclusion of this argument—the part that follows the "therefore"—does not follow from the premises. In supposing that the argument is valid, one fails to distinguish between (a) *what it is that a man means* to say when he uses certain words and (b) his assumptions concerning the adequacy of these words for *expressing* what it is that he means to say; one supposes, mistakenly, that what justifies (b) must be included in what justifies (a). A Frenchman, not yet sure of his English, may utter the words "There are apples in the basket," intending thereby to express his belief that there are potatoes in the basket. If we show him that he has used the word "apples" incorrectly, and hence that he is mistaken in his assumptions about the ways in which English-speaking people use and understand the word "apples," we have not shown him anything relevant to his *belief* that there are apples in the basket.

Logicians now take care to distinguish between the *use* and *mention* of language (e.g., the English word "Socrates" is mentioned in the sentence " 'Socrates' has eight letters" and is used but not mentioned, in "Socrates is a Greek").[23]But the distinction has not always been observed in writings on epistemology.

11. If we decide, then, that there is a class of beliefs or statements which are "self-justifying," and that this class is limited to certain beliefs or statements about our own psychological states and about the ways in which we are "appeared to," we may be tempted to return to the figure of the edifice: our knowledge of the world is a structure supported entirely by a foundation of such self-justifying statements or beliefs. We should recall, however, that the answers to our original Socratic questions had *two* parts. When asked "What is your justification for thinking that you know *a?*" one may reply "I am justified in thinking I know *a,* because (1) I know *b* and (2) if I know *b* then I know *a."* We considered our justification for the *first* part of this answer, saying "I am justified in thinking I know *b,* because (1) I know *c* and (2) if I know *c* then I know *b."* And then we considered our justification for the first part of the second answer, and continued in this fashion until we reached the point of self-justification. In thus moving toward "the given," we accumulated, step by step, a backlog of claims that we did not attempt to justify—those claims constituting the *second* part of each of our answers. Hence our original claim—"I know that *a* is true"—does not rest upon "the given" alone; it also rests upon all of those other claims that we made en route. And it is not justified unless these other claims are justified.

A consideration of these other claims will lead us, I think, to at least three additional types of "stopping place," which are concerned, respectively, with memory, perception, and what Kant called the a priori. I shall comment briefly on the first two.

It is difficult to think of any claim to empirical knowledge, other than the self-justifying statements we have just considered, which does not to some extent rest upon an appeal to memory. But the appeal to memory— "I remember that A occurred"—is not self-justifying. One may ask "And what is your justification for thinking that you remember that A occurred?" and the question will have an answer—even if the answer is only the self-justifying "I think that I remember that A occurred." The statement "I remember that A occurred" does, of course, imply "A occurred"; but "I think that I remember that A occurred" does not imply "A occurred" and hence does not imply "I remember that A occurred." For we can remember occasions—at least we think we can remember them—when we learned, concerning some event we had thought we remembered, that the event had not occurred at all, and consequently that we had not really remembered it. When we thus find that one memory conflicts with another, or, more accurately, when we thus find that one thing that we think we remember conflicts with another thing that we think we remember, we may correct one or the other by making further inquiry; but the results of any such inquiry will always be justified in part by other memories, or by other things that we think that we remember. How then are we to choose between what seem to be conflicting memories? Under what conditions does "I think that I remember that A occurred" serve to justify "I remember that A occurred"?

The problem is one of formulating a rule of evidence—a rule specifying the conditions under which statements about what we think we remember can justify statements about what we do remember. A possible solution, in very general terms, is "When we think that we remember, then we are justified in believing that we do remember, provided that what we think we remember does not conflict with anything else that we think we remember; when what we think we remember does conflict with something else we think we remember, then, of the two conflicting memories (more accurately, ostensible memories) the one that is justified is the one that fits in better with the other things that we think we remember." Ledger Wood made the latter point by saying that the justified memory is the one which "coheres with the system of related memories"; C. I. Lewis used "congruence" instead of "coherence."[24] But we cannot say precisely what is meant by "fitting in," "coherence," or "congruence" until certain controversial questions of confirmation theory and the logic of probability have been answered. And it may be that the rule of evidence is too liberal; perhaps we should say, for example, that when two ostensible memories conflict neither one of them is justified. But these are questions which have not yet been satisfactorily answered.

If we substitute "perceive" for "remember" in the foregoing, we can formulate a similar set of problems about perception; these problems, too, must await solution.[25]

The problems involved in formulating such rules of evidence, and in determining the validity of these rules, do not differ in any significant way from those which arise in connection with the formulation, and validity, of the rules of logic. Nor do they differ from the problems posed by the moral and religious "cognitivists" (the "nonintuitionistic cognitivists"). The status of ostensible memories and perceptions, with respect to that experience which is their "source," is essentially like that which such "cognitivists" claim for judgments having an ethical or theological subject matter. Unfortunately, it is also like that which other "enthusiasts" claim for still other types of subject matter.

12. What, then, is the status of the doctrine of "the given"—of the "myth of the given"? In my opinion, the doctrine is correct in saying that there are some beliefs or statements which are "self-justifying" and that among such beliefs and statements are some which concern appearances or

"ways of being appeared to"; but the "phenomenalistic version" of the doctrine is mistaken in implying that our knowledge may be thought of as an edifice which is supported by appearances alone.[26] The cognitive significance of "the empirically given" was correctly described—in a vocabulary rather different from that which I have been using—by John Dewey:

> The alleged primacy of sensory meanings is mythical. They are primary only in logical status; they are primary as tests and confirmation of inferences concerning matters of fact, not as historic originals. For, while it is not usually needful to carry the check or test of theoretical calculations to the point of irreducible sensa, colors, sounds, etc., these sensa form a limit approached in careful analytic certifications, and upon critical occasions it is necessary to touch the limit. . . . Sensa are the class of irreducible meanings which are employed in verifying and correcting other meanings. We actually set out with much coarser and more inclusive meanings and not till we have met with failure from their use do we even set out to discover those ultimate and harder meanings which are sensory in character.[27]

The Socratic questions leading to the concept of "the given" also lead to the concept of "rules of evidence." Unfortunately some of the philosophers who stressed the importance of the former concept tended to overlook that of the latter.

Notes

1. Philosophers in other traditions also noted these confusions. See, for example, John Wild, "The Concept of the Given in Contemporary Philosophy," *Philosophy and Phenomenological Research* 1 (1940): 70–82.
2. The expression "myth of the given" was used by Wilfrid Sellars in "Empiricism and the Philosophy of Mind," in *Science, Perception and Reality.*
3. Dewey also said that, instead of trying to provide "Foundations for Knowledge," the philosopher should apply "what is known to intelligent conduct of the affairs of human life" to "the problems of men." John Dewey, *Problems of Men* (Philosophical Library, 1946), pp. 6–7.
4. C. I. Lewis, *Mind and the World-Order,* p. 29.
5. Ibid., p. 19. Cf. Hans Reichenbach, *Experience and Prediction* (U. of Chicago Press, 1938), p. 6; C. J. Ducasse, "Some Observations Concerning the Nature of Probability," *Journal of Philosophy* 38 (1941), esp. 400–401.
6. Hans Reichenbach, "Are Phenomenal Reports Absolutely Certain?," *Philosophical Review* 61 (1952): 147–59; the quotation is from p. 150.
7. Brand Blanshard, *The Nature of Thought,* vol. 2, p. 276.
8. C. G. Hempel, "On the Logical Positivists' Theory of Truth," *Analysis* (1935): 49–59; the quotation is from p. 57.
9. Rudolf Carnap, "Truth and Confirmation," in *Readings in Philosophical Analysis,* ed. Herbert Feigl and W. S. Sellars (Appleton, 1949), p. 125. The portions of the article quoted above first appeared in "Wahrheit und Bewährung," *Actes du congrès internationale de philosophie scientifique,* Vol. 4 (Paris, 1936), 18–23.

10. Cf. Nelson Goodman, *The Structure of Appearance* (Harvard, 1951), p. 104.

11. C. G. Hempel, "Some Theses on Empirical Certainty," *Review of Metaphysics* 5 (1952): 621–29; the quotation is from p. 621.

12. Ibid., p. 628. Hempel's remarks were made in an "Exploration" in which he set forth several theses about "empirical certainty" and then replied to objections by Paul Weiss, Roderick Firth, Wilfrid Sellars and myself.

13. C. J. Ducasse, "Propositions, Truth, and the Ultimate Criterion of Truth," *Philosophy and Phenomenological Research* 4 (1939): 317–40; the quotation is from p. 339.

14. Cf. Norman Malcolm, "Knowledge of Other Minds," *Journal of Philosophy* 55 (1958): 969–78. Reprinted in Malcolm, *Knowledge and Certainty*.

15. The principle behind this way of looking at the matter is defended in detail by Max Black in *Language and Philosophy* (Cornell, 1949), p. 16ff.

16. One of the best criticisms of the "appearance" (or "sense-datum") terminology was O. K. Bouwsma's "Moore's Theory of Sense-Data," in *The Philosophy of G. E. Moore,* ed. Schilpp, pp. 201–21. In *Perceiving: A Philosophical Study,* I tried to call attention to certain facts about appearing which, I believe, Bouwsma may have overlooked.

17. Augustine, *Contra academicos,* xi, 26; translated by Sister Mary Patricia Garvey as *Saint Augustine Against the Academicians* (Marquette, 1942); the quotations are from pp. 68–69.

18. Reichenbach, *Experience and Prediction,* p. 176.

19. It may follow, however, that "the vaunted incorrigibility of the sense-datum language can be achieved only at the cost of its perfect utility as a means of communication" (Max Black, *Problems of Analysis* [Cornell, 1954], p. 66), and doubtless, as Black added, it would be "misleading, to say the least" to speak of a "language that cannot be communicated"—cf. Wilfrid Sellars, "Empiricism and the Philosophy of Mind"—but these points do affect the epistemological question at issue.

20. This doctrine was modified in Lewis's later *An Analysis of Knowledge and Valuation* in a way which enabled him to preserve the theory of the given.

21. *The Nature of Thought,* pp. 269–70. Blanshard added, however, that "for all the ordinary purposes of life" we *can* justify some beliefs by showing that they cohere "with the system of present knowledge"; and therefore, he said, his theory should not be described as being "simply sceptical" (vol. II, p. 271). Cf. W. H. Werkmeister, *The Basis and Structure of Knowledge* (Harper, 1948), part 2.

22. Quoted by A. E. Murphy in "Dewey's Epistemology and Metaphysics," in *The Philosophy of John Dewey,* ed. P. A. Schilpp (Northwestern, 1939), p. 203. Dewey's theory of inquiry, however, was not intended to be an epistemology and he did not directly address himself to the question with which we are here concerned.

23. Cf. W. V. Quine, *Mathematical Logic* (Norton, 1940; rev. ed. Harvard, 1951), sec. 4.

24. Ledger Wood, *The Analysis of Knowledge* (Princeton, 1941), p. 81; C. I. Lewis, *An Analysis of Knowledge and Valuation,* p. 334.

25. Important steps toward solving them were taken by Nelson Goodman in "Sense and Certainty," *Philosophical Review* 61 (1952): 160–67; and by Israel Scheffler in "On Justification and Commitment," *Journal of Philosophy* 51 (1954): 180–90. The former paper is reprinted in *Philosophy of Knowledge,* ed. Roland Houde and J. P. Mullally (Lippincott, 1960), 97–103.

26. Alternatives to the general metaphor of the edifice are proposed by W. V. Quine in the introduction to *Methods of Logic* (Holt, 1950; rev. ed., 1959), in *From a Logical Point of View* (Harvard, 1953), and in *Word and Object* (Wiley, 1960).

27. John Dewey, *Experience and Nature*, 2nd ed. (Norton, 1929), p. 327.

3   Two Types of Foundationalism

WILLIAM P. ALSTON

Foundationalism is often stated as the doctrine that knowledge constitutes a structure the foundations of which support all the rest but
themselves need no support. To make this less metaphorical we need to
specify the mode of support involved. In contemporary discussions of
foundationalism knowledge is thought of in terms of true-justified-belief
(with or without further conditions); thus the mode of support involved is
justification, and what gets supported a belief.[1] The sense in which a
foundation needs no support is that it is not justified by its relation to
other justified beliefs; in that sense it does not "rest on" other beliefs.
Thus we may formulate foundationalism as follows:

> I. Our justified beliefs form a structure, in that some beliefs (the foundations)
> are justified by something other than their relation to other justified beliefs;
> beliefs that *are* justified by their relation to other beliefs all depend for their
> justification on the foundations.

Notice that nothing is said about *knowledge* in this formulation. Since the
structure alleged by foundationalism is a structure of the justification of
belief, the doctrine can be stated in terms of that component of knowledge
alone. Indeed, one who thinks that knowledge has nothing to do with
justified belief is still faced with the question of whether foundationalism
is a correct view about the structure of epistemic justification.

Two emendations will render this formulation more perspicuous. First,
a useful bit of terminology. Where what justifies a belief includes[2] the
believer's having certain other justified beliefs, so related to the first belief
as to embody reasons or grounds for it, we may speak of *indirectly
(mediately) justified belief.* And, where what justifies a belief does not
include any such constituent, we may speak of *directly (immediately)
justified belief.* Correspondingly, a case of knowledge in which the
justification requirement is satisfied by indirect (mediate) justification will
be called *indirect (mediate) knowledge,* and a case in which the justification requirement is satisfied by direct (immediate) justification will be
called *direct (immediate) knowledge.*

Reprinted from *The Journal of Philosophy* 73 (1976): 165–85, by permission of the author
and the publisher. Copyright 1976 by *The Journal of Philosophy.*

Second, we should make more explicit how mediate justification is thought to rest on immediately justified belief. The idea is that, although the other beliefs involved in the mediate justification of a given belief may themselves be mediately justified, if we continue determining at each stage how the supporting beliefs are justified, we will arrive, sooner or later, at directly justified beliefs. This will not, in general, be a single line of descent; typically the belief with which we start will rest on several beliefs, each of which in turn will rest on several beliefs. So the general picture is that of multiple branching from the original belief.

With this background we may reformulate foundationalism as follows (turning the "foundation" metaphor on its head):

II. Every mediately justified belief stands at the origin of a (more or less) multiply branching tree structure at the tip of each branch of which is an immediately justified belief.

II can be read as purely hypothetical (*if* there are any mediately justified beliefs, then . . .) or with existential import (there are mediately justified beliefs, and . . .). Foundationalists typically make the latter claim, and I shall understand the doctrine to carry existential import.

II can usefully be divided into two claims:

(A) There are directly justified beliefs.
(B) A given person has a stock of directly justified beliefs sufficient to generate chains of justification that terminate in whatever indirectly justified beliefs he has.

In other words, (A) there are foundations, and (B) they suffice to hold up the building.

In this essay we shall restrict our attention to A. More specifically, we shall be concerned with a certain issue over what it takes for a belief to serve as a foundation.

I. The Second-Level Argument

Let's approach this issue by confronting foundationalism with a certain criticism, a recent version of which can be found in Bruce Aune.[3]

> The line of reasoning behind the empiricist's assumption is, again, that while intra-language rules may validly take us from premise to conclusion, they cannot themselves establish empirical truth. If the premises you start with are false, you will have no guarantee that the conclusions you reach are not false either. Hence, to attain knowledge of the actual world, you must ultimately have premises whose truth is acceptable independently of any inference and whose status is accordingly indubitable. Only by having such premises can you gain a starting point that would make inference worthwhile. For convenience, these indispensable basic premises may be called "intrinsically acceptable."

The possibility of empirical knowledge may then be said to depend on the availability of intrinsically acceptable premises.

If this line of thought is sound, it follows that utter skepticism can be ruled out only if one can locate basic empirical premises that are intrinsically acceptable. Although philosophers who attack skepticism in accordance with this approach generally think they are defending common sense, it is crucial to observe that they cannot actually be doing so. The reason for this is that, from the point of view of common experience, there is no plausibility at all in the idea that intrinsically acceptable premises, as so defined, ever exist. Philosophers defending such premises fail to see this because they always ignore the complexity of the situation in which an empirical claim is evaluated.

I have already given arguments to show that introspective claims are not, in themselves, intrinsically infallible; they may be regarded as virtually certain if produced by a reliable (sane, clear-headed) observer, but their truth is not a consequence of the mere fact that they are confidently made. To establish a similar conclusion regarding the observation claims of everyday life only the sketchiest arguments are needed. Obviously the mere fact that such a claim is made does not assure us of its truth. If we know that the observer is reliable, made his observation in good light, was reasonably close to the object, and so on, then we may immediately regard it as acceptable. But its acceptability is not intrinsic to the claim itself . . . I would venture to say that any spontaneous claim, observational or introspective, carries almost no presumption of truth, when considered entirely by itself. If we accept such a claim as true, it is only because of our confidence that a complex body of background assumptions— concerning observers, standing conditions, the kind of object in question— and, often, a complex mass of further observations all point to the conclusion that it is true.

Given these prosaic considerations, it is not necessary to cite experimental evidence illustrating the delusions easily brought about by, for example, hypnosis to see that no spontaneous claim is acceptable wholly on its own merits. On the contrary, common experience is entirely adequate to show that clear-headed men never accept a claim merely because it is made, without regard to the peculiarities of the agent and of the conditions under which it is produced. For such men, the acceptability of every claim is always determined by inference. If we are prepared to take these standards of acceptability seriously, we must accordingly admit that the traditional search for intrinsically acceptable empirical premises is completely misguided [p. 41–43].

Now the target of Aune's critique differs in several important respects from the foundationalism defined above. First and most obviously, Aune supposes that any "intrinsically acceptable premises" will be infallible and indubitable, and some of his arguments are directed specifically against these features.[4] Second, there is an ambiguity in the term "intrinsically acceptable." Aune introduces it to mean "whose truth is acceptable independently of any inference"; this looks roughly equivalent to our "directly justified." However, in arguing against the supposition that the "observation claims of everyday life" are intrinsically acceptable, he says that "the mere fact that such a claim is made does not assure us of its truth," thereby implying that to be intrinsically acceptable a claim would have to be justified just by virtue of being made. Now it is clear that a belief (claim) of which this is true is directly justified, but the converse does not hold. A perceptual belief will also be directly justified, as that term was explained above, if what justifies it is the fact that the perceiver "is reliable, made his observation in good light, was reasonably close to the object, and so on," *provided it is not also required that he be justified in believing that these conditions are satisfied.* Thus this argument of Aune's has no tendency to show that perceptual beliefs cannot be directly justified, but only that they cannot enjoy that special sort of direct justification which we may term "self-justification."[5]

However, some of Aune's arguments would seem to be directed against any immediate justification, and a consideration of these will reveal a third and more subtle discrepancy between Aune's target(s) and my version of foundationalism. Near the end of the passage Aune says:

> If we accept such a claim [observational or introspective] as true, it is only because of our confidence that a complex of background assumptions . . . all point to the conclusion that it is true.

And again:

> For such men [clear-headed men], the acceptability of every claim is always determined by inference.

It certainly looks as if Aune is arguing that whenever a claim (belief) is justified it is justified by inference (by relation to other justified beliefs), and that would be the denial of "There are directly justified beliefs." But look more closely. Aune is discussing not what would justify the issuer of an introspective or observational claim in his belief, but rather what it would take to justify "us" in accepting his claim; he is arguing from a third-person perspective. Now it does seem clear that *I* cannot be immediately justified in accepting *your* introspective or observational claim as true. If I am so justified it is because I am justified in supposing that you issued a claim of that sort, that you are in a normal condition and know the language, and (if it is an observational claim) that conditions were favorable for your accurately perceiving that sort of thing. But that is only because *I*, in contrast to you, am justified in believing that *p* (where what you claimed is that *p*, and where I have no independent access to *p*) only if I am justified in supposing that you are justified in believing that *p*. My access to *p* is through your access. It is just because *my* justification in believing that *p* presupposes my being justified in believing that you are justified, that my justification has to be indirect. That is why I have to look into such matters as conditions of observation, and your normality. Thus what Aune is really pointing to is the necessity for "inferential" backing for any higher-level belief to the effect that someone is justified in believing that *p*. (I shall call such higher-level beliefs *epistemic beliefs*.)

His argument, if it shows anything, shows that no epistemic belief can be immediately justified. But it does nothing to show that the original observer's or introspector's belief that p was not immediately justified. Hence his argument is quite compatible with the view that an introspective belief is self-justified and with the view that an observational belief is justified just by being formed in favorable circumstances.

As a basis for further discussion I should like to present my own version of an argument against the possibility of immediate justification for epistemic beliefs—what I shall call the *second-level argument:*

A1 Where S's belief that p is mediately justified, any jurisdiction for the belief that S *is justified in believing that p* is obviously mediate. For one could not be justified in this latter belief unless it were based on a justified belief that S is justified in accepting the grounds on which his belief that p is based. But even where S is immediately justified in believing that p, the higher-level belief will still be mediately justified, if at all. For in taking a belief to be justified, we are evaluating it in a certain way.[6] And, like any evaluative property, epistemic justification is a supervenient property, the application of which is based on more fundamental properties. A belief is justified because it possesses what Roderick Firth has called "warrant-increasing properties."[7] Hence in order for me to be justified in believing that S's belief that p is justified, I must be justified in certain other beliefs, viz., that S's *belief that p* possesses a certain property, Q and that Q renders its possessor justified. (Another way of formulating this last belief is: a belief that there is a valid epistemic principle to the effect that any belief that is Q is justified.) Hence in no case can an epistemic belief that S is justified in believing that p, itself be immediately justified.

Before proceeding I shall make two comments on this argument and its conclusion.

(1) It may appear that the conclusion of the argument is incompatible with the thesis that one cannot be justified in believing that p without also being justified in believing that one is justified in believing that p. For if being immediately justified in believing that p necessarily carried with it being justified in believing that I am justified in believing that p, it would seem that this latter justification would be equally immediate. I would not shirk from such an incompatibility, since I feel confident in rejecting that thesis. It is not clear, however, that there is any such incompatibility. It all depends on how we construe the necessity. If, e.g., it is that my being justified in believing that p necessarily puts me into possession of the *grounds* I need for being justified in the higher-level belief, then that is quite compatible with our conclusion that the latter can only be mediately justified.

(2) The conclusion should not be taken to imply that one must perform any conscious inference to be justified in an epistemic belief, or even that one must be explicitly aware that the lower-level belief has an appropriate warrant-increasing property. Here as in other areas, one's grounds can be

possessed more or less implicitly. Otherwise we would have precious little mediate knowledge.

I have already suggested that the second-level argument is not really directed against II. To be vulnerable to this argument, a foundationalist thesis would have to require of foundations not only that *they* be immediately justified, but also that the believer be immediately justified in believing that they are immediately justified. A position that does require this we may call *iterative foundationalism*, and we may distinguish it from the earlier form *(simple foundationalism)* as follows (so far as concerns the status of the foundations):

> Simple Foundationalism: For any epistemic subject, S, there are p's such that S is immediately justified in believing that p.

> Iterative Foundationalism: For any epistemic subject, S, there are p's such that S is immediately justified in believing that p and S is immediately justified in believing that he is immediately justified in believing that p.[8]

It would not take much historical research to show that both positions have been taken. What I want to investigate here is which of them there is most reason to take. Since the classic support for foundationalism has been the regress argument, I shall concentrate on determining which form emerges from that line of reasoning.

II. The Regress Argument

The regress argument seeks to show that the only alternatives to admitting epistemic foundations are circularity of justification or an equally unpalatable infinite regress of justification. It may be formulated as follows:

A2 Suppose we are trying to determine whether S is mediately justified in believing that p. To be so justified he has to be justified in believing certain other propositions, q, r, . . . that are suitably related to p (so as to constitute adequate grounds for p). Let's say we have identified a set of such propositions each of which S believes. Then he is justified in believing that p only if he is justified in believing each of those propositions.[9] And, for each of these propositions q, r, . . . that he is not immediately justified in believing, he is justified in believing it only if he is justified in believing some other propositions that are suitably related to it. And for each of these latter propositions
. . .
   Thus in attempting to give a definitive answer to the original question we are led to construct a more or less extensive true structure, in which the original belief and every other putatively mediately justified belief form nodes from which one or more branches issue, in such a way that every branch is a part of some branch that issues from the original belief. Now the question is: what form must be assumed by the structure in order that S be

mediately justified in believing that *p?* There are the following conceivable forms for a given branch:

A. It terminates in an immediately justified belief.
B. It terminates in an unjustified belief.
C. The belief that *p* occurs at some point (past the origin), so that the branch forms a loop.
D. The branch continues infinitely.

Of course some branches might assume one form and others another.

The argument is that the original belief will be mediately justified only if every branch assumes form A. Positively, it is argued that on this condition the relevant necessary condition for the original belief's being mediately justified is satisfied, and, negatively, it is argued that if any branch assumes any of the other forms, is not.

A. Where every branch has form A, this necessary condition is satisfied for every belief in the structure. Since each branch terminates in an immediately justified belief that is justified without necessity for further justified beliefs, the regress is ended along each branch. Hence justification is transferred along each branch right back to the original belief.

B. For any branch that exhibits form B, no element, even the origin, is justified, at least by this structure. Since the terminus is not justified, the prior element, which is justified only if the terminus is, is not justified. And, since it is not justified, its predecessor, which is justified only if it is, is not justified either. And so on, right back to the origin, which therefore itself fails to be justified.

C. Where we have a branch that forms a closed loop, again nothing on that branch, even the origin, is justified, so far as its justification depends on this tree structure. For what the branch "says" is that the belief that *p* is justified only if the belief that *r* is justified, and that belief is justified only if . . . , and the belief that *z* is justified only if the belief that *p* is justified. So what this chain of necessary conditions tells us is that the belief that *p* is justified only if the belief that *p* is justified. True enough, but that still leaves it completely open whether the belief that *p* is justified.

D. If there is a branch with no terminus, that means that no matter how far we extend the branch the last element is still a belief that is mediately justified if at all. Thus, as far as this structure goes, wherever we stop adding elements we have still not shown that the relevant necessary condition for the mediate justification of the original belief is satisfied. Thus the structure does not exhibit the original belief as mediately justified.

Hence the original belief is mediately justified only if every branch in the tree structure terminates in an immediately justified belief. Hence every mediately justified belief stands at the origin of a tree structure at the tip of each branch of which is an immediately justified belief.[10]

Now this version of the argument, analogues of which occur frequently in the literature,[11] supports only simple foundationalism. It has no tendency to show that there is immediately justified epistemic belief. So long as *S* is directly justified in believing some *t* for each branch of the tree, that will be quite enough to stop the regress; for all that is needed is that he *be* justified in believing *t* without thereby incurring the need to be justified in believing some further proposition. But perhaps there are other versions that yield the stronger conclusion. Indeed, in surveying the literature one will discover versions that differ from A2 in one or both of the following respects:

1. Their starting points (the conditions of which they seek to establish) are cases of being justified in believing that one knows (is justified in believing) that *p*, rather than, more generally, cases of being justified in believing that *p*.

2. They are concerned to establish what is necessary for *showing* that *p*, rather than what is necessary for *being justified* in believing that *p*.

Let's consider whether regress arguments with one or the other of these features will yield iterative foundationalism.

First let's consider an argument that differs from A2 only in the first respect. In his essay "Theory of Knowledge" in a volume devoted to the history of twentieth-century American philosophy, R. M. Chisholm[12] launches a regress argument as follows:

> To the question "What justification do I have for thinking that I know that *a* is true?" one may reply: "I know that *b* is true, and if I know that *b* is true then I also know that *a* is true." and to the question "What justification do I have for thinking I know that *b* is true?" one may reply: "I know that *c* is true, and if I know that *c* is true then I also know that *b* is true." Are we thus led, sooner or later, to something, *n*, of which one may say "What justifies me in thinking I know that *n* is true is simply the fact that *n* is true"? [p. 263; see Chap. 2 above].

Chisholm then supports an affirmative answer to this last question by excluding other alternatives in a manner similar to that of A2.

Now the crucial question is: why does Chisholm conclude not just that mediate justification of claims to know requires *some* immediately justified beliefs, but that it requires immediately justified *epistemic* beliefs? Of course, having granted the general position that any mediately justified belief rests on some immediately justified belief(s), it is natural to suppose that mediately justified *epistemic* beliefs will rest on immediately justified *epistemic* beliefs. But we should not assume that all cases of mediate knowledge rest on foundations that are similar in content. On the contrary, every version of foundationalism holds that from a certain set of basic beliefs one erects a superstructure that is vastly different from these foundations. From knowledge of sense data one derives knowledge of public objects, from knowledge of present occurrences one derives knowledge of the past and future, and so on. So why suppose that *if* mediate epistemic beliefs rest on foundations, those foundations will be epistemic beliefs? We would need some special reason for this. And neither Chisholm nor, to my knowledge, anyone else has given any such reason. All rely on essentially the same argument as A2, which at most yields the weaker conclusion. They seem to have just assumed uncritically that the foundations on which epistemic beliefs rest are themselves epistemic.[13]

Thus, altering the regress argument in the first way does not provide grounds for iterative foundationalism. Let's turn to the second modification. In order to maximize our chances, let's combine it with the first, and consider what it would take to *show*, for some *p*, that I am justified in believing that *p*.[14] It is easy to see how one might be led into this. One who accepted the previous argument might still feel dissatisfied with simple foundationalism. "You have shown," he might say, "that it is *possible* to be justified in believing that *p* without having any immediately justified epistemic belief. But are we *in fact* justified in believing any *p*? To answer that question you will have to *show*, for some *p*, *that* you are justified in believing it. And the question is, what is required for that? Is it possible to do that without immediately justified epistemic belief?"

Now if we are to show, via a regress argument, that immediately justified epistemic belief is necessary for showing that I am justified in believing any *p*, it must be because some requirement for showing sets up a regress that can only be stopped if we have such beliefs. What could that requirement be? Let's see what is required for showing that *p*. Clearly, to show that *p* I must adduce some other (possibly compound) proposition, *q*. What restrictions must be put on a *q* and my relations thereto?

1. It is true that *q*.[15]
2. *q* constitutes adequate grounds for *p*.

These requirements give rise to no regress, or at least none that is vicious. Even if no proposition can be true without some other proposition's being true, there is nothing repugnant about the notion of an infinity of true propositions. Hence we may pass on.

3. I am justified in believing that *q*.[16]

This requirement clearly does give rise to a regress, viz., that already brought out in A2. We have seen that immediately justified epistemic belief is not required to end that regress; so again we may pass on.

4. I am justified in believing that I am justified in believing that *q*.

I am not prepared to admit this requirement, my reasons being closely connected with the point that one may be justified in believing that *q* without even believing that one is so justified, much less being justified in believing that one is so justified. However, it is not necessary to discuss that issue here. Even if 4 is required, it will simply set up a regress of the sort exemplified by Chisholm's argument, an argument we have seen to have no stronger conclusion than simple foundationalism.

    5. I am able to show that q.

This looks more promising. Clearly this requirement gives rise to a regress that is different from that of A2. If I can show that p by citing q only if I am able to show that q, and if, in turn, I am able to show that q by citing r only if I am able to show that r, it is clear that we will be able to avoid our familiar alternatives of circularity and infinite regress, only if at some point I arrive at a proposition that I can show to be correct without appealing to some other proposition. In deciding whether this argument provides support for iterative foundationalism, we must consider first whether requirement 5 is justified and, second, whether immediately justified epistemic belief would stop the regress so generated.

The requirement looks plausible. For, if I cannot show that q, then it looks as if I won't be able to settle whether or not it is the case that q, and in that case how can I claim to have settled the question about p? But this plausibility is specious, stemming from one of the protean forms assumed by that confusion of levels typified by the confusion of knowing that p with knowing that one knows that p. It's quite true that an inability to show that q will prevent me from showing *that I have shown that p;* for to do the latter I have to show that the grounds I have cited for p are correct. But why suppose that it also prevents me from showing that p? Can't I prove a theorem in logic without being able to prove that I have proved it? The former requires only an ability to wield the machinery of first-order logic, which one may possess without the mastery of metalogic required for the second. Similarly, it would seem that I can show that p, by adducing true adequate grounds I am justified in accepting, without being able to *show* that those grounds are true.

This conclusion is reinforced by the point that it is all too possible to *have* adequate grounds for a belief without being able to articulate them. Having observed Jones for a while, I may *have* adequate reasons for supposing him to be unsure of himself, without being able to specify just what features of his bearing and behavior provide those reasons. A philosophically unsophisticated person (and many of the philosophically sophisticated as well) may be amply justified in believing that there is a tree in front of his wide-open eyes, but not be able to show that he is so justified. I may be justified in believing that Louis IX reigned in the thirteenth century, since I acquired that belief on excellent authority, but not now be able to specify that authority, much less *show* that it is reliable. Of course in the case under discussion, I am able to articulate my grounds for p, for *ex hypothesi* I have adduced adequate grounds for p. But to suppose that it is reasonable to require that I be able to *show* that those grounds are true, and the grounds of these grounds, and . . . is to ignore the elementary point that a person may *have* adequate grounds for q and so be in an epistemically sound position vis-à-vis q, without being able to articulate those grounds. The latter ability is the exception rather than the rule with mediately justified belief.

But even if requirement 5 were justified and the show-regress were launched, immediately justified epistemic beliefs would be powerless to stop it. Let's say that I originally set out to show that I am justified in believing that a, and in the regress of showings thus generated I eventually cite as a ground *that I am immediately justified in believing that z* (call this higher-level proposition "Z"), where I am in fact immediately justified in believing that Z. How will this latter fact enable me to *show* that Z? As a result of being immediately justified in believing that Z, I may have no doubt about the matter; I may feel no need to show *myself* that Z. But of course that doesn't imply that I *have shown* that Z. However immediate my justification for accepting Z, I haven't *shown* that Z unless I adduce grounds for it that meet the appropriate conditions. And once I do that we are off to the races again. The regress has not been stopped. In the nature of the case it cannot be stopped. In this it differs from the original regress of *being* justified. *Showing* by its very nature requires the exhibition of grounds. Furthermore, grounds must be different from the proposition to be shown. (This latter follows from the "pragmatic" aspect of the concept of showing. To show that p is to present grounds that one can justifiably accept without already accepting p. Otherwise showing would lack the point that goes toward making it what it is.) Hence, there are no conceivable conditions under which I could show that p without citing other propositions that, by requirement 5, I must be able to show. If we accept requirement 5, if an infinite structure of abilities to show is ruled out, and if circularity is unacceptable, it follows that it is impossible ever to show anything. (That would seem to be an additional reason for rejecting 5.) Since immediately justified epistemic belief would do nothing to stop the regress, this kind of regress argument can provide no support for iterative foundationalism.

III. Functions of Foundationalism

Thus, although simple foundationalism is strongly supported by A2, we have failed to find any argument that supports iterative foundationalism. And the second-level argument strikes at the latter but not the former. Hence it would seem that foundationalism has a chance of working only in its simple form. This being the case, it is of some interest to determine the extent to which simple foundationalism satisfies the demands and aspirations that foundationalism is designed to satisfy, other than stopping the regress of justification. I shall consider two such demands.

Answering Skepticism. Skepticism assumes various forms, many of which no sort of foundationalism could sensibly be expected to answer. For example, the extreme skeptic who refuses to accept anything until it has been shown to be true, and who will not allow his opponent any premises to use for this purpose, obviously cannot be answered whatever one's position. Talking with him is a losing game. Again there are more limited skepticisms in which one sort of knowledge is questioned (e.g., knowledge of the conscious states of other persons) but others are left unquestioned (e.g., knowledge of the physical environment). Here the answering will be done, if at all, by finding some way of deriving knowledge of the questioned sort from knowledge of the unquestioned sort. The role of a general theory of knowledge will be limited to laying down criteria for success in the derivation, and differences over what is required for foundations would seem to make no difference to such criteria.

The kind of "answer to skepticism" that one might suppose to be affected by our difference is that in which the skeptic doubts that we have any knowledge, a successful answer being a demonstration there is some. One may think that the possession of immediate epistemic knowledge will put us in a better position to do that job. Whether it does, and if so how, depends on what it takes to show that one knows something. The discussion of showing in section II yielded the following conditions for *S*'s showing that *p*:

1. It is true that *p*.
2. *S* cites in support of *p* a certain proposition *q* such that:
   A. It is true that *q*.
   B. *q* is an adequate ground for *p*.
   C. *S* is justified in believing *q*.

We rejected the further condition that *S* be able to show that *q*. However, since we are here concerned with showing something to a skeptic, it may be that some further requirement should be imposed. After all, we could hardly expect a skeptic to abandon his doubt just on the *chance* that his interlocuter is correct in the grounds he gives. The skeptic will want to be given some reason for supposing those grounds to be correct, and this does not seem unreasonable. But we can't go back to the unqualified requirement that every ground adduced be established or even establishable, without automatically making showing impossible. Fortunately there is an intermediate requirement that might satisfy a reasonable skeptic while not rendering all showing impossible. Let's require that *S* be able to show that *r* for any *r* among his grounds concerning which his audience has any real doubt. This differs from the unqualified requirement in leaving open the possibility that there will be grounds concerning which no reasonable person who has reflected on the matter will have any doubt; and if there be such it may still be possible for S to succeed in showing that p. Thus we may add to our list of conditions:

D.   If there is real doubt about q, S is able to show that q.

Now when p is "S knows that a," the question is whether one or more of these conditions is satisfiable only if S has immediately justified epistemic beliefs. Let's consider the conditions in turn. As for 1, S can in fact know that a without having any directly justified epistemic belief, even if it should be the case that one can't know that a without knowing that one knows that a. For, as we saw in section II, there is no reason to doubt that all justified beliefs that one knows or is justified in believing something are themselves *mediately* justified. As for 2A and 2B, there should be no temptation to suppose that they depend on iterative foundationalism. Surely the grounds I adduce for the claim to know that a can be true and adequate without my having any immediately justified epistemic beliefs. Even if one or more of the grounds should themselves be claims to knowledge, the question of what is required for their truth can be handled in the same way as requirement 1. And adequacy, being a matter of relations between propositions, cannot depend on what sort of justification S has for one or another belief. As for 2C, the discussion in sections I and II failed to turn up any reasons for supposing that immediately justified epistemic belief is required for my being justified in believing anything. That leaves 2D. But this has already been covered. To satisfy 2D I have to be able to *show* that (some of) my grounds are true. But that will not require conditions that are different in kind from those already discussed. Hence we may conclude that iterative foundationalism is not a presupposition of our showing that we do have knowledge. Of course it remains an open question whether we are in fact capable of showing that we know something. But if we are incapable, it is not because of the lack of immediately justified epistemic belief.

Self-consciously Reconstructing Knowledge from the Foundations. What I have in mind here is the enterprise classically exemplified by Descartes in the *Meditations*. There Descartes first sets out to identify those items for which there could not be any grounds for doubt. Having done so, he seeks to use these items as a basis for showing that other items are known as well. Now we cannot assimilate Descartes to our scheme without some adjustments. For one thing, Descartes required indubitability and infallibility of his foundations. For another, he was not working with a true-justified-belief conception of knowledge. Translating Descartes into the conception of knowledge we are using and ignoring the extra demands of indubitability and infallibility, it is clear that Descartes takes his foundational beliefs to be immediately justified. I am justified in believing that I exist or that I am presently thinking about epistemology, regardless of what else I may be justified in believing. I am so justified just by the fact that the belief "records" the content of a clear and distinct intuition of the fact that makes the belief true. Hence, in order to *identify* a belief, *B*, as foundational Descartes must be justified in the higher-level belief that *B* is immediately justified. And if he is to perform this identification at the outset of his reconstruction, when nothing is recognized as mediately justified, this justification must be immediate, since he lacks a suitable body of other beliefs on which to base it.[17] Hence this enterprise is possible only if one can be immediately justified in taking a certain belief to be immediately justified. Here, then, is a point at which iterative foundationalism is genuinely needed.[18]

If iterative foundationalism is both without strong support and subject to crushing objections, it looks as if we will have to do without a self-conscious reconstruction of knowledge. How grievous a loss is this? Why should anyone want to carry out such a reconstruction? Well, if knowledge does have a foundational structure it seems intolerable that we should be unable to spell this out. And it may seem that such a spelling out would have to take the present form. But that would be an illusion. If there are foundations, one can certainly identify them and determine how other sorts of knowledge are based on them without first taking on the highly artificial stance by Descartes in the *Meditations*. One can approach this problem, as one approaches any other, making use of whatever relevant knowledge or justified belief one already possesses. In that case immediate epistemic knowledge is by no means required, just as we have seen it is not required to show that one is justified in holding certain beliefs.

The Cartesian program has been branded as unrealistic on more grounds than one. And if I am right in holding that the simple form of foundationalism is the most we can have, I have provided one more ground. If iterative foundationalism is false, we can still have as much epistemic knowledge as you like, but only after we have acquired quite a lot of first-level knowledge. And why should that not satisfy any epistemic aspirations that are fitting for the human condition?

IV. Envoi

As we have seen, the main reason for adopting foundationalism is the seeming impossibility of a belief's being mediately justified without resting ultimately on immediately justified belief. And the main reason for rejecting it (at least the main antecedent reason, apart from the difficulties of working it out) is that reason one version of which we found in the quotation from Aune. That is, it appears that the foundationalist is committed to adopting beliefs in the absence of any reasons for regarding them as acceptable. And this would appear to be the sheerest dogmatism. It is the aversion to dogmatism, to the apparent arbitrariness of putative foundations, that leads many philosophers to embrace some form of coherence or contextualist theory, in which no belief is deemed acceptable unless backed by sound reason.

The main burden of this paper is that with simple foundationalism one can have the best of both arguments; one can stop the regress of justification without falling into dogmatism. We have already seen that Aune's form of the dogmatism argument does not touch Simple Foundationalism. For that form of the argument attacks only the ungrounded acceptance of claims *to knowledge or justification,* and simple foundationalism is not committed to the immediate justification of any such higher-level claims. But one may seek to apply the same argument to lower-level beliefs. Even simple foundationalism, the critic may say, must allow that some beliefs may be accepted in the absence of any reasons for supposing them to be true. And this is still arbitrary dogmatism. But the simple foundationalist has an answer. His position does not require anyone to accept any belief without having a reason for doing so. Where a person *is* immediately justified in believing that *p,* he may find adequate reasons for the higher-level belief that he is immediately justified in believing that *p.* And if he has adequate reasons for accepting this epistemic proposition, it surely is not arbitrary of him to accept the proposition that *p.* What better reason could he have for accepting it?

Lest the reader dismiss this answer as a contemptible piece of sleight-of-hand, let me be more explicit about what is involved. Though the simple foundationalist requires *some* immediately justified beliefs in order to terminate the regress of justification, his position permits him to recognize that all epistemic beliefs require mediate justification. Therefore, for any belief that one is immediately justified in believing, one *may* find adequate reasons for accepting the proposition that one is so justified. The curse (of dogmatism) is taken off immediate justification at the lower level, just by virtue of the fact that propositions at the higher level are acceptable only on the basis of reasons. A foundational belief, *b,* is immediately justified just because some valid epistemic principle lays down conditions for its being justified which do not include the believer's having certain other justified beliefs. But the believer will be justified in believing *that* he is immediately justified in holding *b* only if he has *reasons* for regarding that principle as valid and for regarding *b* as falling under that principle. And if he does have such reasons he certainly cannot be accused of arbitrariness or dogmatism in accepting *b.* The absence of reasons for *b* is "compensated" for by the reasons for the correlated higher-level belief. Or, better, the sense in which one can have reasons for accepting an immediately justified belief is necessarily different from that in which one can have reasons for accepting a mediately justified belief. Reasons in the former case are necessarily "meta" in character; they have to do with reasons for regarding the belief as justified. Whereas in the latter case, though one *may* move up a level and find reasons for the higher-level belief that the original belief is mediately justified, it is also required that one have adequate reasons for the lower-level belief itself.

We should guard against two possible misunderstandings of the above argument. First, neither simple foundationalism nor any other epistemology can guarantee that one will, or can, find adequate reasons for a given epistemic proposition, or for any other proposition. The point rather is that there is nothing in the position that rules out the possibility that, for any immediately justified belief that one has, one can find adequate reasons for the proposition that one is so justified. Second, we should not take the critic to be denying the obvious point that people are often well advised, in the press of everyday life, to adopt beliefs for which they do not have adequate reasons. We should interpret him as requiring only that an *ideal* epistemic subject will adopt beliefs only for good and sufficient reason. Hence he insists that our epistemology must make room for this possibility. And, as just pointed out, Simple Foundationalism does so.

The dogmatism arguments may be urged with respect to *showing* that *p,* as well as with respect to accepting the proposition that *p.* That is, the critic may argue that foundationalism is committed to the view that "foundations cannot be argued for." Suppose that in trying to show that *p* I adduce some grounds, and, the grounds being challenged, I try to show that they are true, and . . . in this regress I finally arrive at some foundation *f.* Here, according to the critic, the foundationalist must hold that the most I can (properly) do is simply *assert f,* several times if necessary, and with increasing volume. And again this is dogmatism. But again Simple Foundationalism is committed to no such thing. It leaves something for the arguer to do even here; viz., try to establish the higher-level proposition that he is immediately justified in believing that *f.* And, if he succeeds in doing this, what more could we ask? Unless someone demands that he go on to establish the grounds appealed to in that argument—to which again the simple foundationalist has no objection in principle. Of course, as we saw earlier, the demand that one establish every ground in a demonstration is a self-defeating demand. But the point is that the simple foundationalist need not, any more than the coherence theorist, mark out certain points at which the regress of showing *must* come to an end. He allows the possibility of one's giving reasons for an assertion whenever it is appropriate to do so, even if that assertion is of a foundation.

But, like many positions that give us the best of both worlds, this one may be too good to be true. Although I am convinced that simple foundationalism is the most defensible form of foundationalism, especially if it also divests itself of other gratuitous claims for foundations, such as infallibility and incorrigibility,[19] I do not claim that it can actually be made to work. Though it escapes the main antecedent objection, it still faces all the difficulties involved in finding enough immediately justified beliefs to ground all our mediately justified beliefs. And on this rock I suspect it will founder. Meanwhile, pending a final decision on that question, it is the version on which both constructive and critical endeavors should be concentrated.

Notes

1. Contemporary writers on foundationalism do not seem to notice that Descartes and Locke have a quite different view of knowledge and, hence, that, if they hold that knowledge rests on foundations, this will mean something rather different.

2. Only "includes," because other requirements are also commonly imposed for mediate justification, e.g., that the first belief be "based" on the others, and, by some epistemologists, that the believer realize that the other beliefs do constitute adequate grounds for the first.

3. *Knowledge, Mind and Nature* (New York: Random House, 1967).

4. See the distinctions between infallibility, indubitability, and immediacy in my "Varieties of Privileged Access," *American Philosophical Quarterly*, 8, no. 3 (July 1971): 223–41.

5. In "Varieties of Privileged Access" I used the term "self-warrant" for a belief that is justified by virtue of being a belief of a certain sort.

6. For one attempt to explain the distinctively epistemic dimension of evaluation, see R. M. Chisholm, "On the Nature of Empirical Evidence," in Chisholm and R. J. Swartz, eds., *Empirical Knowledge* (Englewood Cliffs, N.J.: Prentice-Hall, 1973), 225–230.

7. In "Coherence, Certainty, and Epistemic Priority," *Journal of Philosophy* 61, no. 19 (Oct. 15, 1964): 545–57.

8. One should not confuse the respect in which Iterative is stronger than Simple Foundationalism with other ways in which one version of the position may be stronger than another. These include at least the following (a) whether it is required of foundations that they be infallible, indubitable, or incorrigible; (b) whether foundations have to be self-justified, or whether some weaker form of direct justification is sufficient; (c) how strongly the foundations support various portions of the superstructure. I am convinced that none of these modes of strength requires any of the others, but I will not have time to argue that here. Note too that our version of the regress argument (to be presented in a moment) does nothing to support the demand for foundations that are strong in any of these respects.

9. I am adopting the simplifying assumption that, for each mediately justified belief, there is only one set of adequate grounds that S justifiably believes. The argument can be formulated so as to allow for "overjustification," but at the price of further complexity.

10. The weakest link in this argument is the rejection of D. So far as I am aware, this alternative is never adequately explained, and much less is adequate reason given for its rejection. Usually, I fear, *being justified* is confused with exhibiting one's justification, and it is argued (irrelevantly) that one cannot do the latter for an infinite sequence of propositions. It is interesting in this connection that in two very recent attacks on foundationalism the infinite regress rejected by the regress argument is construed as a regress of *showing justification,* and in different ways the critics argue that the impossibility of completing an infinite sequence of such showings does not imply that there may not *be* an infinite sequence of mediate justification. See Keith Lehrer, *Knowledge,* pp. 15–16; and Frederick L. Will, *Induction and Justification,* pp. 176–85.

An adequate treatment of the argument would involve looking into the possibility of an infinite structure of belief and the patterns of justification that can obtain there. Pending such an examination, the most one can say for the argument is that it is clear that mediate justification is possible on alternative A and not clear that it is possible on alternative D.

11. See, e.g., Bertrand Russell, *Human Knowledge, Its Scope and Limits,* p. 171; Anthony Quinton, *The Nature of Things,* p. 119.

12. *Philosophy* (Englewood Cliffs, N.J.: Prentice-Hall, 1964). Because of the ambiguity of the term "knowledge claim," formulations and criticisms of the argument are often ambiguous in the present respect. When we ask how a "knowledge claim" is justified, we may be asking what it takes to justify an assertion that *p* or we may be asking what it takes to justify a claim that one knows that *p.* Thus, e.g., we find Arthur Danto beginning the argument by speaking of *m* being justified in asserting *s* but then sliding into a consideration of what it takes to justify "claims to know" *(Analytical Philosophy of Knowledge,* pp. 26–38).

13. Lest this assumption still seem obvious to some of my readers, let me take a moment to indicate how mediate epistemic knowledge might conceivably be derived from nonepistemic foundations. Let's begin the regress with Chisholm and follow the line of the first ground he mentions: that I justifiably believe that *b.* (To simplify this exposition I am replacing "know" with "justifiably believe" throughout.) By continuing to raise the same question we will at last arrive at a *c* such that I have *immediate* justification for believing that *c.* Here my justification (for believing that I justifiably believe that *c)* will shift from one or more other justified beliefs to the appropriate "warrant-increasing" property. What is then required at the next stage is a justification for supposing the belief that *c* to have this property, and for supposing that this property does confer warrant. It is highly controversial just how claims like these are to be justified, but, in any event, at this point we have exited from the arena of explicit claims to being justified in a certain belief; what needs justification from here on are beliefs as to what is in fact the case, and beliefs as to what principles of evaluation are valid, not beliefs as to my epistemic relation to these matters. And, without attempting to go into the details, it seems plausible that, if a foundationalist view is tenable at all, these sorts of beliefs will rest on the same sort of foundation as other factual and evaluative beliefs.

14. I have not located a clear-cut example of a regress argument with this starting point and with the conclusion in question. Nevertheless, the prospect seems tempting enough to be worth deflating. Moreover, it forces us to raise interesting quesions concerning the concept of showing.

Just as the ambiguity of "knowledge claim" led to versions of the regress argument being indeterminate with respect to the earlier feature, so the process-product ambiguity of terms like "justification" and "justified" often make it uncertain whether a philosopher is talking about what it takes for a belief to *be* justified or about what it takes to *justify* a belief in the sense of *showing* it to be justified. See, e.g., C. I. Lewis, *An Analysis of Knowledge and Valuation*, p. 187; Leonard Nelson, "The Impossibility of the 'Theory of Knowledge,' " in Chisholm and Swartz, *op. cit.*, p. 8.

15. It may also be required that *p* be true, on the ground that it makes no sense to speak of my having shown what is not the case. ("Show" is a success concept.) I neglect this point since it has no bearing on our present problem.

16. One may contest this requirement on the grounds that, if I have produced what is in fact a true adequate ground, that is all that should be demanded. And it may be that there is some "objective" concept of showing of which this is true. Nevertheless where we are interested in whether *Jones* has shown that *p* (rather than just whether "it has been shown that *p*," where perhaps all we are interested in is whether there *are* true adequate grounds), it seems that we must adopt this requirement in order to exclude wildly accidental cases in which Jones is asserting propositions at random and just happens to hit the mark.

17. To be sure, this short treatment leaves open the abstract possibility that the first such higher-level belief might be justified by some of the lower-level beliefs among the current foundations (if indeed the rules of the game permit their use in justification without first having been justifiably recognized as immediately justified). But it is clear that the foundational beliefs Descartes recognizes are radically unsuitable for this employment.

18. Descartes apparently felt that he was required not only to *identify* his foundations as such before building anything on them, but also to *show* at that stage that each of the foundations had the required status. And not even iterative foundationalism could help him with that. In the attempt to show that he immediately knows that, e.g., 2 plus 2 equals 4, he is inevitably and notoriously led to make use of premises the knowledge of which needs to be shown just as much or as little as the proposition with which he begins.

19. For a position that approximates this, see Anthony Quinton, *The Nature of Things*, Part II.

4   Can Empirical Knowledge Have a Foundation?

LAURENCE BONJOUR

The idea that empirical knowledge has, and must have, a *foundation* has been a common tenet of most major epistemologists, both past and present. There have been, as we shall see further below, many importantly different variants of this idea. But the common denominator among them, the central thesis of epistemological foundationism as I shall understand it here, is the claim that certain empirical beliefs possess a degree of epistemic justification or warrant which does not depend, inferentially or otherwise, on the justification of other empirical beliefs, but is instead somehow immediate or intrinsic. It is these noninferentially justified beliefs, the unmoved (or self-moved) movers of the epistemic realm, as Chisholm has called them,[1] that constitute the foundation upon which the rest of empirical knowledge is alleged to rest.

In recent years, the most familiar foundationist views have been subjected to severe and continuous attack. But this attack has rarely been aimed directly at the central foundationist thesis itself, and new versions of foundationism have been quick to emerge, often propounded by the erst-while critics themselves. Thus foundationism has become a philosophical hydra, difficult to come to grips with and seemingly impossible to kill. The purposes of this essay are, first, to distinguish and clarify the main dialectical variants of foundationism, by viewing them as responses to one fundamental problem which is both the main motivation and the primary obstacle for foundationism; and second, as a result of this discussion to offer schematic reasons for doubting whether any version of foundationism is finally acceptable.

The main reason for the impressive durability of foundationism is not any overwhelming plausibility attaching to the main foundationist thesis in itself, but rather the existence of one apparently decisive argument which seems to rule out all nonskeptical alternatives to foundationism, thereby showing that *some* version of foundationism must be true (on the

Reprinted from the *American Philosophical Quarterly* 15 (1978): 1–13, by permission of the editor and the author. Copyright 1978, *American Philosophical Quarterly*.

assumption that skepticism is false). In a recent statement by Quinton, this argument runs as follows:

> If any beliefs are to be justified at all, . . . there must be some terminal beliefs that do not owe their . . . credibility to others. For a belief to be justified it is not enough for it to be accepted, let alone merely entertained: there must also be good reason for accepting it. Furthermore, for an inferential belief to be justified the beliefs that support it must be justified themselves. There must, therefore, be a kind of belief that does not owe its justification to the support provided by others. Unless this were so no belief would be justified at all, for to justify any belief would require the antecedent justification of an infinite series of beliefs. The terminal . . . beliefs that are needed to bring the regress of justification to a stop need not be strictly self-evident in the sense that they somehow justify themselves. All that is required is that they should not owe their justification to any other beliefs.[2]

I shall call this argument *the epistemic regress argument,* and the problem which generates it, the *epistemic regress problem.* Since it is this argument which provides the primary rationale and argumentative support for foundationism, a careful examination of it will also constitute an exploration of the foundationist position itself. The main dialectical variants of foundationism can best be understood as differing attempts to solve the regress problem, and the most basic objection to the foundationist approach is that it is doubtful that any of these attempts can succeed. (In this essay, I shall be concerned with the epistemic regress argument and the epistemic regress problem only as they apply to empirical knowledge. It is obvious that an analogous problem arises also for *a priori* knowledge, but there it seems likely that the argument would take a different course. In particular, a foundationist approach might be inescapable in an account of *a priori* knowledge.)

I

This epistemic regress problem arises directly out of the traditional conception of knowledge as *adequately justified true belief*[3]—whether this be taken as a fully adequate definition of knowledge or, in light of the apparent counterexamples discovered by Gettier,[4] as merely a necessary but not sufficient condition. (I shall assume throughout that the elements of the traditional conception are at least necessary for knowledge.) Now the most natural way to justify a belief is by producing a justificatory argument: belief *A* is justified by citing some other (perhaps conjunctive) belief *B,* from which *A* is inferable in some acceptable way and which is thus offered as a reason for accepting *A*.[5] Call this *inferential justification.* It is clear, as Quinton points out in the passage quoted above, that for *A* to be genuinely justified by virtue of such a justificatory argument, *B* must itself be justified in some fashion; merely being inferable from an unsupported guess or hunch, e.g., would confer no genuine justification upon *A*.

Two further points about inferential justification, as understood here, must be briefly noted. First, the belief in question need not have been *arrived at* as the result of an inference in order to be inferentially justified. This is obvious, since a belief arrived at in some other way (e.g., as a result of wishful thinking) may later come to be maintained solely because it is now seen to be inferentially justifiable. Second, less obviously, a person for whom a belief is inferentially justified need not have explicitly rehearsed the justificatory argument in question to others or even to himself. It is enough that the inference be available to him if the belief is called into question by others or by himself (where such availability may itself be less than fully explicit) and that the availability of the inference be, in the final analysis, his reason for holding the belief.[6] It seems clear that many beliefs which are quite sufficiently justified to satisfy the justification criterion for knowledge depend for their justification on inferences which have not been explicitly formulated and indeed which could not be explicitly formulated without considerable reflective effort (e.g., my current belief that this is the same piece of paper upon which I was typing yesterday).[7]

Suppose then that belief *A* is (putatively) justified via inference, thus raising the question of how the justifying premise-belief *B* is justified. Here again the answer may be in inferential terms: *B* may be (putatively) justified in virtue of being inferable from some further belief *C*. But then the same question arises about the justification of *C*, and so on, threatening an infinite and apparently vicious regress of epistemic justification. Each belief is justified only if an epistemically prior belief is justified, and that epistemically prior belief is justified only if a still prior belief is justified, etc., with the apparent result that justification can never get started—and hence that there is no justification and no knowledge. The foundationist claim is that only through the adoption of some version of foundationism can this skeptical consequence be avoided.

Prima facie, there seem to be only four basic possibilities with regard to the eventual outcome of this potential regress of epistemic justification: (i) the regress might terminate with beliefs for which no justification of any kind is available, even though they were earlier offered as justifying premises; (ii) the regress might proceed infinitely backwards with ever more new premise-beliefs being introduced and then themselves requiring justification; (iii) the regress might circle back upon itself, so that at some point beliefs which appeared earlier in the sequence of justifying arguments are appealed to again as premises; (iv) the regress might terminate because beliefs are reached which are justified—unlike those in alternative (i)— but whose justification does not depend inferentially on other empirical beliefs and thus does not raise any further issue of justification with respect to such beliefs.[8] The foundationist opts for the last alternative. His argument is that the other three lead inexorably to the skeptical result, and that the second and third have additional fatal defects as well, so that some version of the fourth, foundationist alternative must be correct (assuming that skepticism is false).

With respect to alternative (i), it seems apparent that the foundationist is correct. If this alternative were correct, empirical knowledge would rest ultimately on beliefs which were, from an epistemic standpoint at least, entirely arbitrary and hence incapable of conferring any genuine justification. What about the other two alternatives?

The argument that alternative (ii) leads to a skeptical outcome has in effect already been sketched in the original formulation of the problem. One who opted for this alternative could hope to avoid skepticism only by claiming that the regress, though infinite, is not vicious; but there seems to be no plausible way to defend such a claim. Moreover, a defense of an infinite regress view as an account of how empirical knowledge is actually justified—as opposed to how it might in principle be justified—would have to involve the seemingly dubious thesis that an ordinary knower holds a literally infinite number of distinct beliefs. Thus it is not surprising that no important philosopher, with the rather uncertain exception of Peirce,[9] seems to have advocated such a position.

Alternative (iii), the view that justification ultimately moves in a closed curve, has been historically more prominent, albeit often only as a dialectical foil for foundationism. At first glance, this alternative might seem even less attractive than the second. Although the problem of the knower having to have an infinite number of beliefs is no longer present, the regress itself, still infinite, now seems undeniably vicious. For the justification of each of the beliefs which figure in the circle seems now to presuppose *its own* epistemically prior justification: such a belief must, paradoxically, be justified before it can be justified. Advocates of views resembling alternative (iii) have generally tended to respond to this sort of objective by adopting a holistic conception of justification in which the justification of individual beliefs is subordinated to that of the closed systems of beliefs which such a view implies; the property of such systems usually appealed to as a basis for justification is internal *coherence*. Such coherence theories attempt to evade the regress problem by abandoning the view of justification as essentially involving a linear order of dependence (though a non-linear view of justification has never been worked out in detail).[10] Moreover, such a coherence theory of empirical knowledge is subject to a number of other familiar and seemingly decisive objections.[11] Thus alternative (iii) seems unacceptable, leaving only alternative (iv), the foundationist alternative, as apparently viable.

As thus formulated, the epistemic regress argument makes an undeniably persuasive case for foundationism. Like any argument by elimination however, it cannot be conclusive until the surviving alternative has itself been carefully examined. The foundationist position may turn out to be subject to equally serious objections, thus forcing a reexamination of the other alternatives, a search for a further non-skeptical alternative, or conceivably the reluctant acceptance of the skeptical conclusion.[12] In particular, it is not clear on the basis of the argument thus far whether and how foundationism can itself solve the regress problem; and thus the possibility exists that the epistemic regress argument will prove to be a two-edged sword, as lethal to the foundationist as it is to his opponents.

II

The most straightforward interpretation of alternative (iv) leads directly to a view which I will here call *strong foundationism.* According to strong foundationism, the foundational beliefs which terminate the regress of justification possess sufficient epistemic warrant, independently of any appeal to inference from (or coherence with) other empirical beliefs, to satisfy the justification condition of knowledge and qualify as acceptable justifying premises for further beliefs. Since the justification of these *basic beliefs,* as they have come to be called, is thus allegedly not dependent on that of any other empirical belief, they are uniquely able to provide secure starting-points for the justification of empirical knowledge and stopping-points for the regress of justification.

The position just outlined is in fact a fairly modest version of strong foundationism. Strong foundationists have typically made considerably stronger claims on behalf of basic beliefs. Basic beliefs have been claimed not only to have sufficient non-inferential justification to qualify as knowledge, but also to be *certain, infallible, indubitable,* or *incorrigible* (terms which are usually not very carefully distinguished).[13] And most of the major attacks on foundationism have focused on these stronger claims. Thus it is important to point out that nothing about the basic strong foundationist response to the regress problem demands that basic beliefs be more than adequately justified. There might of course be other reasons for requiring that basic beliefs have some more exalted epistemic status or for thinking that in fact they do. There might even be some sort of indirect argument to show that such a status is a consequence of the sorts of epistemic properties which are directly required to solve the regress problem. But until such an argument is given (and it is doubtful that it can be), the question of whether basic beliefs are or can be certain, infallible, etc., will remain a relatively unimportant side-issue.

Indeed, many recent foundationists have felt that even the relatively modest version of strong foundationism outlined above is still too strong. Their alternative, still within the general aegis of the foundationist position, is a view which may be called *weak foundationism*. Weak foundationism accepts the central idea of foundationism—viz. that certain empirical beliefs possess a degree of independent epistemic justification or warrant which does not derive from inference or coherence relations. But the weak foundationist holds that these foundational beliefs have only a quite low degree of warrant, much lower than that attributed to them by even modest strong foundationism and insufficient by itself to satisfy the justification condition for knowledge or to qualify them as acceptable justifying premises for other beliefs. Thus this independent warrant must somehow be augmented if knowledge is to be achieved, and the usual appeal here is to coherence with other such minimally warranted beliefs. By combining such beliefs into larger and larger coherent systems, it is held, their initial, minimal degree of warrant can gradually be enhanced until knowledge is finally achieved. Thus weak foundationism, like the pure coherence theories mentioned above, abandons the linear conception of justification.[14]

Weak foundationism thus represents a kind of hybrid between strong foundationism and the coherence views discussed earlier, and it is often thought to embody the virtues of both and the vices of neither. Whether or not this is so in other respects, however, relative to the regress problem weak foundationism is finally open to the very same basic objection as strong foundationism, with essentially the same options available for meeting it. As we shall see, the key problem for any version of foundationism is whether it can itself solve the regress problem which motivates its very existence, without resorting to essentially *ad hoc* stipulation. The distinction between the two main ways of meeting this challenge both cuts across and is more basic than that between strong and weak foundationism. This being so, it will suffice to concentrate here on strong foundationism, leaving the application of the discussion to weak foundationism largely implicit.

The fundamental concept of strong foundationism is obviously the concept of a basic belief. It is by appeal to this concept that the threat of an infinite regress is to be avoided and empirical knowledge given a secure foundation. But how can there be any empirical beliefs which are thus basic? In fact, though this has not always been noticed, the very idea of an epistemically basic empirical belief is extremely paradoxical. For on what basis is such a belief to be justified, once appeal to further empirical beliefs is ruled out? Chisholm's theological analogy, cited earlier, is most appropriate: a basic belief is in effect an epistemological unmoved (or self-moved) mover. It is able to confer justification on other beliefs, but apparently has no need to have justification conferred on it. But is such a status any easier to understand in epistemology than it is in theology? How can a belief impart epistemic "motion" to other beliefs unless it is itself in "motion"? And, even more paradoxically, how can a belief epistemically "move" itself?

This intuitive difficulty with the concept of a basic empirical belief may be elaborated and clarified by reflecting a bit on the concept of epistemic justification. The idea of justification is a generic one, admitting in principle of many specific varieties. Thus the acceptance of an empirical belief might be morally justified, i.e., justified as morally obligatory by reference to moral principles and standards; or pragmatically justified, i.e., justified by reference to the desirable practical consequences which will result from such acceptance; or religiously justified, i.e., justified by reference to specified religious texts or theological dogmas; etc. But none of these other varieties of justification can satisfy the justification condition for knowledge. Knowledge requires *epistemic* justification, and the distinguishing characteristic of this particular species of justification is, I submit, its essential or internal relationship to the cognitive goal of truth. Cognitive doings are epistemically justified, on this conception, only if and to the extent that they are aimed at this goal—which means roughly that one accepts all and only beliefs which one has good reason to think are true.[15] To accept a belief in the absence of such a reason, however appealing or even mandatory such acceptance might be from other standpoints, is to neglect the pursuit of truth; such acceptance is, one might say, *epistemically irresponsible*. My contention is that the idea of being epistemically responsible is the core of the concept of epistemic justification.[16]

A corollary of this conception of epistemic justification is that a satisfactory defense of a particular standard of epistemic justification must consist in showing it to be truth-conducive, i.e., in showing that accepting beliefs in accordance with its dictates is likely to lead to truth (and more likely than any proposed alternative). Without such a meta-justification, a proposed standard of epistemic justification lacks any underlying rationale. Why after all should an epistemically responsible inquirer prefer justified beliefs to unjustified ones, if not that the former are more likely to be true? To insist that a certain belief is epistemically justified, while confessing in the same breath that this fact about it provides no good reason to think that it is true, would be to render nugatory the whole concept of epistemic justification.

These general remarks about epistemic justification apply in full measure to any strong foundationist position and to its constituent account of basic beliefs. If basic beliefs are to provide a secure foundation for empirical knowledge, if inference from them is to be the sole basis for the justification of other empirical beliefs, then that feature, whatever it may be, in virtue of which a belief qualifies as basic must also constitute a good reason for thinking that the belief is true. If we let 'ϕ' represent this

feature, then for a belief B to qualify as basic in an acceptable foundationist account, the premises of the following justificatory argument must
themselves be at least justified:[17]

(i) Belief B has feature ϕ.
(ii) Beliefs having feature ϕ are highly likely to be true.

Therefore, B is highly likely to be true.

Notice further that while either premise taken separately might turn out
to be justifiable on an *a priori* basis (depending on the particular choice of
ϕ), it seems clear that they could not both be thus justifiable. For B is *ex
hypothesi* an empirical belief, and it is hard to see how a particular
empirical belief could be justified on a purely *a priori* basis.[18] And if we
now assume, reasonably enough, that for B to be justified for a particular
person (at a particular time) it is necessary, not merely that a justification
for B exist in the abstract, but that the person in question be in cognitive
possession of that justification, we get the result that B is not basic after
all since its justification depends on that of at least one other empirical
belief. If this is correct, strong foundationism is untenable as a solution to
the regress problem (and an analogous argument will show weak foundationism to be similarly untenable).

The foregoing argument is, no doubt, exceedingly obvious. But how is
the strong foundationist to answer it? *Prima facie,* there seem to be only
two general sorts of answer which are even remotely plausible, so long as
the strong foundationist remains within the confines of the traditional
conception of knowledge, avoids tacitly embracing skepticism, and does
not attempt the heroic task of arguing that an empirical belief could be
justified on a purely *a priori* basis. First, he might argue that although it is
indeed necessary for a belief to be justified and *a fortiori* for it to be basic
that a justifying argument of the sort schematized above be in principle
available in the situation, it is *not* always necessary that the person for
whom the belief is basic (or anyone else) know or even justifiably believe
that it is available; instead, in the case of basic beliefs at least, it is
sufficient that the premises for an argument of that general sort (or for
some favored particular variety of such argument) merely be *true,*
whether or not that person (or anyone else) justifiably believes that they
are true. Second, he might grant that it is necessary both that such
justification exist and that the person for whom the belief is basic be in
cognitive possession of it, but insist that his cognitive grasp of the
premises required for that justification does not involve further empirical
beliefs which would then require justification, but instead involves cognitive states of a more rudimentary sort which do not themselves require
justification: *intuitions or immediate apprehensions.* I will consider each
of these alternatives in turn.

III

The philosopher who has come the closest to an explicit advocacy of the view that basic beliefs may be justified even though the person for whom they are basic is not in any way in cognitive possession of the appropriate justifying argument is D. M. Armstrong. In his recent book, *Belief, Truth and Knowledge,*[19] Armstrong presents a version of the epistemic regress problem (though one couched in terms of knowledge rather than justification) and defends what he calls an "Externalist" solution:

> According to 'Externalist' accounts of non-inferential knowledge, what makes a true non-inferential belief a case of *knowledge* is some natural relation which holds between the belief-state . . . and the situation which makes the belief true. It is a matter of a certain relation holding between the believer and the world [157].

Armstrong's own candidate for this "natural relation" is "that there must be a *law-like connection* between the state of affairs *Bap* [i.e. *a*'s believing that *p*] and the state of affairs that makes '*p*' true such that, given *Bap*, it must be the case that *p*." [166] A similar view seems to be implicit in Dretske's account of perceptual knowledge in *Seeing and Knowing,* with the variation that Dretske requires for knowledge not only that the relation in question obtain, but also that the putative knower *believe* that it obtains—though *not* that this belief be justified.[20] In addition, it seems likely that various views of an ordinary-language stripe which appeal to facts about how language is learned either to justify basic belief or to support the claim that no justification is required would, if pushed, turn out to be positions of this general sort. Here I shall mainly confine myself to Armstrong, who is the only one of these philosophers who is explicitly concerned with the regress problem.

There is, however, some uncertainty as to how views of this sort in general and Armstrong's view in particular are properly to be interpreted. On the one hand, Armstrong might be taken as offering an account of how basic beliefs (and perhaps others as well) satisfy the adequate-justification condition for knowledge; while on the other hand, he might be taken as simply repudiating the traditional conception of knowledge and the associated concept of epistemic justification, and offering a surrogate conception in its place—one which better accords with the "naturalistic" world-view which Armstrong prefers.[21] But it is only when understood in the former way that externalism (to adopt Armstrong's useful term) is of any immediate interest here, since it is only on that interpretation that it constitutes a version of foundationism and offers a direct response to the anti-foundationist argument set out above. Thus I shall mainly focus on this interpretation of externalism, remarking only briefly at the end of the present section on the alternative one.

Understood in this way, the externalist solution to the regress problem is quite simple: the person who has a basic belief need not be in possession of any justified reason for his belief and indeed, except in Dretske's version, need not even think that there is such a reason; the status of his belief as constituting knowledge (if true) depends solely on the external relation and not at all on his subjective view of the situation. Thus there are no further empirical beliefs in need of justification and no regress.

Now it is clear that such an externalist position succeeds in avoiding the regress problem and the anti-foundationist argument. What may well be doubted, however, is whether this avoidance deserves to be considered a *solution*, rather than an essentially *ad hoc* evasion, of the problem. Plainly the sort of "external" relation which Armstrong has in mind would, if known, provide a basis for a justifying argument along the lines sketched earlier, roughly as follows:

(i)   Belief B is an instance of kind K.
(ii) Beliefs of kind K are connected in a law-like way with the sorts of states of affairs which would make them true, and therefore are highly likely to be true.

Therefore, B is highly likely to be true.

But precisely what generates the regress problem in the first place is the requirement that for a belief B to be epistemically justified for a given person P, it is necessary, not just that there be justifiable or even true premises available in the situation which could in principle provide a basis for a justification of B, but that P himself know or at least justifiably believe some such set of premises and thus be in a position to employ the corresponding argument. The externalist position seems to amount merely to waiving this general requirement in cases where the justification takes a certain form, and the question is why this should be acceptable in these cases when it is not acceptable generally. (If it were acceptable generally, then it would seem that any true belief would be justified for any person, and the distinction between knowledge and true belief would collapse.) Such a move seems rather analogous to solving a regress of causes by simply stipulating that although most events must have a cause, events of a certain kind need not.

Whatever plausibility attaches to externalism seems to derive from the fact that if the external relation in question genuinely obtains, then P will not go wrong in accepting the belief, and it is, in a sense, not an accident that this is so. But it remains unclear how these facts are supposed to justify P's acceptance of B. It is clear, of course, that an external observer who knew both that P accepted B and that there was a law-like connection between such acceptance and the truth of B would be in a position to construct an argument to justify *his own* acceptance of *B*. *P* could thus serve as a useful epistemic instrument, a kind of cognitive thermometer, for such an external observer (and in fact the example of a thermometer is exactly the analogy which Armstrong employs to illustrate the relationship which is supposed to obtain between the person who has the belief and the external state of affairs [166ff.]). But *P* himself has no reason at all for thinking that *B* is likely to be true. From his perspective, it *is* an accident that the belief is true.[22] And thus his acceptance of *B* is no more rational or responsible from an epistemic standpoint than would be the acceptance of a subjectively similar belief for which the external relation in question failed to obtain.[23]

Nor does it seem to help matters to move from Armstrong's version of externalism, which requires only that the requisite relationship between the believer and the world obtain, to the superficially less radical version apparently held by Dretske, which requires that *P* also believe that the external relation obtains, but does not require that this latter belief be justified. This view may seem slightly less implausible, since it at least requires that the person have some idea, albeit unjustified, of why *B* is likely to be true. But this change is not enough to save externalism. One way to see this is to suppose that the person believes the requisite relation to obtain on some totally irrational and irrelevant basis, e.g. as a result of reading tea leaves or studying astrological charts. If *B* were an ordinary, non-basic belief, such a situation would surely preclude its being justified, and it is hard to see why the result should be any different for an allegedly basic belief.

Thus it finally seems possible to make sense of externalism only by construing the externalist as simply abandoning the traditional notion of epistemic justification and along with it anything resembling the traditional conception of knowledge. (As already remarked, this may be precisely what the proponents of externalism intend to be doing, though most of them are not very clear on this point.) Thus consider Armstrong's final summation of his conception of knowledge:

> *Knowledge of the truth of particular matters of fact* is a belief which must be true, where the 'must' is a matter of law-like necessity. Such knowledge is a reliable representation or 'mapping' of reality [220].

Nothing is said here of reasons or justification or evidence or having the right to be sure. Indeed the whole idea, central to the western epistemological tradition, of knowledge as essentially the product of reflective, critical, and rational inquiry has seemingly vanished without a trace. It is possible of course that such an altered conception of knowledge may be inescapable or even in some way desirable, but it constitutes a solution to the regress problem or any problem arising out of the traditional conception of knowledge only in the radical and relatively uninteresting sense that to reject that conception is also to reject the problems arising out of it. In this essay, I shall confine myself to less radical solutions.

IV

The externalist solution just discussed represents a very recent approach to the justification of basic beliefs. The second view to be considered is, in contrast, so venerable that it deserves to be called the standard foundationist solution to the problem in question. I refer of course to the traditional doctrine of cognitive givenness, which has played a central role in epistemological discussions at least since Descartes. In recent years, however, the concept of the given, like foundationism itself, has come under serious attack. One upshot of the resulting discussion has been a realization that there are many different notions of givenness, related to each other in complicated ways, which almost certainly do not stand or fall together. Thus it will be well to begin by formulating the precise notion of givenness which is relevant in the present context and distinguishing it from some related conceptions.

In the context of the epistemic regress problem, givenness amounts to the idea that basic beliefs are justified by reference not to further *beliefs*, but rather to states of affairs in the world which are "immediately apprehended" or "directly presented" or "intuited." This justification by reference to non-cognitive states of affairs thus allegedly avoids the need for any further justification and thereby stops the regress. In a way, the basic gambit of givenism (as I shall call positions of this sort) thus resembles that of the externalist positions considered above. In both cases the justificatory appeal to further beliefs which generates the regress problem is avoided for basic beliefs by an appeal directly to the non-cognitive world; the crucial difference is that for the givenist, unlike the externalist, the justifying state of affairs in the world is allegedly apprehended *in some way* by the believer.

The givenist position to be considered here is significantly weaker than more familiar versions of the doctrine of givenness in at least two different respects. In the first place, the present version does not claim that the given (or, better, the apprehension thereof) is certain or even incorrigible. As discussed above, these stronger claims are inessential to the strong foundationist solution to the regress problem. If they have any importance at all in this context it is only because, as we shall see, they might be thought to be entailed by the only very obvious intuitive picture of how the view is supposed to work. In the second place, givenism as understood here does not involve the usual stipulation that only one's private mental and sensory states can be given. There may or may not be other reasons for thinking that this is in fact the case, but such a restriction is not part of the position itself. Thus both positions like that of C. I. Lewis, for whom the given is restricted to private states apprehended with certainty, and positions like that of Quinton, for whom ordinary physical states of affairs are given with no claim of certainty or incorrigibility being involved, will count as versions of givenism.

As already noted, the idea of givenness has been roundly criticized in recent philosophical discussion and widely dismissed as a piece of philosophical mythology. But much at least of this criticism has to do with the claim of certainty on behalf of the given or with the restriction to private, subjective states. And some of it at least has been mainly concerned with issues in the philosophy of mind which are only distantly related to our present epistemological concerns. Thus even if the objections offered are cogent against other and stronger versions of givenness, it remains unclear whether and how they apply to the more modest version at issue here. The possibility suggests itself that modest givenness may not be a myth, even if more ambitious varieties are, a result which would give the epistemological foundationist all he really needs, even though he has usually, in a spirit of philosophical greed, sought considerably more. In what follows, however, I shall sketch a line of argument which, if correct, will show that even modest givenism is an untenable position.[24]

The argument to be developed depends on a problem within the givenist position which is surprisingly easy to overlook. I shall therefore proceed in the following way. I shall first state the problem in an initial way, then illustrate it by showing how it arises in one recent version of givenism, and finally consider whether any plausible solution is possible. (It will be useful for the purposes of this discussion to make two simplifying assumptions, without which the argument would be more complicated, but not essentially altered. First, I shall assume that the basic belief which is to be justified by reference to the given or immediately apprehended state of affairs is just the belief that this same state of affairs obtains. Second, I shall assume that the given or immediately apprehended state of affairs is not itself a belief or other cognitive state.)

Consider then an allegedly basic belief that-p which is supposed to be justified by reference to a given or immediately apprehended state of affairs that-p. Clearly what justifies the belief is not the state of affairs simpliciter, for to say that would be to return to a form of externalism. For the givenist, what justifies the belief is the *immediate apprehension* or *intuition* of the state of affairs. Thus we seem to have three items present in the situation: the belief, the state of affairs which is the object of the belief, and the intuition or immediate apprehension of that state of affairs. The problem to be raised revolves around the nature of the last of these items, the intuition or immediate apprehension (hereafter I will use mainly the former term). It *seems* to be a cognitive state, perhaps somehow of a more rudimentary sort than a belief, which involves the thesis or assertion that-*p*. Now if this is correct, it is easy enough to understand in a rough sort of way how an intuition can serve to justify a belief with this same assertive content. The problem is to understand why the intuition, involving as it does the cognitive thesis that-*p*, does not *itself* require justification. And if the answer is offered that the intuition is justified by reference to the state of affairs that-*p*, then the question will be why this would not require a second intuition or other apprehension of the state of affairs to justify the original one. For otherwise one and the same cognitive state must somehow constitute both an apprehension of the state of affairs and a justification of that very apprehension, thus pulling itself up by its own cognitive bootstraps. One is reminded here of Chisholm's claim that certain cognitive states justify themselves,[25] but that extremely paradoxical remark hardly constitutes an explanation of how this is possible.

If, on the other hand, an intuition is not a cognitive state and thus involves no cognitive grasp of the state of affairs in question, then the need for a justification for the intuition is obviated, but at the serious cost of making it difficult to see how the intuition is supposed to justify the belief. If the person in question has no cognitive grasp of that state of affairs (or of any other) by virtue of having such an intuition, then how does the intuition give him a *reason* for thinking that his belief is true or likely to be true? We seem again to be back to an externalist position, which it was the whole point of the category of intuition or givenness to avoid.

As an illustration of this problem, consider Quinton's version of givenism, as outlined in his book *The Nature of Things*.[26] As noted above, basic beliefs may, according to Quinton, concern ordinary perceptible states of affairs and need not be certain or incorrigible. (Quinton uses the phrase "intuitive belief" as I have been using "basic belief" and calls the linguistic expression of an intuitive belief a "basic statement"; he also seems to pay very little attention to the difference between beliefs and statements, shifting freely back and forth between them, and I will generally follow him in this.) Thus "this book is red" might, in an appropriate context, be a basic statement expressing a basic or intuitive belief. But how are such basic statements (or the correlative beliefs) supposed to be justified? Here Quinton's account, beyond the insistence that they are not justified by reference to further beliefs, is seriously unclear. He says rather vaguely that the person is "aware" [129] or "directly aware" [139] of the appropriate state of affairs, or that he has "direct knowledge" [126] of it, but he gives no real account of the nature or epistemological status of this state of "direct awareness" or "direct knowledge," though it seems clear that it is supposed to be a cognitive state of some kind. (In particular, it is not clear what "direct" means, over and above "non-inferential.")[27]

The difficulty with Quinton's account comes out most clearly in his discussion of its relation to the correspondence theory of truth:

> The theory of basic statements is closely connected with the correspondence theory of truth. In its classical form that theory holds that to each true statement, whatever its form may be, a fact of the same form corresponds. The theory of basic statements indicates the point at which correspondence is established, at which the system of beliefs makes its justifying contact with the world [139].

And further on he remarks that the truth of basic statements "is directly determined by their correspondence with fact" [143]. (It is clear that "determined" here means "epistemically determined.") Now it is a familiar but still forceful idealist objection to the correspondence theory of truth that if the theory were correct we could never know whether any of our beliefs were true, since we have no perspective outside our system of beliefs from which to see that they do or do not correspond. Quinton, however, seems to suppose rather blithely that intuition or direct awareness provides just such a perspective, from which we can in some cases apprehend both beliefs and world and judge whether or not they correspond. And he further supposes that the issue of justification somehow does not arise for apprehensions made from this perspective, though without giving any account of how or why this is so.

My suggestion here is that no such account can be given. As indicated above, the givenist is caught in a fundamental dilemma: if his intuitions or immediate apprehensions are construed as cognitive, then they will be both capable of giving justification and in need of it themselves; if they are non-cognitive, then they do not need justification but are also apparently incapable of providing it. This, at bottom, is why epistemological givenness is a myth.[28]

Once the problem is clearly realized, the only possible solution seems to be to split the difference by claiming that an intuition is a semi-cognitive or quasi-cognitive state,[29] which resembles a belief in its capacity to confer justification, while differing from a belief in not requiring justification itself. In fact, some such conception seems to be implicit in most if not all givenist positions. But when stated thus baldly, this "solution" to the problem seems hopelessly contrived and *ad hoc*. If such a move is acceptable, one is inclined to expostulate, then once again any sort of regress could be solved in similar fashion. Simply postulate a final term in the regress which is sufficiently similar to the previous terms to satisfy, with respect to the penultimate term, the sort of need or impetus which originally generated the regress; but which is different enough from previous terms so as not itself to require satisfaction by a further term. Thus we would have semi-events, which could cause but need not be caused; semi-explanatia, which could explain but need not be explained; and semi-beliefs, which could justify but need not be justified. The point is not that such a move is always incorrect (though I suspect that it is), but simply that the nature and possibility of such a convenient regress-stopper needs at the very least to be clearly and convincingly established and explained before it can constitute a satisfactory solution to any regress problem.

The main account which has usually been offered by givenists of such semi-cognitive states is well suggested by the terms in which immediate or intuitive apprehensions are described: "immediate," "direct," "presentation," etc. The underlying idea here is that of *confrontation:* in intuition, mind or consciousness is directly confronted with its object, without the intervention of any sort of intermediary. It is in this sense that the object is *given* to the mind. The root metaphor underlying this whole picture is vision: mind or consciousness is likened to an immaterial eye, and the object of intuitive awareness is that which is directly before the mental eye and open to its gaze. If this metaphor were to be taken seriously, it would become relatively simple to explain how there can be a cognitive state which can justify but does not require justification. (If the metaphor is to be taken seriously enough to do the foundationist any real good, it becomes plausible to hold that the intuitive cognitive states which result would after all have to be infallible. For if all need for justification is to be precluded, the envisaged relation of confrontation seemingly must be conceived as too intimate to allow any possibility of error. To the extent that this is so, the various arguments which have been offered against the notion of infallible cognitive states count also against this version of givenism.)

Unfortunately, however, it seems clear that the mental eye metaphor will not stand serious scrutiny. The mind, whatever else it may be, is not an eye or, so far as we know, anything like an eye. Ultimately the metaphor is just far too simple to be even minimally adequate to the complexity of mental phenomena and to the variety of conditions upon which such phenomena depend. This is not to deny that there is considerable intuitive appeal to the confrontational model, especially as applied to perceptual consciousness, but only to insist that this appeal is far too vague in its import to adequately support the very specific sorts of epistemological results which the strong foundationist needs. In particular, even if empirical knowledge at some point involves some sort of confrontation or seeming confrontation, this by itself provides no clear reason for attributing epistemic justification or reliability, let alone certainty, to the cognitive states, whatever they may be called, which result.

Moreover, quite apart from the vicissitudes of the mental eye metaphor, there are powerful independent reasons for thinking that the attempt to defend givenism by appeal to the idea of a semi-cognitive or quasi-cognitive state is fundamentally misguided. The basic idea, after all, is to distinguish two aspects of a cognitive state, its capacity to justify other states and its own need for justification, and then try to find a state which possesses only the former aspect and not the latter. But it seems clear on reflection that these two aspects cannot be separated, that it is one and the same feature of a cognitive state, viz., its assertive content, which both enables it to confer justification on other states and also requires that it be justified itself. If this is right, then it does no good to introduce semi-cognitive states in an attempt to justify basic beliefs, since to whatever extent such a state is capable of conferring justification, it will to that very same extent require justification. Thus even if such states do exist, they are of no help to the givenist in attempting to answer the objection at issue here.[30]

Hence the givenist response to the anti-foundationist argument seems to fail. There seems to be no way to explain how a basic cognitive state, whether called a belief or an intuition, can be directly justified by the world without lapsing back into externalism—and from there into skepticism. I shall conclude with three further comments aimed at warding off certain likely sorts of misunderstanding. First. It is natural in this connection to attempt to justify basic beliefs by appealing to *experience*. But there is a familiar ambiguity in the term "experience," which in fact glosses over the crucial distinction upon which the foregoing argument rests. Thus "experience" may mean either an *experiencing* (i.e., a cognitive state) or something *experienced* (i.e., an object of cognition). And once this ambiguity is resolved, the concept of experience seems to be of no particular help to the givenist. Second. I have concentrated, for the sake of simplicity, on Quinton's version of givenism in which ordinary physical states of affairs are among the things which are given. But the logic of the argument would be essentially the same if it were applied to a more traditional version like Lewis's in which it is private experiences which are given; and I cannot see that the end result would be different—though it might be harder to discern, especially in cases where the allegedly basic belief is a belief about another cognitive state. Third. Notice carefully that the problem raised here with respect to givenism is a logical problem (in a broad sense of "logical"). Thus it would be a mistake to think that it can be solved simply by indicating some sort of state which seems intuitively to have the appropriate sorts of characteristics; the problem is to understand how it is *possible* for any state to have those characteristics. (The mistake would be analogous to one occasionally made in connection with the free-will problem: the mistake of attempting to solve the logical problem of how an action can be not determined but also not merely random by indicating a subjective act of effort or similar state, which seems intuitively to satisfy such a description.)

Thus foundationism appears to be doomed by its own internal momentum. No account seems to be available of how an empirical belief can be genuinely justified in an epistemic sense, while avoiding all reference to further empirical beliefs or cognitions which themselves would require justification. How then is the epistemic regress problem to be solved? The natural direction to look for an answer is to the coherence theory of empirical knowledge and the associated non-linear conception of justification which were briefly mentioned above.[31] But arguments by elimination are dangerous at best: there may be further alternatives which have not yet been formulated, and the possibility still threatens that the epistemic regress problem may in the end be of aid and comfort only to the skeptic.[32]

Notes

1. Roderick M. Chisholm, *Theory of Knowledge*, 1st. ed., p. 30.
2. Anthony Quinton, *The Nature of Things*, p. 119. This is an extremely venerable argument, which has played a central role in epistemological discussion at least since Aristotle's statement of it in the *Posterior Analytics*, Book I, ch. 2–3. (Some have found an anticipation of the argument in the *Theaetetus* at 209E–210B, but Plato's worry in that passage appears to be that the proposed definition of knowledge is circular, not that it leads to an infinite regress of justification.)
3. "Adequately justified" because a belief could be justified to some degree without being sufficiently justified to qualify as knowledge (if true). But it is far from clear just how much justification is needed for adequacy. Virtually all recent epistemologists agree that certainty is not required. But the lottery paradox shows that adequacy cannot be understood merely in terms of some specified level of probability. (For a useful account of the lottery paradox, see Robert Ackermann, *Belief and Knowledge*, pp. 39–50.) Armstrong, in *Belief, Truth and Knowledge*, argues that what is required is that one's reasons for the belief be "conclusive," but the precise meaning of this is less than clear. Ultimately, it may be that the concept of knowledge is simply too crude for refined epistemological discussion, so that it may be necessary to speak instead of degrees of belief and corresponding degrees of justification. I shall assume (perhaps controversially) that the proper solution to this problem will not affect the issues to be discussed here, and speak merely of the reasons or justification making the belief *highly likely* to be true, without trying to say exactly what this means.
4. See Edmund Gettier, "Is Justified True Belief Knowledge?" Chap. 11 below. Also Ackermann, *Belief and Knowledge*, chap. 5, and the corresponding references.
5. For simplicity, I will speak of inference relations as obtaining between beliefs rather than, more accurately, between the propositions which are believed. "Inference" is to be understood here in a very broad sense; any relation between two beliefs which allows one, if accepted, to serve as a good reason for accepting the other will count as inferential.
6. It is difficult to give precise criteria for when a given reason is *the* reason for a person's holding a belief. G. Harman, in *Thought*, argues that for a person to believe for a given reason is for that reason to *explain* why he holds that belief. But this suggestion, though heuristically useful, hardly yields a usable criterion.
7. Thus it is a mistake to conceive the regress as a *temporal* regress, as it

would be if each justifying argument had to be explicitly given before the belief in question was justified.

8. Obviously these views could be combined, with different instances of the regress being handled in different ways. I will not consider such combined views here. In general, they would simply inherit all of the objections pertaining to the simpler views.

9. Peirce seems to suggest a virtuous regress view in "Questions Concerning Certain Faculties Claimed for Man," *Collected Papers,* 5, pp. 135–55. But the view is presented metaphorically and it is hard to be sure exactly what it comes to or to what extent it bears on the present issue.

10. The original statement of the non-linear view was by Bernard Bosanquet in *Implication and Linear Inference* (London, 1920). For more recent discussions, see Gilbert Harman, *Thought;* and Nicholas Rescher, "Foundationalism, Coherentism, and the Idea of Cognitive Systematization."

11. I have attempted to show how a coherence view might be defended against the most standard of these objections in "The Coherence Theory of Empirical Knowledge." (See Chap. 5 below.)

12. The presumption against a skeptical outcome is strong, but I think it is a mistake to treat it as absolute. If no non-skeptical theory can be found which is at least reasonably plausible in its own right, skepticism might become the only rational alternative.

13. For some useful distinctions among these terms, see William Alston, "Varieties of Privileged Access."

14. For discussions of weak foundationism, see Bertrand Russell, *Human Knowledge,* part 2, chap. 2, and part 5, chaps. 6 and 7; Nelson Goodman, "Sense and Certainty," *Philosophical Review* 61 (1952): 160–67; Israel Scheffler, *Science and Subjectivity,* chapter 5; and Roderick Firth, "Coherence, Certainty, and Epistemic Priority."

15. How good a reason must one have? Presumably some justification accrues from any reason which makes the belief even minimally more likely to be true than not, but considerably more than this would be required to make the justification adequate for knowledge. (See note 3, above.) (The James-Clifford controversy concerning the "will to believe" is also relevant here. I am agreeing with Clifford to the extent of saying that epistemic justification requires some positive reason in favor of the belief and not just the absence of any reason against.)

16. For a similar use of the notion of epistemic irresponsibility, see Ernest Sosa, "How Do You Know?," p. 117.

17. In fact, the premises would probably have to be true as well, in order to avoid Gettier-type counterexamples. But I shall ignore this refinement here.

18. On a Carnap-style *a priori* theory of probability it could, of course, be the case that very general empirical propositions were more likely to be true than not, i.e., that the possible state-descriptions in which they are true outnumber those in which they are false. But clearly this would not make them likely to be true in a sense which would allow the detached assertion of the proposition in question (on pain of contradiction), and this fact seems to preclude such justification from being adequate for knowledge.

19. Armstrong, *Belief, Truth and Knowledge,* chaps. 11–13. Bracketed page references in this section are to this book.

20. Fred I. Dretske, *Seeing and Knowing,* chap. 3, especially pp. 126–39. It is

difficult to be quite sure of Dretske's view, however, since he is not concerned in this book to offer a general account of knowledge. Views which are in some ways similar to those of Armstrong and Dretske have been offered by Goldman and by Unger. See Alvin Goldman, "A Causal Theory of Knowing," *The Journal of Philosophy* 64 (1967): 357–72; and Peter Unger, "An Analysis of Factual Knowledge," *The Journal of Philosophy* 65 (1968): 157–70. But both Goldman and Unger are explicitly concerned with the Gettier problem and not at all with the regress problem, so it is hard to be sure how their views relate to the sort of externalist view which is at issue here.

21. On the one hand, Armstrong seems to argue that it is *not* a requirement for knowledge that the believer have "sufficient evidence" for his belief, which sounds like a rejection of the adequate-justification condition. On the other hand, he seems to want to say that the presence of the external relation makes it rational for a person to accept a belief, and he seems (though this is not clear) to have *epistemic* rationality in mind; and there appears to be no substantial difference between saying that a belief is epistemically rational and saying that it is epistemically justified.

22. One way to put this point is to say that whether a belief is likely to be true or whether in contrast it is an accident that it is true depends significantly on how the belief is described. Thus it might be true of one and the same belief that it is "a belief connected in a law-like way with the state of affairs which it describes" and also that it is "a belief adopted on the basis of no apparent evidence"; and it might be likely to be true on the first description and unlikely to be true on the second. The claim here is that it is the believer's own conception which should be considered in deciding whether the belief is justified. (Something analogous seems to be true in ethics: the moral worth of a person's action is correctly to be judged only in terms of that person's subjective conception of what he is doing and not in light of what happens, willy-nilly, to result from it.)

23. Notice, however, that if beliefs standing in the proper external relation should happen to possess some subjectively distinctive feature (such as being spontaneous and highly compelling to the believer), and if the believer were to notice empirically, that beliefs having this feature were true a high proportion of the time, he would then be in a position to construct a justification for a new belief of that sort along the lines sketched at the end of section II. But of course a belief justified in that way would no longer be basic.

24. I suspect that something like the argument to be given here is lurking somewhere in Sellars's "Empiricism and the Philosophy of Mind" (reprinted in Sellars, *Science, Perception, and Reality,* pp. 127–96), but it is difficult to be sure. A more recent argument by Sellars which is considerably closer on the surface to the argument offered here is contained in "The Structure of Knowledge," his Machette Foundation Lectures given at the University of Texas in 1971, in Hector-Neri Castaneda, ed., *Action, Knowledge, and Reality: Critical Studies in Honor of Wilfrid Sellars* (Indianapolis, 1975), Lecture III, sections 3–4. A similar line of argument was also offered by Neurath and Hempel. See Otto Neurath, "Protocol Sentences," tr. in A. J. Ayer, ed., *Logical Positivism* (New York, 1959), pp. 199–208; and Carl G. Hempel, "On the Logical Positivists' Theory of Truth," *Analysis* 2 (1934–5): 49–59. The Hempel paper is in part a reply to a foundationist critique of Neurath by Schlick in "The Foundation of Knowledge," also translated in Ayer, *Logical Positivism,* pp. 209–27. Schlick replied to Hempel in "Facts and Propositions," and Hempel responded in "Some Remarks on

'Facts' and Propositions," both in *Analysis,* 2 (1934–35): 65–70 and 93–96, respectively. Though the Neurath-Hempel argument conflates issues having to do with truth and issues having to do with justification in a confused and confusing way, it does bring out the basic objection to givenism.

25. Chisholm, "Theory of Knowledge," in Chisholm *et al., Philosophy* (Englewood Cliffs, N.J., 1964), pp. 270ff. [Cf. Chapter 2 above.]

26. Ibid. Bracketed page references in this section will be to this book.

27. Quinton does offer one small bit of clarification here, by appealing to the notion of ostensive definition and claiming in effect that the sort of awareness involved in the intuitive justification of a basic belief is the same as that involved in a situation of ostensive definition. But such a comparison is of little help, for at least two reasons. First, as Wittgenstein, Sellars, and others have argued, the notion of ostensive definition is itself seriously problematic. Indeed, an objection quite analogous to the present one against the notion of a basic belief could be raised against the notion of an ostensive definition; and this objection, if answerable at all, could not only be answered by construing the awareness involved in ostension in such a way as to be of no help to the foundationist in the present discussion. Second, more straightforwardly, even if the notion of ostensive definition were entirely unobjectionable, there is no need for the sort of awareness involved to be *justified.* If all that is at issue is learning the meaning of a word (or acquiring a concept), then justification is irrelevant. Thus the existence of ostensive definitions would not show how there could be basic beliefs.

28. Notice, however, that to reject an epistemological given does not necessarily rule out other varieties of givenness which may have importance for other philosophical issues. In particular, there may still be viable versions of givenness which pose an obstacle to materialist views in the philosophy of mind. For useful distinctions among various versions of givenness and a discussion of their relevance to the philosophy of mind, see James W. Cornman, "Materialism and Some Myths about Some Givens," *The Monist* 56 (1972): 215–33.

29. Compare the Husserlian notion of a "pre-predicative awareness."

30. It is interesting to note that Quinton seems to offer an analogous critique of givenness in an earlier paper, "The Problem of Perception," reprinted in Robert J. Swartz, ed., *Perceiving, Sensing, and Knowing* (Garden City, New York, 1965), pp. 497–526; cf. especially p. 503.

31. For a discussion of such a coherence theory, see my "The Coherence Theory of Empirical Knowledge" (Chapter 5, this volume).

32. I am grateful to my friends Jean Blumenfeld, David Blumenfeld, Hardy Jones, Jeff Pelletier, and Martin Perlmutter for extremely helpful comments on an earlier version of this essay.

5   The Coherence Theory of Empirical Knowledge

LAURENCE BONJOUR

In a paper written for a commemorative symposium on the philosophy of C. I. Lewis, Roderick Firth remarks that Lewis liked to confront his Harvard epistemology students with a fundamental choice between a foundation theory of knowledge based on "the given," like that advocated so ably in Lewis's own books, and "a coherence theory like that of Bosanquet."[1] As Firth notes, there are many different philosophical views which have been called "coherence theories," including theories of truth and of meaning; but what Lewis seems to have had primarily in mind is a coherence theory of *epistemic justification*: the view that the epistemic warrant or authority of empirical statements derives *entirely* from coherence and not at all from any sort of "foundation."[2] Since Lewis's strong version of foundationism is by now everywhere in eclipse, it seems appropriate to examine the Bosanquetian alternative.

The purpose of this essay is to explore, and tentatively defend, a view of the Bosanquetian sort, which I shall call "the coherence theory of empirical knowledge" (hereafter CTEK). As discussed here, the CTEK is not to be identified with any specific historical view, though it has obvious affinities with some. It is intended rather as an idealized reconstruction of a relatively pure coherence theory, one which avoids all versions of foundationism.[3]

Views like the CTEK, though often employed as dialectical bogeymen, have rarely been treated as serious epistemological alternatives, since they have been thought to be subject to obvious and overwhelming objections. Thus the essential first step in a defense of such a view is to provide a sketch of its overall shape and rationale and show on this basis that these supposedly fatal objections can be answered. Such a preliminary defense of the CTEK, aimed at establishing its epistemological viability, is the goal of this essay.

Reprinted from *Philosophical Studies* 30 (1976): 281–312, by permission of the publisher and the author. Copyright 1976, D. Reidel Publishing Company.

I

The main watershed which divides the CTEK from opposing epistemological views is a familiar problem which I shall call "the regress problem." This problem arises directly out of the justification condition of the traditional explication of knowledge as adequately justified true belief.[4] The most obvious way in which beliefs are justified is *inferential justification*. In its most explicit form, inferential justification consists in providing an argument from one or more other beliefs as premises to the justificandum belief as conclusion.[5] But it is obviously a necessary condition for such inferential justification that the beliefs appealed to as premises be themselves *already* justified in some fashion; that a belief follows from unjustified premises lends it no justification. Now the premise-beliefs might also be justified inferentially, but such justification would only introduce further premise-beliefs which would have to be justified in some way, thus leading apparently to an infinite, vicious regress of epistemic justification. The justification of one belief would require the *logically antecedent* justification of one or more other beliefs, which in turn would require the logically antecedent justification of still further beliefs, etc. The result, seemingly inescapable so long as all justification is inferential in character, would be that justification could never even get started and hence that no belief would ever be genuinely justified.[6] Any adequate epistemological position must provide a solution to this problem, a way of avoiding the skeptical result—and the character of that solution will determine, more than anything else, the basic structure of the position.

One can find in the epistemological literature three main strategies for coping with the regress problem as it applies to empirical knowledge.[7]

(i) The historically most popular solution has been what may be called "strong foundationism," one version of the basic foundationist approach to epistemological issues. The basic thesis of foundationism in all of its forms is that certain empirical, contingent beliefs have a degree of epistemic warrant or justification which is non-inferential in character, i.e., which does not derive from other beliefs via inference in a way that would require those other beliefs to be antecedently justified. Strong foundationism is the view that the non-inferential warrant of these beliefs is sufficient *by itself* to satisfy the adequate-justification condition of knowledge and to qualify them as acceptable premises for the inferential justification of further beliefs. Thus these "basic beliefs" constitute the "foundation" upon which the rest of our empirical knowledge is based; the regress of justification terminates when such beliefs are reached.

Strong foundationism has many variants in recent philosophy which differ from each other in important ways, and many recent attacks on strong foundationism really apply to only some of these variants. One issue which divides these variants is whether basic beliefs are, or need be, infallible, indubitable, and/or incorrigible, i.e., whether and to what extent they are subject to subsequent rejection in the way in which non-basic beliefs are.[8] A second issue is whether basic beliefs are always about subjective experience or whether they may sometimes be about ordinary physical objects. A third issue, perhaps the most important, is whether and how basic beliefs are themselves justified. The traditional view is Lewis's: they are justified by reference to "given" experience (so that their justification is derivative from other cognitive or at least quasi-cognitive states, but not from further *beliefs*). But other proponents of strong foundationist theories have appealed instead to facts about language-learning or about the causal antecedents of the belief (facts which need not be known to the person for whom the belief is justified—on pain of further regress); and some philosophers have seemed to hold, paradoxically, that basic beliefs need not be justified at all in order to constitute knowledge and provide suitable justifying premises for further beliefs, that the issue of their justification "does not arise."[9] What all such views have in common is the idea that basic beliefs, if justified at all, are not justified via any sort of inferential appeal to further beliefs that would require those further beliefs to be justified and would thus unleash the regress.

(ii) The main traditional alternative to strong foundationism is the CTEK. In first approximation, the CTEK involves two main theses. The first is that *all* epistemic justification for individual empirical beliefs is inferential in character and hence that there are no basic beliefs and no foundations for knowledge. The second is the twofold claim (a) that the regress of justification does not go on forever, which would involve an infinite number of distinct beliefs, but rather circles back upon itself, thus forming a closed system; and (b) that the primary unit of epistemic justification is such a system, which is justified in terms of its internal coherence. The main historical proponents of the CTEK were the absolute idealists, though they tended at times to conflate (or confuse) the CTEK with a coherence account of *truth*. A similar view was also held by certain of the logical positivists, especially Neurath and Hempel.[10] Among contemporary philosophers views resembling the CTEK to some extent have been held by Quine, Sellars, and others.[11] To most philosophers, however, the CTEK has seemed to be afflicted with insuperable difficulties.

(iii) The third view, a relative newcomer to the philosophical scene, amounts to an interesting hybrid of a foundation theory of knowledge with the CTEK; it may be called "weak foundationism." On this view, certain empirical beliefs ("initially credible beliefs") have a modicum of epistemic warrant which is non-inferential in character. But these beliefs are not basic beliefs, as that phrase was understood above, since their degree of non-inferential warrant is insufficient by itself to satisfy the adequate-justification condition of knowledge or to qualify them as acceptable justifying premises for other beliefs; this initial modicum of justification must be augmented by a further appeal to coherence before knowledge is achieved. Thus the solution to the regress problem is presumably (though this is seldom spelled out) that the regress moves ultimately in a circle, as in the CTEK, but that the warrant for the coherent system of beliefs which results derives *both* from coherence and from the non-inferential warrant of certain of its component beliefs. Versions of weak foundationism have been suggested by Russell and Goodman, and developed by Scheffler and, much more extensively, by Rescher.[12]

It is the regress problem which has provided the main motivation and much of the argumentative support for foundationist views. Most philosophers have thought that the CTEK was obviously incapable of providing an adequate solution to the problem and hence that some version of foundationism must be true. This argument by elimination has led them to overlook serious problems which pertain not only to particular versions of foundationism, but to the overall foundationist position itself.

II

The underlying motivation for the CTEK is the conviction that all foundationist accounts of empirical knowledge are untenable. The crucial problem is much the same for both versions of foundationism: what is the source or rationale of the non-inferential epistemic warrant which allegedly attaches to a basic belief (in strong foundationism) or to an initially credible belief (in weak foundationism)? If an empirical, contingent belief *B*, one which is not knowable *a priori*, is to have such warrant for a given person, it seems that he must have some *reason* for thinking that *B* is true or likely to be true (the degree of likelihood required depending on whether *B* is held to be basic or only initially credible). And it is hard to see what such a reason could consist in other than the justified beliefs both (a) that *B* has some property or feature Φ, and (b) that beliefs having the property or feature Φ are likely, to the appropriate degree, to be true. Such justified beliefs would provide the basis for a justifying argument for *B*, and reliance on them would of course mean that *B* was not basic or initially credible after all. But how can a person be justified in accepting a contingent belief if he does not believe, and *a fortiori* does not know, anything about it which makes it at all likely to be true? A standard of epistemic justification which yields this result would seem clearly to have severed the vital connection between epistemic justification and truth, thus leaving itself without any ultimate rationale. It is for reasons of this sort that the CTEK holds that the justification of particular empirical beliefs is always inferential in character, and that there can in principle be no basic (or initially credible) empirical beliefs and no foundation for empirical knowledge.[13]

This picture of the CTEK, however, though accurate as far as it goes, is seriously misleading because it neglects the systematic or holistic character of the view. The best way to see this is to return to the regress problem.

Having rejected foundationism, the CTEK must hold that the regress of justification moves in a circle (or at least a closed curve), since this is the only alternative to a genuinely infinite regress involving an infinite number of distinct beliefs. But this response to the regress problem will seem obviously inadequate to one who approaches the issue with foundationist preconceptions. For surely, it will be argued, such an appeal to circularity does not solve the regress problem. Each step in the regress is an argument whose premises must be justified *before* they can confer justification on the conclusion. To say that the regress moves in a circle is to say that at some point one (or more) of the beliefs which figured earlier as conclusions is now appealed to as a justifying premise. And this situation, far from solving the regress problem, yields the patently absurd result that the justification of such a belief (qua conclusion) depends on *its own* logically prior justification (qua premise): it cannot be justified unless it is *already* justified. And thus neither it nor anything which depends on it can be justified. Since justification is always finally circular in this way according to the CTEK, there can be on that view no genuine justification and no knowledge.

The tacit premise in this seemingly devastating line of argument is the idea that inferential justification is essentially *linear* in character, involving a linear sequence of beliefs along which warrant is transferred from the earlier beliefs in the sequence to the later beliefs via connections of inference. It is this linear conception of inferential justification that ultimately generates the regress problem. If it is accepted, the idea that justification moves in a circle will be obviously unacceptable, and only *strong* foundationism will be left as an alternative. (Even weak foundationism cannot accept a purely linear view of justification, since its initially credible beliefs are not sufficiently justified to serve as first premises for everything else.) Thus the basic response of the CTEK to the regress problem is not the appeal to circularity, which would be futile by itself, but rather the rejection of the linear conception of inferential justification.[14]

The alternative is a holistic or systematic conception of inferential justification (and hence of empirical justification in general, since all empirical justification is inferential for the CTEK): beliefs are justified by being inferentially related to other beliefs in the overall context of a coherent system. To make this view clear, it is necessary to distinguish two levels at which issues of justification can be raised. Thus the issue at hand may be merely the justification of a particular belief, or a small set of beliefs, in the context of a cognitive system whose overall justification is taken for granted; or it may be the global issue of the justification of the cognitive system itself. According to the CTEK it is the latter, global issue which is fundamental for the determination of epistemic justification. Confusion arises, however, because it is only issues of the former, more limited, sort which tend to be raised explicitly in actual cases.

At the level at which only the justification of a particular belief (or small set of such beliefs) is at issue, justification appears linear. A given justificandum belief is justified explicitly by citing other premise-beliefs from which it may be inferred. Such premise-beliefs can themselves be challenged, with justification being provided for them in the same fashion. But there is no serious danger of a regress at this level since the justification of the overall epistemic system (and thus of at least most of its component beliefs) is *ex hypothesi* not at issue. One thus quickly reaches premise-beliefs which are dialectically acceptable in that context.

If on the other hand no dialectically acceptable stopping point is reached, if the premise-beliefs which are offered by way of justification continue to be challenged, then the epistemic dialogue would, if ideally continued, eventually move in a circle, giving the appearance of a regress and in effect challenging the entire cognitive system. At this global level, however, the CTEK no longer conceives the relation between the various particular beliefs as one of linear dependence, but rather as one of mutual or reciprocal support. There is no ultimate relation of epistemic priority among the members of such a system and consequently no basis for a true regress. The component beliefs are so related that each can be justified in terms of the others; the direction in which the justifying argument actually moves depends on which belief is under scrutiny in a particular context. The apparent circle of justification is not vicious because the justification of particular beliefs depends finally not on other particular beliefs, as in the linear conception of justification, but on the overall system and its coherence.

Thus the fully explicit justification of a particular belief would involve four distinct steps of argument, as follows:

1. The inferability of that particular belief from other particular beliefs, and further inference relations among particular beliefs.
2. The coherence of the overall system of beliefs.
3. The justification of the overall system of beliefs.
4. The justification of the particular belief in question, by virtue of its membership in the system.

According to the CTEK, each of these steps depends on the ones which precede it. It is the neglecting of steps 2 and 3, the ones pertaining explicitly to the cognitive system, that is the primary source of the linear conception of justification and thus of the regress problem. This is a seductive mistake. Since the very same inferential connections between particular beliefs are involved in both step 1 and step 4, it is fatally easy to conflate these two, leaving out the two intermediary steps which involve explicit reference to the system.

Of the three transitions represented in this schematic argument, only the third, from step 3 to step 4, is reasonably unproblematic, depending as it does on the inferential relations that obtain between the justificandum belief and other beliefs of the system; in effect it is this transition that is made when an inferential justification is offered in an ordinary context. But the other two transitions are highly problematic, and the issues which they raise are crucial for understanding and assessing the CTEK.

The transition from step 1 to step 2, from the inference relations obtaining between particular beliefs to the coherence of the system as a whole, is rendered problematic by the serious vagueness and unclarity of the central conception of coherence. It is clear that coherence depends on the various sorts of inferential, evidential, and explanatory relations which exist among the members of a set of propositions, especially upon the more systematic of these. Thus various detailed investigations by philosophers and logicians of such topics as explanation, confirmation, etc., may be taken to provide some of the essential ingredients of a general account of coherence. But the main job of giving such a general account, and in particular one which will provide a basis for *comparative* assessments of coherence, has scarcely been begun.[15] Nevertheless, while the absence of such an account represents a definite lacuna in the CTEK, it cannot provide the basis for a decisive or even a very serious objection to the theory. This is so because coherence (or something very closely resembling it) is, and seemingly must be, a basic ingredient of rival epistemological theories as well. We have already seen that weak foundationism makes an explicit appeal to coherence. And it seems that even strong foundationism must appeal to coherence if it is to make sense of knowledge of the past, theoretical knowledge, etc. In fact, all of the leading proponents of alternatives to the CTEK employ the notion of coherence (sometimes by other names)[16] in their accounts.

Thus the problem of giving an adequate account of coherence is one which may safely be neglected by the sort of preliminary defense of the CTEK which is offered here. There are, however, some essential points concerning the concept which should be noted. First, coherence is not to be equated with consistency. A coherent system must be consistent, but a consistent system need not be very coherent. Coherence has to do with systematic connections between the components of a system, not just with their failure to conflict.[17] Second, coherence will obviously be a matter of degree. For a system of beliefs to be justified, according to the CTEK, it must not be merely coherent to some extent, but more coherent than any currently available alternative.[18] Third, coherence is closely connected with the concept of explanation. Exactly what the connection is I shall not try to say here. But it is clear that the coherence of a system is enhanced to the extent that observed facts (in a sense to be explicated below) can be explained within it and reduced to the extent that this is not the case. Since explanation and prediction are at the very least closely allied, much the same thing can be said about prediction as well.

The problems relating to the other problematic transition in the schematic argument, that from step 2 to step 3, are more immediately serious. What is at issue here is the fundamental question of the connection between coherence and justification: why, if a body of beliefs is coherent, is it thereby epistemically justified? The force of this question is best brought out by formulating three related objections to the CTEK, centering on this point, which are usually thought to destroy all plausibility which it might otherwise have:

(I) According to the CTEK, the system of beliefs which constitutes empirical knowledge is justified *solely* by reference to coherence. But coherence will never suffice to pick out one system of beliefs, since there will always be many other alternative, incompatible systems of belief which are equally coherent and hence equally justified according to the CTEK.

(II) According to the CTEK, empirical beliefs are justified only in terms of relations to other beliefs and to the system of beliefs; at no point does any relation to the world come in. But this means that the alleged system of empirical knowledge is deprived of all *input* from the world. Surely such a self-enclosed system of beliefs cannot constitute empirical knowledge.

(III) An adequate epistemological theory must establish a connection between its account of justification and its account of *truth;* i.e., it must be shown that justification, as viewed by that theory, is *truth-conducive,* that one who seeks justified beliefs is at least likely to find true ones. But the only way in which the CTEK can do this is by adopting a coherence theory of truth and the absurd idealistic metaphysics which goes along with it.

Of these three objections, (III) is the most basic and (I) is the most familiar. It is (II), however, which must be dealt with first, since the answer to it is essential for dealing with the other two objections. Fundamentally, the point made in (II) must simply be accepted: there must be some sort of input into the cognitive system from the world. Thus the answer to (II) must consist in showing how the CTEK can allow for such input. I shall attempt to lay the groundwork for this in the next section by offering a schematic account of how the crucial concept of *observation* fits into the CTEK, following which I shall return in the final section to the objections.

III

It may be thought that the suggestion that there is room in the CTEK for an appeal to observation involves an immediate contradiction in terms. For surely, the argument might go, it is essential to the very conception of observation that observational beliefs are *non-inferential* in character; and it is equally essential to the conception of the CTEK, as explained above, that *all* justified beliefs are *inferential*. Thus the CTEK can accord no significant epistemic role to observation (which surely constitutes an immediate *reductio ad absurdum* of the theory).

But this argument is mistaken. It rests on a confusion between two quite different ways in which a belief may be said to be inferential (or non-inferential). In the first place, there is the issue of how the belief was arrived at, of its *origin* in the thinking of the person in question: was it arrived at via an actual process of reasoning or inference from other beliefs, or in some other way? In the second place, there is the issue of how the belief is *justified* or *warranted* (if at all): is it justified by virtue of inferential relations to other beliefs, or in some other way? Thus there are two distinct senses in which a belief may be inferential (and corresponding senses in which it may be non-inferential). And the immediate force of the above objection rests on a failure to distinguish these senses, for it is in the *first* sense (inferential or non-inferential *origin*) that an observational belief is paradigmatically non-inferential; while it is in the *second* sense (inferential or non-inferential *warrant*) that the CTEK insists that all justified belief must be inferential. And there is nothing absurd about the idea that a belief might be arrived at in some non-inferential way (e.g., as a hunch) and only subsequently justified, via inference.

Proponents of the foundation theory will no doubt argue that this distinction at best only momentarily staves off the force of the objection, since observational beliefs are in fact non-inferential in both senses, even if somewhat more obviously so in the first sense, so that the contradiction remains. The CTEK, on the other hand, holds that observational beliefs are non-inferential in only the first sense, that their epistemic authority or warrant derives from inferential relations to other beliefs and thus ultimately from coherence, in the way outlined above. The immediate task here is to elaborate this latter view by showing in some detail how the justification of observational beliefs might be plausibly viewed as deriving from inference. In doing so I shall neglect, for the moment, the systematic dimension of coherence and concentrate more narrowly on the inferential relations which pertain immediately to observation, according to the CTEK.

It is best to begin by considering some examples before attempting a more general account. Consider, as a first example, the following simple case. As I look at my desk, I come to have the belief, among many others, that there is a red book on the desk. This belief is *cognitively spontaneous:* it is not arrived at via any sort of conscious ratiocinative process, but simply occurs to me, strikes me, in a coercive manner over which I have no control; thus it is clearly non-inferential in the first of the two senses distinguished above. Let us suppose, as would ordinarily be the case, that this belief is indeed an instance of knowledge. The question now becomes: how is it justified or warranted? The strong foundationist will claim either that the belief is itself a basic belief, or else that it is justified via inference from a further belief, presumably about my experience, which is basic. But what account can the CTEK offer as an alternative? What sort of inferential justification might be available for such a belief?

Once the question is put in this way, the main elements of the answer are, I think, readily discernible. First, the belief in question is a visual belief, i.e., it is produced by my sense of sight; and I am, or at least can be, introspectively aware of this fact. Second, the conditions of observation are of a specifiable sort: the lighting is good, my eyes are functioning normally, and there are no interfering circumstances; and again, I know or can know these facts about the conditions, via other observations and introspections. Finally, it is a true law about me (and indeed about a large class of relevantly similar observers) that my spontaneous visual beliefs in such conditions about that sort of subject matter (viz., medium-sized physical objects) are highly reliable, i.e., very likely to be true; and, once more, I know this law. Putting these elements together, I am in a position to offer the following justification for my belief:

(i) I have a spontaneous visual belief that there is a red book on the desk.
(ii) Spontaneous visual beliefs about the color and general classification of medium-sized physical objects are, in (specified) conditions, very likely to be true.
(iii) The conditions are as specified in (ii).

Therefore, my belief that there is a red book on the desk is very likely to be true.
Therefore, (probably) there is a red book on the desk.[19]

There are two points which may be noted quickly about this justifying argument. First, all of the premises are empirical. Second, instead of assuming a listing of the conditions, I could have spoken instead in (ii) and (iii) of "standard conditions"; this would have had the effect of reducing the empirical content of (ii) and packing this content instead into (iii), but would have altered nothing of any real significance.

Consider now, more briefly, some contrasting examples. In all of the following cases I fail to have knowledge, despite the presence of a spontaneous visual belief. According to the account offered by the CTEK, the reason that I fail to know is that in each case one of the essential premises for an analogous justifying argument is unavailable to me. (a) Far on the other side of the campus a figure is coming toward me. I spontaneously believe that it is my friend George, and in fact it is; but the belief is not knowledge, because beliefs produced under those conditions (i.e., at very great distance) are not generally reliable, i.e., not likely enough to be true. (b) Watching the traffic, I spontaneously believe that the car going by is a Lotus, and in fact it is; but the belief is not knowledge, although the conditions of observation are excellent, because I am not very familiar with cars and my perceptual beliefs about them are not very reliable. (I am apt to think that almost any fancy sports car is a Lotus.) (c) Peering into the darkness, I spontaneously believe that there is a man in the bushes, and in fact there is; but the belief is not knowledge, both because the conditions are poor and because I am a bit paranoid and quite apt to imagine people in the bushes who are not there. (d) In a fun house (a house of mirrors), I spontaneously believe that there is a little fat man directly in front of me, across the room, and in fact there is; but the belief is not knowledge, because I do not know the conditions of perception (which are in fact quite normal) and hence am unable to supply the appropriate premise.

I submit that the contrast between these latter cases where I fail to have knowledge and the former one where I do have knowledge, and between analogous cases of the same sort, provides good evidence that arguments like the one sketched above are indeed involved in the justification of observation knowledge. It is an interesting exercise to attempt to give an account of the difference between such cases in strong foundationist terms.

There is one other sort of case which needs to be discussed. Looking at my desk, I come to know that there is no blue book on it. This knowledge clearly results from observation, but the sort of account sketched above is inapplicable, since I do not have a spontaneous visual belief that there is no blue book on the desk, I do not somehow see the absence of such a book; rather I simply fail to see its presence, i.e., I fail to have a spontaneous visual belief that there *is* a blue book on the desk, and my belief that there is not is an inference from my failure to spontaneously believe that there is. What this example illustrates is that spontaneous visual beliefs are reliable in two distinct senses: not only are they (in specifiable circumstances, about specifiable subject matter) very likely to be true, but they are also very likely to be produced (in specifiable circumstances, about specifiable subject matter[20]), if they would be true if produced. It is this second sort of reliability that allows me to reason, in the case in point:

(i) I have no spontaneous visual belief that there is a blue book on my desk.

(ii) If there were a blue book on my desk, then, in (specified) conditions, it is highly likely that such a belief would be produced.

(iii) The conditions are as specified in (ii)

Therefore, (probably) there is not a blue book on my desk.

Clearly knowledge justified in this way is closely connected with observation, whether or not it should itself be called observational. (It is also an interesting question, which I shall not pause to discuss here, whether all negative observational or observation-related knowledge must be justified in this indirect fashion.)

The crucial point, for present purposes, is that all of the premises of this justifying argument (as of the earlier one) are empirical premises, including most especially the crucial general premise (ii) in each argument. It is not an *a priori* truth, but rather an empirical discovery, that certain sorts of cognitively spontaneous beliefs are epistemically reliable and others are not; that waking visual beliefs are reliable and that visual beliefs produced in dreams, though similar in other respects, are not reliable. There are possible worlds in which the positions of these two sorts of experience are exactly reversed, in which reliable visual beliefs occur during sleep and unreliable ones while awake. (In such worlds, of course, the causal genesis of dreams, and of waking visual beliefs as well, will no doubt be different in important ways, but this difference need not be reflected in the subjective character of the beliefs or in the known conditions.) Thus the reason that visual perceptual beliefs are epistemically justified or warranted is that we have empirical background knowledge which tells us that beliefs of that specific sort are epistemically reliable. This is the basic claim of the CTEK for *all* varieties of observation.

On the basis of these examples, I offer the following tentative sketch of a concept of observation compatible with the CTEK. According to this view, any mode of observation must involve three essential elements.

First, there must be a process of some sort which produces cognitively spontaneous beliefs about a certain range of subject matter. The process involved may be very complicated, involving such things as sense organs; the state of the mind and/or brain as a result of previous training or innate capacities; perhaps also the sorts of entities or events which philosophers have variously referred to by such terms as "immediate experience," "raw feels," and "sensa;" instruments of various kinds; perhaps even occult abilities of some sort (such as clairvoyance); etc.

Second, the beliefs thus produced must be *reliable* with respect to the subject matter in question in the two distinct ways discussed above (under specifiable conditions): on the one hand, it must be very likely that such beliefs, when produced, are true (if the requisite conditions are satisfied); and, on the other hand, if the person is in a situation in which a particular belief about that range of subject matter would be true (and if the requisite conditions are satisfied), then it must be very likely that such a belief will in fact be produced. This second sort of reliability is crucial; on it depends, in large part at least, the possibility of negative observational knowledge.

Third, and most important from the standpoint of the CTEK, the person must *know* all of these things, at least in a rough and ready way. He must be able to recognize beliefs which result from the process in question (though he need not know anything about the details of the process). He must know that such beliefs are reliable in the two senses specified. And he must know in a given case that any necessary conditions for reliability are satisfied. He will then be in a position, in a particular case, to offer the following justification for such a spontaneous belief:

(i) I have a spontaneous belief that P (about subject matter S) which is an instance of kind K.
(ii) Spontaneous beliefs about S which are instances of K are very likely to be true, if conditions C are satisfied.
(iii) Conditions C are satisfied.

Therefore, my belief that P is (probably) true.
Therefore, (probably) P.

And he will also be in a position to argue for a negative conclusion on the basis of observation, in the following way:

(i) I have no spontaneous belief that P (about subject matter S) which is an instance of kind K.
(ii) If P, then if conditions C are satisfied, it is very likely that I would have a spontaneous belief that P which was an instance of K.
(iii) Conditions C are satisfied.

Therefore, (probably) not-P.

These two schematic arguments are the basic schemata for the justification of observational knowledge, according to the CTEK.

The foregoing account of observation is obviously highly schematic and would require much more discussion to be complete. For present purposes, however, it will suffice to add five supplementary comments, by way of clarification, elaboration, and anticipation of possible objections, following which I shall return to a discussion of the main objection to the CTEK.

First. It needs to be asked what the exact status of the various inferences outlined above is supposed to be, relative to the actual cognitive state of a person who has observational knowledge. For it is only too obvious that such a person need not go explicitly through any such process of inference in order to have observational knowledge (on pain of making actual instances of observational knowledge vanishingly rare). But it is equally obvious that the inferences in question, in order to be a correct account of the observational knowledge of such a person, must be somehow relevant to his particular cognitive state and not merely an account which could be added, totally from the outside, by a philosopher. Thus the claim of the CTEK here (and indeed the analogous claim of foundation theories for the inferences which they typically postulate) must be that such inferences are in some way tacitly or implicitly involved in the cognitive state of a person who has observational knowledge, even though he does not rehearse them explicitly and indeed might well be unable to do so even if challenged. It is not necessary that the belief actually originate via inference, however tacit or even unconscious; but it must be the case that a tacit grasp of the *availability* of the inference is the basis for the continuing acceptance of the belief and for the conviction that it is warranted. It has to be claimed, in other words, that such inferences are indeed an adequate philosophical unpacking or explication of what is really involved in the observational knowledge of an ordinary person, even though he may never be explicitly conscious of them. Such a claim on the part of the CTEK, as also on the part of foundation theories, is obviously very difficult to establish. Ultimately, it must simply be asserted that careful reflection on actual cases of observational knowledge will reveal that something like this is tacitly involved, though ultimately it may have to be conceded that any philosophically adequate account of knowledge is an idealization which is only loosely approximated by ordinary cognition. (It is worth remarking, however, that the inferential apparatus postulated by the CTEK, on the above account, is surely more common-sensical and less esoteric than is the analogous apparatus typically postulated by the foundation theories.)

Second. It is obvious that the knowledge represented by the third premises of the illustrative and schematic justifying arguments set out above, viz., the knowledge of the conditions of observation, will itself normally be largely or wholly based on observation and must be justified in the same way. This means that the element of coherence enters in immediately—with many observational beliefs, which may be from the same sense or from different senses, serving (directly or indirectly) as premises for each other's justification.

Third. As was emphasized above, the second premises of the various arguments are empirical premises. More specifically, each such premise is an empirical *law* about certain classes of beliefs. But it is obvious that such laws cannot be viewed in general as having been arrived at inductively, since no inductive argument as ordinarily construed would be possible unless one was *already* in a position to make warranted observations. Confirming evidence *is* available from within the coherent system for such laws, and any such law can be empirically tested within the context of the others; but the cognitive system as a whole could not have been developed piecemeal from the ground up.[21]

Fourth. A more difficult problem is how the first premises of the various arguments are to be justified. It is obvious that such premises, for the most part at least, are to be regarded as the products of introspection, but how is introspective knowledge to be understood within the CTEK? It is tempting to treat introspection as just one more mode of observation, which would then be justified along the lines of the justification-schemata set forth above. Unfortunately, however, this will not quite do. Justifying an introspective belief along those lines would require as a first premise the claim that one had a spontaneous introspective belief of a certain sort. Thus, to return to the original example of my perceiving a red book on my desk, if premise (i) of the justifying argument for the claim is taken as the introspective belief to be justified, the first premise of the justifying argument would have to be:

(i) I have a spontaneous introspective belief that I have a spontaneous visual belief that there is a red book on the desk.

This is all right by itself. But now if justification is demanded for this premise, and one attempts to give it along similar lines, the first premise required for the new justifying argument will be:

(i) I have a spontaneous introspective belief that I have a spontaneous introspective belief that I have a spontaneous visual belief that there is a red book on the desk.

And since the challenge can be repeated again and again, we are seemingly off on a new regress, one which cannot be handled by the strategy set forth above, since the chain of arguments clearly does not move in a circle. I am not convinced that this regress is logically vicious, but it does not represent a plausible account of our actual introspective knowledge.[22]

How then is introspective knowledge to be handled by the CTEK—that is if it is to avoid collapsing back into the foundationist view that introspective beliefs are basic? The key to the answer is that although an introspective belief *could* be justified along the lines of the earlier justification-schema, only one of the three premises of such an argument is really indispensable for the work of justification. Thus premise (iii), concerning conditions of observation, can be dispensed with because introspection, unlike other modes of observation, is almost entirely impervious to conditions. And premise (i), the premise which produced our current difficulty, can also be dispensed with. It is a fact about human perceivers that their beliefs about introspective matters are in accord with and reflect their spontaneous introspective beliefs. This is a weak and unproblematic version of privileged access, which is traceable to the fact that in introspective matters we are always in the proper position to have spontaneous beliefs; and thus, unlike the situation with other modes of observation, there is no chance for a disparity between our potential spontaneous beliefs and our other beliefs about the same introspective subject matter to develop. Consequently the reliability which attaches to spontaneous introspective beliefs also attaches to beliefs about introspective subject matter generally, whether spontaneous or not, and there is thus no need for premise (i) which stipulates that I have such a spontaneous belief.

Thus the only premise that is essential for a justification of introspective beliefs along the lines of CTEK is the one corresponding to premise (ii) of the schematic argument, with the references to conditions of observation and to cognitive spontaneity excised:

(*) Introspective beliefs (of certain sorts) are very likely to be true.

Here the phrase "introspective beliefs" is to be taken to mean simply "beliefs about introspective subject matter"; such beliefs need not be cognitively spontaneous. It is premise (*) that underlies introspective knowledge, according to the CTEK.[23]

The appeal to premise (*) may perhaps give the appearance that the CTEK is only verbally distinct from foundationalism, for it might be taken to be equivalent to treating introspective beliefs as basic or at least as initially credible. This would be a mistake. The basic difference is that premise (*), according to the CTEK, is an *empirical* premise, which must and does receive justification from within the rest of our cognitive system and which is subject to being reassessed and modified in light of that system. This fact about (*) is reflected in the parenthetical clause; all instances of introspection are not equally reliable, and the distinction among them must be made empirically. When an introspective belief is justified by appeal to premise (*), the appeal is still ultimately to coherence. Therefore, according to the CTEK, although introspective beliefs do play a unique and pivotal role in empirical knowledge, they do not constitute a foundation for that knowledge, as that notion has traditionally been understood; the basic thesis of foundationism can still be consistently rejected. (Indeed, the CTEK does *not* insist that some premise like premise (*) must be maintained by any acceptable cognitive system. It is logically conceivable that no such premise might be true, that no variety of introspection might be consistently reliable, so that *any* premise of this sort would fail to yield coherent results in the long run. This point will be considered further below, together with its bearing on the possibility of empirical knowledge.)

Fifth. It is worth noting explicitly that the conception of observation advanced here is implicitly much broader than the standard conceptions of sense-perception and introspection. On this view any process of empirical belief-production whose results are epistemically reliable counts as a mode of observation, whether or not it involves the traditional senses. Thus, for example, if there are people who have spontaneous clairvoyance or telepathic beliefs which are reliable, then for such people clairvoyance or telepathy is at least a potential mode of observation (though they must *know* that the beliefs in question are reliable if they are to have knowledge on this basis). Or, more interestingly, if (as often seems to be the case) a scientist who masters the use of an instrument such as a Geiger counter or cloud chamber develops the capacity to have reliable spontaneous beliefs about theoretical entities and processes such as radioactivity or subatomic particles,[24] then these beliefs count as observational on the present account and can be justified directly, without reference to sense-experience, along the lines sketched above.

IV

This schematic account of the role of observation in the CTEK provides the essential ingredient for answering the three objections to that theory that were set out in Section II, above. The first two objections can be dealt with very simply and directly, while the third will require a more extended discussion and even then must be dealt with here in a less conclusive fashion.

I begin with objection (II), which alleges that a consequence of the CTEK is that empirical knowledge has no *input* from the world. In light of the discussion of observation, it should now be clear that the CTEK can allow for input into the cognitive system from the world, while insisting that this input must be understood in *causal* rather than epistemic terms. The world impinges upon the system of knowledge by causing cognitively spontaneous beliefs of various sorts, but these beliefs are epistemically justified or warranted only from within the system, along the lines set out above. And, in principle at least, any sort of causal impact of the world that is capable of producing such beliefs in a reliable way is capable of being justified as a species of observation.

Moreover, such observational beliefs need not merely augment the overall system, but may force the alteration or abandonment of parts of it—either because the observational belief is directly inconsistent with one or more other beliefs in the system or because such alteration will enhance the overall coherence of the system. (Of course the observational belief could itself be rejected for a similar reason, though if this is done very often the law which specifies the degree of reliability of that sort of observational belief will also have to be revised.) In this way, the CTEK provides an account of how a system of beliefs can be tested against the results of observation.[25]

Thus the CTEK clearly allows for the *possibility* of input from the world into the cognitive system, a possibility which is in fact realized in our cognitive system. But does it not also admit the possibility of empirical knowledge without such input? Suppose that a cognitive system either fails to attribute reliability to any observational beliefs at all, or else fails to attribute reliability to those introspective beliefs which are needed for the reliable recognition of other reliable observational beliefs. Such a state of affairs might be built into the system from the outset, or might result gradually from repeated revision of the system if conflicts between putative observations and other component beliefs were always adjudicated by rejecting the observation. Clearly such a system would fail to have any effective input from the world. And yet on the account of the CTEK given so far, it seems that such a system (or rather the contingent part thereof) might constitute empirical knowledge if only it were sufficiently coherent. And surely this is an absurd result.

This point is essentially sound. Any adequate account of empirical knowledge must *require,* not merely allow, input from the world into the cognitive system—for without such input any agreement between the system and the world would be purely fortuitous, and thus the beliefs of the system would not be knowledge. Thus the CTEK must require that for a cognitive system to be even a candidate for the status of empirical knowledge, it must include laws attributing a high degree of reliability to a reasonable variety of kinds of cognitively spontaneous beliefs, including those kinds of introspective beliefs which are required for the recognition of other sorts of reliable cognitively spontaneous beliefs. Call this "the observation requirement." It provides the basic answer to objection (II).[26]

It is important to understand clearly the status of this requirement within the CTEK. The need for the requirement is *a priori:* it is an *a priori* truth, according to the CTEK, that a cognitive system must attribute reliability to cognitively spontaneous beliefs to the degree indicated *if* it is to contain empirical knowledge. But it is *not* an *a priori* truth that the antecedent of this conditional is satisfied and hence also not an *a priori* truth that its consequent must be satisfied. Whether any cognitively spontaneous beliefs are in fact reliable is an empirical issue to be decided within the cognitive system purely on the basis of coherence. It is logically conceivable, according to the CTEK, that no variety of cognitively spontaneous belief is sufficiently reliable and hence that any system satisfying the observation requirement would become incoherent in the long run, so that coherence could be preserved only by denying reliability to enough cognitively spontaneous beliefs to violate the observation requirement. The observation requirement does *not* say that such a result must be incorrect, but only that if it were correct there would be no empirical knowledge.

Thus the observation requirement functions within the CTEK as a regulative meta-principle of epistemological assessment. It does not impinge directly on the operations of the coherence machinery, but rather provides a partial basis for categorizing the results of that process. This is the main difference between the CTEK and that very weak version of weak foundationism which would attribute initial credibility to all cognitively spontaneous beliefs and then require the preservation of a reasonably high proportion of them. For such a version of foundationism, it is true *prior* to the workings of coherence that cognitively spontaneous beliefs have this minimal degree of credibility—for which no empirical justification is thus ever offered. Whereas for the CTEK *all* epistemic warrant for empirical propositions is ultimately a matter of coherence.[27]

What then is the status of those contingent and seemingly empirical beliefs which appear within a cognitive system that violates the observation requirement? I would suggest that their status is quite analogous to, if not indeed identical with, that of imaginative or fictional accounts. It is a consequence of the holism advocated by the CTEK that the distinction between the category of empirical description and these other categories is not to be drawn with respect to particular beliefs but only with regard to systems of beliefs. And the empirical thrust of a cognitive system is precisely the implicit claim that its component beliefs will agree, in general at least, with those classes of cognitively spontaneous beliefs which it holds to be reliable. Thus the observation requirement might be viewed as a weak analogue of the old positivist verifiability criterion of empirical meaningfulness, now transposed so as to apply to systems rather than to individual statements.

The answer to objection (I), the alternative coherent system objection, is already implicit in the foregoing discussion. For once it is clear that the CTEK involves the possibility that a system which is coherent at one time may be rendered incoherent by subsequent observational input, and once the requirement is accepted that any putative system of empirical knowledge must allow for this possibility, objection (I) in effect divides into two parts. Part one is the claim that *at a given moment* there may be many equally coherent empirical systems among which the CTEK provides no basis for decision. This claim is correct, but does not provide any basis for a serious objection, since the same thing will be true for any theory of knowledge imaginable. The important issue is whether these equally coherent systems will remain equally coherent and still distinct under the impact of observation in the long run.[28] Thus the second and crucial part of objection (I) will be the claim that even in the long run, and with the continuing impact of observation, there will be multiple, equally coherent empirical systems among which it will not be possible to decide. But, once the role of observation in the CTEK is appreciated, there seems little if any reason to accept this claim. The role of observation undercuts the idea that such alternatives can be simply constructed at will: such systems might be coherent at the beginning, but there is no reason to think that they would remain so as observations accumulate. This point is obvious enough if the observational components of the different systems involve the same concepts. But even if the observational components, or even the entire systems, involve different concepts so that they are not directly commensurable, there is no reason to think that one objective world will go on providing coherent input to incompatible systems in the long run.[29]

This brings us to objection (III), surely the most penetrating and significant of the three. Objection (III) contends that the CTEK will be unable to establish the vital connection between justification and truth, will be unable to show that its account of justification is truth-conducive, unless it also adopts the coherence theory of *truth*. It is certainly correct that a connection of this sort must be established by any adequate epistemology, even though this issue is rarely dealt with in a fully explicit fashion. Truth is after all the *raison d'être* of the cognitive enterprise. The only possible ultimate warrant for an account of epistemic justification must therefore consist in showing that accepting such an account and seeking beliefs which are in accord with it is likely to yield the truth, or at least more likely than would be the case on any alternative account. And the objection is also right that one who adopts a coherence theory of justification is in danger of being driven dialectically to espouse the coherence theory of truth as well. For the easiest and most straightforward way to establish a connection between a coherence account of justification and truth itself is to simply identify truth with justification-in-the-long-run, i.e., with coherence-in-the-long-run. Essentially this move was made by the absolute idealists and, in a different way, by Peirce. I assume here that such a coherence theory of truth is mistaken, that truth is to be understood at least roughly along the lines of the traditional correspondence theory. But if this is right, then the only way finally to justify the CTEK and answer objection (III) is to provide an argument to show that following the epistemic standards set by the CTEK is, in the long run, *likely* at least to lead to correspondence.[30]

I believe that it is possible to give such an argument, though I cannot undertake to provide a detailed account of it here. The main difficulty is an extrinsic one: no one has succeeded so far in giving an adequate account of the correspondence theory of truth,[31] and such an account is an indispensable ingredient of the envisaged argument. It is possible, however, to provide a rough sketch of the way in which the argument would go, given a very rough and intuitive conception of the correspondence theory: a proposition is true if it accords with an actual situation in the world, and otherwise false. (The argument is relative to the assumption that the observation requirement can be satisfied; if there were no possibility of reliable input from the world, then no set of epistemic standards would be likely to yield the truth.)

Suppose then that we have a hypothetical cognitive system which is coherent and satisfies the observation requirement as stipulated above, but fails to accord with reality. Our task is to show that such a system is unlikely to *remain* coherent (and continue to satisfy the observation requirement) unless it is revised in the direction of greater accord with reality. The way in which such revision *might* take place is obvious enough. If the lack of accord between the system and reality involves observable matters, then if the appropriate observations are actually made, they will produce inconsistency or incoherence within the system and force its revision. If the observations themselves are not rejected by such a revision, then the effect is to bring the system more into accord with reality. And this process *might* be repeated over and over until complete accord with reality is achieved in the very long run.

This, as I say, is what *might* happen. But is it *likely* to happen? The best way to show that it is likely to happen is to consider in turn each of the various seemingly plausible ways in which it might fail to happen, despite the lack of accord between system and reality stipulated above, and show that these are all *un*likely.

First. The process described above, whereby the system is revised in the direction of greater accord with the world, depends essentially on the occurrence of observational beliefs which conflict with other parts of the system and thus force the revision of the system. But any such revision involves a choice as to which of the conflicting beliefs to retain, and the system will come to accord more closely with reality only if this choice results in the retention of the observational beliefs and the exclusion of their competitors. Thus the most obvious way in which such revision in the direction of truth might fail to occur is that the choice be made consistently in favor of the non-observational beliefs in question, rejecting the observational beliefs. In the short run, it is quite likely that such a revision would produce a more justified result than would the alternate choice in favor of observation. But this could not happen in the long run. For if an inquirer or community of inquirers were to follow in the long run such a policy, deliberate or not, of resolving most such decisions in favor of the antecedent system and against the observational belief, this would inevitably have the effect of undermining the law that such observations are reliable and thus eventually violating the observation requirement. Thus this first possibility may be ruled out.

Second. Another way in which the envisaged revision in favor of truth might fail to take place is that, although the situations in the world which conflicted with the system were in fact observable, it might be the case that the inquirer or inquirers in question were simply never in the proper position to make the requisite observations, and so the conflict between the system and world would never be discovered. This possibility cannot be completely ruled out. But the longer the period of inquiry in question becomes, the more unlikely it is that this situation would continue, and this unlikelihood is increased as the supposed discrepancy between system and world is made larger.

Third. So far the assumption has been that the lack of accord between system and world involves aspects of the world which are observable. But suppose that this is not the case, that the aspects of the world in question are unobservable. There are various ways in which this might be so. First, and most basically, it might be the case that the aspects in question simply had no causal effects which were detectable by the sense organs or sensitive faculties of our community of inquirers, so that there would be no way that such inquirers could learn to observe those aspects. Second, it might be the case that, although the aspects in question did have causal impact on our inquirers, these inquirers simply had not learned to make observations of the appropriate sort. Third, it might be the case that although the aspects in question were in principle observable by our inquirers, there were barriers of some sort which prevented them from actually making the observations. Such barriers would include distance in space or time, impossibly hostile environments of various sorts, etc.

This sort of situation must be acknowledged as possible and even likely. The question is whether it could be overcome, given only the resources allowed by the CTEK, and if so, how likely it is that such an overcoming would occur.[32] The answer to the first part of the question is that it *could* be overcome, in either of two ways. In the first place, the unobservability of the aspects of the world in question might be overcome: the barriers might be transcended, the inquirers might learn to make the requisite observations, and/or new instruments might be developed which would create an appropriate causal linkage between these aspects and the sense organs of our observers. (See the remarks about instrumental observation at the end of Section III.) All of these things could happen, but there is no way to show that they are likely to happen in general. Thus the more important way in which the situation of unobservability might be overcome is by the development of *theories* concerning the unobservable aspects of the world. It is via theory construction that we come to know about the unobservable aspects of the world.

But is there any reason to think that such theory construction is likely to take place? The only possible answer on behalf of the CTEK, as indeed on behalf of any theory of knowledge, is that if enough aspects of the world are observable and if the unobservable aspects of the world have enough causal impact on the observable ones, then a fully coherent account of the observable aspects will in the long run lead to theories about the unobservable aspects. The main consideration here is that coherence essentially involves both prediction and explanation. An account of the observable world which was unable to predict and explain the observable effects of unobservable entities and processes would be to that extent incoherent. Thus to suppose that an ideally coherent account could be given of the observable aspects without any mention of the unobservable aspects would be in effect to suppose both that the world divides into two parts with no significant causal interaction between the two, and that this division coincides with that between the observable and the unobservable. And this is surely unlikely, even if one does not bring in the fact that the observable/unobservable line is not fixed once and for all.[33]

Fourth. There is one other apparently possible way to be considered in which there could be a lack of accord between one's cognitive system and reality without revision in the direction of truth being likely to take place. This alleged possibility is difficult to make fully clear, but it goes at least roughly as follows. Suppose that the conceptual picture which is given by the cognitive system, though failing to accord with the world, is isomorphic with it in the following way: for each kind of thing K, property of things P, etc., in the world, there is a corresponding but distinct kind of thing K^*, property of things P^*, etc., in the conceptual picture, and analogously for other kinds, properties, and whatever other categories of things are found in the world. The observational dispositions of the community of inquirers are such that they have observational beliefs about K^*s when what they are actually observing is As, etc. Under these conditions, the conceptual picture of the world would be fully coherent and would be in no danger of being rendered incoherent by observations, and yet *ex hypothesi* it would fail to accord with the world.[34]

Notice, however, that for this situation to occur, the laws, conceptual connections, etc., which pertain to the conceptually depicted kinds, properties, etc., must exactly mirror those which pertain to the actual kinds, properties, etc., of the world. If it is a true law in the world that instances of K_1 are always accompanied by instances of K_2, then it must be a law in the conceptual depiction that instances of K_1^* are always accompanied by instances of K_2^*, etc. For any discrepancy in such inferential patterns between the conceptual depiction and the world would be a basis for a potential conflicting observation. But despite this exact mirroring of all inferential patterns, it must still be the case that the kinds, properties, etc., of the world are not identical with those of the system. Thus one possible response by a proponent of the CTEK would be simply the denial that this sort of situation is indeed possible, on the grounds that the associated inferential patterns determine the kinds, properties, etc., completely, so that if these are the same there is no room left for a difference between the conceptually depicted world and the actual world. I think that there is merit in this claim, but a defense of it is impossible here.[35] In any case, it will suffice for present purposes merely to make the weaker claim that this sort of situation in which the inference patterns match but the kinds, etc., are still different is very unlikely, i.e., that the fact that one set of inference patterns mirror the other is a very good reason for supposing that the kinds, etc., are identical.

The foregoing considerations are an attempt to make plausible the following conclusion: it is highly unlikely, though not impossible, that a cognitive system which failed to accord with the world and which satisfied the observation requirement would be coherent and remain coherent under the impact of new observation, unless it was gradually revised in the direction of greater accord with the world. This is so because all of the apparent ways in which such revision could fail to take place represent highly unlikely situations.[36] This is obviously only a sketch of a line of argument which would have to be greatly elaborated in various ways to be really adequate. Here it is intended only to suggest the sort of answer which the CTEK can make to objection (III), how it can establish the truth-conduciveness of its view of justification, without resorting to the desperate expedient of the coherence theory of truth.

Thus the standard objections to views like the CTEK turn out to be in fact far less conclusive than has usually been thought, and it is reasonable to suppose that they can be successfully answered, once the role of observation in the theory is fully understood and appreciated. This in turn suggests that views like the CTEK are potentially viable accounts of empirical knowledge, worthy of far more serious attention than they have usually been given.[37]

Notes

1. Roderick Firth, "Coherence, Certainty, and Epistemic Priority." Reprinted in Chisholm and Swartz, eds., *Empirical Knowledge,* p. 459.

2. Ibid., pp. 460, 463.

3. Whether or not the view presented here is an entirely *pure* coherence theory is mainly an issue of taxonomy. As will be seen, it does *not* hold that the only factor which determines the acceptability of a set of propositions as putative empirical knowledge is its internal coherence. It does claim, however, that the epistemic justification attaching to an empirical proposition always derives entirely from considerations of coherence—and thus is never immediate or intrinsic, as the foundationist claims.

4. That this cannot be a complete conception of knowledge is evident from the work of Gettier and those who have followed his lead. See Edmund Gettier, "Is Justified True Belief Knowledge?" But none of this literature has seriously challenged the view that the traditional conditions are at least *necessary* for knowledge, and that is enough to generate the problem to be discussed here.

5. The notion of an argument is to be taken very broadly here. Any sort of

inferential relation between a belief (or set of beliefs) *A* and a further belief *B* which allows *B* to be justified relative to a justified acceptance of *A* will provide a basis for a justifying argument.

6. Notice that the important regress here is *logical* or *epistemic,* rather than *temporal,* in character. If it were a requirement for a belief to be justified that the justifying argument be explicitly given (perhaps only in thought) by the person in question, then clearly there would be a vicious temporal regress of justification in which no stopping place was ever reached (so long as all justification is inferential). But there is no reason to assume in this way that an explicit process of justification must actually take place before a belief is justified. It is enough, it would seem, that there be a justification which could be supplied if demanded and which in fact is the reason for the holding of the belief; but this need not be made explicit (to others or even to oneself) until and unless the issue is raised.

7. The restriction to empirical knowledge is to be understood throughout the discussion of this paper, even where not made explicit. In particular, it is clear that a coherence theory of *a priori* knowledge would be hopeless, since at least some *a priori* inferential connections must be presupposed by any account of coherence.

8. On the distinction between infallibility, indubitability, and incorrigibility, see William Alston, "Varieties of Privileged Access."

9. For Lewis's view, see his *Analysis of Knowledge and Valuation,* chaps. 2, 7. An appeal to language-learning is made by Quinton in his paper "The Foundations of Knowledge," reprinted in Chisholm and Swartz. An example of the view that the issue of justification does not arise is J.L. Austin, *Sense and Sensibilia* (Oxford: Oxford University Press, 1962). These are only examples of two positions which are widely held.

10. The clearest specimen of this idealist view is Brand Blanshard, *The Nature of Thought.* See also F. H. Bradley, *Essays on Truth and Reality* (Oxford: Oxford University Press, 1914); and Bernard Bosanquet, *Implication and Linear Inference* (London: Macmillan, 1920). For the positivists, see Otto Neurath, "Protocol Sentences," translated in A. J. Ayer, ed. *Logical Positivism* (New York: The Free Press, 1959); pp. 199–208; and Carl G. Hempel, "On the Logical Positivists' Theory of Truth," *Analysis* 2 (1934–35): 49–59. The Hempel paper is in part a reply to a foundationist critique of Neurath by Schlick in "The Foundation of Knowledge," also translated in *Logical Positivism,* pp. 209–27. Schlick replied to Hempel in "Facts and Propositions," and Hempel responded in "Some Remarks on 'Facts' and Propositions," both in *Analysis* 2 (1934–35): 65–70 and 93–96, respectively.

11. See W. V. O. Quine, "Two Dogmas of Empiricism," in his *From a Logical Point of View* (Cambridge: Harvard University Press, 1953); also his *Word and Object* (New York: John Wiley & Sons, 1960), chap. 1; and Gilbert Harman, "Quine on Meaning and Existence II," *Review of Metaphysics* 21 (1967–68): 343–67. Sellars's writings on this subject are voluminous, but the most important are: "Empiricism and the Philosophy of Mind" (especially Section VIII) and "Some Reflections on Language Games," both reprinted in his *Science, Perception and Reality;* "Givenness and Explanatory Coherence," *Journal of Philosophy* 70 (1973): 612–24; and "The Structure of Knowledge," his Machette Lectures, given at the University of Texas in the spring of 1971, especially Part 3, "Epistemic Principles." The view offered in this paper is closest to Sellars's and is, at certain points, strongly influenced by it, though I am very unsure how much of it Sellars

would agree with. Others who have advocated somewhat similar views include Hall, Aune, Harman, and Lehrer. For Hall's view see his *Our Knowledge of Fact and Value* (Chapel Hill: University of North Carolina Press, 1961). Aune's views are to be found in his book *Knowledge, Mind, and Nature*. For Harman, see his book *Thought*. For Lehrer, see his *Knowledge*.

12. See Bertrand Russell, *Human Knowledge*, Part 2, chap. 2, and Part 5, chaps. 6 and 7; Nelson Goodman, "Sense and Certainty," *Philosophical Review* 61 (1952): 160–67; Israel Scheffler, *Science and Subjectivity*, chap. 5; and Nicholas Rescher, *The Coherence Theory of Truth*. Despite the title, Rescher's position in the book just cited is not a version of the CTEK and still less of a coherence theory of truth. In a later book, *Methodological Pragmatism*, Rescher seems to waver between a version of the CTEK and a version of weak foundationism. See my critical study, "Rescher's Idealistic Pragmatism," in the *Review of Metaphysics* 29 (1976). Firth, in the paper cited in note 1, also opts, rather tentatively, for a version of weak foundationism.

13. Of course some of the justifying premises might be *a priori* in character. But the CTEK denies that this is ever the case for *all* of the premises which would be necessary to justify an empirical belief.

14. The original critique of the linear account of inference was by Bosanquet in *Implication and Linear Inference*. A more recent version is offered by Rescher in "Foundationalism, Coherentism, and the Idea of Cognitive Systematization." Harman's account of inference in *Thought* is in many ways a modernized version of Bosanquet.

15. A useful, though preliminary, account is contained in Hall, *op. cit.* See also Harman, *op. cit.*, and Lehrer, *op. cit.*, for further useful discussion.

16. Thus Lewis calls it "congruence" and Chisholm calls it "concurrence." See Lewis, *op. cit.*, chap. 11, and Chisholm, *Theory of Knowledge*, chap. 3.

17. This point might seem too obvious to be worth making, but it has occasionally been overlooked, e.g., by Scheffler, *op. cit.*, chap. 5. And Rescher's very idiosyncratic account of coherence in *The Coherence Theory of Truth* in effect is based only on consistency.

18. It is difficult to provide an exact gloss for the phrase "currently available alternative." The rough idea is that the currently available alternatives are those which would be considered by a reasonably careful and reflective inquirer. They do not include all of the theoretically possible alternative systems which might ideally be constructed; this would place justification as well as truth beyond our ken, since we could never in fact consider and certainly could never know that we had considered all such alternatives. On the other hand, the set of currently available alternatives may well include more than have actually occurred to a given inquirer or community of inquirers; there is an implicit epistemic obligation to seek out such alternatives.

19. I take this to be an instance of what Sellars calls "trans-level inference." See, e.g., *Science, Perception, and Reality*, p. 88.

20. The relevant conditions here need not be the same as for the other sort of reliability and indeed normally will not be.

21. Here I am expanding on some suggestive remarks of Sellars in "Givenness and Explanatory Coherence."

22. The reason for doubting that the regress is vicious is that in this special instance it seems possible to give the whole infinite series of arguments in a finite way. Thus premises (ii) and (iii) seem to be invariant for all the arguments in the

series, and the various premises (i) can be recursively specified, since each is simply premise (i) of the previous argument with one more occurrence of the belief operator prefixed; thus the whole series of arguments can be recursively specified. Moreover, it might be argued on this basis that one who gives explicitly the first argument in the series thereby tacitly gives, or at least commits himself to, all the others: he has asserted the invariant premises (ii) and (iii), and by asserting the first premise (i), he commits himself to all the other premises (i) by the principle of epistemic logic whose violation yields "Moore's paradox." Thus the main objection to construing the justification of introspection as involving this infinite hierarchy of arguments is not simply that it is infinite, but rather that it is highly questionable that people do in fact believe, even dispositionally, the infinite set of first premises. And if this is so, then the series of arguments cannot be taken as an account of how introspective beliefs are in fact justified, even though it is possibly acceptable as an account of how they *could* be justified. If, on the other hand, one finds it plausible, as does e.g. Lehrer (*op. cit.*, p. 229), to hold that anyone who believes that *P* also believes that he believes that *P*, then it becomes plausible to hold that the infinite series of first premises is believed whenever the first one is. In this case the infinite series of arguments would represent a possible alternative to the account of the justification of introspection given in the text.

23. It might be thought that the justification of an introspective belief using premise (*) would still require the additional premise that the person indeed has the introspective belief in question—which would suffice to generate a regress. There is no doubt that the thesis that the person has the introspective belief in question figures in the justification. I would argue, however, that it does not figure as a *premise*, which would then require further justification, because the existence of that belief is *presupposed* by the very raising of the issue of justification in the first place.

24. Of course such beliefs will still, in the normal case, be *causally* dependent on normal sensory processes. My point is that the trained scientist, unlike the novice, need not *first* have an ordinary observational belief about the state of the instrument and *then* infer to the theoretical belief; instead the latter belief may itself be arrived at non-inferentially.

25. A complete account here would have to discuss intentional action and how it relates to one's cognitive system, since such action is obviously needed in most cases in order to put oneself in the correct position to make a relevant observation. I shall neglect this additional topic here. For some useful discussion see Sellars, "Some Reflections on Language Games."

26. The observation requirement, as stated, may seem too weak. It may be thought that at least two further requirements should be added: (a) that each of the kinds of cognitively spontaneous beliefs in question result from a unique causal process; and (b) that the various causal processes in question actually produce reliable beliefs. These additional requirements are indeed part of the notion of observation as set forth above. But they need not be made a part of this requirement, because failure to satisfy them will make it extremely unlikely that a cognitive system will both remain coherent and continue to satisfy the observation requirement as stated, in the long run. (A point worth adding is that the ability to have epistemically reliable cognitively spontaneous beliefs is presumably acquired via training, linguistic or otherwise, since it presupposes the grasp of a conceptual system. Such training, however, though presumably a causally neces-

sary condition for the satisfaction of the observation requirement, is not a part of it.)

The observation requirement should also be understood to include the requirement, common to all adequate theories of knowledge, that a user of the system must make a reasonable attempt to seek out relevant observations if his results are to be justified.

27. It may still be questioned whether the CTEK, even if not a version of foundationism, is truly a *pure* coherence theory. Would it not be a purer coherence view to say simply that the most coherent system is justified, without adding the observation requirement? But although such a view would superficially involve a purer appeal to coherence at the empirical level, it would—if the claim that input from the world is an *a priori* requirement for empirical knowledge is correct—be *a priori* mistaken, and thus incoherent at the meta-epistemic level of epistemological reflection. Thus the CTEK seems to be as pure a coherence theory as is defensible.

28. I assume here, without discussion, that one can make sense of the notion of identity through change for cognitive systems.

29. This point is elaborated from a slightly different perspective in the discussion of truth and objection (III) which follows.

30. For an argument that this cannot be done, and hence that the CTEK cannot avoid a coherence theory of truth, see Blanshard, *op. cit.*, chaps. 25–26.

31. Sellars's writings on truth, if I read him right, are an attempt to provide such an account of truth from an epistemological perspective which is similar to that offered here. See "Truth and 'Correspondence,' " reprinted in *Science, Perception and Reality;* and also his *Science and Metaphysics* (London: Routledge & Kegan Paul, 1968), chap. 5. See also my "Sellars on Truth and Picturing," *International Philosophical Quarterly* 13 (1973): 243–65.

32. Notice, however, that exactly the same problem will afflict any foundation theory whose basic (or initially credible) beliefs are limited to those which can count as observational for the CTEK. Since the category of basic beliefs is usually more, rather than less, restricted than this, this will mean virtually all foundation theories. And since foundation theories have no appeal at this point other than coherence, they will be able to solve this problem only if a solution is also available to the CTEK.

33. For a suggestive account of the rationale of theory construction in this spirit, see Sellars, "The Language of Theories," in *Science, Perception and Reality*.

34. This argument was suggested to me by Richard Diaz.

35. Sellars's views on meaning would provide a basis for such an argument. See especially his "Inference and Meaning," *Mind* 62 (1953): 313–38. On Sellars's account the coherence account of justification thus rests on a coherence theory of meaning.

36. There are of course other logically possible ways in which a lack of accord could exist between a cognitive system and reality without observation operating to correct the system in the ways suggested. The assumption operative here and in the earlier discussion of objection (I) is that a mechanism for producing cognitively spontaneous beliefs is unlikely to yield coherent results in the long run unless it genuinely reflects objective reality. It is certainly not necessary that this be so: coherent results might conceivably be produced by hallucination, by a

Cartesian demon, or even by pure chance. The claim here is only that all of these things are unlikely to happen, that each would represent an improbable coincidence relative to the envisaged situation.

37. Extremely helpful comments on an earlier version of this essay were offered by my colleagues Hardy Jones and Martin Perlmutter.

6   The Raft and the Pyramid: Coherence versus Foundations in the Theory of Knowledge

ERNEST SOSA

Contemporary epistemology must choose between the solid security of the ancient foundationalist pyramid and the risky adventure of the new coherentist raft. Our main objective will be to understand, as deeply as we can, the nature of the controversy and the reasons for and against each of the two options. But first of all we take note of two underlying assumptions.

1. Two Assumptions

(A1) Not everything believed is known, but nothing can be known without being at least believed (or accepted, presumed, taken for granted, or the like) in some broad sense. What additional requirements must a belief fill in order to be knowledge? There are surely at least the following two: (a) it must be true, and (b) it must be justified (or warranted, reasonable, correct, or the like).

(A2) Let us assume, moreover, with respect to the second condition A1(b): first, that it involves a normative or evaluative property; and, second, that the relevant sort of justification is that which pertains to knowledge: epistemic (or theoretical) justification. Someone seriously ill may have two sorts of justification for believing he will recover: the practical justification that derives from the contribution such belief will make to his recovery and the theoretical justification provided by the lab results, the doctor's diagnosis and prognosis, and so on. Only the latter is relevant to the question whether he knows.

Reprinted from *Midwest Studies in Philosophy, Vol. 5: Studies in Epistemology* (Minneapolis: University of Minnesota Press, 1980), 3–25, by permission of the author and the publisher. Copyright 1980, University of Minnesota Press.

2. Knowledge and Criteria

a. There are two key questions of the theory of knowledge:
    (i) What do we know?
    (ii) How do we know?
    The answer to the first would be a list of bits of knowledge or at least of types of knowledge: of the self, of the external world, of other minds, and so on. An answer to the second would give criteria (or canons, methods, principles, or the like) that would explain how we know whatever it is that we do know.

b. In developing a theory of knowledge, we can begin either with a(i) or with a(ii). Particularism would have us begin with an answer to a(i) and only then take up a(ii) on the basis of that answer. Quite to the contrary, methodism would reverse that order. The particularist thus tends to be antiskeptical on principle. But the methodist is as such equally receptive to skepticism and to the contrary. Hume, for example, was no less a methodist than Descartes. Each accepted, in effect, that only the obvious and what is proved deductively on its basis can possibly be known.

c. What, then, is the obvious? For Descartes it is what we know by intuition, what is clear and distinct, what is indubitable and credible with no fear of error. Thus for Descartes basic knowledge is always an infallible belief in an indubitable truth. All other knowledge must stand on that basis through deductive proof. Starting from such criteria (canons, methods, etc.), Descartes concluded that knowledge extended about as far as his contemporaries believed.[1] Starting from similar criteria, however, Hume concluded that both science and common sense made claims far beyond their rightful limits.

d. Philosophical posterity has rejected Descartes's theory for one main reason: that it admits too easily as obvious what is nothing of the sort. Descartes's reasoning is beautifully simple: God exists; no omnipotent perfectly good being would descend to deceit; but if our common sense beliefs were radically false, that would represent deceit on His part. Therefore, our common sense beliefs must be true or at least cannot be radically false. But in order to buttress this line of reasoning and fill in details, Descartes appeals to various principles that appear something less than indubitable.

e. For his part, Hume rejects all but a miniscule portion of our supposed common sense knowledge. He establishes first that there is no way to prove such supposed knowledge on the basis of what is obvious at any given moment through reason or experience. And he concludes, in keeping with this methodism, that in point of fact there really is no such knowledge.

3. Two Metaphors: The Raft and the Pyramid

Both metaphors concern the body or system of knowledge in a given mind. But the mind is of course a more complex marvel than is sometimes supposed. Here I do not allude to the depths plumbed by Freud, nor even to Chomsky's. Nor need we recall the labyrinths inhabited by statesmen and diplomats, nor the rich patterns of some novels or theories. We need look no further than the most common, everyday beliefs. Take, for instance, the belief that driving tonight will be dangerous. Brief reflection should reveal that any of us with that belief will join to it several other closely related beliefs on which the given belief depends for its existence or (at least) its justification. Among such beliefs we could presumably find some or all of the following: that the road will be icy or snowy; that driving on ice or snow is dangerous; that it will rain or snow tonight; that the temperature will be below freezing; appropriate beliefs about the forecast and its reliability; and so on.

How must such beliefs be interrelated in order to help justify my belief about the danger of driving tonight? Here foundationalism and coherentism disagree, each offering its own metaphor. Let us have a closer look at this dispute, starting with foundationalism.

Both Descartes and Hume attribute to human knowledge an architectonic structure. There is a nonsymmetric relation of physical support such that any two floors of a building are tied by that relation: one of the two supports (or at least helps support) the other. And there is, moreover, a part with a special status: the foundation, which is supported by none of the floors while supporting them all.

With respect to a body of knowledge K (in someone's possession), foundationalism implies that K can be divided into parts K_1, K_2, . . . such that there is some nonsymmetric relation R (analogous to the relation of physical support) which orders those parts in such a way that there is one—call it F—that bears R to every other part while none of them bears R in turn to F.

According to foundationalism, each piece of knowledge lies on a pyramid such as the following:

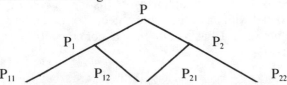

The nodes of such a pyramid (for a proposition P relative to a subject S and a time t) must obey the following requirements:

    a. The set of all nodes that succeed (directly) any given node must serve jointly as a base that properly supports that node (for S at t).

   b. Each node must be a proposition that S is justified in believing at *t*.
   c. If a node is not self-evident (for S at *t*), it must have successors (that serve jointly as a base that properly supports that node).
   d. Each branch of an epistemic pyramid must terminate.

For the foundationalist Descartes, for instance, each terminating node must be an indubitable proposition that S believes at *t* with no possibility of error. As for the nonterminal nodes, each of them represents inferential knowledge, derived by deduction from more basic beliefs.

Such radical foundationalism suffers from a fatal weakness that is twofold: (a) there are not so many perfectly obvious truths as Descartes thought; and (b) once we restrict ourselves to what is truly obvious in any given context, very little of one's supposed common sense knowledge can be proved on that basis. If we adhere to such radical foundationalism, therefore, we are just wrong in thinking we know so much.

Note that in citing such a "fatal weakness" of radical foundationalism, we favor particularism as against the methodism of Descartes and Hume. For we reject the methods or criteria of Descartes and Hume when we realize that they plunge us in a deep skepticism. If such criteria are incompatible with our enjoyment of the rich body of knowledge that we commonly take for granted, then as good particularists we hold on to the knowledge and reject the criteria.

If we reject radical foundationalism, however, what are we to put in its place? Here epistemology faces a dilemma that different epistemologists resolve differently. Some reject radical foundationalism but retain some more moderate form of foundationalism in favor of a radically different coherentism. Coherentism is associated with idealism—of both the German and the British variety—and has recently acquired new vigor and interest.

The coherentists reject the metaphor of the pyramid in favor of one that they owe to the positivist Neurath, according to whom our body of knowledge is a raft that floats free of any anchor or tie. Repairs must be made afloat, and though no part is untouchable, we must stand on some in order to replace or repair others. Not every part can go at once.

According to the new metaphor, what justifies a belief is not that it be an infallible belief with an indubitable object, nor that it have been proved deductively on such a basis, but that it cohere with a comprehensive system of beliefs.

4. A Coherentist Critique of Foundationalism

What reasons do coherentists offer for their total rejection of foundationalism? The argument that follows below summarizes much of what is alleged against foundationalism. But first we must distinguish between subjective states that incorporate a propositional attitude and those that do not. A propositional attitude is a mental state of someone with a proposition for its object: beliefs, hopes, and fears provide examples. By way of contrast, a headache does not incorporate any such attitude. One can of course be conscious of a headache, but the headache itself does not constitute or incorporate any attitude with a proposition for its object. With this distinction in the background, here is the antifoundationalist argument, which has two lemmas—a(iv) and b(iii)—and a principal conclusion.

a.   (i)   If a mental state incorporates a propositional attitude, then it does not give us direct contact with reality, e.g., with pure experience, unfiltered by concepts or beliefs.

    (ii)   If a mental state does not give us direct contact with reality, then it provides no guarantee against error.

    (iii)   If a mental state provides no guarantee against error, then it cannot serve as a foundation for knowledge.

    (iv)   Therefore, if a mental state incorporates a propositional attitude, then it cannot serve as a foundation for knowledge.

b.   (i)   If a mental state does not incorporate a propositional attitude, then it is an enigma how such a state can provide support for any hypothesis, raising its credibility selectively by contrast with its alternatives. (If the mental state has no conceptual or propositional content, then what logical relation can it possibly bear to any hypothesis? Belief in a hypothesis would be a propositional attitude with the hypothesis itself as object. How can one depend logically for such a belief on an experience with no propositional content?)

    (ii)   If a mental state has no propositional content and cannot provide logical support for any hypothesis, then it cannot serve as a foundation for knowledge.

    (iii)   Therefore, if a mental state does not incorporate a propositional attitude, then it cannot serve as a foundation for knowledge.

c.   Every mental state either does or does not incorporate a propositional attitude.

d.   Therefore, no mental state can serve as a foundation for knowledge. (From a(iv), b(iii), and c.)

According to the coherentist critic, foundationalism is run through by this dilemma. Let us take a closer look.[2]

In the first place, what reason is there to think, in accordance with premise b(i), that only propositional attitudes can give support to their own kind? Consider practices—e.g., broad policies or customs. Could not

some person or group be justified in a practice because of its consequences: that is, could not the consequences of a practice make it a good
practice? But among the consequences of a practice may surely be found,
for example, a more just distribution of goods and less suffering than there
would be under its alternatives. And neither the more just distribution nor
the lower degree of suffering is a propositional attitude. This provides an
example in which propositional attitudes (the intentions that sustain the
practice) are justified by consequences that are not propositional attitudes. That being so, is it not conceivable that the justification of belief
that matters for knowledge be analogous to the objective justification by
consequences that we find in ethics?

Is it not possible, for instance, that a belief that there is something red
before one be justified in part because it has its origins in one's visual
experience of red when one looks at an apple in daylight? If we accept
such examples, they show us a source of justification that serves as such
without incorporating a propositional attitude.

As for premise a(iii), it is already under suspicion from our earlier
exploration of premise b(i). A mental state M can be nonpropositional and
hence not a candidate for so much as truth, much less infallibility, while it
serves, in spite of that, as a foundation of knowledge. Leaving that aside,
let us suppose that the relevant mental state is indeed propositional. Must
it then be infallible in order to serve as a foundation of justification and
knowledge? That is so far from being obvious that it seems more likely
false when compared with an analogue in ethics. With respect to beliefs,
we may distinguish between their being true and their being justified.
Analogously, with respect to actions, we may distinguish between their
being optimal (best of all alternatives, all things considered) and their
being (subjectively) justified. In practical deliberation on alternatives for
action, is it inconceivable that the most *eligible* alternative *not* be objectively the best, all things considered? Can there not be another alternative—perhaps a most repugnant one worth little if any consideration—
that in point of fact would have a much better total set of consequences
and would thus be better, all things considered? Take the physician
attending to Frau Hitler at the birth of little Adolf. Is it not possible that if
he had acted less morally, that would have proved better in the fullness of
time? And if that is so in ethics, may not its likeness hold good in
epistemology? Might there not be justified (reasonable, warranted) beliefs
that are not even true, much less infallible? That seems to me not just a
conceivable possibility, but indeed a familiar fact of everyday life, where
observational beliefs too often prove illusory but no less reasonable for
being false.

If the foregoing is on the right track, then the antifoundationalist is far
astray. What has led him there?

As a diagnosis of the antifoundationalist argument before us, and more particularly of its second lemma, I would suggest that it rests on an Intellectualist Model of Justification.

According to such a model, the justification of belief (and psychological states generally) is parasitical on certain logical relations among propositions. For example, my belief (i) that the streets are wet, is justified by my pair of beliefs (ii) that it is raining, and (iii) that if it is raining, the streets are wet. Thus we have a structure such as this:

B(Q) is justified by the fact that B(Q) is grounded on (B(P), B(P⊃Q)).

And according to an Intellectualist Model, this is parasitical on the fact that

P and (P⊃Q) together logically imply Q.

Concerning this attack on foundationalism I will argue (a) that it is useless to the coherentist, since if the antifoundationalist dilemma impales the foundationalist, a form of it can be turned against the coherentist to the same effect; (b) that the dilemma would be lethal not only to foundationalism and coherentism but also to the very possibility of substantive epistemology; and (c) that a form of it would have the same effect on normative ethics.

(a) According to coherentism, what justifies a belief is its membership in a coherent and comprehensive set of beliefs. But whereas being grounded on B(P) and B(P⊃Q) is a property of a belief B(Q) that yields immediately the logical implication of Q and P and (P⊃Q) as the logical source of that property's justificatory power, the property of being a member of a coherent set is not one that immediately yields any such implication.

It may be argued, nevertheless, (i) that the property of being a member of a coherent set would supervene in any actual instance on the property of being a member of a particular set *a* that is in fact coherent, and (ii) that this would enable us to preserve our Intellectualist Model, since (iii) the justification of the member belief B(Q) by its membership in *a* would then be parasitical on the logical relations among the beliefs in *a* which constitute the coherence of that set of beliefs, and (iv) the justification of B(Q) by the fact that it is part of a coherent set would then be *indirectly* parasitical on logical relations among propositions after all.

But if such an indirect form of parasitism is allowed, then the experience of pain may perhaps be said to justify belief in its existence parasitically on the fact that P logically implies P! The Intellectualist Model seems either so trivial as to be dull, or else sharp enough to cut equally against both foundationalism and coherentism.

(b) If (i) only propositional attitudes can justify such propositional attitudes as belief, and if (ii) to do so they must in turn be justified by yet other propositional attitudes, it seems clear that (iii) there is no hope of contructing a complete epistemology, one which would give us, in theory, an account of what the justification of any justified belief would supervene on. For (i) and (ii) would rule out the possibility of a finite regress of justification.

(c) If only propositional attitudes can justify propositional attitudes, and if to do so they must in turn be justified by yet other propositional attitudes, it seems clear that there is no hope of constructing a complete normative ethics, one which would give us, in theory, an account of what the justification of any possible justified action would supervene upon. For the justification of an action presumably depends on the intentions it embeds and the justification of these, and here we are already within the net of propositional attitudes from which, for the Intellectualist, there is no escape.

It seems fair to conclude that our coherentist takes his antifoundationalist zeal too far. His antifoundationalist argument helps expose some valuable insights but falls short of its malicious intent. The foundationalist emerges showing no serious damage. Indeed, he now demands equal time for a positive brief in defense of his position.

5. The Regress Argument

a. The regress argument in epistemology concludes that we must countenance beliefs that are justified in the absence of justification by other beliefs. But it reaches that conclusion only by rejecting the possibility in principle of an infinite regress of justification. It thus opts for foundational beliefs justified in some noninferential way by ruling out a chain or pyramid of justification that has justifiers, and justifiers of justifiers, and so on *without end*. One may well find this too short a route to foundationalism, however, and demand more compelling reasons for thus rejecting an infinite regress as vicious. We shall find indeed that it is not easy to meet this demand.

b. We have seen how even the most ordinary of everyday beliefs is the tip of an iceberg. A closer look below the surface reveals a complex structure that ramifies with no end in sight. Take again my belief that driving will be dangerous tonight, at the tip of an iceberg, (I), that looks like this:

(I)

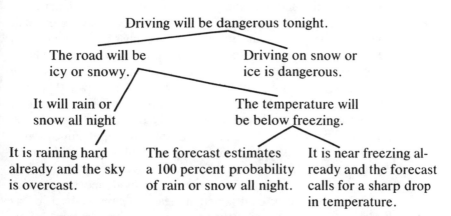

Driving will be dangerous tonight.

The road will be icy or snowy.

Driving on snow or ice is dangerous.

It will rain or snow all night

The temperature will be below freezing.

It is raining hard already and the sky is overcast.

The forecast estimates a 100 percent probability of rain or snow all night.

It is near freezing already and the forecast calls for a sharp drop in temperature.

The immediate cause of my belief that driving will be hazardous tonight is the sound of raindrops on the windowpane. All but one or two members of the underlying iceberg are as far as they can be from my thoughts at the time. In what sense, then, do they form an iceberg whose tip breaks the calm surface of my consciousness?

Here I will assume that the members of (I) are beliefs of the subject, even if unconscious or subconscious, that causally buttress and thus justify his prediction about the driving conditions.

Can the iceberg extend without end? It may appear obvious that it cannot do so, and one may jump to the conclusion that any piece of knowledge must be ultimately founded on beliefs that are *not* (inferentially) justified or warranted by other beliefs. This is a doctrine of *epistemic foundationalism*.

Let us focus not so much on the *giving* of justification as on the *having* of it. *Can* there be a belief that is justified in part by other beliefs, some of which are in turn justified by yet other beliefs, and so on without end? Can there be an endless regress of justification?

c. There are several familiar objections to such a regress:

(i) *Objection:* "It is incompatible with human limitations. No human subject could harbor the required infinity of beliefs." *Reply:* It is mere presumption to fathom with such assurance the depths of the mind, and especially its unconscious and dispositional depths. Besides, our object here is the nature of epistemic justification in itself and not only that of such justification as is accessible to humans. Our question is not whether humans could harbor an infinite iceberg of justification. Our question is rather whether *any* mind, no matter how deep, could do so. Or is it ruled out *in principle* by the very nature of justification?

(ii) *Objection:* "An infinite regress is indeed ruled out in principle, for if justification were thus infinite how could it possibly end? *Reply:* (i) If the end mentioned is *temporal,* then why must there be such an end? In the first place, the subject may be eternal. Even if he is not eternal, moreover, why must belief acquisition and justification occur seriatim? What precludes an infinite body of beliefs acquired at a single stroke? Human limitations may rule this out for humans, but we have yet to be shown that it is precluded in principle, by the very nature of justification. (ii) If the end mentioned is justificatory, on the other hand, then to ask how justification could possibly end is just to beg the question.

(iii) *Objection:* "Let us make two assumptions: first, that S's belief of q justifies his belief of p only if it works together with a justified belief on his part that q provides good evidence for p; and, second, that if S is to be justified in believing p on the basis of his belief of q and is to be justified in believing q on the basis of his belief of r, then S must be justified in believing that r provides good evidence for p via q. These assumptions imply that an actual regress of justification requires belief in an infinite proposition. Since no one (or at least no human) can believe an infinite proposition, no one (no human) can be a subject of such an actual regress."[3]

Reply: Neither of the two assumptions is beyond question, but even granting them both, it may still be doubted that the conclusion follows. It is true that each finitely complex belief of form "r provides good evidence for p via $q_1 \ldots q_n$" will *omit* how some members of the full infinite regress are epistemically tied to belief of p. But that seems irrelevant given the fact that for each member r of the regress, such that r is tied epistemically to belief of p, there *is* a finite belief of the required sort ("r provides good evidence for p via $q_1 \ldots q_n$") that ties the two together. Consequently, there is no apparent reason to suppose—even granted the two assumptions—that an infinite regress will require a single belief in an infinite proposition, and not just an infinity of beliefs in increasingly complex finite propositions.

(iv) *Objection:* "But if it is allowed that justification extend infinitely, then it is too easy to justify any belief at all or too many beliefs altogether. Take, for instance, the belief that there are perfect numbers greater than 100. And suppose a mind powerful enough to believe every member of the following sequence:

(σ1) There is at least one perfect number > 100
There are at least two perfect numbers > 100
      "   three   "   "

If such a believer has no other belief about perfect numbers save the belief that a perfect number is a whole number equal to the sum of its whole factors, then surely he is *not* justified in believing that there are perfect numbers greater than 100. He is quite unjustified in believing any of the members of sequence (σ1), in spite of the fact that a challenge to any can be met easily by appeal to its successor. Thus it cannot be allowed after all that justification extend infinitely, and an infinite regress is ruled out."

Reply: We must distinguish between regresses of justification that are actual and those that are merely potential. The difference is *not* simply that an actual regress is composed of actual beliefs. For even if all members of the regress are actual beliefs, the regress may still be *merely potential* in the following sense: while it is true that *if* any member *were* justified then its predecessors *would* be, still none is in fact justified. Anyone with our series of beliefs about perfect numbers in the absence of any further relevant information on such numbers would presumably be the subject of such a merely potential justificatory regress.

(v) *Objection:* "But defenders of infinite justificatory regresses cannot distinguish thus between actual regresses and those that are merely potential. There is no real distinction to be drawn between the two. For if any regress ever justifies the belief at its head, then every regress must always do so. But obviously not every regress does so (as we have seen by examples), and hence no regress can do so."[4]

Reply: One can in fact distinguish between actual justificatory regresses and merely potential ones, and one can do so both abstractly and by examples.

What an actual regress has that a merely potential regress lacks is the property of containing only justified beliefs as members. What they both share is the property of containing no member without successors that would jointly justify it.

Recall our regress about perfect numbers greater than 100; i.e., there is at least one; there are at least two; there are at least three; and so on. Each member has a successor that would justify it, but no member is justified (in the absence of further information external to the regress). That is therefore a merely potential infinite regress. As for an actual regress, I see no compelling reason why someone (if not a human, then some more powerful mind) could not hold an infinite series of actually justified beliefs as follows:

(σ2) There is at least one even number
     There are at least two even numbers
            "   three   "

It may be that no one could be the subject of such a series of justified beliefs unless he had a proof that there is a denumerable infinity of even numbers. But even if that should be so, it would not take away the fact of the infinite regress of potential justifiers, each of which is actually justified, and hence it would not take away the fact of the actual endless regress of justification.

The objection under discussion is confused, moreover, on the nature of the issue before us. Our question is *not* whether there can be an infinite potential regress, each member of which would be justified by its successors, such that the belief at its head is justified in virtue of its position there, at the head of such a regress. The existence and even the possibility of a single such regress with a belief at its head that was *not* justified in virtue of its position there would of course settle that question in the negative. Our question is, rather, whether there can be an actual infinite regress of justification, and the fact that a belief at the head of a potential regress might still fail to be justified despite its position does *not* settle this question. For even if there can be a merely potential regress with an unjustified belief at its head, that leaves open the possibility of an infinite regress, each member of which is justified by its immediate successors working jointly, where every member of the regress is in addition actually justified.

6. The Relation of Justification and Foundationalist Strategy

The foregoing discussion is predicated on a simple conception of justification such that a set of beliefs β conditionally justifies (*would* justify) a belief X iff, necessarily, if all members of β are justified then X is also justified (if it exists). The fact that on such a conception of justification actual endless regresses—such as ($\sigma2$)—seem quite possible blocks a straightforward regress argument in favor of foundations. For it shows that an actual infinite regress cannot be dismissed out of hand.

Perhaps the foundationalist could introduce some relation of justification—presumably more complex and yet to be explicated—with respect to which it could be argued more plausibly that an actual endless regress is out of the question.

There is, however, a more straightforward strategy open to the foundationalist. For he *need not* object to the possibility of an endless regress of justification. His essential creed is the more positive belief that every justified belief must be at the head of a terminating regress. Fortunately, to affirm the universal necessity of a terminating regress is *not* to deny the bare possibility of a nonterminating regress. For a single belief can trail at once regresses of both sorts: one terminating and one not. Thus the proof of the denumerably infinite cardinality of the set of evens may provide for a powerful enough intellect a *terminating* regress for each member of the *endless* series of justified beliefs:

> (σ2) There is at least one even number
>   There are at least two even numbers
>   "   three   "

At the same time, it is obvious that each member of (σ2) lies at the head of an actual endless regress of justification, on the assumption that each member is conditionally justified by its successor, which is in turn actually justified.

"Thank you so much," the foundationalist may sneer, "but I really do not need that kind of help. Nor do I need to be reminded of my essential creed, which I know as well as anyone. Indeed my rejection of endless regresses of justification is only a means of supporting my view that every justified belief must rest ultimately on foundations, on a terminating regress. You reject that strategy much too casually, in my view, but I will not object here. So we put that strategy aside. And now, my helpful friend, just what do we put in its place?"

Fair enough. How then could one show the need for foundations if an endless regress is not ruled out?

7. Two Levels of Foundationalism

a. We need to distinguish, first, between two forms of foundationalism: one *formal,* the other *substantive.* A type of *formal foundationalism* with respect to a normative or evaluative property φ is the view that the conditions (actual and possible) within which φ would apply can be specified in general, perhaps recursively. *Substantive foundationalism* is only a particular way of doing so, and coherentism is another.

Simpleminded hedonism is the view that:

(i) every instance of pleasure is good,
(ii) everything that causes something good is itself good, and
(iii) everything that is good is so in virtue of (i) or (ii) above.

Simpleminded hedonism is a type of formal foundationalism with respect to the good.

Classical foundationalism in epistemology is the view that:

(i) every infallible, indubitable belief is justified.
(ii) every belief deductively inferred from justified beliefs is itself justified, and
(iii) every belief that is justified is so in virtue of (i) or (ii) above.

Classical foundationalism is a type of formal foundationalism with respect to epistemic justification.

Both of the foregoing theories—simpleminded hedonism in ethics, and classical foundationalism in epistemology—are of course flawed. But they both remain examples of formal foundationalist theories.

b. One way of arguing in favor of formal foundationalism in epistemology is to formulate a convincing formal foundationalist theory of justification. But classical foundationalism in epistemology no longer has for many the attraction that it had for Descartes, nor has any other form of epistemic foundationalism won general acceptance. Indeed epistemic foundationalism has been generally abandoned, and its advocates have been put on the defensive by the writings of Wittgenstein, Quine, Sellars, Rescher, Aune, Harman, Lehrer, and others. It is lamentable that in our headlong rush away from foundationalism we have lost sight of the different types of foundationalism (formal vs. substantive) and of the different grades of each type. Too many of us now see it as a blur to be decried and avoided. Thus our present attempt to bring it all into better focus.

c. If we cannot argue from a generally accepted foundationalist theory, what reason is there to accept formal foundationalism? There is no reason to think that the conditions (actual and possible) within which an object is spherical are generally specifiable in nongeometric terms. Why should we think that the conditions (actual and possible) within which a belief is epistemically justified are generally specifiable in nonepistemic terms?

So far as I can see, the main reason for accepting formal foundationalism in the absence of an actual, convincing formal foundationalist theory is the very plausible idea that epistemic justification is subject to the supervenience that characterizes normative and evaluative properties generally. Thus, if a car is a good car, then any physical replica of that car must be just as good. If it is a good car in virtue of such properties as being economical, little prone to break down, etc., then surely any exact replica would share all such properties and would thus be equally good. Similarly, if a belief is epistemically justified, it is presumably so in virtue of its character and its basis in perception, memory, or inference (if any). Thus any belief exactly like it in its character and its basis must be equally well justified. Epistemic justification is supervenient. The justification of a belief supervenes on such properties of it as its content and its basis (if any) in perception, memory, or inference. Such a doctrine of supervenience may itself be considered, with considerable justice, a grade of foundationalism. For it entails that every instance of justified belief is founded on a number of its nonepistemic properties, such as its having a certain basis in perception, memory, and inference, or the like.

But there are higher grades of foundationalism as well. There is, for instance, the doctrine that the conditions (actual and possible) within which a belief would be epistemically justified *can be specified* in general, perhaps recursively (and by reference to such notions as perception, memory, and inference).

A higher grade yet of formal foundationalism requires not only that the conditions for justified belief be specifiable, in general, but that they be specifiable by a simple, comprehensive theory.

d. Simpleminded hedonism is a formal foundationalist theory of the highest grade. If it is true, then in every possible world goodness supervenes on pleasure and causation in a way that is recursively specifiable by means of a very simple theory.

Classical foundationalism in epistemology is also a formal foundationalist theory of the highest grade. If it is true, then in every possible world epistemic justification supervenes on infallibility cum indubitability and deductive inference in a way that is recursively specifiable by means of a very simple theory.

Surprisingly enough, coherentism may also turn out to be formal foundationalism of the highest grade, provided only that the concept of coherence is itself both simple enough and free of any normative or evaluative admixture. Given these provisos, coherentism explains how epistemic justification supervenes on the nonepistemic in a theory of remarkable simplicity: a belief is justified if it has a place within a system of beliefs that is coherent and comprehensive.

It is a goal of ethics to explain how the ethical rightness of an action supervenes on what is not ethically evaluative or normative. Similarly, it is a goal of epistemology to explain how the epistemic justification of a belief supervenes on what is not epistemically evaluative or normative. If coherentism aims at this goal, that imposes restrictions on the notion of coherence, which must now be conceived innocent of epistemically evaluative or normative admixture. Its substance must therefore consist of such concepts as explanation, probability, and logical implication—with these conceived, in turn, innocent of normative or evaluative content.

e. We have found a surprising kinship between coherentism and substantive foundationalism, both of which turn out to be varieties of a deeper foundationalism. This deeper foundationalism is applicable to any normative or evaluative property ϕ, and it comes in three grades. The *first* or lowest is simply the supervenience of ϕ: the idea that whenever something has ϕ its having it is founded on certain others of its properties which fall into certain restricted sorts. The *second* is the explicable supervenience of ϕ: the idea that there are formulable principles that explain in quite general terms the conditions (actual and possible) within which ϕ applies. The *third* and highest is the easily explicable supervenience of φ: the idea that there is a *simple* theory that explains the conditions within which φ applies. We have found the coherentist and the substantive foundationalist sharing a primary goal: the development of a formal foundationalist theory of the highest grade. For they both want a simple theory that explains precisely how epistemic justification supervenes, in general, on the nonepistemic. This insight gives us an unusual viewpoint on some recent attacks against foundationalism. Let us now consider as an example a certain simple form of argument distilled from the recent antifoundationalist literature.[5]

8. Doxastic Ascent Arguments

Several attacks on foundationalism turn on a sort of "doxastic ascent" argument that calls for closer scrutiny.[6] Here are two examples:

A. A belief B is foundationally justified for S in virtue of having property F only if S is justified in believing (1) that most at least of his beliefs with property F are true, and (2) that B has property F. But this means that belief B is not foundational after all, and indeed that the very notion of (empirical) foundational belief is incoherent.

   It is sometimes held, for example, that perceptual or observational beliefs are often justified through their origin in the exercise of one or more of our five senses in standard conditions of perception. The advocate of doxastic ascent would raise a vigorous protest, however, for in his view the mere fact of such sensory prompting is impotent to justify the belief prompted. Such prompting must be coupled with the further belief that one's senses work well in the circumstances, or the like. For we are dealing here with *knowledge,* which requires not blind faith but *reasoned* trust. But now surely the further belief about the reliability of one's senses itself cannot rest on blind faith but requires its own backing of reasons, and we are off on the regress.

B. A belief B of proposition P is foundationally justified for S only if S is justified in believing that there are no factors present that would cause him to make mistakes on the matter of the proposition P. But, again, this means that belief B is not foundational after all and indeed that the notion of (empirical) foundational belief is incoherent.

From the vantage point of formal foundationalism, neither of these arguments seems persuasive. In the first place, as we have seen, what makes a belief foundational (formally) is its having a property that is nonepistemic (not evaluative in the epistemic or cognitive mode), and does not involve inference from other beliefs, but guarantees, via a necessary principle, that the belief in question is justified. A belief B is made foundational by having some such nonepistemic property that yields its justification. Take my belief that I am in pain in a context where it is caused by my being in pain. The property that my belief then has, of being a self-attribution of pain caused by one's own pain is, let us suppose, a nonepistemic property that yields the justification of any belief that has it. So my belief that I am in pain is in that context foundationally justified. Along with my belief that I am in pain, however, there come other beliefs that are equally well justified, such as my belief that someone is in pain. Thus I am foundationally justified in believing that I am in pain only if I am justified in believing that someone is in pain. Those who object to foundationalism as in A or B above are hence mistaken in thinking that their premises would refute foundationalism. The fact is that they would not touch it. For a belief is no less foundationally justified for having its justification yoked to that of another closely related belief.

The advocate of arguments like A and B must apparently strengthen his premises. He must apparently claim that the beliefs whose justification is entailed by the foundationally justified status of belief B must in some sense function as a *necessary source* of the justification of B. And this would of course preclude giving B foundationally justified status. For if the *being justified* of those beliefs is an *essential* part of the source of the justification of B, then it is ruled out that there be a wholly *non-epistemic* source of B's justification.

That brings us to a second point about A and B, for it should now be clear that these cannot be selectively aimed at foundationalism. In particular, they seem neither more nor less valid objections to coherentism than to foundationalism, or so I will now argue about each of them in turn.

A'. A belief X is justified for S in virtue of membership in a coherent set only if S is justified in believing (1) that most at least of his beliefs with the property of thus cohering are true, and (2) that X has that property.

Any coherentist who accepts A seems bound to accept A'. For what could he possibly appeal to as a relevant difference? But A' is a quicksand of endless depth. (How is he justified in believing A'(1)? Partly through justified belief that *it* coheres? And what would justify *this?* And so on . . .)

B'. A belief X is justified for S only if S is justified in believing that there are no factors present that would cause him to make mistakes on the subject matter of that belief.

Again, any coherentist who accepts B seems bound to accept B'. But this is just another road to the quicksand. (For S is justified in believing that there are no such factors only if . . . and so on.)

Why are such regresses vicious? The key is again, to my mind, the doctrine of supervenience. Such regresses are vicious because they would be logically incompatible with the supervenience of epistemic justification on such nonepistemic facts as the totality of a subject's beliefs, his cognitive and experiential history, and as many other nonepistemic facts as may seem at all relevant. The idea is that there is a set of such nonepistemic facts surrounding a justified belief such that no belief could possibly have been surrounded by those very facts without being justified. Advocates of A or B run afoul of such supervenience, since they are surely committed to the more general views derivable from either A or B by deleting 'foundationally' from its first sentence. In each case the more general view would then preclude the possibility of supervenience, since it would entail that the source of justification *always* includes an *epistemic* component.

9. Coherentism and Substantive Foundationalism

a. The notions of coherentism and substantive foundationalism remain unexplicated. We have relied so far on our intuitive grasp of them. In this section we shall consider reasons for the view that substantive foundationalism is superior to coherentism. To assess these reasons, we need some more explicit account of the difference between the two.

By coherentism we shall mean any view according to which the ultimate sources of justification for any belief lie in relations among that belief and other beliefs of the subject: explanatory relations, perhaps, or relations of probability or logic.

According to substantive foundationalism, as it is to be understood here, there are ultimate sources of justification other than relations among beliefs. Traditionally these additional sources have pertained to the special content of the belief or its special relations to the subjective experience of the believer.

b. The view that justification is a matter of relations among beliefs is open to an objection from alternative coherent systems or detachment from reality, depending on one's perspective. From the latter perspective the body of beliefs is held constant and the surrounding world is allowed to vary, whereas from the former perspective it is the surrounding world that is held constant while the body of beliefs is allowed to vary. In either case, according to the coherentist, there could be no effect on the justification for any belief.

Let us sharpen the question before us as follows. Is there reason to think that there is at least one system B', alternative to our actual system of beliefs B, such that B' contains a belief X with the following properties:

(i) in our present nonbelief circumstances we would not be justified in having belief X even if we accepted along with that belief (as our total system of beliefs) the entire belief system B' in which it is embedded (no matter how acceptance of B' were brought about); and

(ii) that is so despite the fact that belief X coheres within B' at least as fully as does some actual justified belief of ours within our actual belief system B (where the justification of that actual justified belief is alleged by the coherentist to derive solely from its coherence within our actual body of beliefs B).

The coherentist is vulnerable to counterexamples of this sort right at the surface of his body of beliefs, where we find beliefs with minimal coherence, whose detachment and replacement with contrary beliefs would have little effect on the coherence of the body. Thus take my belief that I have a headache when I do have a splitting headache, and let us suppose that this *does* cohere within my present body of beliefs. (Thus I have no reason to doubt my present introspective beliefs, and so on. And if my belief does *not* cohere, so much the worse for coherentism, since my belief is surely justified.) Here then we have a perfectly justified or warranted belief. And yet such a belief may well have relevant relations of explanation, logic, or probability with at most a small set of other beliefs of mine at the time: say, that I am not free of headache, that I am in pain, that someone is in pain, and the like. If so, then an equally coherent alternative is not far to seek. Let everything remain constant, *including* the splitting headache, except for the following: replace the belief that I have a headache with the belief that I do *not* have a headache, the belief that I am in pain with the belief that I am *not* in pain, the belief that someone is in pain with the belief that someone is *not* in pain, and so on. I contend that my resulting hypothetical system of beliefs would cohere as fully as does my actual system of beliefs, and yet my hypothetical belief that I do *not* have a headache would not therefore be justified. What makes this difference concerning justification between my actual belief that I have a headache and the hypothetical belief that I am free of headache, each as coherent as the other within its own system, if not the actual splitting headache? But the headache is *not* itself a belief nor a relation among beliefs and is thus in no way constitutive of the internal coherence of my body of beliefs.

Some might be tempted to respond by alleging that one's belief about whether or not one has a headache is always *infallible*. But since we could devise similar examples for the various sensory modalities and propositional attitudes, the response given for the case of headache would have to be generalized. In effect, it would have to cover "peripheral" beliefs generally—beliefs at the periphery of one's body of beliefs, minimally coherent with the rest. These peripheral beliefs would all be said to be infallible. That is, again, a possible response, but it leads to a capitulation by the coherentist to the radical foundationalist on a crucial issue that has traditionally divided them: the infallibility of beliefs about one's own subjective states.

What is more, not all peripheral beliefs are about one's own subjective states. The direct realist is probably right that some beliefs about our surroundings are uninferred and yet justified. Consider my present belief that the table before me is oblong. This presumably coheres with such other beliefs of mine as that the table has the same shape as the piece of paper before me, which is oblong, and a different shape than the window frame here, which is square, and so on. So far as I can see, however, there is no insurmountable obstacle to replacing that whole set of coherent beliefs with an equally coherent set as follows: that the table before me is square, that the table has the same shape as the square window frame, and a different shape than the piece of paper, which is oblong, and so on. The important points are (a) that this replacement may be made without changing the rest of one's body of beliefs or any aspect of the world beyond, including one's present visual experience of something oblong, not square, as one looks at the table before one; and (b) that it is so, in part, because of the fact (c) that the subject need not have any beliefs about his present sensory experience.

Some might be tempted to respond by alleging that one's present experience is *self-intimating,* i.e., always necessarily taken note of and reflected in one's beliefs. Thus if anyone has visual experience of something oblong, then he believes that he has such experience. But this would involve a further important concession by the coherentist to the radical foundationalist, who would have been granted two of his most cherished doctrines: the infallibility of introspective belief and the self-intimation of experience.

10. The Foundationalist's Dilemma

The antifoundationalist zeal of recent years has left several forms of foundationalism standing. These all share the conviction that a belief can be justified not only by its coherence within a comprehensive system but also by an appropriate combination of observational content and origin in the use of the senses in standard conditions. What follows presents a dilemma for any foundationalism based on any such idea.

a. We may surely suppose that beings with observational mechanisms radically unlike ours might also have knowledge of their environment. (That seems possible even if the radical difference in observational mechanisms precludes overlap in substantive concepts and beliefs.)

b. Let us suppose that there is such a being, for whom experience of type φ (of which we have no notion) has a role with respect to his beliefs of type φ analogous to the role that our visual experience has with respect to our visual beliefs. Thus we might have a schema such as the following:

Human	*Extraterrestial being*
Visual experience	φ experience
Experience of something red	Experience of something F
Belief that there is something red before one	Belief that there is something F before one

c. It is often recognized that our visual experience intervenes in two ways with respect to our visual beliefs: as cause and as justification. But these are not wholly independent. Presumably, the justification of the belief that something here is red derives at least in part from the fact that it originates in a visual experience of something red that takes place in normal circumstances.

d. Analogously, the extraterrestial belief that something here has the property of being F might be justified partly by the fact that it originates in a φ experience of something F that takes place in normal circumstances.

e. A simple question presents the foundationalist's dilemma: regarding the epistemic principle that underlies our justification for believing that something here is red on the basis of our visual experience of something red, is it proposed as a fundamental principle or as a derived generalization? Let us compare the famous Principle of Utility of value theory, according to which it is best for that to happen which, of all the possible alternatives in the circumstances, would bring with it into the world the greatest balance of pleasure over pain, joy over sorrow, happiness over unhappiness, content over discontent, or the like. Upon this fundamental principle one may then base various generalizations, rules of thumb, and maxims of public health, nutrition, legislation, etiquette, hygiene, and so on. But these are all then derived generalizations which rest for their validity on the fundamental principle. Similarly, one may also ask, with respect to the generalizations advanced by our foundationalist, whether these are proposed as fundamental principles or as derived maxims or the like. This sets him face to face with a dilemma, each of whose alternatives is problematic. If his proposals are meant to have the status of secondary or derived maxims, for instance, then it would be quite unphilosophical to stop there. Let us turn, therefore, to the other alternative.

f. On reflection it seems rather unlikely that epistemic principles for the justification of observational beliefs by their origin in sensory experience could have a status more fundamental than that of derived generalizations. For by granting such principles fundamental status we would open the door to a multitude of equally basic principles with no unifying factor. There would be some for vision, some for hearing, etc., without even mentioning the corresponding extraterrestial principles.

g. It may appear that there is after all an idea, however, that unifies our multitude of principles. For they all involve sensory experience and sensible characteristics. But what is a sensible characteristic? Aristotle's answer appeals to examples: colors, shapes, sounds, and so on. Such a notion might enable us to unify perceptual epistemic principles under some more fundamental principle such as the following.

> If σ is a sensible characteristic, then the belief that there is something with σ before one is (prima facie) justified if it is based on a visual experience of something with σ in conditions that are normal with respect to σ.

h. There are at least two difficulties with such a suggestion, however, and neither one can be brushed aside easily. First, it is not clear that we can have a viable notion of sensible characteristics on the basis of examples so diverse as colors, shapes, tones, odors, and so on. Second, the authority of such a principle apparently derives from contingent circumstances concerning the reliability of beliefs prompted by sensory experiences of certain sorts. According to the foundationalist, our visual beliefs are justified by their origin in our visual experience or the like. Would such beliefs be equally well justified in a world where beliefs with such an origin were nearly always false?

i. In addition, finally, even if we had a viable notion of such characteristics, it is not obvious that fundamental knowledge of reality would have to derive causally or otherwise from sensory experience of such characteristics. How could one impose reasonable limits on extraterrestial mechanisms for noninferential acquisition of beliefs? Is it not possible that such mechanisms need not always function through sensory experience of any sort? Would such beings necessarily be denied any knowledge of the surroundings and indeed of any contingent spatio-temporal fact?

Let us suppose them to possess a complex system of true beliefs concerning their surroundings, the structures below the surface of things, exact details of history and geography, all constituted by concepts none of which corresponds to any of our sensible characteristics. What then? Is it not possible that their basic beliefs should all concern fields of force, waves, mathematical structures, and numerical assignments to variables in several dimensions? This is no doubt an exotic notion, but even so it still seems conceivable. And if it is in fact possible, what then shall we say of the noninferential beliefs of such beings? Would we have to concede the existence of special epistemic principles that can validate their noninferential beliefs? Would it not be preferable to formulate more abstract principles that can cover both human and extraterrestial foundations? If such more abstract principles are in fact accessible, then the less general principles that define the human foundations and those that define the extraterrestial foundations are both derived principles whose validity depends on that of the more abstract principles. In this the human and extraterrestial epistemic principles would resemble rules of good nutrition for an infant and an adult. The infant's rules would of course be quite unlike those valid for the adult. But both would still be based on a more fundamental principle that postulates the ends of well-being and good health. What more fundamental principles might support both human and extraterrestial knowledge in the way that those concerning good health and well-being support rules of nutrition for both the infant and adult?

11. Reliabilism: An Ethics of Moral Virtues and an Epistemology of Intellectual Virtues

In what sense is the doctor attending Frau Hitler justified in performing an action that brings with it far less value than one of its accessible alternatives? According to one promising idea, the key is to be found in the rules that he embodies through stable dispositions. His action is the result of certain stable virtues, and there are no equally virtuous alternative *dispositions* that, given his cognitive limitations, he might have embodied with equal or better total consequences, and that would have led him to infanticide in the circumstances. The important move for our purpose is the stratification of justification. Primary justification attaches to virtues and other dispositions, to stable dispositions to act, through their greater contribution of value when compared with alternatives. Secondary justification attaches to particular acts in virtue of their source in virtues or other such justified dispositions.

The same strategy may also prove fruitful in epistemology. Here primary justification would apply to *intellectual* virtues, to stable dispositions for belief acquisition, through their greater contribution toward getting us to the truth. Secondary justification would then attach to particular beliefs in virtue of their source in intellectual virtues or other such justified dispositions.[7]

That raises parallel questions for ethics and epistemology. We need to consider more carefully the concept of a virtue and the distinction between moral and intellectual virtues. In epistemology, there is reason to think that the most useful and illuminating notion of intellectual virtue will prove broader than our tradition would suggest and must give due weight not only to the subject and his intrinsic nature but also to his environment and to his epistemic community. This is a large topic, however, to which I hope some of us will turn with more space, and insight, than I can now command.[8]

Summary

1. *Two assumptions:* (A1) that for a belief to constitute knowledge it must be (a) true and (b) justified; and (A2) that the justification relevant to whether or not one knows is a sort of epistemic or theoretical justification to be distinguished from its practical counterpart.

2. *Knowledge and criteria.* Particularism is distinguished from methodism: the first gives priority to particular examples of knowledge over general methods or criteria, whereas the second reverses that order. The methodism of Descartes leads him to an elaborate dogmatism whereas that of Hume leads him to a very simple skepticism. The particularist is, of course, antiskeptical on principle.

3. *Two metaphors: the raft and the pyramid.* For the foundationalist every piece of knowledge stands at the apex of a pyramid that rests on stable and secure foundations whose stability and security do not derive from the upper stories or sections. For the coherentist a body of knowledge is a free-floating raft every plank of which helps directly or indirectly to keep all the others in place, and no plank of which would retain its status with no help from the others.

4. *A coherentist critique of foundationalism.* No mental state can provide a foundation for empirical knowledge. For if such a state is propositional, then it is fallible and hence no secure foundation. But if it is *not* propositional, then how can it possibly serve as a foundation for belief? How can one infer or justify anything on the basis of a state that, having no propositional content, must be logically dumb? An analogy with ethics suggests a reason to reject this dilemma. Other reasons are also advanced and discussed.

5. *The regress argument.* In defending his position, the foundationalist often attempts to rule out the very possibility of an infinite regress of justification (which leads him to the necessity for a foundation). Some of his arguments to that end are examined.
6. *The relation of justification and foundationalist strategy.* An alternative foundationalist strategy is exposed, one that does not require ruling out the possibility of an infinite regress of justification.
7. *Two levels of foundationalism.* Substantive foundationalism is distinguished from formal foundationalism, three grades of which are exposed: first, the supervenience of epistemic justification; second, its explicable supervenience; and, third, its supervenience explicable by means of a simple theory. There turns out to be a surprising kinship between coherentism and substantive foundationalism, both of which aim at a formal foundationalism of the highest grade, at a theory of the greatest simplicity that explains how epistemic justification supervenes on nonepistemic factors.
8. *Doxastic ascent arguments.* The distinction between formal and substantive foundationalism provides an unusual viewpoint on some recent attacks against foundationalism. We consider doxastic ascent arguments as an example.
9. *Coherentism and substantive foundationalism.* It is argued that substantive foundationalism is superior, since coherentism is unable to account adequately for the epistemic status of beliefs at the "periphery" of a body of beliefs.
10. *The foundationalist's dilemma.* All foundationalism based on sense experience is subject to a fatal dilemma.
11. *Reliabilism.* An alternative to foundationalism of sense experience is sketched.

Notes

1. But Descartes's methodism was at most partial. James Van Cleve has supplied the materials for a convincing argument that the way out of the Cartesian circle is through a particularism of basic knowledge. See James Van Cleve, "Foundationalism, Epistemic Principles, and the Cartesian Circle." But this is, of course, compatible with methodism on inferred knowledge. Whether Descartes subscribed to such methodism is hard (perhaps impossible) to determine, since in the end he makes room for all the kinds of knowledge required by particularism. But his language when he introduces the method of hyperbolic doubt, and the order in which he proceeds, suggest that he did subscribe to such methodism.

2. Cf. Laurence Bonjour, "The Coherence Theory of Empirical Knowledge," Chapter 5 above, and, especially, Michael Williams, *Groundless Belief;* and Bonjour, "Can Empirical Knowledge Have a Foundation?," Chapter 4 above.

3. Cf. Richard Foley, "Inferential Justification and the Infinite Regress," *American Philosophical Quarterly* 15 (1978): 311–16.

4. Cf. John Post, "Infinite Regresses of Justification and of Explanation," *Philosophical Studies* 34 (1980).

5. The argument of this whole section is developed in greater detail in my paper "The Foundations of Foundationalism."

6. For some examples of the influence of doxastic ascent arguments, see Wilfrid Sellars's writing in epistemology: "Empiricism and the Philosophy of Mind," especially section VIII, and particularly p. 168. Also I. T. Oakley, "An Argument for Skepticism Concerning Justified Belief," *American Philosophical Quarterly* 13 (1976): 221–28; and Bonjour, "Can Empirical Knowledge Have a Foundation?," Chapter 4 above.

7. This puts in a more traditional perspective the contemporary effort to develop a "causal theory of knowing." From our viewpoint, this effort is better understood not as an attempt to *define* propositional knowledge, but as an attempt to formulate fundamental principles of justification.

Cf. the work of D. Armstrong, *Belief, Truth and Knowledge*, and that of F. Dretske, A. Goldman, and M. Swain, whose relevant already published work is included in *Essays on Knowledge and Justification,* ed. G. Pappas and M. Swain (Ithaca and London, 1978). But the theory is still under development by Goldman and by Swain, who have reached general conclusions about it similar to those suggested here, though not necessarily—so far as I know—for the same reasons or in the same overall context.

8. I am indebted above all to Roderick Chisholm: for his writings and for innumerable discussions. The main ideas in the present essay were first presented in a seminar of 1976–77 at the University of Texas. I am grateful to Anthony Anderson, David and Jean Blumenfeld, Laurence Bonjour, and Martin Perlmutter, who made that seminar a valuable stimulus. Subsequent criticism by my colleague James Van Cleve has also been valuable and stimulating.

7   What Is Justified Belief?

ALVIN I. GOLDMAN

The aim of this essay is to sketch a theory of justified belief. What I
have in mind is an explanatory theory, one that explains in a general way
why certain beliefs are counted as justified and others as unjustified.
Unlike some traditional approaches, I do not try to prescribe standards
for justification that differ from, or improve upon, our ordinary standards.
I merely try to explicate the ordinary standards, which are, I believe,
quite different from those of many classical, e.g., "Cartesian," accounts.

Many epistemologists have been interested in justification because of
its presumed close relationship to knowledge. This relationship is intended to be preserved in the conception of justified belief presented here.
In previous papers on knowledge,[1] I have denied that justification is
necessary for knowing, but there I had in mind "Cartesian" accounts of
justification. On the account of justified belief suggested here, it *is*
necessary for knowing, and closely related to it.

The term "justified," I presume, is an evaluative term, a term of
appraisal. Any correct definition or synonym of it would also feature
evaluative terms. I assume that such definitions or synonyms might be
given, but I am not interested in them. I want a set of *substantive*
conditions that specify when a belief is justified. Compare the moral term
"right." This might be defined in other ethical terms or phrases, a task
appropriate to meta-ethics. The task of normative ethics, by contrast, is
to state substantive conditions for the rightness of actions. Normative
ethics tries to specify non-ethical conditions that determine when an
action is right. A familiar example is act-utilitarianism, which says an
action is right if and only if it produces, or would produce, at least as
much net happiness as any alternative open to the agent. These necessary
and sufficient conditions clearly involve no ethical notions. Analogously,
I want a theory of justified belief to specify in non-epistemic terms when a
belief is justified. This is not the only kind of theory of justifiedness one

Reprinted from *Justification and Knowledge*, ed. G. S. Pappas (Dordrecht: D. Reidel, 1979),
1–23, by permission of the author and the publisher. Copyright 1979, D. Reidel Publishing
Company.

might seek, but it is one important kind of theory and the kind sought here.

In order to avoid epistemic terms in our theory, we must know which terms are epistemic. Obviously, an exhaustive list cannot be given, but here are some examples: "justified," "warranted," "has (good) grounds," "has reason (to believe)," "knows that," "sees that," "apprehends that," "is probable" (in an epistemic or inductive sense), "shows that," "establishes that," and "ascertains that." By contrast, here are some sample non-epistemic expressions: "believes that," "is true," "causes," "it is necessary that," "implies," "is deducible from," and "is probable" (either in the frequency sense or the propensity sense). In general, (purely) doxastic, metaphysical, modal, semantic, or syntactic expressions are not epistemic.

There is another constraint I wish to place on a theory of justified belief, in addition to the constraint that it be couched in non-epistemic language. Since I seek an explanatory theory, i.e., one that clarifies the underlying source of justificational status, it is not enough for a theory to state "correct" necessary and sufficient conditions. Its conditions must also be appropriately deep or revelatory. Suppose, for example, that the following sufficient condition of justified belief is offered: "If S senses redly at t and S believes at t that he is sensing redly, then S's belief at t that he is sensing redly is justified." This is not the kind of principle I seek; for, even if it is correct, it leaves unexplained *why* a person who senses redly and believes that he does, believes this justifiably. Not every state is such that if one is in it and believes one is in it, this belief is justified. What is distinctive about the state of sensing redly, or "phenomenal" states in general? A theory of justified belief of the kind I seek must answer this question, and hence it must be couched at a suitably deep, general, or abstract level.

A few introductory words about my *explicandum* are appropriate at this juncture. It is often assumed that whenever a person has a justified belief, he knows that it is justified and knows what the justification is. It is further assumed that the person can state or explain what his justification is. On this view, a justification is an argument, defense, or set of reasons that can be given in support of a belief. Thus, one studies the nature of justified belief by considering what a person might *say* if asked to defend, or justify, his belief. I make none of these sorts of assumptions here. I leave it an open question whether, when a belief *is* justified, the believer *knows* it is justified. I also leave it an open question whether, when a belief is justified, the believer can *state* or *give* a justification for it. I do not even assume that when a belief is justified there is something "possessed" by the believer which can be called a "justification." I do assume that a justified belief gets its status of being justified from some processes or properties that make it justified. In short, there must be some justification-conferring processes or properties. But this does not imply that there must be an argument, or reason, or anything else, "possessed" at the time of belief by the believer.

I

A theory of justified belief will be a set of principles that specify truth-conditions for the schema $\ulcorner$ S's belief in p at time t is justified $\urcorner$, i.e., conditions for the satisfaction of this schema in all possible cases. It will be convenient to formulate candidate theories in a recursive or inductive format, which would include (A) one or more base clauses, (B) a set of recursive clauses (possibly null), and (C) a closure clause. In such a format, it is permissible for the predicate "is a justified belief" to appear in recursive clauses. But neither this predicate, nor any other epistemic predicate, may appear in (the antecedent of) any base clause.[2]

Before turning to my own theory, I want to survey some other possible approaches to justified belief. Identification of problems associated with other attempts will provide some motivation for the theory I shall offer. Obviously, I cannot examine all, or even very many, alternative attempts. But a few sample attempts will be instructive.

Let us concentrate on the attempt to formulate one or more adequate base-clause principles.[3] Here is a classical candidate:

(1) If S believes p at t, and p is indubitable for S (at t), then S's belief in p at t is justified.

To evaluate this principle, we need to know what "indubitable" means. It can be understood in at least two ways. First, "p is indubitable for S" might mean: "S has no *grounds* for doubting p." Since "ground" is an epistemic term, however, principle (1) would be inadmissible in this reading, for epistemic terms may not legitimately appear in the antecedent of a base-clause. A second interpretation would avoid this difficulty. One might interpret "p is indubitable for S" psychologically, i.e., as meaning "S is psychologically incapable of doubting p." This would make principle (1) admissible, but would it be correct? Surely not. A religious fanatic may be psychologically incapable of doubting the tenets of his faith, but that doesn't make his belief in them justified. Similarly, during the Watergate affair, someone may have been so blinded by the aura of the presidency that even after the most damaging evidence against Nixon had emerged he was still incapable of doubting Nixon's veracity. It doesn't follow that his belief in Nixon's veracity was justified.

A second candidate base-clause principle is this:

(2) If S believes p at t and p is self-evident, then S's belief in p at t is justified.

To evaluate this principle, we again need an interpretation of its crucial term, in this case "self-evident." On one standard reading, "evident" is a synonym for "justified." "*Self*-evident" would therefore mean something like "directly justified," "intuitively justified," or "non-derivatively justified." On this reading "self-evident" is an epistemic phrase, and principle (2) would be disqualified as a base-clause principle.

However, there are other possible readings of "p is self-evident" on which it isn't an epistemic phrase. One such reading is: "It is impossible to understand p without believing it."[4] According to this interpretation, trivial analytic and logical truths might turn out to be self-evident. Hence, any belief in such a truth would be a justified belief, according to (2).

What does "it is *impossible* to understand p without believing it" mean? Does it mean "*humanly* impossible"? That reading would probably make (2) an unacceptable principle. There may well be propositions which humans have an innate and irrepressible disposition to believe, e.g., "Some events have causes." But it seems unlikely that people's inability to refrain from believing such a proposition makes every belief in it justified.

Should we then understand "impossible" to mean "impossible in principle," or "logically impossible"? If that is the reading given, I suspect that (2) is a vacuous principle. I doubt that even trivial logical or analytic truths will satisfy this definition of "self-evident." Any proposition, we may assume, has two or more components that are somehow organized or juxtaposed. To understand the proposition one must "grasp" the components and their juxtaposition. Now in the case of *complex* logical truths, there are (human) psychological operations that suffice to grasp the components and their juxtaposition but do not suffice to produce a belief that the proposition is true. But can't we at least *conceive* of an analogous set of psychological operations even for simple logical truths, operations which perhaps are not in the repertoire of human cognizers but which might be in the repertoire of some conceivable beings? That is, can't we conceive of psychological operations that would suffice to grasp the components and componential-juxtaposition of these simple propositions but do not suffice to produce *belief* in the propositions? I think we can conceive of such operations. Hence, for any proposition you choose, it will be possible for it to be understood without being believed.

Finally, even if we set these two objections aside, we must note that self-evidence can at best confer justificational status on relatively few beliefs, and the only plausible group are beliefs in necessary truths. Thus, other base-clause principles will be needed to explain the justificational status of beliefs in contingent propositions.

The notion of a base-clause principle is naturally associated with the idea of "direct" justifiedness, and in the realm of contingent propositions first-person-current-mental-state propositions have often been assigned this role. In Chisholm's terminology, this conception is expressed by the notion of a *"self-presenting"* state or proposition. The sentence "I am thinking," for example, expresses a self-presenting proposition. (At least I shall *call* this sort of content a "proposition," though it only has a truth value given some assignment of a subject who utters or entertains the content and a time of entertaining.) When such a proposition is true for person *S* at time *t*, *S* is justified in believing it at *t:* in Chisholm's terminology, the proposition is "evident" for *S* at *t*. This suggests the following base-clause principle.

(3) If *p* is a self-presenting proposition, and *p* is true for *S* at *t*, and *S* believes *p* at *t*, then *S*'s belief in *p* at *t* is justified.

What, exactly, does "self-presenting" mean? In the second edition of *Theory of Knowledge*, Chisholm offers this definition: "*h* is self-presenting for *S* at *t* = df. h* is true at *t;* and necessarily, if *h* is true at *t*, then *h* is evident for *S* at *t*."[5] Unfortunately, since "evident" is an epistemic term, "self-presenting" also becomes an epistemic term on this definition, thereby disqualifying (3) as a legitimate base-clause. Some other definition of self-presentingness must be offered if (3) is to be a suitable base-clause principle.

Another definition of self-presentation readily comes to mind. "Self-presentation" is an approximate synonym of "self-intimation," and a proposition may be said to be self-intimating if and only if whenever it is true of a person that person believes it. More precisely, we may give the following definition:

(SP) Proposition *p* is self-presenting if and only if: necessarily, for any *S* and any *t*, if *p* is true for *S* at *t*, then *S* believes *p* at *t*.

On this definition, "self-presenting" is clearly not an epistemic predicate, so (3) would be an admissible principle. Moreover, there is initial plausibility in the suggestion that it is *this* feature of first-person-current-mental-state propositions—viz., their truth guarantees their being believed—that makes beliefs in them justified.

Employing this definition of self-presentation, is principle (3) correct? This cannot be decided until we define self-presentation more precisely. Since the operator "necessarily" can be read in different ways, there are different forms of self-presentation and correspondingly different versions of principle (3). Let us focus on two of these readings: a *"nomological"* reading and a *"logical"* reading. Consider first the nomological reading. On this definition a proposition is self-presenting just in case it is nomologically necessary that if *p* is true for *S* at *t*, then *S* believes *p* at *t*.[6]

Is the nomological version of principle (3)—call it "(3_N)"—correct? Not at all. We can imagine cases in which the antecedent of (3_N) is satisfied, but we would not say that the belief is justified. Suppose, for example, that *p* is the proposition expressed by the sentence "I am in brain-state *B*," where "*B*" is shorthand for a certain highly specific neural state description. Further suppose it is a nomological truth that anyone in brain-state *B* will ipso facto *believe* he is in brain-state *B*. In other words, imagine that an occurrent belief with the content "I am in brain-state *B*" is realized whenever one is in brain-state *B*.[7] According to (3_N), any such belief is justified. But that is clearly false. We can readily imagine circumstances in which a person goes into brain-state *B* and therefore has the belief in question, though this belief is by no means justified. For example, we can imagine that a brain-surgeon operating on *S* artificially induced brain-state *B*. This results, phenomenologically, in *S*'s suddenly believing—out of the blue—that he is in brain-state *B*, without any relevant antecedent beliefs. We would hardly say, in such a case, that *S*'s belief that he is in brain-state *B* is justified.

Let us turn next to the logical version of (3)—call it "(3_L)"—in which a proposition is defined as self-presenting just in case it is logically necessary that if *p* is true for *S* at *t*, then *S* believes *p* at *t*. This stronger version of principle (3) might seem more promising. In fact, however, it is no more successful than (3_N). Let *p* be the proposition "I am awake" and assume that it is logically necessary that if this proposition is true for some person *S* and time *t*, then *S* believes *p* at *t*. This assumption is consistent with the further assumption that *S* frequently believes *p* when it is false, e.g., when he is dreaming. Under these circumstances, we would hardly accept the contention that *S*'s belief in this proposition is always justified. Nor should we accept the contention that the belief is justified when it is *true*. The truth of the proposition logically guarantees that the belief is *held*, but why should it guarantee that the belief is *justified?*

The foregoing criticism suggests that we have things backwards. The idea of self-presentation is that truth guarantees belief. This fails to confer justification because it is compatible with there being belief without truth. So what seems necessary—or at least sufficient—for justification is that belief should guarantee truth. Such a notion has usually gone under the label of *"infallibility"* or *"incorrigibility."* It may be defined as follows:

(INC) Proposition *p* is incorrigible if and only if: necessarily, for any *S* and any *t*, if *S* believes *p* at *t*, then *p* is true for *S* at *t*.

Using the notion of incorrigibility, we may propose principle (4).

(4) If *p* is an incorrigible proposition, and *S* believes *p* at *t*, then *S*'s belief in *p* at *t* is justified.

As was true of self-presentation, there are different varieties of incorrigibility, corresponding to different interpretations of "necessarily." Accordingly, we have different versions of principle (4). Once again, let us concentrate on a nomological and a logical version, (4_N) and (4_L) respectively.

We can easily construct a counterexample to (4_N) along the lines of the belief-state/brain-state counterexample that refuted (3_N). Suppose it is nomologically necessary that if anyone believes he is in brain-state B then it is true that he is in brain-state B, for the only way this belief-state is realized is through brain-state B itself. It follows that "I am in brain-state B" is a nomologically incorrigible proposition. Therefore, according to (4_N), whenever anyone believes this proposition at any time, that belief is justified. But we may again construct a brain-surgeon example in which someone comes to have such a belief but the belief isn't justified.

Apart from this counterexample, the general point is this. Why should the fact that S's believing p guarantees the truth of p imply that S's belief is justified? The nature of the guarantee might be wholly fortuitous, as the belief-state/brain-state example is intended to illustrate. To appreciate the point, consider the following related possibility. A person's mental structure might be such that whenever he believes that p will be true (of him) a split second later, then p is true (of him) a split second later. This is because, we may suppose, his believing it brings it about. But surely we would not be compelled in such a circumstance to say that a belief of this sort is justified. So why should the fact that S's believing p guarantees the truth of p *precisely at the time of belief* imply that the belief is justified? There is no intuitive plausibility in this supposition.

The notion of *logical* incorrigibility has a more honored place in the history of conceptions of justification. But even principle (4_L), I believe, suffers from defects similar to those of (4_N). The mere fact that belief in p logically guarantees its truth does not confer justificational status on such a belief.

The first difficulty with (4_L) arises from logical or mathematical truths. Any true proposition of logic or mathematics is logically necessary. Hence, any such proposition p is logically incorrigible, since it is logically necessary that, for any S and any t, if S believes p at t then p is true (for S at t). Now assume that Nelson believes a certain very complex mathematical truth at time t. Since such a proposition is logically incorrigible, (4_L) implies that Nelson's belief in this truth at t is justified. But we may easily suppose that this belief of Nelson is not at all the result of proper mathematical reasoning, or even the result of appeal to trustworthy authority. Perhaps Nelson believes this complex truth because of utterly confused reasoning, or because of hasty and ill-founded conjecture. Then his belief is not justified, contrary to what (4_L) implies.

The case of logical or mathematical truths is admittedly peculiar, since the truth of these propositions is assured independently of any beliefs. It might seem, therefore, that we can better capture the idea of "belief logically guaranteeing truth" in cases where the propositions in question are *contingent*. With this in mind, we might restrict (4_L) to *contingent* incorrigible propositions. Even this amendment cannot save (4_L), however, since there are counterexamples to it involving purely contingent propositions.

Suppose that Humperdink has been studying logic—or, rather, pseudo-logic—from Elmer Fraud, whom Humperdink has no reason to trust as a logician. Fraud has enunciated the principle that any disjunctive proposition consisting of at least 40 distinct disjuncts is very probably true. Humperdink now encounters the proposition *p*, a contingent proposition with 40 disjuncts, the 7th disjunct being "I exist." Although Humperdink grasps the proposition fully, he doesn't notice that it is entailed by "I exist." Rather, he is struck by the fact that it falls under the disjunction rule Fraud has enunciated (a rule I assume Humperdink is not *justified* in believing). Bearing this in mind, Humperdink forms a belief in *p*. Now notice that *p* is logically incorrigible. It is logically necessary that if anyone believes *p*, then *p* is true (of him at that time). This simply follows from the fact that, first, a person's believing anything entails that he exists, and second, "I exist" entails *p*. Since *p* is logically incorrigible, principle (4_L) implies that Humperdink's belief in *p* is justified. But surely, given our example, that conclusion is false. Humperdink's belief in *p* is not at all justified.

One thing that goes wrong in this example is that while Humperdink's belief in *p* logically implies its truth, Humperdink doesn't *recognize* that his believing it implies its truth. This might move a theorist to revise (4_L) by adding the requirement that *S* "recognize" that *p* is logically incorrigible. But this, of course, won't do. The term "recognize" is obviously an epistemic term, so the suggested revision of (4_L) would result in an inadmissible base-clause.

II

Let us try to diagnose what has gone wrong with these attempts to produce an acceptable base-clause principle. Notice that each of the foregoing attempts confers the status of "justified" on a belief without restriction on *why* the belief is held, i.e., on what *causally initiates* the belief or *causally sustains* it. The logical versions of principles (3) and (4), for example, clearly place no restriction on causes of belief. The same is true of the nomological versions of (3) and (4), since nomological requirements can be satisfied by simultaneity or cross-sectional laws, as illustrated by our brain-state/belief-state examples. I suggest that the absence of causal requirements accounts for the failure of the foregoing principles. Many of our counterexamples are ones in which the belief is caused in some strange or unacceptable way, e.g., by the accidental movement of a brain-surgeon's hand, by reliance on an illicit, pseudo-logical principle, or by the blinding aura of the presidency. In general, a strategy for defeating a noncausal principle of justifiedness is to find a case in which the principle's antecedent is satisfied but the belief is caused by some faulty belief-forming process. The faultiness of the belief-forming process will incline us, intuitively, to regard the belief as unjustified. Thus, correct principles of justified belief must be principles that make causal requirements, where "cause" is construed broadly to include sustainers as well as initiators of belief (i.e., processes that determine, or help to overdetermine, a belief's continuing to be held).[8]

The need for causal requirements is not restricted to base-clause principles. Recursive principles will also need a causal component. One might initially suppose that the following is a good recursive principle: "If S justifiably believes q at t, and q entails p, and S believes p at t, then S's belief in p at t is justified." But this principle is unacceptable. S's belief in p doesn't receive justificational status simply from the fact that p is entailed by q and S justifiably believes q. If what causes S to believe p at t is entirely different, S's belief in p may well not be justified. Nor can the situation be remedied by adding to the antecedent the condition that S justifiably believes that q entails p. Even if he believes this, and believes q as well, he might not put these beliefs together. He might believe p as a result of some other wholly extraneous considerations. So once again, conditions that fail to require appropriate causes of a belief don't guarantee justifiedness.

Granted that principles of justified belief must make reference to causes of belief, what kinds of causes confer justifiedness? We can gain insight into this problem by reviewing some faulty processes of belief-formation, i.e., processes whose belief-outputs would be classed as unjustified. Here are some examples: confused reasoning, wishful thinking, reliance on emotional attachment, mere hunch or guesswork, and hasty generalization. What do these faulty processes have in common? They share the feature of *unreliability:* they tend to produce *error* a large proportion of the time. By contrast, which species of belief-forming (or belief-sustaining) processes are intuitively justification-conferring? They include standard perceptual processes, remembering, good reasoning, and introspection. What these processes seem to have in common is *reliability:* the beliefs they produce are generally true. My positive proposal, then, is this. The justificational status of a belief is a function of the reliability of the process or processes that cause it, where (as a first approximation) reliability consists in the tendency of a process to produce beliefs that are true rather than false.

To test this thesis further, notice that justifiedness is not a purely categorical concept, although I treat it here as categorical in the interest of simplicity. We can and do regard certain beliefs as more justified than others. Furthermore, our intuitions of comparative justifiedness go along with our beliefs about the comparative reliability of the belief-causing processes.

Consider perceptual beliefs. Suppose Jones believes he has just seen a mountain-goat. Our assessment of the belief's justifiedness is determined by whether he caught a brief glimpse of the creature at a great distance, or whether he had a good look at the thing only 30 yards away. His belief in the latter sort of case is *(ceteris paribus)* more justified than in the former sort of case. And, if his belief is true, we are more prepared to say he *knows* in the latter case than in the former. The difference between the two cases seems to be this. Visual beliefs formed from brief and hasty scanning, or where the perceptual object is a long distance off, tend to be wrong more often than visual beliefs formed from detailed and leisurely scanning, or where the object is in reasonable proximity. In short, the visual processes in the former category are less reliable than those in the latter category. A similar point holds for memory beliefs. A belief that results from a hazy and indistinct memory impression is counted as less justified than a belief that arises from a distinct memory impression, and our inclination to classify those beliefs as *"knowledge"* varies in the same way. Again, the reason is associated with the comparative reliability of the processes. Hazy and indistinct memory impressions are generally less reliable indicators of what actually happened, so beliefs formed from such impressions are less likely to be true than beliefs formed from distinct impressions. Further, consider beliefs based on inference from observed samples. A belief about a population that is based on random sampling, or on instances that exhibit great variety, is intuitively more justified than a belief based on biased sampling, or on instances from a narrow sector of the population. Again, the degree of justifiedness seems to be a function of reliability. Inferences based on random or varied samples will tend to produce less error or inaccuracy than inferences based on non-random or non-varied samples.

Returning to a categorical concept of justifiedness, we might ask just *how* reliable a belief-forming process must be in order that its resultant beliefs be justified. A precise answer to this question should not be expected. Our conception of justification is *vague* in this respect. It does seem clear, however, that *perfect* reliability isn't required. Belief-forming processes that *sometimes* produce error still confer justification. It follows that there can be justified beliefs that are false.

I have characterized justification-conferring processes as ones that have a "tendency" to produce beliefs that are true rather than false. The term "tendency" could refer either to *actual* long-run frequency, or to a "propensity," i.e., outcomes that would occur in merely *possible* realizations of the process. Which of these is intended? Unfortunately, I think our ordinary conception of justifiedness is vague on this dimension too. For the most part, we simply assume that the "observed" frequency of truth versus error would be approximately replicated in the actual long-run, and also in relevant counterfactual situations, i.e., ones that are highly "realistic" or conform closely to the circumstances of the actual world. Since we ordinarily assume these frequencies to be roughly the same, we make no concerted effort to distinguish them. Since the purpose of my present theorizing is to capture our ordinary conception of justifiedness, and since our ordinary conception is vague on this matter, it is appropriate to leave the theory vague in the same respect.

We need to say more about the notion of a belief-forming *"process."* Let us mean by a "process" a *functional operation* or procedure, i.e., something that generates a *mapping* from certain states—"inputs"—into other states—"outputs." The outputs in the present case are states of believing this or that proposition at a given moment. On this interpretation, a process is a *type* as opposed to a *token*. This is fully appropriate, since it is only types that have statistical properties such as producing truth 80 percent of the time; and it is precisely such statistical properties that determine the reliability of a process. Of course, we also want to speak of a process as *causing* a belief, and it looks as if types are incapable of being causes. But when we say that a belief is caused by a given process, understood as a functional procedure, we may interpret this to mean that it is caused by the particular *inputs* to the process (and by the intervening events "through which" the functional procedure carries the inputs into the output) on the occasion in question.

What are some examples of belief-forming "processes" construed as functional operations? One example is reasoning processes, where the inputs include antecedent beliefs and entertained hypotheses. Another example is functional procedures whose inputs include desires, hopes, or emotional states of various sorts (together with antecedent beliefs). A third example is a memory process, which takes as input beliefs or experiences at an earlier time and generates as output beliefs at a later time. For example, a memory process might take as input a belief *at t_1* that Lincoln was born in 1809 and generate as output a belief *at t_n* that Lincoln was born in 1809. A fourth example is perceptual processes. Here it isn't clear whether inputs should include states of the environment, such as the distance of the stimulus from the cognizer, or only events within or on the surface of the organism, e.g., receptor stimulations. I shall return to this point in a moment.

A critical problem concerning our analysis is the degree of generality of the process-types in question. Input-output relations can be specified very broadly or very narrowly, and the degree of generality will partly determine the degree of reliability. A process-type might be selected so narrowly that only one instance of it ever occurs, and hence the type is either completely reliable or completely unreliable. (This assumes that reliability is a function of *actual* frequency only.) If such narrow process-types were selected, beliefs that are intuitively unjustified might be said to result from perfectly reliable processes, and beliefs that are intuitively justified might be said to result from perfectly unreliable processes.

It is clear that our ordinary thought about process-types slices them broadly, but I cannot at present give a precise explication of our intuitive principles. One plausible suggestion, though, is that the relevant processes are *content-neutral*. It might be argued, for example, that the process of *inferring p whenever the Pope asserts p* could pose problems for our theory. If the Pope is infallible, this process will be perfectly reliable; yet we would not regard the belief-outputs of this process as justified. The content-neutral restriction would avert this difficulty. If relevant processes are required to admit as input beliefs (or other states) with *any* content, the aforementioned process will not count, for its input beliefs have a restricted propositional content, viz., *"the Pope asserts p."*

In addition to the problem of "generality" or "abstractness" there is the previously mentioned problem of the *"extent"* of belief-forming processes. Clearly, the causal ancestry of beliefs often includes events outside the organism. Are such events to be included among the "inputs" of belief-forming processes? Or should we restrict the extent of belief-forming processes to *"cognitive"* events, i.e., events within the organism's nervous system? I shall choose the latter course, though with some hesitation. My general grounds for this decision are roughly as follows. Justifiedness seems to be a function of how a cognizer deals with his environmental input, i.e., with the goodness or badness of the operations that register and transform the stimulation that reaches him. ("Deal with," of course, does not mean *purposeful* action, nor is it restricted to *conscious* activity.) A justified belief is, roughly speaking, one that results from cognitive operations that are, generally speaking, good or successful. But *"cognitive"* operations are most plausibly construed as operations of the cognitive faculties, i.e., "information-processing" equipment *internal* to the organism.

With these points in mind, we may now advance the following base-clause principle for justified belief.

(5) If S's believing p at t results from a reliable cognitive belief-forming process (or set of processes), then S's belief in p at t is justified.

Since "reliable belief-forming process" has been defined in terms of such notions as belief, truth, statistical frequency, and the like, it is not an epistemic term. Hence, (5) is an admissible base-clause.

It might seem as if (5) promises to be not only a successful base clause, but the only principle needed whatever, apart from a closure clause. In other words, it might seem as if it is a necessary as well as a sufficient condition of justifiedness that a belief be produced by reliable cognitive belief-forming processes. But this is not quite correct, given our provisional definition of "reliability."

Our provisional definition implies that a reasoning process is reliable only if it generally produces beliefs that are true, and similarly, that a memory process is reliable only if it generally yields beliefs that are true. But these requirements are too strong. A reasoning procedure cannot be expected to produce true belief if it is applied to false premises. And memory cannot be expected to yield a true belief if the original belief it attempts to retain is false. What we need for reasoning and memory, then, is a notion of *"conditional reliability."* A process is conditionally reliable when a sufficient proportion of its output-beliefs are true *given that its input-beliefs are true*.

With this point in mind, let us distinguish *belief-dependent* and *belief-independent* cognitive processes. The former are processes *some* of whose inputs are belief-states.[9] The latter are processes *none* of whose inputs are belief-states. We may then replace principle (5) with the following two principles, the first a base-clause principle and the second a recursive-clause principle.

(6$_A$) If S's belief in p at t results ("immediately") from a belief-independent process that is (unconditionally) reliable, then S's belief in p at t is justified.

(6$_B$) If S's belief in p at t results ("immediately") from a belief-dependent process that is (at least) conditionally reliable, and if the beliefs (if any) on which this process operates in producing S's belief in p at t are themselves justified, then S's belief in p at t is justified.[10]

If we add to (6$_A$) and (6$_B$) the standard closure clause, we have a complete theory of justified belief. The theory says, in effect, that a belief is justified if and only if it is *"well-formed,"* i.e., it has an ancestry of reliable and/or conditionally reliable cognitive operations. (Since a dated belief may be over-determined, it may have a number of distinct ancestral trees. These need not all be full of reliable or conditionally reliable processes. But at least one ancestral tree must have reliable or conditionally reliable processes throughout.)

The theory of justified belief proposed here, then, is an *Historical* or *Genetic* theory. It contrasts with the dominant approach to justified belief, an approach that generates what we may call (borrowing a phrase from Robert Nozick) *"Current Time-Slice"* theories. A Current Time-Slice theory makes the justificational status of a belief wholly a function of what is true of the cognizer *at the time* of belief. An Historical theory makes the justificational status of a belief depend on its prior history. Since my Historical theory emphasizes the reliability of the belief-generating processes, it may be called *"Historical Reliabilism."*

The most obvious examples of Current Time-Slice theories are "Cartesian" Foundationalist theories, which trace all justificational status (at least of contingent propositions) to current mental states. The usual varieties of Coherence theories, however, are equally Current Time-Slice views, since they too make the justificational status of a belief wholly a function of *current* states of affairs. For Coherence theories, however, these current states include all other beliefs of the cognizer, which would not be considered relevant by Cartesian Foundationalism. Have there been other Historical theories of justified belief? Among contemporary writers, Quine and Popper have Historical epistemologies, though the notion of "justification" is not their avowed *explicandum*. Among historical writers, it might seem that Locke and Hume had Genetic theories of sorts. But I think that their Genetic theories were only theories of ideas, not of knowledge or justification. Plato's theory of recollection, however, is a good example of a Genetic theory of knowing.[11] And it might be argued that Hegel and Dewey had Genetic epistemologies (if Hegel can be said to have had a clear epistemology at all).

The theory articulated by (6_A) and (6_B) might be viewed as a kind of "Foundationalism" because of its recursive structure. I have no objection to this label, as long as one keeps in mind how different this "diachronic" form of Foundationalism is from Cartesian, or other "synchronic" varieties of, Foundationalism.

Current Time-Slice theories characteristically assume that the justificational status of a belief is something which the cognizer is able to know or determine at the time of belief. This is made explicit, for example, by Chisholm.[12] The Historical theory I endorse makes no such assumption. There are many facts about a cognizer to which he lacks "privileged access," and I regard the justificational status of his beliefs as one of those things. This is not to say that a cognizer is necessarily ignorant, at any given moment, of the justificational status of his current beliefs. It is only to deny that he necessarily has, or can get, knowledge or true belief about this status. Just as a person can know without knowing that he knows, so he can have justified belief without knowing that it is justified (or believing justifiably that it is justified).

A characteristic case in which a belief is justified though the cognizer doesn't know that it's justified is where the original evidence for the belief has long since been forgotten. If the original evidence was compelling, the cognizer's original belief may have been justified, and this justificational status may have been preserved through memory. But since the cognizer no longer remembers how or why he came to believe, he may not know that the belief is justified. If asked now to justify his belief, he may be at a loss. Still, the belief *is* justified, though the cognizer can't demonstrate or establish this.

The Historical theory of justified belief I advocate is connected in spirit with the causal theory of knowing I have presented elsewhere.[13] I had this in mind when I remarked near the outset of the essay that my theory of justified belief makes justifiedness come out closely related to knowledge. Justified beliefs, like pieces of knowledge, have appropriate histories; but they may fail to be knowledge either because they are false or because they founder on some other requirement for knowing of the kind discussed in the post-Gettier knowledge-trade.

There is a variant of the Historical conception of justified belief that is worth mentioning in this context. It may be introduced as follows. Suppose S has a set B of beliefs at time t_0, and some of these beliefs are *un*justified. Between t_0 and t_1 he reasons from the entire set B to the conclusion p, which he then accepts at t_1. The reasoning procedure he uses is a very sound one, i.e., one that is conditionally reliable. There is a sense or respect in which we are tempted to say that S's belief in p at t_1 is "justified." At any rate, it is tempting to say that the *person* is justified in believing p at t. Relative to his antecedent cognitive state, he did as well as could be expected: the *transition* from his cognitive state at t_0 to his cognitive state at t_1 was entirely sound. Although we may acknowledge this brand of justifiedness—it might be called *"Terminal-Phase Reliabilism"*—it is not a kind of justifiedness so closely related to knowing. For a person to know proposition p, it is not enough that the *final phase* of the process that leads to his belief in p be sound. It is also necessary that some entire history of the process be sound (i.e., reliable or conditionally reliable).

Let us return now to the Historical theory. In the next section, I shall adduce reasons for strengthening it a bit. Before looking at these reasons, however, I wish to review two quite different objections to the theory.

First, a critic might argue that *some* justified beliefs do not derive their justificational status from their causal ancestry. In particular, it might be argued that beliefs about one's current phenomenal states and intuitive beliefs about elementary logical or conceptual relationships do not derive their justificational status in this way. I am not persuaded by either of these examples. Introspection, I believe, should be regarded as a form of retrospection. Thus, a justified belief that I am "now" in pain gets its justificational status from a relevant, though brief, causal history.[14] The apprehension of logical or conceptual relationships is also a cognitive process that occupies time. The psychological process of "seeing" or "intuiting" a simple logical truth is very fast, and we cannot introspectively dissect it into constituent parts. Nonetheless, there are mental operations going on, just as there are mental operations that occur in *idiots savants*, who are unable to report the computational processes they in fact employ.

A second objection to Historical Reliabilism focuses on the reliability element rather than the causal or historical element. Since the theory is intended to cover all possible cases, it seems to imply that for any cognitive process *C*, if *C* is reliable in possible world *W*, then any belief in *W* that results from *C* is justified. But doesn't this permit easy counterexamples? Surely we can imagine a possible world in which wishful thinking is reliable. We can imagine a possible world where a benevolent demon so arranges things that beliefs formed by wishful thinking usually come true. This would make wishful thinking a reliable process in that possible world, but surely we don't want to regard beliefs that result from wishful thinking as justified.

There are several possible ways to respond to this case, and I am unsure which response is best, partly because my own intuitions (and those of other people I have consulted) are not entirely clear. One possibility is to say that in the possible world imagined, beliefs that result from wishful thinking *are* justified. In other words, we reject the claim that wishful thinking could never, intuitively, confer justifiedness.[15]

However, for those who feel that wishful thinking couldn't confer justifiedness even in the world imagined, there are two ways out. First, it may be suggested that the proper criterion of justifiedness is the propensity of a process to generate beliefs that are true *in a non-manipulated environment*, i.e., an environment in which there is no purposeful arrangement of the world either to accord or conflict with the beliefs that are formed. In other words, the suitability of a belief-forming process is only a function of its success in *"natural"* situations, not situations of the sort involving benevolent or malevolent demons or any other such manipulative creatures. If we reformulate the theory to include this qualification, the counterexample in question will be averted.

Alternatively, we may reformulate our theory, or reinterpret it, as follows. Instead of construing the theory as saying that a belief in possible world *W* is justified if and only if it results from a cognitive process that is reliable in *W*, we may construe it as saying that a belief in possible world *W* is justified if and only if it results from a cognitive process that is reliable in *our world*. In short, our conception of justifiedness is derived as follows. We note certain cognitive processes in the actual world, and form beliefs about which of these are reliable. The ones we believe to be reliable are then regarded as justification-conferring processes. In reflecting on hypothetical beliefs, we deem them justified if and only if they result from processes already picked out as justification-conferring, or processes very similar to those. Since wishful thinking is not among these processes, a belief formed in a possible world *W* by wishful thinking would not be deemed justified, even if wishful thinking is reliable *in* W. I am not sure that this is a correct reconstruction of our intuitive conceptual scheme, but it would accommodate the benevolent demon case, at least if the proper thing to say in that case is that the wishful-thinking-caused beliefs are unjustified.

Even if we adopt this strategy, however, a problem still remains. Suppose that wishful thinking turns out to be reliable *in the actual world!*[16] This might be because, unbeknownst to us at present, there is a benevolent demon who, lazy until now, will shortly start arranging things so that our wishes come true. The long-run performance of wishful thinking will be very good, and hence even the new construal of the theory will imply that beliefs resulting from wishful thinking (in *our* world) are justified. Yet this surely contravenes our intuitive judgment on the matter.

Perhaps the moral of the case is that the standard format of a "conceptual analysis" has its shortcomings. Let me depart from that format and try to give a better rendering of our aim and the theory that tries to achieve that aim. What we really want is an *explanation* of why we count, or would count, certain beliefs as justified and others as unjustified. Such an explanation must refer to our *beliefs* about reliability, not to the actual *facts*. The reason we *count* beliefs as justified is that they are formed by what we *believe* to be reliable belief-forming processes. Our beliefs about which belief-forming processes are reliable may be erroneous, but that does not affect the adequacy of the explanation. Since we *believe* that wishful thinking is an unreliable belief-forming process, we regard beliefs formed by wishful thinking as unjustified. What matters, then, is what we *believe* about wishful thinking, not what is *true* (in the long run) about wishful thinking. I am not sure how to express this point in the standard format of conceptual analysis, but it identifies an important point in understanding our theory.

III

Let us return, however, to the standard format of conceptual analysis, and let us consider a new objection that will require some revisions in the theory advanced until now. According to our theory, a belief is justified in case it is caused by a process that is in fact reliable, or by one we generally believe to be reliable. But suppose that although one of S's beliefs satisfies this condition, S has no reason to believe that it does. Worse yet, suppose S has reason to believe that his belief is caused by an *un*reliable process (although *in fact* its causal ancestry is fully reliable). Wouldn't we deny in such circumstances that S's belief is justified? This seems to show that our analysis, as presently formulated, is mistaken.

Suppose that Jones is told on fully reliable authority that a certain class of his memory beliefs are almost all mistaken. His parents fabricate a wholly false story that Jones suffered from amnesia when he was seven but later developed *pseudo*-memories of that period. Though Jones listens to what his parents say and has excellent reason to trust them, he persists in believing the ostensible memories from his seven-year-old past. Are these memory beliefs justified? Intuitively, they are not justified. But since these beliefs result from genuine memory and original perceptions, which are adequately reliable processes, our theory says that these beliefs are justified.

Can the theory be revised to meet this difficulty? One natural suggestion is that the actual reliability of a belief's ancestry is not enough for justifiedness; in addition, the cognizer must be *justified in believing* that the ancestry of his belief is reliable. Thus one might think of replacing (6_A), for example, with (7). (For simplicity, I neglect some of the details of the earlier analysis.)

(7) If S's belief in p at t is caused by a reliable cognitive process, and S justifiably believes at t that his p-belief is so caused, then S's belief in p at t is justified.

It is evident, however, that (7) will not do as a base clause, for it contains the epistemic term "justifiably" in its antecedent.

A slightly weaker revision, without this problematic feature, might next be suggested, viz.,

(8) If S's belief in p at t is caused by a reliable cognitive process, and S believes at t that his p-belief is so caused, then S's belief in p at t is justified.

But this won't do the job. Suppose that Jones believes that his memory beliefs are reliably caused despite all the (trustworthy) contrary testimony of his parents. Principle (8) would be satisfied, yet we wouldn't say that these beliefs are justified.

Next, we might try (9), which is stronger than (8) and, unlike (7), formally admissible as a base clause.

(9) If S's belief in p at t is caused by a reliable cognitive process, and S believes at t that his p-belief is so caused, and this meta-belief is caused by a reliable cognitive process, then S's belief in p at t is justified.

A first objection to (9) is that it wrongly precludes unreflective creatures—creatures like animals or young children, who have no beliefs about the genesis of their beliefs—from having justified beliefs. If one shares my view that justified belief is, at least roughly, *well-formed* belief, surely animals and young children can have justified beliefs.

A second problem with (9) concerns its underlying rationale. Since (9) is proposed as a substitute for (6_A), it is implied that the reliability of a belief's own cognitive ancestry does not make it justified. But, the suggestion seems to be, the reliability of a *meta-belief*'s ancestry confers justifiedness on the first-order belief. Why should that be so? Perhaps one is attracted by the idea of a "trickle-down" effect: if an $n+1$–level belief is justified, its justification trickles down to an n–level belief. But even if the trickle-down theory is correct, it doesn't help here. There is no assurance from the satisfaction of (9)'s antecedent that the meta-belief itself is *justified*.

To obtain a better revision of our theory, let us re-examine the Jones case. Jones has strong evidence against certain propositions concerning his past. He doesn't *use* this evidence, but if he *were* to use it properly, he would stop believing these propositions. Now the proper use of evidence would be an instance of a (conditionally) reliable process. So what we can say about Jones is that he *fails* to use a certain (conditionally) reliable process that he could and should have used. Admittedly, had he used this process, he would have "worsened" his doxastic states: he would have replaced some true beliefs with suspension of judgment. Still, he couldn't have known this in the case in question. So he failed to do something which, epistemically, he should have done. This diagnosis suggests a fundamental change in our theory. The justificational status of a belief is not only a function of the cognitive process *actually* employed in producing it, it is also a function of processes that could and should be employed.

With these points in mind, we may tentatively propose the following revision of our theory, where we again focus on a base-clause principle but omit certain details in the interest of clarity.

> (10) If S's belief in p at t results from a reliable cognitive process, and there is no reliable or conditionally reliable process available to S which, had it been used by S in addition to the process actually used, would have resulted in S's not believing p at t, then S's belief in p at t is justified.

There are several problems with this proposal. First, there is a technical problem. One cannot use an additional belief-forming (or doxastic-state-forming) process *as well as* the original process if the additional one would result in a different doxastic state. One wouldn't be using the original process at all. So we need a slightly different formulation of the relevant counterfactual. Since the basic idea is reasonably clear, however, I won't try to improve on the formulation here. A second problem concerns the notion of *"available"* belief-forming (or doxastic-state-forming) processes. What is it for a process to be "available" to a cognizer? Were scientific procedures "available" to people who lived in pre-scientific ages? Furthermore, it seems implausible to say that all "available" processes ought to be used, at least if we include such processes as gathering *new* evidence. Surely a belief can sometimes be justified even if additional evidence-gathering would yield a different doxastic attitude. What I think we should have in mind here are such additional processes as calling previously acquired evidence to mind, assessing the implications of that evidence, etc. This is admittedly somewhat vague, but here again our ordinary notion of justifiedness is vague, so it is appropriate for our analysans to display the same sort of vagueness.

This completes the sketch of my account of justified belief. Before concluding, however, it is essential to point out that there is an important use of "justified" which is not captured by this account but can be captured by a closely related one.

There is a use of "justified" in which it is not implied or presupposed that there is a *belief* that is justified. For example, if *S* is trying to decide whether to believe *p* and asks our advice, we may tell him that he is "justified" in believing it. We do not thereby imply that he *has* a justified *belief*, since we know he is still suspending judgment. What we mean, roughly, is that he *would* or *could* be justified if he were to believe *p*. The justificational status we ascribe here cannot be a function of the causes of *S*'s believing *p*, for there is no belief by *S* in *p*. Thus, the account of justifiedness we have given thus far cannot explicate *this* use of "justified." (It doesn't follow that this use of "justified" has no connection with causal ancestries. Its proper use may depend on the causal ancestry of the cognizer's cognitive state, though not on the causal ancestry of his believing *p*.)

Let us distinguish two uses of "justified": an *ex post* use and an *ex ante* use. The *ex post* use occurs when there exists a belief, and we say of *that belief* that it is (or isn't) justified. The *ex ante* use occurs when no such belief exists, or when we wish to ignore the question of whether such a belief exists. Here we say of the *person,* independent of his doxastic state vis-à-vis *p*, that *p* is (or isn't) suitable for him to believe.[17]

Since we have given an account of *ex post* justifiedness, it will suffice if we can analyze *ex ante* justifiedness in terms of it. Such an analysis, I believe, is ready at hand. *S* is *ex ante* justified in believing *p* at *t* just in case his total cognitive state at *t* is such that from that state he could come to believe *p* in such a way that this belief would be *ex post* justified. More precisely, he is *ex ante* justified in believing *p* at *t* just in case a reliable belief-forming operation is available to him such that the application of that operation to his total cognitive state at *t* would result, more or less immediately, in his believing *p* and this belief would be *ex post* justified. Stated formally, we have the following:

(11) Person *S* is *ex ante* justified in believing *p* at *t* if and only if there is a reliable belief-forming operation available to *S* which is such

that if *S* applied that operation to this total cognitive state at *t*, *S* would believe *p* at *t*-plus-delta (for a suitably small delta) and that belief would be *ex post* justified.

For the analysans of (11) to be satisfied, the total cognitive state at *t* must have a suitable causal ancestry. Hence, (11) is implicitly an Historical account of *ex ante* justifiedness.

As indicated, the bulk of this essay was addressed to *ex post* justifiedness. This is the appropriate analysandum if one is interested in the connection between justifiedness and knowledge, since what is crucial to whether a person *knows* a proposition is whether he has an actual *belief* in the proposition that is justified. However, since many epistemologists are interested in *ex ante* justifiedness, it is proper for a general theory of justification to try to provide an account of that concept as well. Our theory does this quite naturally, for the account of *ex ante* justifiedness falls out directly from our account of *ex post* justifiedness.[18]

Notes

1. "A Causal Theory of Knowing"; "Innate Knowledge," in S. P. Stich, ed., *Innate Ideas* (Berkeley: University of California Press, 1975); and "Discrimination and Perceptual Knowledge."

2. Notice that the choice of a recursive format does not prejudice the case for or against any particular theory. A recursive format is perfectly general. Specifically, an explicit set of necessary and sufficient conditions is just a special case of a recursive format, i.e., one in which there is no recursive clause.

3. Many of the attempts I shall consider are suggested by material in William P. Alston, "Varieties of Privileged Access."

4. Such a definition (though without the modal term) is given, for example, by W. V. Quine and J. S. Ullian in *The Web of Belief*, p. 21. Statements are said to be self-evident just in case "to understand them is to believe them."

5. Page 22.

6. I assume, of course, that "nomologically necessary" is *de re* with respect to "*S*" and "*t*" in this construction. I shall not focus on problems that may arise in this regard, since my primary concerns are with different issues.

7. This assumption violates the thesis that Davidson calls "The Anomalism of the Mental." Cf. "Mental Events" in L. Foster and J. W. Swanson, eds., *Experience and Theory* (Amherst: University of Massachusetts Press, 1970). But it is unclear that this thesis is a necessary truth. Thus, it seems fair to assume its falsity in order to produce a counterexample. The example neither entails nor precludes the mental–physical identity theory.

8. Keith Lehrer's example of the gypsy lawyer is intended to show the inappropriateness of a causal requirement. (See *Knowledge*, pp. 124–25.) But I find this example unconvincing. To the extent that I clearly imagine that the lawyer fixes his belief solely as a result of the cards, it seems intuitively wrong to say that he *knows*—or has a *justified belief*—that his client is innocent.

9. This definition is not exactly what we need for the purposes at hand. As

Ernest Sosa points out, introspection will turn out to be a belief-dependent process, since sometimes the input into the process will be a belief (when the introspected content is a belief). Intuitively, however, introspection is not the sort of process which may be merely conditionally reliable. I do not know how to refine the definition so as to avoid this difficulty, but it is a small and isolated point.

10. It may be objected that principles (6_A) and (6_B) are jointly open to analogues of the lottery paradox. A series of processes composed of reliable but less-than-perfectly-reliable processes may be extremely unreliable. Yet applications of (6_A) and (6_B) would confer justifiedness on a belief that is caused by such a series. In reply to this objection, we might simply indicate that the theory is intended to capture our ordinary notion of justifiedness, and this ordinary notion has been formed without recognition of this kind of problem. The theory is not wrong *as* a theory of the ordinary (naive) conception of justifiedness. On the other hand, if we want a theory to do more than capture the ordinary conception of justifiedness, it might be possible to strengthen the principles to avoid lottery-paradox analogues.

11. I am indebted to Mark Pastin for this point.

12. Cf. *Theory of Knowledge*, 2nd ed., pp. 17, 114–16.

13. Cf. "A Causal Theory of Knowing." The reliability aspect of my theory also has its precursors in earlier papers of mine on knowing: "Innate Knowledge" and "Discrimination and Perceptual Knowledge."

14. The view that introspection is retrospection was taken by Ryle, and before him (as Charles Hartshorne points out to me) by Hobbes, Whitehead, and possibly Husserl.

15. Of course, if people in world *W* learn *inductively* that wishful thinking is reliable, and regularly base their beliefs on this inductive inference, it is quite unproblematic and straightforward that their beliefs are justified. The only interesting case is where their beliefs are formed *purely* by wishful thinking, without using inductive inference. The suggestion contemplated in this paragraph of the text is that, in the world imagined, even pure wishful thinking would confer justifiedness.

16. I am indebted here to Mark Kaplan.

17. The distinction between *ex post* and *ex ante* justifiedness is similar to Roderick Firth's distinction between *doxastic* and *propositional* warrant. See his "Are Epistemic Concepts Reducible to Ethical Concepts?" in Alvin I. Goldman and Jaegwon Kim, eds., *Values and Morals, Essays in Honor of William Frankena, Charles Stevenson, and Richard Brandt* (Dordrecht: D. Reidel, 1978).

18. Research on this essay was begun while the author was a fellow of the John Simon Guggenheim Memorial Foundation and of the Center for Advanced Study in the Behavioral Sciences. I am grateful for their support. I have received helpful comments and criticism from Holly S. Goldman, Mark Kaplan, Fred Schmitt, Stephen P. Stich, and many others at several universities where earlier drafts of the paper were read.

8   Reliability and Justified Belief

JOHN L. POLLOCK

The central problem of epistemology is to give an account of when beliefs are justified. Traditional epistemological theories are "internalist" in the sense that they make justification entirely a matter of what beliefs one has and what sensory states, mnemonic states, etc., one is in. But there is a currently popular move in epistemology to import "external" considerations of reliability into matters of justification. The feeling is that if a particular belief-forming mechanism is to issue in justified belief, then "surely it must be reliable." Thus it is proposed that reliability is either a necessary condition, or a sufficient condition, or both, for justified belief.[1]

It cannot be denied that the reliabilist view has a certain amount of intuitive support. This can be illustrated by considering some rather common objections to my own internalist view. My view is that epistemic justification proceeds in terms of reasons, some prima facie and some conclusive, and that the reasons associated with a particular concept are constitutive of that concept. Those reasons cannot be derived from anything more basic. In particular, they cannot be derived from truth conditions. Concepts do not generally have informative truth conditions. Instead, an informative characterization of a concept must often proceed in terms of its "justification conditions."[2] Against this, the reliabilist protests that justification conditions cannot be basic, because if they were then there would be no reason to regard justified beliefs as probably true. The implication is that justification conditions must be derived from truth conditions together with facts about the circumstances under which it is probable that beliefs will be true. This is a very common view, but in my estimation it is completely mistaken.

The simplest and most intuitive objection to reliabilism is that justification is a normative notion and this precludes reliability from playing any direct role in justification. Reliability cannot be a necessary condition for justification, because a person can have every reason to think that his beliefs are reliable when in fact they are not. Consider the venerable brain in a vat: suppose a person is kidnapped in his sleep and his brain is

Reprinted from the *Canadian Journal of Philosophy* 14 (1984): 103–14, by permission of the author and the editor. Copyright 1984, *Canadian Journal of Philosophy*.

removed from his body and placed in a vat where it is stimulated artificially. If the artificial stimulation is done skillfully enough so that there is no apparent incoherence in his experience, surely when the victim awakes he is justified in beliefs he has about the normality of his immediate surroundings, although such beliefs are totally unreliable. The reason he is justified is, roughly, that he could not be expected to know better. He satisfies the normative requirements of justification, and that is good enough.

We can also appeal to the normative character of justification to argue that reliability is not a sufficient condition for justification, although here the argument is somewhat less compelling. Roderick Firth recounts the D. H. Lawrence story of the boy who is able to predict the winners of horse races by riding his rocking horse.[3] Eventually, of course, the boy may acquire inductive evidence for believing that his predictions are reliable, and that will give him a straightforward internalist reason for believing his own predictions. But even before he reaches that stage, we are pulled in the direction of saying he knows the winner. This is because his predictions are reliable. Nevertheless, even those who urge that the boy knows which horse will win are inclined to say that he knows this without having justified belief. His belief is not justified because he has *no right to believe his own prediction*. This is again a reflection of the normative character of justification.[4]

I feel that the appeal to the normative character of justification constitutes a decisive objection to reliabilism, but the dedicated reliabilist is not apt to be moved by it. So let us turn to some objections of a more formal nature which I think must be deemed conclusive. I will argue that there is no way to construct an intelligible notion of reliability which does the job required by the reliabilist. The reliabilist has been tripped up by misconceptions about probability.

Reliability is a probabilistic notion. To say that one's belief in a proposition is reliable (in the present circumstances) is to say, roughly, that given the way one acquired the belief, it is probable that it is true. Without further elaboration, we can already see that reliability cannot, in general, be either a necessary or a sufficient condition for justification. This turns upon the lottery paradox together with consideration of the role of reasoning in justification. If we consider a lottery consisting of one million tickets each with an equal chance of being drawn, and Louie the Loser believes of each ticket that it will not be drawn, then it seems that each of his beliefs is probably true. The reliabilist would have us conclude from this that each of Louie's beliefs is justified. But that cannot be right. If each of a set of beliefs is justified for a person, and he correctly reasons from them to a conclusion, then either the conclusion becomes justified for him as well, or else some of his initial beliefs become unjustified. Louie could reason from the beliefs regarding the individual tickets to the conclusion that no ticket will be drawn. Presumably we will all agree that he would not be justified in believing that conclusion on this basis. It follows that, at least after he has gone through this reasoning, Louie is not justified in believing of each ticket that it will not be drawn. But his having gone through the reasoning in no way affects the probability of those beliefs being true, and so does not affect questions of reliability. His beliefs are still reliable, but they are not justified.[5] Consequently, reliability cannot be a sufficient condition for justification. To demand that it is would be to deny the essential role of reasoning in justified belief.[6]

A related argument establishes that reliability cannot be a necessary condition for justification either. We often become justified in believing a conclusion by reasoning to it from other beliefs we are already justified in holding. But from the fact that our premises are reliable, it does not follow that our conclusion is reliable. In general, by conjoining a number of beliefs which are both justified and reliable, we can arrive at a conclusion which is justified but as improbable and hence unreliable as we desire. This is a simple consequence of the probability calculus, which tells us that if the conjuncts of a conjunction are independent of one another, then the probability of the conjunction is less than the probability of either conjunct. Consequently, reliability cannot be a necessary condition for justified belief.

The fact that reliability is neither necessary nor sufficient for justified belief is an inevitable consequence of the role that reasoning plays in justification. It does not show that reliabilism is thoroughly mistaken, however. The reliabilist can avoid this difficulty by restricting his theory. We can distinguish between *discursive beliefs,* which are those held as a result of reasoning, and *non-discursive beliefs,* which are the result of belief-forming mechanisms like perception, memory, etc. Although reliability can be neither a necessary nor a sufficient condition for justified belief in general, it is somewhat more plausible to suppose that it is either a necessary or a sufficient condition for non-discursive belief to be justified. The lottery argument employed above can be generalized to show that reliability is not a sufficient condition for justification even in the case of non-discursive beliefs. If a person finds himself reasoning from a set of reliable non-discursive beliefs to a conclusion he knows to be false, he cannot justifiably continue to hold all of the non-discursive beliefs despite their being reliable. But the more serious question is whether reliability might be a *necessary* condition for justification in the case of non-discursive belief. In order to resolve this we must consider more carefully just what is meant by talk of the reliability of a belief.

Reliability is a probabilistic notion, so we must begin by talking about probability. There is an important distinction to be made between *definite* and *indefinite* probability. A definite probability is the probability that a particular proposition is true. For example, we can talk about the probability that Jones will die of heart disease. Definite probabilities are "single-case" probabilities. Indefinite probability, on the other hand, is the probability of an unspecified object of one sort being also of another sort. For example, we can talk about the probability of a smoker dying of heart disease. The latter is not about any particular smoker, but about smokers in general. In symbolizing probabilities, we write definite probabilities in the form "prob(P)" where P is a closed formula (i.e., contains no free variables). We write indefinite probabilities in the form "prob(Ax/Bx)," making essential use of free variables. Indefinite probabilities have been regarded variously as relating classes, properties, predicates, etc.

Different theories of probability take differing attitudes toward definite and indefinite probabilities. Subjectivist or personal theories take definite probabilities to be basic, and if they talk about them at all they attempt to somehow reduce indefinite probabilities to definite probabilities.[7] On the other hand, objective theories of probability take indefinite probabilities to be basic, either identifying them with or somehow basing them upon relative frequencies, and then infer definite probabilities from indefinite probabilities by what is called "direct inference."

Analogous to the distinction between definite and indefinite probabilities, we can draw a distinction between what I will call *general reliability* and *single-case reliability*. General reliability attaches to belief-forming mechanisms like perception, memory, etc. The general reliability of a mechanism M under circumstances of type C is just the indefinite probability of a belief formed by M under circumstances of type C being true. For example, we can say that the general reliability of color vision under conditions of good light is high because the probability of a person being right about the color of something he sees under those conditions is high. On the other hand, single-case reliability attaches to particular beliefs. The single-case reliability of a particular belief is the definite probability that it is true. I regard the notion of general reliability as unproblematic, but for reasons that will emerge below, it is extremely difficult to make sense of a notion of single-case reliability that has any particular bearing on epistemology.

The reliabilist alleges that reliability is a necessary condition for justified non-discursive belief. But the reliability of what? It might first be proposed that what is required is the general reliability of one's belief-forming mechanism (without reference to the current circumstances). In other words, for a non-discursive belief formed by a particular mechanism to be justified, it might be required that the indefinite probability of a belief formed by that mechanism being true is high. But now, suppose we have a belief-forming mechanism that is reliable under some circumstances and unreliable under others, with the circumstances in which it is unreliable being the more common. Then the mechanism is generally unreliable. For example, consider color vision on a planet where the light is generally quite dim. Color vision will then be unreliable in general, but still reliable in those relatively rare circumstances in which the light is good. The residents of this planet may be aware of all this, and distrust their color vision except when the light is good. Then what are we to say about the justification of their beliefs based upon color vision in good lighting? Surely the reliabilist will not insist that they are automatically unjustified because color vision is generally unreliable.

This example can be viewed as raising the question of what counts as a belief-forming mechanism. Perhaps we should say that the residents of our dark world are employing the mechanism of color-vision-in-good-light rather than just color vision, and that the former is generally reliable. Equivalently, the reliabilist can reformulate his requirement as demanding that justified non-discursive beliefs be based upon belief-forming mechanisms that are generally reliable under the present circumstances rather than generally reliable simpliciter. But now there is a problem concerning what counts as "reliability under the present circumstances." Perhaps we should require that the believer be in circumstances of some type C such that his belief-forming mechanism is generally reliable in circumstances of type C. But what if the believer is also in narrower circumstances of type C* such that the belief-forming mechanism is unreliable in circumstances of type C*? Presumably, the reliabilist would want that to preclude justification. The present circumstances can be specified more and more narrowly without limit, so it appears that the reliabilist should formulate his theory as follows:

(R1) S's non-discursive belief in P is justified only if it is based upon a belief-forming mechanism M which is such that:
(1) the present circumstances are of some type C in which M is generally reliable; and
(2) if the present circumstances are of some type C* which is narrower than C then M is also generally reliable under circumstances of type C*.

(R1) cannot possibly be correct. It implies that a non-discursive belief is justified only if it is true. This is because one feature of the present circumstances is a characterization of the belief as a belief in P, and another feature is the truth value of P. If P is false, then clause (2) requires that the probability is high of a belief being true given that it is produced by M under circumstances of type C *and is a belief in P and P is false*. But in fact, by the probability calculus, that probability is zero, and so clause (2) is not satisfied. The conclusion that justified beliefs must be true is totally unacceptable. For example, we often excuse a person on the grounds that he was justified in believing that the consequences of his behavior would be other than they were.

There seems to be no way to avoid the preceding problem if we attempt to base a reliabilist theory on general reliability. If a reliabilist theory is to be defensible, it must be based upon single-case reliability. Then the requirement will be:

(R2) S's non-discursive belief in P is justified only if it is reliable.

Recall that a belief is reliable iff the definite probability that it is true is high. In evaluating (R2) we must consider what kind of definite probability we are talking about. Different theories of probability lead to different kinds of definite probabilities. Objective theories insist that definite probabilities be derived from indefinite probabilities by some kind of "direct inference." Although theories of direct inference are problematic, the use of some kind of direct inference is both common and intuitive.[8] For example, knowing that the probability of a red-haired male in Arizona getting skin cancer is .4, we may infer (prima facie) that the probability of Robert (who is a red-haired male living in Arizona) getting skin cancer is .4. The kind of definite probability at which we arrive by such direct inference is inherently epistemic. We are attempting to ascertain the probability of a person of Robert's description getting skin cancer, where in that description we include everything we are justified in believing about Robert.[9] Accordingly, the definite probability of Robert's getting skin cancer is conditional upon everything we are justified in believing about Robert. But *everything* we are justified in believing can be regarded as being about Robert and hence relevant to this probability.[10] Thus the definite probabilities at which we arrive by direct inference are conditional on the set of all our justified beliefs. This makes (R2) true but trivially so. If S is justified in believing P, then P is entailed by the set of S's justified beliefs, and hence the probability of P on the set of S's justified beliefs is 1. This robs (R2) of the content it is supposed to have. (R2) is supposed to impose some substantive constraint on justified belief.

If (R2) is to have any content, it must appeal to some kind of definite probability other than the epistemic variety at which we arrive by direct inference. The only obvious way to construct an objective non-epistemic kind of definite probability is to make it conditional upon everything that is true, rather than upon justified belief.[11] But this kind of probability is trivial. It is always either zero or one, because the probability of P will always be evaluated relative to a class of propositions containing either P or its negation. This is just a variation on the previously noted difficulty regarding general reliability.

I do not believe that there is any way to interpret single-case reliability in terms of objective probability which makes (R2) reasonable. The difficulty is that there is no suitable kind of objective definite probability. This leads naturally to the consideration of subjective probability. Can we defend (R2) by interpreting single-case reliability in terms of subjective probability? Subjective probability is supposed to be a measure of either degree of belief or degree of rational belief. A person's degree of belief in a proposition P is defined to be the greatest number r (or the least upper bound of these numbers) such that the person would accept a bet on the truth of P at odds of r to $1-r$. A few subjectivists identify S's subjective probability for P with S's degree of belief in P. Most do not, however, because it is recognized that the degrees of belief of actual people do not conform to the probability calculus, i.e., they are "incoherent." It is alleged that insofar as a person's degrees of belief do not conform to the probability calculus, that person is irrational. Most subjectivists then go on to identify S's subjective probability for P with the degree of belief S *rationally ought to have* in P, rather than the degree of belief he actually has.

Subjective probability is very popular among philosophers. I suspect that this is due less to its intrinsic merit than to the fact that it looks good in comparison to most theories of objective probability. Unless they simply identify probabilities with relative frequencies, advocates of objective probability have encountered enormous problems in trying to tell us how to ascertain the values of objective probabilities. This is where subjective probability has seemed to shine. It tells us exactly how to measure probabilities—in terms of betting quotients. I think that for this reason more than any other, subjectivism has gained great popularity. Unfortunately, this apparent advantage of subjective probability over objective probability is chimerical. This claim to virtue ignores the distinction between actual degrees of belief and rational degrees of belief. It is true that we can measure actual degrees of belief in terms of betting quotients, but actual degrees of belief do not satisfy the probability calculus. This is why most subjectivists insist that they are talking about rational degrees of belief. Unfortunately, they have given us no recipe for computing the degrees of belief people ought to have on the basis of the degrees of belief they actually have. Given a person's incoherent actual degrees of belief, there are infinitely many different ways to make them coherent. Which way is the right way? Without some answer to this question, subjective probability as rational degree of belief is incalculable, and subjective probability is no better off than objective probability. In fact, I think there is reason to doubt that the notion of *the* rational degree of belief a person ought to have in a proposition makes sense. Numerous philosophers have objected to the claim that incoherent degrees of belief are irrational, but even if we grant that they are, is there any reason to suppose that there is a unique way they ought to be altered to make them rational? I see no reason to think so.

Subjective probability is a very weak foundation to base a theory upon. It is doubtful that there is any such thing as subjective probability in the sense of *the* rational degree of belief in a proposition. Grasping at straws, the reliabilist might try instead to base (R2) on actual degree of belief, foregoing coherence. On this proposal, S's belief in P is reliable iff the degree of belief in P is high. But whose degree of belief—S's, or the speaker's? We might try each proposal. First:

(R2.1) S's non-discursive belief in P is justified only if *I* have a high degree of belief in P.

(R2.1) is absurd quite apart from the fact that it would make assessments of justification systematically ambiguous. It is absurd because it would make it impossible for us to grant that a person is justified in believing something which we, from our loftier perspective, know to be false. The other possibility is:

(R2.2) S's non-discursive belief in P is justified only if S has a high degree of belief in P.

This is equally indefensible. People do not always behave rationally, and one form their irrationality can take is failing to believe what they have good reason to believe. More moderately, they may believe something only very tentatively and with reluctance, when in fact they have the best of reasons for believing it. But that is precisely what (R2.2) denies.

There is no way to build a reliabilist theory on subjective probability. Even if good sense could be made of subjective probability, it cannot capture what the reliabilist is trying to get at. Reliability is supposed to be something objective, something about how good a person is at getting things right, and not just a matter of how strongly he believes things. As such, it must be concluded that no sense can be made of single-case reliability. Reliability is at base a general notion. Repeatable processes are reliable—individual beliefs are not. This brings us back to general reliability. There is no way to make general reliability a necessary condition for justified beliefs. The best we can do is (R1), and (R1) is false. Why then is there this persistent intuition that reliability is somehow tied up with justification?

I think that there is an important connection between justification and reliability. Reliability can be neither a necessary nor a sufficient condition for justification, but it is involved in a more complex way. Justification is a matter of having good reasons for beliefs. There are two kinds of reasons—conclusive reasons and prima facie reasons. Prima facie reasons are defeasible. There are two kinds of defeaters for prima facie reasons. The simplest are *rebutting defeaters*. If P is a prima facie reason for believing Q, a rebutting defeater is any reason for believing ~Q. Rebutting defeaters are familiar. Everyone who has talked about prima facie reasons has recognized the existence of rebutting defeaters. But rebutting defeaters are not enough. There must be *undercutting defeaters*. Undercutting defeaters attack the connection between P and Q rather than attacking Q itself. For example, "*x* looks red to me" gives me a prima facie reason to believe that x is red. If Jones tells me that, despite appearance, x is green, that is a rebutting defeater for my prima facie reason. But if instead I discover that there are red lights shining on x and the red lights can make something look red when it isn't, this is also a defeater but not a rebutting defeater. This is an undercutting defeater. In general, an undercutting defeater is any reason for denying that P wouldn't be true unless Q were true.[12]

Considerations of reliability enter epistemology in the guise of undercutting defeaters. For example, one undercutting defeater for "x looks red to me" as a prima facie reason for "x is red" consists of discovering that I am in circumstances of type C and that in circumstances of type C, an object's looking red is not a reliable indication that it is red. To generalize this, note that prima facie reasons come in *reason schemes* rather than piecemeal. That is, not only is "x looks red to me" a prima facie reason for "x is red," but also "y looks red to me" is a prima facie reason for "y is red," and so on. In general, a reason scheme has the form:

(RS)   For any x, $P(x)$ is a prima facie reason for $Q(x)$.

(RD)   I am in circumstances of type C, and something's being P in circumstances of type C is not a reliable indication that it is Q.

As with any defeater, (RD)'s merely being true is not sufficient to defeat an instance of (RS). What is required is that I either do or should believe (RD).

In discussing reliabilism, we were led to formulate (R1). In doing so, we had to make (R1) accommodate the intuition that reliability (or unreliability) in circumstances of type C should not count for anything if our belief-forming mechanism is unreliable (or reliable) in circumstances of a narrower type. But in (R1), that had the surprising and unacceptable consequence that you can never be justified in holding a false nondiscursive belief. That was the downfall of reliabilism. The general intuition which (R1) failed to capture can be accommodated much more naturally in terms of defeaters. What it amounts to is the observation that (RD) is a defeasible defeater. Discovering:

(RDD)   I am in circumstances of type C* narrower than C, and something's being P in circumstances of type C* is a reliable indication that it is Q.

defeats the defeater and reinstates the original reason. In this way, we accommodate the intuition that appeal to narrower circumstances takes precedence over appeal to broader circumstances, while avoiding the absurd consequences of (R1).

In my opinion, reliability defeaters are the source of the persistent intuition that reasons must be reliable in order to confer justification. As we have seen, there is no way to make reliability a necessary condition for justification. Instead, lack of reliability is a defeater. If we have no reason to suspect that our reasons are unreliable, then we are justified in basing beliefs upon them; but if we acquire reason for thinking that our reasons are unreliable, that defeats our reasoning and prevents our reasons from conferring justification. That is the sense in which reasons must be reliable in order to confer justification. There is no way for there to be any tighter connection between justification and reliability.[13]

Notes

1. Theories of this general sort are proposed by Laurence Bonjour, "External-ist Theories of Empirical Knowledge"; Alvin Goldman, "What Is Justified Belief?" and "The Internalist Conception of Justification"; Wilfrid Sellars, "Giv-enness and Explanatory Coherence," and "More on Givenness and Explanatory Coherence"; Marshall Swain "Justification and the Basis of Belief," and "Justifi-cation and Reliable Belief."
2. This theory is defended at length in *Knowledge and Justification*.
3. I have been unable to trace the source of this example, although I have repeatedly heard it attributed to Firth. Apparently Firth takes this to be an example of knowledge without justification.
4. My own inclination is to deny in addition that the boy has propositional knowledge. He does know who the winner will be, but only in the sense of knowing *how* to pick the winner. In the same sense a bicycle rider may know *what* to do in order to keep from falling over, but not be able to write a treatise on bicycle riding. This is practical knowledge rather than theoretical knowledge.
5. My own view is that they were not justified in the first place, but we need not press that point here.
6. There are philosophers who do deny that role, most notably Henry Kyburg.
7. See Robert Pargetter and Frank Jackson, "Indefinite Probability State-ments," *Synthese* 26 (1973): 205–17; and Brian Skyrms, *Causal Necessity* (New Haven, CT: Yale University Press, 1980).
8. I have attempted to construct a satisfactory theory of direct inference in "A Theory of Direct Inference," *Theory and Decision* 15 (1983): 29–96.
9. For a more precise account of the epistemic nature of these definite probabilities, see my "A Theory of Direct Inference."
10. Formally, if P is about Robert and Q is any other proposition, then (P&Q) is also about Robert.
11. This seems to be what is suggested by Reichenbach and Salmon when they talk about objectively homogeneous reference classes.
12. The principal defense of my view of epistemic justification is to be found in *Knowledge and Justification,* but see also "A Plethora of Epistemological Theo-ries" (in *Justification and Knowledge*) for some recent refinements. In my earlier publications I called rebutting defeaters "Type 1 defeaters" and undercutting defeaters "Type II defeaters." Despite my repeatedly pointing out the need for undercutting defeaters, they have been almost universally overlooked by episte-mologists. For example, in "A Version of Foundationalism" (in *Midwest Studies in Philosophy* 5 [1980]: 543–64), Chisholm adumbrates a theory which is similar to mine in many respects, but which lacks undercutting defeaters.
13. I am indebted to Stewart Cohen for helpful discussions on this topic.

9

A Contextualist Theory of Epistemic Justification

DAVID B. ANNIS

I. Foundationalism, Coherentism, and Contextualism

Foundationalism is the theory that every empirical statement which is justified ultimately must derive at least some of its justification from a special class of basic statements which have at least some degree of justification independent of the support such statements may derive from other statements. Such *minimal* foundationalism does not require certainty or incorrigibility; it does not deny the revisability of *all* statements, and it allows an important role for intrasystematic justification or coherence.[1] The main objections to foundationalism have been (a) the denial of the existence of basic statements and (b) the claim that even if such statements were not mythical, such an impoverished basis would never justify all the various statements we normally take to be justified.

Opposed to foundationalism has been the coherence theory of justification. According to coherentism a statement is justified if and only if it coheres with a certain kind of system of statements. Although there has been disagreement among coherentists in explaining what coherence is and specifying the special system of statements, the key elements in these explanations have been consistency, connectedness, and comprehensiveness. The chief objection to the theory has been that coherence within a consistent and comprehensive set of statements is not sufficient for justification.[2] Theorists of epistemic justification have tended to stress foundationalism and coherentism and in general have overlooked or ignored a third kind of theory, namely, *contextualism*. The contextualist denies that there are basic statements in the foundationalist's sense and that coherence is sufficient for justification. According to contextualism both theories overlook contextual parameters essential to justification. In what follows I develop a version of a contextualist theory.[3]

Reprinted from the *American Philosophical Quarterly* 15 (1978): 213–19, by permission of the author and the editor. Copyright 1978, *American Philosophical Quarterly*.

II. The Basic Model—Meeting Objections

The basic model of justification to be developed here is that of a person's being able to meet certain objections. The objections one must meet and whether or not they are met are relative to certain goals. Since the issue is that of epistemic justification, the goals are epistemic in nature. With respect to one epistemic goal, accepting some statement may be reasonable, whereas relative to a different goal it may not be. Two of our epistemic goals are having true beliefs and avoiding having false beliefs. Other epistemic goals such as simplicity, conservation of existing beliefs, and maximization of explanatory power will be assumed to be subsidiary to the goals of truth and the avoidance of error.[4]

Given these goals, if a person S claims that some statement h is true, we may object (A) that S is not in a position to know that h or (B) that h is false. Consider (A). Suppose we ask S how he knows that h and he responds by giving us various reasons $e_1, e_2, \ldots, e_n$ for the truth of h. We may object that one of his reasons e_1-e_n is false, e_1-e_n does not provide adequate support for h, S's specific reasoning from e_1-e_n to h is fallacious, or that there is evidence i such that the conjunction of e_1-e_n and i does not provide adequate support for h. These objections may be raised to his reasons for e_1-e_n as well as to his responses to our objections.

There are also cases where a person is not required to give reasons for his claim that h is true. If S claims to see a brown book across the room, we usually do not require reasons. But we may still object that the person is not in a position to know by arguing, for example, that the person is not reliable in such situations. So even in cases where we do not in general require reasons, objections falling into categories (A) or (B) can be raised.

But it would be too strong a condition to require a person to be able to meet all *possible* objections falling into these categories. In some distant time new evidence may be discovered as the result of advances in our scientific knowledge which would call into question the truth of some statement h. Even though we do not in fact have that evidence now, it is logically possible that we have it, so it is a possible objection to h now. If the person had to meet the objection, he would have to be in a different and better epistemic position than the one he is presently in, that is, he would have to have new evidence in order to respond to the objection. The objectors also would have to be in a better position to raise the objection. But the objections to be raised and answered should not require the participants to be in a new epistemic position. What is being asked is whether the person in his present position is justified in believing h. Thus the person only has to answer *current* objections, that is, objections based on the current evidence available.

Merely uttering a question that falls into one of our categories does not make it an objection S must answer. To demand a response the objection must be an expression of a *real* doubt. According to Peirce, doubt is an uneasy and dissatisfied state from which we struggle to free ourselves. Such doubt is the result of "some surprising phenomenon, some experience which either disappoints an expectation, or breaks in upon some habit of expectation."[5] As Dewey puts it, it is only when "jars, hitches, breaks, blocks, . . . incidents occasioning an interruption of the smooth straight forward course of behavior" occur that doubt arises.[6] Thus for *S* to be held accountable for answering an objection, it must be a manifestation of a real doubt where the doubt is occasioned by a real life situation. Assuming that the subjective probabilities a person assigns reflect the person's actual epistemic attitudes and that these are the product of his confrontation with the world, the above point may be expressed as follows. *S* is not required to respond to an objection if *in general* it would be assigned a low probability by the people questioning *S*.

If an objection must be the expression of a real doubt caused by the jars of a real life situation, then such objections will be primarily *local* as opposed to *global*. Global objections call into question the totality of beliefs held at a certain time or a whole realm of beliefs, whereas local objections call into question a specific belief. This is not to say that a real situation might not occur that would prompt a global objection. If having experienced the nuclear radiation of a third world war, there were a sudden and dramatic increase in the error rate of perceptual beliefs of the visual sort, we would be more hesitant about them as a class.

It must be assumed that the objecting audience has the epistemic goals of truth and the avoidance of error. If they were not critical truth seekers, they would not raise appropriate objections. To meet an objection *i*, *S* must respond in such a way as to produce within the objecting group a general but not necessarily universal rejection of *i* or at least the general recognition of the diminished status of *i* as an objection. In the latter case *S* may, for example, point out that although *i* might be true, it only decreases the support of e_i (one of his reasons for believing *h*) a very small amount, and hence he is still justified in believing *h*. There are of course many ways in which *S* can handle an objection. He might indicate that it is not of the type (A) or (B) and so is not relevant. He may respond that it is just an *idle* remark not prompted by real doubt; that is, there is no reason for thinking that it is true. He may ask the objector for his reasons, and he can raise any of the objections of the type (A) or (B) in response. Again the give and take is based on real objections and responses.

III. The Social Nature of Justification

When asking whether *S* is justified in believing *h*, this has to be considered relative to an *issue-context*. Suppose we are interested in whether Jones, an ordinary non-medically trained person, has the general information that polio is caused by a virus. If his response to our question is that he remembers the paper reporting that Salk said it was, then this is good enough. He has performed adequately given the issue-context. But suppose the context is an examination for the M.D. degree. Here we expect a lot more. If the candidate simply said what Jones did, we would take him as being very deficient in knowledge. Thus relative to one issue-context a person may be justified in believing h but not justified relative to another context.

The issue-context is what specific issue involving h is being raised. It determines the level of understanding and knowledge that S must exhibit, and it determines an appropriate objector-group. For example in the context of the examination for the M.D. degree, the appropriate group is not the class of ordinary non-medically trained people, but qualified medical examiners.

The importance (value or utility) attached to the outcome of accepting h when it is false or rejecting h when it is true is a component of the issue-context. Suppose the issue is whether a certain drug will help cure a disease in humans without harmful effects. In such a situation we are much more demanding than if the question were whether it would help in the case of animals. In both cases the appropriate objector-group would be the same, namely, qualified researchers. But they would require quite a bit more proof in the former case. Researchers do in fact strengthen or weaken the justificatory conditions in relation to the importance of the issue. If accepting h when h is false would have critical consequences, the researcher may increase the required significance level in testing h.

Man is a social animal, and yet when it comes to the justification of beliefs philosophers tend to ignore this fact. But this is one contextual parameter that no adequate theory of justification can overlook. According to the contextualist model of justification sketched above, when asking whether some person S is justified in believing h, we must consider this relative to some specific issue-context which determines the level of understanding and knowledge required. This in turn determines the appropriate objector-group. For S to be justified in believing h relative to the issue-context, S must be able to meet all current objections falling into (A) and (B) which express a real doubt of the qualified objector-group where the objectors are critical truth seekers. Thus social information—the beliefs, information, and theories of others—plays an important part in justification, for it in part determines what objections will be raised, how a person will respond to them, and what responses the objectors will accept.

Perhaps the most neglected component in justification theory is the *actual* social practices and norms of justification of a culture or community of people. Philosophers have looked for universal and a priori principles of justification. But consider this in the context of scientific inquiry. There certainly has been refinement in the methods and techniques of discovery and testing in science. Suppose that at a time *t* in accordance with the best methods then developed for discovery and testing in a scientific domain by critical truth seekers, *S* accepts theory *T*. It is absurd to say that *S* is not justified in accepting *T* since at a later time a refinement of those techniques would lead to the acceptance of a different theory. Thus relative to the standards at *t*, *S* is justified in accepting *T*.

The same conclusion follows if we consider a case involving two different groups existing at the same time instead of two different times as in the above example. Suppose *S* is an Earth physicist and accepts *T* on the basis of the best methods developed by Earth physicists at *t*. Unknown to us the more advanced physicists on Twin Earth reject *T*. *S* is still justified in accepting *T*.

To determine whether *S* is justified in believing *h* we must consider the actual standards of justification of the community of people to which he belongs. More specifically we determine whether *S* is justified in believing *h* by specifying an issue-context raised within a community of people *G* with certain social practices and norms of justification. This determines the level of understanding and knowledge *S* is expected to have and the standards he is to satisfy. The appropriate objector-group is a subset of *G*. To be justified in believing *h*, *S* must be able to meet their objections in a way that satisfies their practices and norms.

It follows that justification theory must be *naturalized*. In considering the justification of beliefs we cannot neglect the actual social practices and norms of justification of a group. Psychologists, sociologists, and anthropologists have started this study, but much more work is necessary.[7]

The need to naturalize justification theory has been recognized in recent philosophy of science. Positivists stressed the *logic* of science—the structure of theories, confirmation, explanation—in abstraction from science as actually carried on. But much of the main thrust of recent philosophy of science is that such an approach is inadequate. Science as *practiced* yields justified beliefs about the world. Thus the study of the actual practices, which have changed through time, cannot be neglected. The present tenor in the philosophy of science is thus toward a historical and methodological realism.[8]

From the fact that justification is relative to the social practices and norms of a group, it does not follow that they cannot be criticized nor that justification is somehow subjective. The practices and norms are epistemic and hence have as their goals truth and the avoidance of error. Insofar as they fail to achieve these goals they can be criticized. For example the Kpelle people of Africa rely more on the authority of the elders than we do. But this authority could be questioned if they found it led to too many false perceptual beliefs. An objection to a practice must of course be real; that is, the doubt must be the result of some jar or hitch in our experience of the world. Furthermore such objections will always be local as opposed to global. Some practice or norm and our experiences of the world yield the result that another practice is problematic. A real objection presupposes some other accepted practice. This however does not commit us to some form of subjectivism. Just as there is no theory-neutral observation language in science, so there is no standard-neutral epistemic position that one can adopt. But in neither case does it follow that objectivity and rational criticism are lost.[9]

IV. The Regress Argument

Philosophers who have accepted foundationalism have generally offered a version of the infinite regress argument in support of it. Two key premises in the argument are the denial of a coherence theory of justification and the denial that an infinite sequence of reasons is sufficient to justify a belief. But there is another option to the conclusion of the argument besides foundationalism. A contextualist theory of the sort offered above stops the regress and yet does not require basic statements in the foundationalist's sense.

Suppose that the Joneses are looking for a red chair to replace a broken one in their house. The issue-context is thus not whether they can discern subtle shades of color. Nor is it an examination in physics where the person is expected to have detailed knowledge of the transmission of light and color perception. Furthermore nothing of great importance hinges on a correct identification. Mr. Jones, who has the necessary perceptual concepts and normal vision, points at a red chair a few feet in front of him and says "here is a red one." The appropriate objector-group consists of normal perceivers who have general knowledge about the standard conditions of perception and perceptual error. In such situations which we are all familiar with, generally, there will be no objections. His claim is accepted as justified. But imagine that someone objects that there is a red light shining on the chair so it may not be red. If Jones cannot respond to this objection when it is real, then he is not in an adequate cognitive position. But suppose he is in a position to reply that he knows about the light and the chair is still red since he saw it yesterday in normal light. Then we will accept his claim.

A belief is *contextually basic* if, given an issue-context, the appropriate objector-group does not require the person to have reasons for the belief in order to be in a position to have knowledge. If the objector-group requires reasons, then it is not basic in the context. Thus in the first situation above Jones's belief that there is a red chair here is contextually-basic, whereas it is not basic in the second situation.

Consider the case either where the objector-group does not require S to have reasons for his belief that h in order to be in a position to have knowledge and where they accept his claim, or the case where they require reasons and accept his claim. In either case there is no regress of reasons. If an appropriate objector-group, the members of which are critical truth seekers, have no real doubts in the specific issue-context, then the person's belief is justified. The belief has withstood the test of verifically motivated objectors.

V. Objections to the Theory

There are several objections to the contextualist theory offered, and their main thrust is that the conditions for justification imposed are too stringent. The objections are as follows. First according to the theory offered, to be justified in believing h one must be able to meet a restricted class of objections falling into categories (A) and (B). But this ignores the distinction between *being* justified and *showing* that one is justified. To be justified is just to satisfy the principles of justification. To show that one is justified is to demonstrate that one satisfies these principles, and this is much more demanding.[10] For example S might have evidence that justifies his belief that h even though he is not able to articulate the evidence. In this case S would not be able to show that he was justified.

Second, if to be justified in believing h requires that one be able to meet the objection that h is false, then the theory ignores the distinction between truth and justification. A person can be justified in believing a statement even though it is false.

Finally the theory requires S to be in a position to answer all sorts of objections from a variety of perspectives. But this again is to require too much. For example assume that two scientists in different countries unaware of each other's work perform a certain experiment. The first scientist, S_1, gets one result and concludes that h. The second scientist, S_2, does not get the result (due to incorrect measurements). To require of S_1 that he be aware of S_2's experiment and be able to refute it is to impose an unrealistic burden on him in order for his belief to be justified. It is to build a *defeasibility* requirement into the justification condition. One approach to handling the Gettier problem has been to add the condition that in order to have knowledge, besides having justified true belief, the justification must not be defeated. Although there have been different characterizations of defeasibility, a core component or unrestricted version has been that a statement i defeats the justification evidence e provides h just in case i is true and the conjunction of i and e does not provide adequate support for h.[11] But according to the contextualist theory presented in order for S to be justified in believing h, he must be able to meet the objection that there is defeating evidence.

In reply to the first objection, the theory offered does not ignore the distinction between being justified and showing that one is justified. It is not required of S that he be able to state the standards of justification and demonstrate that he satisfies them. What is required is that he be able to meet real objections. This may *sometimes* require him to discuss standards, but not always. Furthermore the example given is not a counterexample since it is not a case of justified belief. Consider a case where relative to an issue-context we would expect S to have reasons for his belief that h. Suppose when asked how he knows or what his reasons are he is not able to say anything. We certainly would not take him as justified in his belief. We may not be able to articulate all our evidence for h, but we are required to do it for some of the evidence. It is not enough that we have evidence for h; it must be *taken* by us as evidence, and this places us "in the logical space of reasons, of justifying and being able to justify what one says."[12]

The first point in response to the next objection is that *epistemic* justification makes a claim to knowledge. To be *epistemically* justified in believing h is to be in a position to know h. Furthermore if the goals of epistemic justification are truth and the avoidance of error, then one *ought not* accept false statements. From an epistemic point of view to do so is objectionable. Hence the falsity of h at least counts against the person's being justified.

However, the contextualist account offered does not ignore the distinction between truth and justification. Meeting an objection does not entail showing the objection is false. It only requires general agreement on the response. So the objection may still be true. Thus S may be justified in believing h since he can meet the objection when h is in fact false. Furthermore an objection in order to require a response has to be the expression of a real doubt. Since it is possible for verifically motivated objectors not to be aware of the falsity of h, this objection will not be raised, so S may be justified in believing h even though it is false.

The situation is complex, however, since there are cases where the falsity of h implies S is not justified in believing h. Suppose that Jones is at a party and wonders whether his friend Smith is there. Nothing of great importance hinges on his presence; he simply wonders whether he is there. Perhaps he would not mind a chat with Smith. He looks about and asks a few guests. They have not seen him there. In such a situation Jones is justified in believing Smith is not there.

Imagine now that Jones is a police officer looking for Smith, a suspected assassin, at the party. Merely looking about casually and checking with a few guests is certainly not adequate. If Smith turns out to be hiding in one of the closets, we will not conclude that Jones was justified in his belief only it turned out false. He displayed gross negligence in not checking more thoroughly. There are cases where relative to an issue-context we require the person *S* to put himself in such an epistemic position that *h* will not turn out to be false. In this case the falsity of *h* is *non-excusable*. To be justified in believing *h* in non-excusable cases, *S* must be able to meet the objection that *h* is false. This is not required in excusable cases.

Assume that *h* is some very complicated scientific theory and *S* puts himself in the very best evidential position at the time. Even if the truth of *h* is very important, the falsity of *h* is excusable. The complexity of the issue and the fact that *S* put himself in the best position possible excuses *S* from the falsity of *h*, so he is still justified. But not all excusable cases involve a complex *h* nor being in the best position possible. Suppose that Smith has an identical twin brother but the only living person who knows this is the brother. Furthermore there are no records that there was a twin brother. If Jones returns a book to Smith's house and mistakenly gives it to the brother (where the issue-context is simply whether he returned the borrowed book and nothing of great importance hinges on to whom he gave it), he is still justified in his belief that he gave it to his friend Smith. Although Jones could have put himself in a better position (by asking questions about their friendship), there was no reason for him in the context to check further. People did not generally know about the twin brother, and Smith did not notice any peculiar behavior. Given the issue-context, members of the appropriate objector-group would not *expect* Jones to check further. So he evinces no culpability when his belief turns out to be false. Excusability thus depends on the issue-context and what the appropriate objector-group, given their standards of justification and the information available, expect of *S*.

Part of assimilating our epistemic standards, as is the case with both legal and moral standards, is learning the conditions of excusability. Such conditions are highly context-dependent, and it would be extremely difficult if not impossible to formulate rules to express them. In general we learn the conditions of excusability case by case. One need only consider moral and legal negligence to realize the full complexity of excuses, an area still to be studied despite Austin's well-known plea a number of years ago.

In response to the third objection it should be noted that epistemic justification is not to be taken lightly. Accepting *h* in part determines what other things I will believe and do. Furthermore I can infect the minds of others with my falsehoods and thus affect their further beliefs and actions. So to be epistemically justified requires that our claims pass the test of criticism. This point has motivated some philosophers to build a defeasibility requirement into the conditions of justification.[13]

The contextualist theory presented above, however, does not do this. There may be a defeating statement *i*, but *S* need meet this objection only if the objector-group raises it. For them to raise it, *i* must be the expression of real doubt. But it is perfectly possible for verifically motivated people to be unaware of *i*.

Furthermore the concept of epistemic excusability applies to defeating evidence. Suppose there is defeating evidence *i*. *S* may still be justified in his belief that *h* in the issue-context, even though he is unable to meet the objection. Relative to the issue-context, the appropriate objector-group with their standards of justification and available information may not expect of *S* that he be aware of *i*. Perhaps the issue involving *h* is very complicated. Thus his failure to meet the defeating evidence is excusable.

In the experiment case we can imagine issue-contexts where we would expect the first scientist to know of the experiment of the other scientist. But not all issue-contexts demand this. Nevertheless we may still require that he be in a position to say something about the other experiment if informed about it. For example he might indicate that he knows the area well, has performed the experiment a number of times and gotten similar results, it was performed under carefully controlled conditions, so he has every reason for believing that the experiment is replicable with similar results. Thus there must be something wrong with the other experiment. Requiring the scientist to be able to respond in the *minimal* way seems not to be overly demanding.

VI. Summary

Contextualism is an alternative to the traditional theories of foundationalism and coherentism. It denies the existence of basic statements in the foundationalist's sense (although it allows contextually basic statements), and it denies that coherence as it traditionally has been explained is sufficient for justification. Both theories overlook contextual parameters essential to justification, such as the issue-context and thus the value of *h*, social information, and social practices and norms of justification. In particular, the social nature of justification cannot be ignored.

Notes

1. For a discussion of minimal foundationalism see William P. Alston, "Has Foundationalism Been Refuted?"; James W. Cornman, "Foundationalism versus Nonfoundational Theories of Empirical Justification"; David B. Annis, "Epistemic Foundationalism."

2. Recent discussions of coherentism are found in Keith Lehrer, *Knowledge,*

chaps. 7–8; Nicholas Rescher, "Foundationalism, Coherentism, and the Idea of Cognitive Systematization." and his *The Coherence Theory of Truth*. Criticism of Lehrer's coherence theory is to be found in Cornman, "Foundational Versus Nonfoundational Theories of Empirical Justification," and in my review of Lehrer in *Philosophia* 6 (1976): 209–13. Criticism of Rescher's version is found in Mark Pastin's "Foundationalism Redux," unpublished, an abstract of which appears in the *The Journal of Philosophy* 61 (1974): 709–10.

3. Historically the key contextualists have been Peirce, Dewey, and Popper. But contextualist hints, suggestions, and theories are also to be found in Robert Ackermann, *Belief and Knowledge;* Bruce Aune, *Knowledge, Mind and Nature;* John Austin *Sense and Sensibilia* (London, 1962); Isaac Levi, *Gambling with Truth* (New York, 1967); Stephen Toulmin, *The Uses of Argument* (London, 1958) and *Human Understanding* (Princeton, New Jersey, 1972); Carl Wellman, *Challenge and Response: Justification in Ethics* (Carbondale, Illinois, 1971); F. L. Will, *Induction and Justification;* Ludwig Wittgenstein, *Philosophical Investigations* (New York, 1953) and *On Certainty*.

4. For a discussion of epistemic goals see Levi, *Gambling with Truth*.

5. C. S. Peirce, *Collected Papers,* vol. 6, ed. Charles Hartshorne and Paul Weiss (Harvard, 1965), p. 469.

6. John Dewey, *Knowing and the Known* (Boston, 1949), p. 315. See also Wittgenstein's *On Certainty*.

7. See, for example, Michael Cole et al., *The Cultural Context of Learning and Thinking* (New York, 1971).

8. For a discussion of the need to naturalize justification theory in the philosophy of science, see Frederick Suppe, "Afterword—1976" in the 2nd edition of his *The Structure of Scientific Theories* (Urbana, Illinois, 1977).

9. See Frederick Suppe's "The Search for Philosophic Understanding of Scientific Theories" and his "Afterword—1976" in *The Structure of Scientific Theories* for a discussion of objectivity in science and the lack of a theory-neutral observation language.

10. Alston discusses this distinction in "Has Foundationalism Been Refuted?" See also his "Two Types of Foundationalism," Chap. 3 above, and "Self-Warrant: A Neglected Form of Privileged Access."

11. The best discussion of defeasibility is Marshall Swain's "Epistemic Defeasibility."

12. Wilfrid Sellars, *Science, Perception and Reality*, p. 169.

13. Carl Ginet, "What Must Be Added to Knowing to Obtain Knowing That One Knows?," *Synthese* 21 (1970): 163–86.

10 Epistemology Naturalized

W. V. QUINE

Epistemology is concerned with the foundations of science. Conceived thus broadly, epistemology includes the study of the foundations of mathematics as one of its departments. Specialists at the turn of the century thought that their efforts in this particular department were achieving notable success: mathematics seemed to reduce altogether to logic. In a more recent perspective this reduction is seen to be better describable as a reduction to logic and set theory. This correction is a disappointment epistemologically, since the firmness and obviousness that we associate with logic cannot be claimed for set theory. But still the success achieved in the foundations of mathematics remains exemplary by comparative standards, and we can illuminate the rest of epistemology somewhat by drawing parallels to this department.

Studies in the foundations of mathematics divide symmetrically into two sorts, conceptual and doctrinal. The conceptual studies are concerned with meaning, the doctrinal with truth. The conceptual studies are concerned with clarifying concepts by defining them, some in terms of others. The doctrinal studies are concerned with establishing laws by proving them, some on the basis of others. Ideally the more obscure concepts would be defined in terms of the clearer ones so as to maximize clarity, and the less obvious laws would be proved from the more obvious ones so as to maximize certainty. Ideally the definitions would generate all the concepts from clear and distinct ideas, and the proofs would generate all the theorems from self-evident truths.

The two ideals are linked. For, if you define all the concepts by use of some favored subset of them, you thereby show how to translate all theorems into these favored terms. The clearer these terms are, the likelier it is that the truths couched in them will be obviously true, or derivable from obvious truths. If in particular the concepts of mathematics were all reducible to the clear terms of logic, then all the truths of

Reprinted from Quine, *Ontological Relativity and Other Essays* (New York: Columbia University Press, 1969), 68–90, by permission of the author and the publisher. Copyright 1969, Columbia University Press.

mathematics would go over into truths of logic; and surely the truths of logic are all obvious or at least potentially obvious, i.e., derivable from obvious truths by individually obvious steps.

This particular outcome is in fact denied us, however, since mathematics reduces only to set theory and not to logic proper. Such reduction still enhances clarity, but only because of the interrelations that emerge and not because the end terms of the analysis are clearer than others. As for the end truths, the axioms of set theory, these have less obviousness and certainty to recommend them than do most of the mathematical theorems that we would derive from them. Moreover, we know from Gödel's work that no consistent axiom system can cover mathematics even when we renounce self-evidence. Reduction in the foundations of mathematics remains mathematically and philosophically fascinating, but it does not do what the epistemologist would like of it: it does not reveal the ground of mathematical knowledge, it does not show how mathematical certainty is possible.

Still there remains a helpful thought, regarding epistemology generally, in that duality of structure which was especially conspicuous in the foundations of mathematics. I refer to the bifurcation into a theory of concepts, or meaning, and a theory of doctrine, or truth; for this applies to the epistemology of natural knowledge no less than to the foundations of mathematics. The parallel is as follows. Just as mathematics is to be reduced to logic, or logic and set theory, so natural knowledge is to be based somehow on sense experience. This means explaining the notion of body in sensory terms; here is the conceptual side. And it means justifying our knowledge of truths of nature in sensory terms; here is the doctrinal side of the bifurcation.

Hume pondered the epistemology of natural knowledge on both sides of the bifurcation, the conceptual and the doctrinal. His handling of the conceptual side of the problem, the explanation of body in sensory terms, was bold and simple: he identified bodies outright with the sense impressions. If common sense distinguishes between the material apple and our sense impressions of it on the ground that the apple is one and enduring while the impressions are many and fleeting, then, Hume held, so much the worse for common sense; the notion of its being the same apple on one occasion and another is a vulgar confusion.

Nearly a century after Hume's *Treatise,* the same view of bodies was espoused by the early American philosopher Alexander Bryan Johnson.[1] "The word iron names an associated sight and feel," Johnson wrote.

What then of the doctrinal side, the justification of our knowledge of truths about nature? Here, Hume despaired. By his identification of bodies with impressions he did succeed in construing some singular statements about bodies as indubitable truths, yes; as truths about impressions, directly known. But general statements, also singular statements about the future, gained no increment of certainty by being construed as about impressions.

On the doctrinal side, I do not see that we are further along today than where Hume left us. The Humean predicament is the human predicament. But on the conceptual side there has been progress. There the crucial step forward was made already before Alexander Bryan Johnson's day, although Johnson did not emulate it. It was made by Bentham in his theory of fictions. Bentham's step was the recognition of contextual definition, or what he called paraphrasis. He recognized that to explain a term we do not need to specify an object for it to refer to, nor even specify a synonymous word or phrase; we need only show, by whatever means, how to translate all the whole sentences in which the term is to be used. Hume's and Johnson's desperate measure of identifying bodies with impressions ceased to be the only conceivable way of making sense of talk of bodies, even granted that impressions were the only reality. One could undertake to explain talk of bodies in terms of talk of impressions by translating one's whole sentences about bodies into whole sentences about impressions, without equating the bodies themselves to anything at all.

This idea of contextual definition, or recognition of the sentence as the primary vehicle of meaning, was indispensable to the ensuing developments in the foundations of mathematics. It was explicit in Frege, and it attained its full flower in Russell's doctrine of singular descriptions as incomplete symbols.

Contextual definition was one of two resorts that could be expected to have a liberating effect upon the conceptual side of the epistemology of natural knowledge. The other is resort to the resources of set theory as auxiliary concepts. The epistemologist who is willing to eke out his austere ontology of sense impressions with these set-theoretic auxiliaries is suddenly rich: he has not just his impressions to play with, but sets of them, and sets of sets, and so on up. Constructions in the foundations of mathematics have shown that such set-theoretic aids are a powerful addition; after all, the entire glossary of concepts of classical mathematics is constructible from them. Thus equipped, our epistemologist may not need either to identify bodies with impressions or to settle for contextual definition; he may hope to find in some subtle construction of sets upon sets of sense impressions a category of objects enjoying just the formula properties that he wants for bodies.

The two resorts are very unequal in epistemological status. Contextual definition is unassailable. Sentences that have been given meaning as wholes are undeniably meaningful, and the use they make of their component terms is therefore meaningful, regardless of whether any translations are offered for those terms in isolation. Surely Hume and

A. B. Johnson would have used contextual definition with pleasure if they had thought of it. Recourse to sets, on the other hand, is a drastic ontological move, a retreat from the austere ontology of impressions. There are philosophers who would rather settle for bodies outright than accept all these sets, which amount, after all, to the whole abstract ontology of mathematics.

This issue has not always been clear, however, owing to deceptive hints of continuity between elementary logic and set theory. This is why mathematics was once believed to reduce to logic, that is, to an innocent and unquestionable logic, and to inherit these qualities. And this is probably why Russell was content to resort to sets as well as to contextual definition when in *Our Knowledge of the External World* and elsewhere he addressed himself to the epistemology of natural knowledge, on its conceptual side.

To account for the external world as a logical construct of sense data— such, in Russell's terms, was the program. It was Carnap, in his *Der logische Aufbau der Welt* of 1928, who came nearest to executing it.

This was the conceptual side of epistemology; what of the doctrinal? There the Humean predicament remained unaltered. Carnap's constructions, if carried successfully to completion, would have enabled us to translate all sentences about the world into terms of sense data, or observation, plus logic and set theory. But the mere fact that a sentence is *couched* in terms of observation, logic, and set theory does not mean that it can be *proved* from observation sentences by logic and set theory. The most modest of generalizations about observable traits will cover more cases than its utterer can have had occasion actually to observe. The hopelessness of grounding natural science upon immediate experience in a firmly logical way was acknowledged. The Cartesian quest for certainty had been the remote motivation of epistemology, both on its conceptual and its doctrinal side; but that quest was seen as a lost cause. To endow the truths of nature with the full authority of immediate experience was as forlorn a hope as hoping to endow the truths of mathematics with the potential obviousness of elementary logic.

What then could have motivated Carnap's heroic efforts on the conceptual side of epistemology, when hope of certainty on the doctrinal side was abandoned? There were two good reasons still. One was that such constructions could be expected to elicit and clarify the sensory evidence for science, even if the inferential steps between sensory evidence and scientific doctrine must fall short of certainty. The other reason was that such constructions would deepen our understanding of our discourse about the world, even apart from questions of evidence; it would make all cognitive discourse as clear as observation terms and logic and, I must regretfully add, set theory.

It was sad for epistemologists, Hume and others, to have to acquiesce in the impossibility of strictly deriving the science of the external world from sensory evidence. Two cardinal tenets of empiricism remained unassailable, however, and so remain to this day. One is that whatever evidence there *is* for science *is* sensory evidence. The other, to which I shall return, is that all inculcation of meanings of words must rest ultimately on sensory evidence. Hence the continuing attractiveness of the idea of a *logischer Aufbau* in which the sensory content of discourse would stand forth explicitly.

If Carnap had successfully carried such a construction through, how could he have told whether it was the right one? The question would have had no point. He was seeking what he called a *rational reconstruction*. Any construction of physicalistic discourse in terms of sense experience, logic, and set theory would have been seen as satisfactory if it made the physicalistic discourse come out right. If there is one way there are many, but any would be a great achievement.

But why all this creative reconstruction, all this make-believe? The stimulation of his sensory receptors is all the evidence anybody has had to go on, ultimately, in arriving at his picture of the world. Why not just see how this construction really proceeds? Why not settle for psychology? Such a surrender of the epistemological burden to psychology is a move that was disallowed in earlier times as circular reasoning. If the epistemologist's goal is validation of the grounds of empirical science, he defeats his purpose by using psychology or other empirical science in the validation. However, such scruples against circularity have little point once we have stopped dreaming of deducing science from observations. If we are out simply to understand the link between observation and science, we are well advised to use any available information, including that provided by the very science whose link with observation we are seeking to understand.

But there remains a different reason, unconnected with fears of circularity, for still favoring creative reconstruction. We should like to be able to *translate* science into logic and observation terms and set theory. This would be a great epistemological achievement, for it would show all the rest of the concepts of science to be theoretically superfluous. It would legitimize them—to whatever degree the concepts of set theory, logic, and observation are themselves legitimate—by showing that everything done with the one apparatus could in principle be done with the other. If psychology itself could deliver a truly translational reduction of this kind, we should welcome it; but certainly it cannot, for certainly we did not grow up learning definitions of physicalistic language in terms of a prior language of set theory, logic, and observation. Here, then, would be good reason for persisting in a rational reconstruction: we want to estabish the essential innocence of physical concepts, by showing them to be theoretically dispensable.

The fact is, though, that the construction which Carnap outlined in *Der logische Aufbau der Welt* does not give translational reduction either. It would not even if the outline were filled in. The crucial point comes where Carnap is explaining how to assign sense qualities to positions in physical space and time. These assignments are to be made in such a way as to fulfill, as well as possible, certain desiderata which he states, and with growth of experience the assignments are to be revised to suit. This plan, however illuminating, does not offer any key to *translating* the sentences of science into terms of observation, logic, and set theory.

We must despair of any such reduction. Carnap had despaired of it by 1936, when, in "Testability and Meaning,"[2] he introduced so-called *reduction forms* of a type weaker than definition. Definitions had shown always how to translate sentences into equivalent sentences. Contextual definition of a term showed how to translate sentences containing the term into equivalent sentences lacking the term. Reduction forms of Carnap's liberalized kind, on the other hand, do not in general give equivalences; they give implications. They explain a new term, if only partially, by specifying some sentences which are implied by sentences containing the term, and other sentences which imply sentences containing the term.

It is tempting to suppose that the countenancing of reduction forms in this liberal sense is just one further step of liberalization comparable to the earlier one, taken by Bentham, of countenancing contextual definition. The former and sterner kind of rational reconstruction might have been represented as a fictitious history in which we imagined our ancestors introducing the terms of physicalistic discourse on a phenomenalistic and set-theoretic basis by a succession of contextual definitions. The new and more liberal kind of rational reconstruction is a fictitious history in which we imagine our ancestors introducing those terms by a succession rather of reduction forms of the weaker sort.

This, however, is a wrong comparison. The fact is rather that the former and sterner kind of rational reconstruction, where definition reigned, embodied no fictitious history at all. It was nothing more nor less than a set of directions—or would have been, if successful—for accomplishing everything in terms of phenomena and set theory that we now accomplish in terms of bodies. It would have been a true reduction by translation, a legitimation by elimination. *Definire est eliminare*. Rational reconstruction by Carnap's later and looser reduction forms does none of this.

To relax the demand for definition, and settle for a kind of reduction that does not eliminate, is to renounce the last remaining advantage that we supposed rational reconstruction to have over straight psychology; namely, the advantage of translational reduction. If all we hope for is a reconstruction that links science to experience in explicit ways short of translation, then it would seem more sensible to settle for psychology. Better to discover how science is in fact developed and learned than to fabricate a fictitious structure to a similar effect.

The empiricist made one major concession when he despaired of deducing the truths of nature from sensory evidence. In despairing now even of translating those truths into terms of observation and logico-mathematical auxiliaries, he makes another major concession. For suppose we hold, with the old empiricist Peirce, that the very meaning of a statement consists in the difference its truth would make to possible experience. Might we not formulate, in a chapter-length sentence in observational language, all the difference that the truth of a given statement might make to experience, and might we not then take all this as the translation? Even if the difference that the truth of the statement would make to experience ramifies indefinitely, we might still hope to embrace it all in the logical implications of our chapter-length formulation, just as we can axiomatize an infinity of theorems. In giving up hope of such translation, then, the empiricist is conceding that the empirical meanings of typical statements about the external world are inaccessible and ineffable.

How is this inaccessibility to be explained? Simply on the ground that the experiential implications of a typical statement about bodies are too complex for finite axiomatization, however lengthy? No; I have a different explanation. It is that the typical statement about bodies has no fund of experiential implications it can call its own. A substantial mass of theory, taken together, will commonly have experiential implications; this is how we make verifiable predictions. We may not be able to explain why we arrive at theories which make successful predictions, but we do arrive at such theories.

Sometimes also an experience implied by a theory fails to come off; and then, ideally, we declare the theory false. But the failure falsifies only a block of theory as a whole, a conjunction of many statements. The failure shows that one or more of those statements is false, but it does not show which. The predicted experiences, true and false, are not implied by any one of the component statements of the theory rather than another. The component statements simply do not have empirical meanings, by Peirce's standard, but a sufficiently inclusive portion of theory does. If we can aspire to a sort of *logischer Aufbau der Welt* at all, it must be to one in which the texts slated for translation into observational and logico-mathematical terms are mostly broad theories taken as wholes, rather than just terms or short sentences. The translation of a theory would be a ponderous axiomatization of all the experiential difference that the truth of the theory would make. It would be a queer translation, for it would translate the whole but none of the parts. We might better speak in such a case not of translation but simply of observational evidence for theories; and we may, following Peirce, still fairly call this the empirical meaning of the theories.

These considerations raise a philosophical question even about ordinary unphilosophical translation, such as from English into Arunta or Chinese. For, if the English sentences of a theory have their meaning only together as a body, then we can justify their translation into Arunta only together as a body. There will be no justification for pairing off the component English sentences with component Arunta sentences, except as these correlations make the translation of the theory as a whole come out right. Any translations of the English sentences into Arunta sentences will be as correct as any other, so long as the net empirical implications of the theory as a whole are preserved in translation. But it is to be expected that many different ways of translating the component sentences, essentially different individually, would deliver the same empirical implications for the theory as a whole; deviations in the translation of one component sentence could be compensated for in the translation of another component sentence. Insofar, there can be no ground for saying which of two glaringly unlike translations of individual sentences is right.[3]

For an uncritical mentalist, no such indeterminacy threatens. Every term and every sentence is a label attached to an idea, simple or complex, which is stored in the mind. When on the other hand we take a verification theory of meaning seriously, the indeterminacy would appear to be inescapable. The Vienna Circle espoused a verification theory of meaning but did not take it seriously enough. If we recognize with Peirce that the meaning of a sentence turns purely on what would count as evidence for its truth, and if we recognize with Duhem that theoretical sentences have their evidence not as single sentences but only as larger blocks of theory, then the indeterminacy of translation of theoretical sentences is the natural conclusion. And most sentences, apart from observation sentences, are theoretical. This conclusion, conversely, once it is embraced, seals the fate of any general notion of propositional meaning or, for that matter, state of affairs.

Should the unwelcomeness of the conclusion persuade us to abandon the verification theory of meaning? Certainly not. The sort of meaning that is basic to translation, and to the learning of one's own language, is necessarily empirical meaning and nothing more. A child learns his first words and sentences by hearing and using them in the presence of appropriate stimuli. These must be external stimuli, for they must act both on the child and on the speaker from whom he is learning.[4] Language is socially inculcated and controlled; the inculcation and control turn strictly on the keying of sentences to shared stimulation. Internal factors may vary *ad libitum* without prejudice to communication as long as the keying of language to external stimuli is undisturbed. Surely one has no choice but to be an empiricist so far as one's theory of linguistic meaning is concerned.

What I have said of infant learning applies equally to the linguist's learning of a new language in the field. If the linguist does not lean on related languages for which there are previously accepted translation practices, then obviously he had no data but the concomitances of native utterance and observable stimulus situation. No wonder there is indeterminacy of translation—for of course only a small fraction of our utterances report concurrent external stimulation. Granted, the linguist will end up with unequivocal translations of everything; but only by making many arbitrary choices—arbitrary even though unconscious—along the way. Arbitrary? By this I mean that different choices could still have made everything come out right that is susceptible in principle to any kind of check.

Let me link up, in a different order, some of the points I have made. The crucial consideration behind my argument for the indeterminacy of translation was that a statement about the world does not always or usually have a separable fund of empirical consequences that it can call its own. That consideration served also to account for the impossibility of an epistemological reduction of the sort where every sentence is equated to a sentence in observational and logico-mathematical terms. And the impossibility of that sort of epistemological reduction dissipated the last advantage that rational reconstruction seemed to have over psychology.

Philosophers have rightly despaired of translating everything into observational and logico-mathematical terms. They have despaired of this even when they have not recognized, as the reason for this irreducibility, that the statements largely do not have their private bundles of empirical consequences. And some philosophers have seen in this irreducibility the bankruptcy of epistemology. Carnap and the other logical positivists of the Vienna Circle had already pressed the term "metaphysics" into pejorative use, as connoting meaninglessness; and the term "epistemology" was next. Wittgenstein and his followers, mainly at Oxford, found a residual philosophical vocation in therapy: in curing philosophers of the delusion that there were epistemological problems.

But I think that at this point it may be more useful to say rather that epistemology still goes on, though in a new setting and a clarified status. Epistemology, or something like it, simply falls into place as a chapter of psychology and hence of natural science. It studies a natural phenomenon, viz., a physical human subject. This human subject is accorded a certain experimentally controlled input—certain patterns of irradiation in assorted frequencies, for instance—and in the fullness of time the subject delivers as output a description of the three-dimensional external world and its history. The relation between the meager input and the torrential output is a relation that we are prompted to study for somewhat the same reasons that always prompted epistemology; namely, in order to see how evidence relates to theory, and in what ways one's theory of nature transcends any available evidence.

Such a study could still include, even, something like the old rational reconstruction, to whatever degree such reconstruction is practicable; for imaginative constructions can afford hints of actual psychological processes, in much the way that mechanical simulations can. But a conspicuous difference between old epistemology and the epistemological enterprise in this new psychological setting is that we can now make free use of empirical psychology.

The old epistemology aspired to contain, in a sense, natural science; it would construct it somehow from sense data. Epistemology in its new setting, conversely, is contained in natural science, as a chapter of psychology. But the old containment remains valid too, in its way. We are studying how the human subject of our study posits bodies and projects his physics from his data, and we appreciate that our position in the world is just like his. Our very epistemological enterprise, therefore, and the psychology wherein it is a component chapter, and the whole of natural science wherein psychology is a component book—all this is our own construction or projection from stimulations like those we were meting out to our epistemological subject. There is thus reciprocal containment, though containment in different senses: epistemology in natural science and natural science in epistemology.

This interplay is reminiscent again of the old threat of circularity, but it is all right now that we have stopped dreaming of deducing science from sense data. We are after an understanding of science as an institution or process in the world, and we do not intend that understanding to be any better than the science which is its object. This attitude is indeed one that Neurath was already urging in Vienna Circle days, with his parable of the mariner who has to rebuild his boat while staying afloat in it.

One effect of seeing epistemology in a psychological setting is that it resolves a stubborn old enigma of epistemological priority. Our retinas are irradiated in two dimensions, yet we see things as three-dimensional without conscious inference. Which is to count as observation—the unconscious two-dimensional reception or the conscious three-dimensional apprehension? In the old epistemological context the conscious form had priority, for we were out to justify our knowledge of the external world by rational reconstruction, and that demands awareness. Awareness ceased to be demanded when we gave up trying to justify our knowledge of the external world by rational reconstruction. What to count as observation now can be settled in terms of the stimulation of sensory receptors, let consciousness fall where it may.

The Gestalt psychologists' challenge to sensory atomism, which seemed so relevant to epistemology forty years ago, is likewise deactivated. Regardless of whether sensory atoms or Gestalten are what favor the forefront of our consciousness, it is simply the stimulations of our sensory receptors that are best looked upon as the input to our cognitive mechanism. Old paradoxes about unconscious data and inference, old problems about chains of inference that would have to be completed too quickly— these no longer matter.

In the old anti-psychologistic days the question of epistemological priority was moot. What is epistemologically prior to what? Are Gestalten prior to sensory atoms because they are noticed, or should we favor sensory atoms on some more subtle ground? Now that we are permitted to appeal to physical stimulation, the problem dissolves; A is epistemologically prior to B if A is causally nearer than B to the sensory receptors. Or, what is in some ways better, just talk explicitly in terms of causal proximity to sensory receptors and drop the talk of epistemological priority.

Around 1932 there was debate in the Vienna Circle over what to count as observation sentences, or *Protokollsätze*.[5] One position was that they had the form of reports of sense impressions. Another was that they were statements of an elementary sort about the external world, e.g., "A red cube is standing on the table." Another, Neurath's, was that they had the form of reports of relations between percipients and external things: "Otto now sees a red cube on the table." The worst of it was that there seemed to be no objective way of settling the matter: no way of making real sense of the question.

Let us now try to view the matter unreservedly in the context of the external world. Vaguely speaking, what we want of observation sentences is that they be the ones in closest causal proximity to the sensory receptors. But how is such proximity to be gauged? The idea may be rephrased this way: observation sentences are sentences which, as we learn language, are most strongly conditioned to concurrent sensory stimulation rather than to stored collateral information. Thus let us imagine a sentence queried for our verdict as to whether it is true or false, queried for our assent or dissent. Then the sentence is an observation sentence if our verdict depends only on the sensory stimulation present at the time.

But a verdict cannot depend on present stimulation to the exclusion of stored information. The very fact of our having learned the language evinces much storing of information, and of information without which we should be in no position to give verdicts on sentences however observational. Evidently then we must relax our definition of observation sentence to read thus: a sentence is an observation sentence if all verdicts on it depend on present sensory stimulation and on no stored information beyond what goes into understanding the sentence.

This formulation raises another problem: how are we to distinguish between information that goes into understanding a sentence and information that goes beyond? This is the problem of distinguishing between analytic truth, which issues from the mere meanings of words, and synthetic truth, which depends on more than meanings. Now I have long maintained that this distinction is illusory. There is one step toward such a distinction, however, which does make sense: a sentence that is true by mere meanings of words should be expected, at least if it is simple, to be subscribed to by all fluent speakers in the community. Perhaps the controversial notion of analyticity can be dispensed with, in our definition of observation sentence, in favor of this straightforward attribute of community-wide acceptance.

This attribute is of course no explication of analyticity. The community would agree that there have been black dogs, yet none who talk of analyticity would call this analytic. My rejection of the analyticity notion just means drawing no line between what goes into the mere understanding of the sentences of a language and what else the community sees eye-to-eye on. I doubt that an objective distinction can be made between meaning and such collateral information as is community-wide.

Turning back then to our task of defining observation sentences, we get this: an observation sentence is one on which all speakers of the language give the same verdict when given the same concurrent stimulation. To put the point negatively, an observation sentence is one that is not sensitive to differences in past experience within the speech community.

This formulation accords perfectly with the traditional role of the observation sentence as the court of appeal of scientific theories. For by our definition the observation sentences are the sentences on which all members of the community will agree under uniform stimulation. And what is the criterion of membership in the same community? Simply, general fluency of dialogue. This criterion admits of degrees, and indeed we may usefully take the community more narrowly for some studies than for others. What count as observation sentences for a community of specialists would not always so count for a larger community.

There is generally no subjectivity in the phrasing of observation sentences, as we are now conceiving them; they will usually be about bodies. Since the distinguishing trait of an observation sentence is inter-subjective agreement under agreeing stimulation, a corporeal subject matter is likelier than not.

The old tendency to associate observation sentences with a subjective sensory subject matter is rather an irony when we reflect that observation sentences are also meant to be the intersubjective tribunal of scientific hypotheses. The old tendency was due to the drive to base science on something firmer and prior in the subject's experience; but we dropped that project.

The dislodging of epistemology from its old status of first philosophy loosed a wave, we saw, of epistemological nihilism. This mood is reflected somewhat in the tendency of Polányi, Kuhn, and the late Russell Hanson to belittle the role of evidence and to accentuate cultural relativism. Hanson ventured even to discredit the idea of observation, arguing that so-called observations vary from observer to observer with the amount of knowledge that the observers bring with them. The veteran physicist looks at some apparatus and sees an x-ray tube. The neophyte, looking at the same place, observes rather "a glass and metal instrument replete with wires, reflectors, screws, lamps, and pushbuttons."[6] One man's observation is another man's closed book or flight of fancy. The notion of observation as the impartial and objective source of evidence for science is bankrupt. Now my answer to the x-ray example was already hinted a little while back: what counts as an observation sentence varies with the width of community considered. But we can also always get an absolute standard by taking in all speakers of the language, or most.[7] It is ironical that philosophers, finding the old epistemology untenable as a whole, should react by repudiating a part which has only now moved into clear focus.

Clarification of the notion of observation sentence is a good thing, for the notion is fundamental in two connections. These two correspond to the duality that I remarked upon early in this essay: the duality between concept and doctrine, between knowing what a sentence means and knowing whether it is true. The observation sentence is basic to both enterprises. Its relation to doctrine, to our knowledge of what is true, is very much the traditional one: observation sentences are the repository of evidence for scientific hypotheses. Its relation to meaning is fundamental too, since observation sentences are the ones we are in a position to learn to understand first, both as children and as field linguists. For observation sentences are precisely the ones that we can correlate with observable circumstances of the occasion of utterance or assent, independently of variations in the past histories of individual informants. They afford the only entry to a language.

The observation sentence is the cornerstone of semantics. For it is, as we just saw, fundamental to the learning of meaning. Also, it is where meaning is firmest. Sentences higher up in theories have no empirical consequences they can call their own; they confront the tribunal of sensory evidence only in more or less inclusive aggregates. The observation sentence, situated at the sensory periphery of the body scientific, is the minimal verifiable aggregate; it has an empirical content all its own and wears it on its sleeve.

The predicament of the indeterminacy of translation has little bearing on observation sentences. The equating of an observation sentence of our language to an observation sentence of another language is mostly a atter of empirical generalization; it is a matter of identity between the range of stimulations that would prompt assent to the one sentence and he range of stimulations that would prompt assent to the other.[8]

It is no shock to the preconceptions of old Vienna to say that epistemology now becomes semantics. For epistemology remains centered as always on evidence, and meaning remains centered as always on verification; and evidence is verification. What is likelier to shock preconceptions s that meaning, once we get beyond observation sentences, ceases in general to have any clear applicability to single sentences; also that epistemology merges with psychology, as well as with linguistics.

This rubbing out of boundaries could contribute to progress, it seems to me, in philosophically interesting inquiries of a scientific nature. One possible area is perceptual norms. Consider, to begin with, the linguistic phenomenon of phonemes. We form the habit, in hearing the myriad variations of spoken sounds, of treating each as an approximation to one or another of a limited number of norms—around thirty altogether—constituting so to speak a spoken alphabet. All speech in our language can be treated in practice as sequences of just those thirty elements, thus rectifying small deviations. Now outside the realm of language also there is probably only a rather limited alphabet of perceptual norms altogether, toward which we tend unconsciously to rectify all perceptions. These, if experimentally identified, could be taken as epistemological building blocks, the working elements of experience. They might prove in part to be culturally variable, as phonemes are, and in part universal.

Again there is the area that the psychologist Donald T. Campbell calls evolutionary epistemology.[9] In this area there is work by Hüseyin Yilmaz, who shows how some structural traits of color perception could have been predicted from survival value.[10] And a more emphatically epistemological topic that evolution helps to clarify is induction, now that we are allowing epistemology the resources of natural science.[11]

Notes

1. A. B. Johnson, *A Treatise on Language* (New York, 1836; Berkeley, 1947).
2. Carnap, *Philosophy of Science* 3 (1936): 419–71; 4 (1937): 1–40.
3. See Quine, *Ontological Relativity* (New York, 1969), pp. 2ff.
4. See ibid., p. 28.
5. Carnap and Neurath in *Erkenntnis* 3 (1932): 204–28.
6. N. R. Hanson, "Observation and Interpretation," in S. Morgenbesser, ed., *Philosophy of Science Today* (New York: Basic Books, 1966).
7. This qualification allows for occasional deviants such as the insane or the blind. Alternatively, such cases might be excluded by adjusting the level of fluency of dialogue whereby we define sameness of language. (For prompting this note and influencing the development of this essay also in more substantial ways I am indebted to Burton Dreben.)

8. Cf. Quine, *Word and Object* (Cambridge, 1960), pp. 31–46, 68.

9. D. T. Campbell, "Methodological Suggestions from a Comparative Psychology of Knowledge Processes," *Inquiry* 2 (1959): 152–82.

10. Hüseyin Yilmaz, "On Color Vision and a New Approach to General Perception," in E. E. Bernard and M. R. Kare, eds., *Biological Prototypes and Synthetic Systems* (New York: Plenum, 1962); "Perceptual Invariance and the Psychophysical Law," *Perception and Psychophysics* 2 (1967): 533-538.

11. See Quine, "Natural Kinds," in *Ontological Relativity,* chap. 5.

PART II

THE GETTIER PROBLEM

11 Is Justified True Belief Knowledge?

EDMUND GETTIER

Various attempts have been made in recent years to state necessary and sufficient conditions for someone's knowing a given proposition. The attempts have often been such that they can be stated in a form similar to the following:[1]

(a) S knows that P   *IFF*   (i)   *P* is true,
                                (ii) S believes that P, and
                                (iii) S is justified in believing that P.

For example, Chisholm has held that the following gives the necessary and sufficient conditions for knowledge:[2]

(b) S knows that P   *IFF*   (i)   S accepts P,
                                (ii) S has adequate evidence for P, and
                                (iii) P is true.

Ayer has stated the necessary and sufficient conditions for knowledge as follows:[3]

(c) S knows that P   *IFF*   (i)   P is true,
                                (ii) S is sure that P is true, and
                                (iii) S has the right to be sure that P is true.

I shall argue that (a) is false in that the conditions stated therein do not constitute a *sufficient* condition for the truth of the proposition that S knows that P. The same argument will show that (b) and (c) fail if "has adequate evidence for" or "has the right to be sure that" is substituted for "is justified in believing that" throughout.

I shall begin by noting two points. First, in that sense of "justified" in which S's being justified in believing P is a necessary condition of S's

Reprinted from *Analysis* 23 (1963): 121–23, by permission of the author and the publisher. Copyright 1963, Edmund Gettier.

knowing that P, it is possible for a person to be justified in believing a proposition which is in fact false. Second, for any proposition P, if S is justified in believing P and P entails Q and S deduces Q from P and accepts Q as a result of this deduction, then S is justified in believing Q. Keeping these two points in mind, I shall now present two cases in which the conditions stated in (a) are true for some proposition, though it is at the same time false that the person in question knows that proposition.

Case I

Suppose that Smith and Jones have applied for a certain job. And suppose that Smith has strong evidence for the following conjunctive proposition:

   (d) Jones is the man who will get the job, and Jones has ten coins in his pocket.

Smith's evidence for (d) might be that the president of the company assured him that Jones would in the end be selected, and that he, Smith, had counted the coins in Jones's pocket ten minutes ago. Proposition (d) entails:

   (e) The man who will get the job has ten coins in his pocket.

Let us suppose that Smith sees the entailment from (d) to (e) and accepts (e) on the grounds of (d), for which he has strong evidence. In this case, Smith is clearly justified in believing that (e) is true.

But imagine, further, that unknown to Smith, he himself, not Jones, will get the job. And, also, unknown to Smith, he himself has ten coins in his pocket. Proposition (e) is then true, though proposition (d), from which Smith inferred (e), is false. In our example, then, all of the following are true: (*i*) (e) is true, (*ii*) Smith believes that (e) is true, and (*iii*) Smith is justified in believing that (e) is true. But it is equally clear that Smith does not *know* that (e) is true; for (e) is true in virtue of the number of coins in Smith's pocket, while Smith does not know how many coins are in Smith's pocket, and bases his belief in (e) on a count of the coins in Jones's pocket, whom he falsely believes to be the man who will get the job.

Case II

Let us suppose that Smith has strong evidence for the following proposition:

   (f) Jones owns a Ford.

Smith's evidence might be that Jones has at all times in the past within Smith's memory owned a car, and always a Ford, and that Jones has just offered Smith a ride while driving a Ford. Let us imagine, now, that Smith has another friend, Brown, of whose whereabouts he is totally ignorant. Smith selects three place names quite at random and constructs the following three propositions:

(g) Either Jones owns a Ford, or Brown is in Boston.
(h) Either Jones owns a Ford, or Brown is in Barcelona
(i) Either Jones owns a Ford, or Brown is in Brest-Litovsk.

Each of these propositions is entailed by (f). Imagine that Smith realizes the entailment of each of these propositions he has constructed by (f), and proceeds to accept (g), (h), and (i) on the basis of (f). Smith has correctly inferred (g), (h), and (i) from a proposition for which he has strong evidence. Smith is therefore completely justified in believing each of these three propositions. Smith, of course, has no idea where Brown is.

But imagine now that two further conditions hold. First, Jones does *not* own a Ford, but is at present driving a rented car. And second, by the sheerest coincidence, and entirely unknown to Smith, the place mentioned in proposition (h) happens really to be the place where Brown is. If these two conditions hold, then Smith does *not* know that (h) is true, even though (*i*) (h) *is* true, (*ii*) Smith does believe that (h) is true, and (*iii*) Smith is justified in believing that (h) is true.

These two examples show that definition (a) does not state a *sufficient* condition for someone's knowing a given proposition. The same cases, with appropriate changes, will suffice to show that neither definition (b) nor definition (c) do so either.

Notes

1. Plato seems to be considering some such definition at *Theaetetus* 201, and perhaps accepting one at *Meno* 98.
2. Roderick M. Chisholm, *Perceiving: A Philosophical Study,* p. 16.
3. A. J. Ayer, *The Problem of Knowledge.*

12   Knowledge and Explanation

GILBERT HARMAN

Gettier Examples and Probabilistic Rules of Acceptance

In any Gettier example we are presented with cases in which someone infers h from things he knows, h is true, and he is equally justified in making the inference in either case. In the one case he comes to know that h and in the other case he does not. I observe that a natural explanation of many Gettier examples is that the relevant inference involves not only the final conclusion h, but also at least one intermediate conclusion true in the one case but not in the other. And I suggest that any account of inductive inference should show why such intermediate conclusions are essentially involved in the relevant inferences. Gettier cases are thus to be explained by appeal to the principle

> *P* Reasoning that essentially involves false conclusions, intermediate or final, cannot give one knowledge.

It is easy to see that purely probabilistic rules of acceptance do not permit an explanation of Gettier examples by means of principle *P*. Reasoning in accordance with a purely probabilistic rule involves essentially only its final conclusion. Since that conclusion is highly probable, it can be inferred without reference to any other conclusions; in particular, there will be no intermediate conclusion essential to the inference that is true in one case and false in the other.

For example, Mary's friend Mr. Nogot convinces her that he has a Ford. He tells her that he owns a Ford, he shows her his ownership certificate, and he reminds her that she saw him drive up in a Ford. On the basis of this and similar evidence, Mary concludes that Mr. Nogot owns a Ford. From that she infers that one of her friends owns a Ford. In a normal case, Mary might in this way come to know that one of her friends owns a Ford. However, as it turns out in this case, Mary is wrong about

Reprinted from Harman, *Thought* (Princeton: Princeton University Press, 1973), 120–24, 126–41, by permission of the author and the publisher. Copyright 1973, Princeton University Press.

Nogot. His car has just been repossessed and towed away. It is no longer his. On the other hand, Mary's friend Mr. Havit does own a Ford, so she is right in thinking that one of her friends owns a Ford. However, she does not realize that Havit owns a Ford. Indeed, she hasn't been given the slightest reason to think that he owns a Ford. It is false that Mr. Nogot owns a Ford, but it is true that one of Mary's friends owns a Ford. Mary has a justified true belief that one of her friends owns a Ford, but she does not know that one of her friends owns a Ford. She does not know this because principle *P* has been violated. Mary's reasoning essentially involves the false conclusion that Mr. Nogot owns a Ford.[1]

But, if there were probabilistic rules of acceptance, there would be no way to exhibit the relevance of Mary's intermediate conclusion. For Mary could then have inferred her final conclusion (that one of her friends owns a Ford) directly from her original evidence, all of which is true. Mr. Nogot *is* her friend, he *did* say he owns a Ford, he *did* show Mary an ownership certificate, she *did* see him drive up in a Ford, etc. If a purely probabilistic rule would permit Mary to infer from that evidence that her friend Nogot owns a Ford, it would also permit her to infer directly that one of her friends owns a Ford, since the latter conclusion is at least as probable on the evidence as the former. Given a purely probabilistic rule of acceptance, Mary need not first infer an intermediate conclusion and then deduce her final conclusion, since by means of such a rule she could directly infer her final conclusion. The intermediate conclusion would not be essential to her inference, and her failure to know that one of her friends owns a Ford could not be explained by appeal to principle *P*.

A defender of purely probabilistic rules might reply that what has gone wrong in this case is not that Mary *must* infer her conclusion from something false, but rather that, from the evidence that supports her conclusion, she *could* also infer something false, namely that Mr. Nogot owns a Ford. In terms of principle *P,* this would be to count as essential to Mary's inference any conclusion the probabilistic rule would authorize from her starting point. But given any evidence, some false conclusion will be highly probable on that evidence. This follows, e.g., from the existence of lotteries. For example, let *s* be a conclusion saying under what conditions the New Jersey State Lottery was most recently held. Let *q* say what ticket won the grand prize. Then consider the conclusion, *not both s and q.* Call that conclusion *r.* The conclusion *r* is highly probable, given evidence having nothing to do with the outcome of the recent lottery, but *r* is false. If such highly probable false conclusions were always considered essential to an inference, Mary could never come to know anything.

The problem is that purely probabilistic considerations do not suffice to account for the peculiar relevance of Mary's conclusion about Nogot. Various principles might be suggested, but none of them work. For example, we might suspect that the trouble with *r* is that it has nothing to do with whether any of Mary's friends owns a Ford. Even if Mary were to assume that *r* is false, her original conclusion would continue to be highly probable on her evidence. So we might suggest that an inferable conclusion *t* is essential to an inference only if the assumption that *t* was false would block the inference. That would distinguish Mary's relevant intermediate conclusion, that Nogot owns a Ford, from the irrelevant conclusion *r*, since if Mary assumed that Nogot does not own a Ford she could not conclude that one of her friends owns a Ford.

But again, if there is a purely probabilistic rule of acceptance, there will always be an inferable false *t* such that the assumption that it is false would block even inferences that give us knowledge. For let *h* be the conclusion of any inference not concerned with the New Jersey Lottery and let *r* be as above. Then we can let *t* be the conjunction *h&r*. This *t* is highly probable on the same evidence *e* on which *h* is highly probable; *t* is false; and *h* is not highly probable relative to the evidence *e&(not t)*. Any inference would be undermined by such a *t*, given a purely probabilistic rule of acceptance along with the suggested criterion of essential conclusions.

The trouble is that purely probabilistic rules are incompatible with the natural account of Gettier examples by means of principle *P*. The solution is not to attempt to modify *P*, but rather to modify our account of inference.

A Causal Theory

Alvin Goldman suggests that we know only if there is the proper sort of causal connection between our belief and what we know. For example, we perceive that there has been an automobile accident only if the accident is relevantly causally responsible, by way of our sense organs, for our belief that there has been an accident. Similarly, we remember doing something only if having done it is relevantly causally responsible for our current memory of having done it. Although in some cases the fact that we know thus simply begins a causal chain that leads to our belief, in other cases the causal connection is more complicated. If Mary learns that Mr. Havit owns a Ford, Havit's past ownership is causally responsible for the evidence she has and also responsible (at least in part) for Havit's present ownership. Here the relevant causal connection consists in there being a common cause of the belief and of the state of affairs believed in.

Mary fails to know in the original Nogot-Havit case because the causal connection is lacking. Nogot's past ownership is responsible for her evidence but is not responsible for the fact that one of her friends owns a Ford. Havit's past ownership at least partly accounts for why one of her friends now owns a Ford, but it is not responsible for her evidence. Similarly, the man who is told something true by a speaker who does not believe what he says fails to know because the truth of what is said is not causally responsible for the fact that it is said.

General knowledge does not fit into this simple framework. That all emeralds are green neither causes nor is caused by the existence of the particular green emeralds examined when we come to know that all emeralds are green. Goldman handles such examples by counting logical connections among the causal connections. The belief that all emeralds are green is, in an extended sense, relevantly causally connected to the fact that all emeralds are green, since the evidence causes the belief and is logically entailed by what is believed.

It is obvious that not every causal connection, especially in this extended sense, is relevant to knowledge. Any two states of affairs are logically connected simply because both are entailed by their conjunction. If every such connection were relevant, the analysis Goldman suggests would have us identify knowledge with true belief, since there would always be a relevant "causal connection" between any state of true belief and the state of affairs believed in. Goldman avoids this reduction of his analysis to justified true belief by saying that when knowledge is based on inference, relevant causal connections must be "reconstructed" in the inference. Mary knows that one of her friends owns a Ford only if her inference reconstructs the relevant causal connection between evidence and conclusion.

But what does it mean to say that her inference must "reconstruct" the relevant causal connection? Presumably it means that she must infer or be able to infer something about the causal connection between her conclusion and the evidence for it. And this suggests that Mary must make at least two inferences. First she must infer her original conclusion, and second she must infer something about the causal connection between the conclusion and her evidence. Her second conclusion is her "reconstruction" of the causal connection. But how detailed must her reconstruction be? If she must reconstruct every detail of the causal connection between evidence and conclusion, she will never gain knowledge by way of inference. If she need only reconstruct some "causal connection," she will always know, since she will always be able to infer that evidence and conclusion are both entailed by their conjunction.

I suggest that it is a mistake to approach the problem as a problem about what else Mary needs to infer before she has knowledge of her original conclusion. Goldman's remark about reconstructing the causal connection makes more sense as a remark about the kind of inference

Mary needs to reach her original conclusion in the first place. It has something to do with principle *P* and the natural account of the Gettier examples.

Nogot presents Mary with evidence that he owns a Ford. She infers that one of her friends owns a Ford. She is justified in reaching that conclusion and it is true. However, since it is true, not because Nogot owns a Ford, but because Havit does, Mary fails to come to know that one of her friends owns a Ford. The natural explanation is that she must infer that Nogot owns a Ford and does not know her final conclusion unless her intermediate conclusion is true. According to this natural explanation, Mary's inference essentially involves the conclusion that Nogot owns a Ford. According to Goldman, her inference essentially involves a conclusion concerning a causal connection. In order to put these ideas together, we must turn Goldman's theory of knowledge into a theory of inference.

As a first approximation, let us take his remarks about causal connections literally, forgetting for the moment that they include logical connections. Then let us transmute his causal theory of knowing into the theory that inductive conclusions always take the form *X causes Y,* where further conclusions are reached by additional steps of inductive or deductive reasoning. In particular, we may deduce either *X* or *Y* from *X causes Y.*

This causal theory of inferring provides the following account of why knowledge requires that we be right about an appropriate causal connection. A person knows by inference only if all conclusions essential to that inference are true. That is, his inference must satisfy principle *P.* Since he can legitimately infer his conclusion only if he can first infer certain causal statements, he can know only if he is right about the causal connection expressed by those statements. First, Mary infers that her evidence is a causal result of Nogot's past ownership of the Ford. From that she deduces that Nogot has owned a Ford. Then she infers that his past ownership has been causally responsible for present ownership, and she deduces that Nogot owns a Ford. Finally, she deduces that one of her friends owns a Ford. She fails to know because she is wrong when she infers that Nogot's past ownership is responsible for Nogot's present ownership.

Inference to the Best Explanatory Statement

A better account of inference emerges if we replace "cause" with "because." On the revised account, we infer not just statements of the form *X causes Y* but, more generally, statements of the form *Y because X* or *X explains Y.* Inductive inference is conceived as inference to the best of competing explanatory statements. Inference to a causal explanation is a special case.

The revised account squares better with ordinary usage. Nogot's past ownership helps to explain Mary's evidence, but it would sound odd to say that it caused that evidence. Similarly, the detective infers that activities of the butler explain these footprints; does he infer that those activities caused the footprints? A scientist explains the properties of water by means of a hypothesis about unobservable particles that make up the water, but it does not seem right to say that facts about those particles cause the properties of water. An observer infers that certain mental states best explain someone's behavior, but such explanation by reasons might not be causal explanation.

Furthermore, the switch from "cause" to "because" avoids Goldman's *ad hoc* treatment of knowledge of generalizations. Although there is no causal relation between a generalization and those observed instances which provide us with evidence for the generalization, there is an obvious explanatory relationship. That all emeralds are green does not cause a particular emerald to be green, but it can explain why that emerald is green. And, other things being equal, we can infer a generalization only if it provides the most plausible way to explain our evidence.

We often infer generalizations that explain but do not logically entail their instances, since they are of the form *In circumstances C, X's tend to be Y's*. Such generalizations may be inferred if they provide a sufficiently plausible account of observed instances all things considered. For example, from the fact that doctors have generally been right in the past when they have said that someone is going to get measles, I infer that doctors can normally tell from certain symptoms that someone is going to get measles. More precisely, I infer that doctors have generally been right in the past because they can normally tell from certain symptoms that someone is going to get measles. This is a very weak explanation, but it is a genuine one. Compare it with the pseudo-explanation "Doctors are generally right when they say someone has measles because they can normally tell from certain symptoms that someone is going to get measles."

Similarly, I infer that a substance is soluble in water from the fact that it dissolved when I stirred it into some water. That is a real explanation, to be distinguished from the pseudo-explanation "That substance dissolves in water because it is soluble in water." Here too a generalization explains an instance without entailing that instance, since water-soluble substances do not always dissolve in water.

Although we cannot simply deduce instances from this sort of generalization, we can often infer that the generalization will explain some new instance. The inference is warranted if the explanatory claim *that X's tend to be Y's will explain why the next X will be Y* is sufficiently more plausible than competitors such as *interfering factor Q will prevent the next X from being a Y*. For example, the doctor says that you will get measles. Because doctors are normally right about that sort of thing, I infer that you will. More precisely, I infer that doctors normally being able to tell when someone will get measles will explain the doctor's being right in this case. The competing explanatory statements here are not other explanations of the doctor being right, but rather explanations of his being wrong—e.g., because he has misperceived the symptoms, or because you have faked the symptoms of measles, or because these symptoms are the result of some other disease, etc. Similarly, I infer that this sugar will dissolve in my tea. That is, I infer that the solubility of sugar in tea will explain this sugar's dissolving in the present case. Competing explanations would explain the sugar's not dissolving—e.g., because there is already a saturated sugar solution there, because the tea is ice-cold, etc.

Further Examples[2]

I infer that when I scratch this match it will light. My evidence is that this is a Sure-Fire brand match, and in the past Sure-Fire matches have always lit when scratched. However, unbeknownst to me, this particular match is defective. It will not light unless its surface temperature can be raised to 600 degrees, which is more than can be attained by scratching. Fortunately, as I scratch the match, a burst of Q-radiation (from the sun) strikes the tip, raising surface temperature to 600 degrees and igniting the match. Did I know that the match would light? Presumably I did not know. I had justified true belief, but not knowledge. On the present account, the explanation of my failure to know is this: I infer that the match will light in the next instance because Sure-Fire matches generally light when scratched. I am wrong about that; that is not why the match will light this time. Therefore, I do not know that it will light.

It is important that our justification can appeal to a simple generalization even when we have false views about the explanation of that generalization. Consider the man who thinks that barometers fall before a rainstorm because of an increase in the force of gravity. He thinks the gravity pulls the mercury down the tube and then, when the force is great enough, pulls rain out of the sky. Although he is wrong about this explanation, the man in question can come to know that it is going to rain when he sees the barometer falling in a particular case. That a man's belief is based on an inference that cannot give him knowledge (because it infers a false explanation) does not mean that it is not also based on an inference that does give him knowledge (because it infers a true explanation). The man in question has knowledge because he infers not only the stronger explanation involving gravity but also the weaker explanation. He infers that the explanation of the past correlation between falling barometer and rain is that the falling barometer is normally associated with rain. Then he infers that this weak generalization will be what will explain the correlation between the falling barometer and rain in the next instance.

Notice that if the man is wrong about that last point, because the barometer is broken and is leaking mercury, so that it is just a coincidence that rain is correlated with the falling barometer in the next instance, he does not come to know that it is going to rain.

Another example is the mad fiend case. Omar falls down drunk in the street. An hour later he suffers a fatal heart attack not connected with his recent drinking. After another hour a mad fiend comes down the street, spies Omar lying in the gutter, cuts off his head, and runs away. Some time later still, you walk down the street, see Omar lying there, and observe that his head has been cut off. You infer that Omar is dead, and in this way you come to know that he is dead. Now there is no causal connection between Omar's being dead and his head's having been cut off. The fact that Omar is dead is not causally responsible for his head's having been cut off, since if he had not suffered that fatal heart attack he still would have been lying there drunk when the mad fiend came along. And having his head cut off did not cause Omar's death, since he was already dead. Nor is there a straightforward logical connection between Omar's being dead and his having his head cut off. (Given the right sorts of tubes, one might survive decapitation.) So it is doubtful that Goldman's causal theory of knowing can account for your knowledge that Omar is dead.

If inductive inference is inference to the best explanatory statement, your inference might be parsed as follows: "Normally, if someone's head is cut off, that person is dead. This generalization accounts for the fact that Omar's having his head cut off is correlated here with Omar's being dead." Relevant competing explanatory statements in this case would not be competing explanations of Omar's being dead. Instead they would seek to explain Omar's not being dead despite his head's having been cut off. One possibility would be that doctors have carefully connected head and body with special tubes so that blood and air get from body to head and back again. You rule out that hypothesis on grounds of explanatory complications: too many questions left unanswered (why can't you see the tubes? why wasn't it done in the hospital? etc.). If you cannot rule such possibilities out, then you cannot come to know that Omar is dead. And if you do rule them out but they turn out to be true, again you do not come to know. For example, if it is all an elaborate psychological philosophical experiment which however fails, then you do not come to know that Omar is dead even though he is dead.

Statistical Inference

Statistical inference, and knowledge obtained from it, is also better explicated by way of the notion of statistical explanation than by way of the notion of cause or logical entailment. A person may infer that a particular coin is biased because that provides the best statistical explanation of the observed fraction of heads. His conclusion explains his evidence but neither causes nor entails it.

The relevant kind of statistical explanation does not always make what it explains very probable. For example, suppose that I want to know whether I have the fair coin or the weighted coin. It is equally likely that I have either; the probability of getting heads on a toss of the fair coin is $\frac{1}{2}$; and the probability of getting heads on a toss of the weighted coin is $\frac{6}{10}$. I toss the coin 10,000 times. It comes up heads 4,983 times and tails 5,017. I correctly conclude that the coin is the fair one. You would ordinarily think that I could in this way come to know that I have the fair coin. On the theory of inference we have adopted, I infer the best explanation of the observed distribution of heads and tails. But the explanation, that these were random tosses of a fair coin, does not make it probable that the coin comes up heads exactly 4,983 times and tails exactly 5,017 times in 10,000 tosses. The probability of this happening with a fair coin is very small. If we want to accept the idea that inference is inference to the best explanatory statement, we must agree that statistical explanation can cite an explanation that makes what it explains less probable than it makes its denial. In the present case, I do not explain why 4,983 heads have come up rather than some other number of heads. Instead I explain how it happened that 4,983 heads came up, what led to this happening. I do not explain why this happened rather than something else, since the same thing could easily have led to something else.

To consider a different example: you walk into a casino and see the roulette wheel stop at red fifty times in a row. The explanation may be that the wheel is fixed. It may also be that the wheel is fair and this is one of those times when fifty reds come up on a fair wheel. Given a fair wheel we may expect that to happen sometimes (but not very often). But if the explanation is that the wheel is fair and that this is just one of those times, it says what the sequence of reds is the result of, the "outcome" of. It does not say why fifty reds in a row occurred this time rather than some other time, nor why that particular series occurred rather than any of the $2^{50}-1$ other possible series.

This kind of statistical explanation explains something as the outcome of a chance set-up. The statistical probability of getting the explained outcome is irrelevant to whether or not we explain that outcome, since this kind of explanation is essentially pure nondeterministic explanation.

All that is relevant is that the outcome to be explained is one possible outcome given that chance set-up. That is not to say that the statistical probability of an outcome is irrelevant to the explanation of that outcome. It is relevant in this sense: the greater the statistical probability an observed outcome has in a particular chance set-up, the better that set-up explains that outcome.

The point is less a point about statistical explanation than a point about statistical inference. I wish to infer the best of competing statistical explanations of the observed distribution of heads. This observed outcome has different statistical probabilities in the two hypothetical chance set-ups, fair coin or weighted coin. The higher this statistical probability, the better, from the point of view of inference (other things being equal). The statistical probability of an outcome in a particular hypothetical chance set-up is relevant to how good an explanation that chance set-up provides. Here a better explanation is one that is more likely to be inferable. For example, I infer that I have the fair coin. The statistical probability of 4,983 heads on 10,000 tosses of a fair coin is much greater than the statistical probability of that number of heads on 10,000 tosses of the weighted coin. From the point of view of statistical probability, the hypothesis that the coin is fair offers a better explanation of the observed distribution than the hypothesis that the coin is biased. So statistical probability is relevant to statistical explanation. Not that there is no explanation unless statistical probability is greater than $1/2$. Rather that statistical probability provides a measure of the inferability of a statistical explanation.

According to probability theory, if initially the coin is just as likely to be the fair one or the weighted one and the statistical probability of the observed outcome is much greater for the fair coin than for the weighted coin, the probability that the coin is fair, given the observed evidence, will be very high. We might conclude that the statistical probability of the observed outcome given the fair or weighted coin is only indirectly relevant to my inference, relevant only because of the theoretical connections between those statistical probabilities and the evidential probabilities of the two hypotheses about the coin, given the observed evidence. But that would be to get things exactly backward. No doubt there is a connection between high evidential probability and inference; but, as we have seen, it is not because there is a purely probabilistic rule of acceptance.

High probability by itself does not warrant inference. Only explanatory considerations can do that, and the probability relevant to explanation is statistical probability, the probability that is involved in statistical explanation. It is the statistical probabilities of the observed outcome, given the fair and weighted coins, that is directly relevant to inference. The evidential probabilities of the two hypotheses are only indirectly relevant in that they in some sense reflect the inferability of the hypotheses, where that is determined directly by considerations of statistical probability.

Suppose that at first you do not know which of the two coins I have selected. I toss it 10,000 times, getting 4,983 heads and 5,017 tails. You infer that I have the fair coin, and you are right. But the reason for the 4,983 heads is that I am very good at tossing coins to come up whichever way I desire and I deliberately tossed the coin so as to get roughly half heads and half tails. So, even though you have justified true belief, you do not know that I have the fair coin.

If statistical inference were merely a matter of inferring something that has a high probability on the evidence, there would be no way to account for this sort of Gettier example. And if we are to appeal to principle *P*, it must be a conclusion essential to your inference that the observed outcome is the result of a chance set-up involving the fair coin in such a way that the probability of heads is $1/2$. Given a purely probabilistic rule, that conclusion could not be essential, for reasons similar to those that have already been discussed concerning the Nogot-Havit case. On the other hand, if statistical inference is inference to the best explanation and there is such a thing as statistical explanation even where the statistical probability of what is explained is quite low, then your conclusion about the reason for my getting 4,983 heads is seen to be essential to your inference. Since your explanation of the observed outcome is false, principle *P* accounts for the fact that you do not come to know that the coin is the fair coin even though you have justified true belief.

Conclusion

We are led to construe induction as inference to the best explanation, or more precisely as inference to the best of competing explanatory statements. The conclusion of any single step of such inference is always of the form *Y because X* (or *X explains Y*), from which we may deduce either *X* or *Y*. Inductive reasoning is seen to consist in a sequence of such explanatory conclusions.

We have been led to this conception of induction in an attempt to account for Gettier examples that show something wrong with the idea that knowledge is justified true belief. We have tried to find principles of inference which, together with principle *P*, would explain Gettier's deviant cases. Purely probabilistic rules were easily seen to be inadequate. Goldman's causal theory of knowing, which promised answers to some of Gettier's questions, suggested a causal theory of induction: inductive inference as inference to the best of competing causal statements. Our present version is simply a modification of that, with *explanatory* replacing *causal*. Its strength lies in the fact that it accounts for a variety of inferences, including inferences that involve weak generalizations or statistical hypotheses, in a way that explains Gettier examples by means of principle *P*.

Notes

1. See Keith Lehrer, "Knowledge, Truth, and Evidence," *Analysis* 25 (1965): 168–75.

2. See Brian Skyrms, "The Explication of 'X knows that P,' " *The Journal of Philosophy* 64 (1967): 373–89.

13

Knowledge as Justified True Belief

RODERICK CHISHOLM

Introduction

According to one traditional view, knowledge may be defined as follows:

S knows that p = Df p; S believes that p; and S is justified in believing that p.

If in this definition, we take "S is justified in believing that p," as many of us have done, to mean the same as "It is evident for S that p," then the definition is not adequate. For E. L. Gettier has shown that, unless we are willing to be skeptics, we must concede that there is evident true belief that isn't knowledge.[1] Hence, if we understand the traditional definition this way, we are faced with the problem of replacing it. But we could also take Gettier's results as showing that "h is justified for S," as it is to be interpreted in the traditional definition, cannot be taken to mean the same as "h is evident for S." Then we would be faced with the task of finding another analysis of "h is justified for S."

Let us view the problem in the second way. For simplicity, we will assume that all justified true belief is propositional.

Gettier Cases

When might one have a true belief in what is evident without that belief being an instance of knowing? This may happen when a false evident proposition makes evident a proposition that is true.[2] In one of Gettier's examples, we consider a conjunction e of propositions ("Jones keeps a Ford in his garage; Jones has been seen driving a Ford; Jones says he

Reprinted with author's revisions from Chisholm, *The Foundations of Knowing* (Minneapolis: University of Minnesota Press, 1982), 43–49, by permission of the author and publisher. Copyright 1982, University of Minnesota Press.

owns a Ford and he has always been honest and reliable in the past"). This proposition is said to make evident for a certain subject S a false proposition *f* ("Jones owns a Ford").[3] This false proposition *f*, in turn, makes evident for S a true proposition *h* ("Jones owns a Ford or Brown is in Barcelona"). The latter proposition has an evident disjunct that is not true ("Jones owns a Ford") and a true disjunct that is not evident ("Brown is in Barcelona"). Moreover, the true disjunct, we may suppose, is not a proposition that S accepts. The disjunction, then, could be said to derive its truth from its nonevident disjunct and to derive its evidence from its false disjunct. Suppose now that S accepts this disjunctive proposition, *h*, having inferred it from its first disjunct and having no beliefs with respect to the second disjunct. Then he will be accepting a true proposition that is evident to him. But this circumstance hardly warrants our saying that he *knows* the proposition to be true.

But not all "Gettier-type" problems thus involve disjunctions. Consider a second example, proposed by Keith Lehrer.[4]

Smith knows something to be true that he expresses as follows: (*e*) "Nogot is in my office; she told me she owns a Ford; she has always been honest and reliable in the past; I have just seen her stepping out of a Ford." This *e* makes evident the following proposition: (*f*) "Nogot is in my office and owns a Ford." And Smith sees that *f* makes evident for him the following proposition: (*h*) "Someone in my office owns a Ford." We suppose that all three propositions are accepted by Smith.

Now suppose further that Nogot has lied on this occasion—and therefore that *f* is false. Suppose also that, entirely unsuspected by Smith, a third person in his office—Havit—*does* own a Ford. The *e*, *f*, and *h* of this example will be related as are the *e*, *f*, and *h* of the first example: *e* will be a proposition that is known by Smith, but *h*—although it is true, evident, and accepted—will not be a proposition that is known by Smith. In place of the disjunction of the first example, we have in this case an existential generalization, which could be said to derive its truth from an instance of it that is not accepted and to derive its evidence from an instance of it that is accepted but false.

Hence, if we retain the traditional definition of knowledge, we cannot interpret "*h* is justified for S" to mean that *h* is evident for S.

Diagnosis of the Difficulty

We will consider the problem only in reference to the first of the two examples. What we will say holds, *mutatis mutandis*, of the second and of all other Gettier-type cases.

The difficulty arises in part because, as we have noted, the relation of making evident may be nondeductive. That is to say, it is possible for a proposition *e* to make evident a proposition *f* even though *e* is true and *f* is false. The false *f* may then, in turn, make evident a proposition *h* that happens to be true. And this true proposition *h*, in the Gettier cases, is the one that makes difficulties for the traditional definition of knowing.

Could we deal with Gettier's example, then, by stipulating that one proposition cannot make another proposition evident for a given subject unless the first proposition *entails* the second? This move would rule out the *h* of Gettier's example; we would no longer have to say that S *knows* that either Jones owns a Ford or Brown is in Barcelona. But such a move would also have the consequence that S knows very little about the world around him. In fact it would restrict the evident—and therefore what is known—to those Cartesian propositions that are self-presenting and to what can be apprehended a priori.

A more precise diagnosis of the problem would seem to be this: the proposition *h* is based on evidence that nondeductively makes evident a false proposition. So to repair the traditional definition, we may be tempted to say, in effect, that belief in an evident true proposition constitutes knowledge *provided* that the basis for that proposition does *not* make evident any false proposition. But this would have the consequence that the *e* of Gettier's example would not be known. And this is an undesirable consequence. Although the *h* of Gettier's example—"Jones owns a Ford"—should not be counted as knowledge, we *should* say that the conjunction *e* of propositions constituting S's evidence for *h*—i.e., "Jones keeps a Ford in his garage; Jones had been seen riding in a Ford"—is a proposition that S knows to be true. Yet it is based on evidence that makes evident a proposition that is false.

Our definition, then, should have the following consequences in application to Gettier's example:

1) The *h* of that example ("Jones owns a Ford or Brown is in Barcelona") is *not* known by the subject S—even though *h* is evident, true, and accepted by S.
2) The conjunction of propositions *e* ("Jones keeps a Ford in his garage; Jones has been seen riding in a Ford; and . . ."), which Gettier cites as S's evidence for *e*, is a proposition that is known by S.
3) The conjunction *b* of directly evident propositions constituting S's ultimate *basis* for *e* is also a proposition that is known by S.[5]

We can satisfy these conditions by introducing the concept of that which is *defectively evident*. Roughly speaking, we will say (1) that a proposition is defectively evident for a given subject S provided the propositions on which it is based make evident a proposition that is false and (2) that what is known must be evident but not defectively evident. But it will be necessary to characterize the defectively evident somewhat more precisely. To fulfill the desiderata listed above, we shall say that *some* defectively evident propositions—those of a certain sort that we will specify—*can* be known.

Proposed Solution

To explicate the sense in which knowledge may be said to be justified true belief, we make use of the undefined locution, "*e* makes *h* evident for S." We first define the concept of a basic proposition:

b is a basic proposition for S = Df *b* is evident for S; and everything that makes *b* evident for S entails *b*.

We next define the defectively evident:

h is defectively evident for S = Df (i) There is a basic proposition for S that makes *h* evident for S and does not logically imply *h;* and (ii) every such basic proposition makes evident a proposition that is false.

Now we are in a position to define the type of justification presupposed by the traditional definition of knowledge:

S is justified in believing that *p* = Df (i) It is evident for S that *p;* and (ii) if it is defectively evident for S that *p,* then the proposition that *p* is entailed by a conjunction of propositions each of which is evident but not defectively evident for S.

And so we retain the traditional definition of knowledge:

S knows that *p* = Df *p;* S believes that *p;* and S is justified in believing that *p.*

We now return to the three desiderata listed above.

1) The proposition *h* of Gettier's example ("Jones owns a Ford or Brown is in Barcelona") will not be counted as known. It is defectively evident for S—since it is made evident by a basic proposition that makes evident a proposition ("Jones owns a Ford") that is false. It does not satisfy the second condition of the definition of justification.

2) The evident proposition *e* that was cited as S's evidence for *h* ("Jones keeps a Ford in his garage; and . . .") is defectively evident by our definition. But it is justified for S, since it is entailed by a conjunction of propositions each of which is made evident for S by a basic proposition that does not make evident a proposition that is false.

3) And that proposition *b* which is S's directly evident basis for *e* is not defectively evident, for it fails to satisfy condition (i) of the definition of the defectively evident. There is no basic proposition that nondeductively makes *b* evident for S.

This definition does not enable us to say that, whenever a person may be said to know, then that person is also in a position to *know that he knows*. This consequence is as it should be. Because of the facts to which Gettier has called attention, one cannot generally know that one knows. For one cannot generally know whether or not one's evidence is defective.

Conclusion

With these definitions, I believe we have adequately dealt with Gettier's example. What we have said may also be applied to the second example, as well as to the other cases of evident true belief that are not cases of knowing. In all such cases, the object of the evident true belief is a proposition that is defectively evident: it is a proposition such that every proposition, which is basic for that subject and which makes *h* evident for him, also makes evident for him a proposition that is false. And, unlike Gettier's *e* and its basis *b*, it is not a proposition that is entailed by a conjunction of evident propositions each of which is nondefectively evident.

In recent philosophical literature, many "Gettier cases" have been formulated—many examples purporting to be cases of evident true belief that are not cases of knowing. If the examples are indeed cases of evident true belief that are not cases of knowing, then our definitions should ensure that they are not counted as cases of knowing. But the reader may find that, in application to *some* of the examples that have been offered, application of the definitions will *not* have this result.[6] I recommend that, in such cases, she look to the proposition corresponding to the *e* of the original example—the proposition that is supposed to make *h* evident to the subject in question. She will then find, if I am not mistaken, that *e* does *not* make *h* evident. The relation that *e* bears to *h* will be some weaker epistemic relation—that, say, of making *h* beyond reasonable doubt, or perhaps merely that of making *h* such as to have some presumption in its favor. If this is the case, then the example in question will not be an example of *evident* true belief.

Notes

1. E. L. Gettier, "Is Justified True Belief Knowledge?" (See Chapter 11 above.)
2. The relevant sense of "makes evident" is explicated in Chisholm, *The Foundations of Knowing*, chap. 2.
3. It should be noted that our formulation of *e* is intended to contain a blank

and is therefore incomplete. The conjunction of propositions that are explicit in our formulation of *e* is *not* sufficient to make *f* evident for the subject of Gettier's example.

4. Keith Lehrer, "Knowledge, Truth and Evidence," *Analysis* 25 (1965): 168–75.

5. Earl Conee has pointed out to me that my earlier attempts to deal with the Gettier problem do not satisfy the third condition. See his "The Analysis of Knowledge in the Second Edition of *Theory of Knowledge*," *Canadian Journal of Philosophy* 10 (1980): 295–300.

6. Possibly this is true of the example of the pyromaniac proposed by Brian Skyrms in "The Explication of 'X knows that P,' " *Journal of Philosophy* 64 (1967): 373–89. Skyrms considers these two propositions, *e* and *h:* (*e*) "Sure-Fire matches have always and often lit for me when struck except when wet, and this match is a Sure-Fire and is dry"; (*h*) "This match will light now as I strike it." He assumes—mistakenly, it seems to me—that *e* makes *h* evident. I believe the most we can expect of *e* in this connection is that it makes *h* such as to be beyond reasonable doubt.

14   An Alleged Defect in Gettier Counterexamples

RICHARD FELDMAN

A number of philosophers have contended that Gettier counterexamples to the justified true belief analysis of knowledge all rely on a certain false principle. For example, in their recent paper "Knowledge Without Paradox,"[1] Robert G. Meyers and Kenneth Stern argue that "Counterexamples of the Gettier sort all turn on the principle that someone can be justified in accepting a certain proposition h on evidence p even though p is false."[2] They contend that this principle is false, and hence that the counterexamples fail. Their view is that one proposition, p, can justify another, h, only if p is true. With this in mind, they accept the justified true belief analysis.

D. M. Armstrong defends a similar view in *Belief, Truth and Knowledge*.[3] He writes:

> This simple consideration seems to make redundant the ingenious argument of . . . Gettier's . . . article . . . Gettier produces counterexamples to the thesis that justified true belief is knowledge by producing true beliefs based on justifiably believed grounds, . . . but where these grounds are in fact *false.* But because possession of such grounds could not constitute possession of *knowledge*, I should have thought it obvious that they are too weak to serve as suitable grounds.[4]

Thus he concludes that Gettier's examples are defective because they rely on the false principle that false propositions can justify one's belief in other propositions. Armstrong's view seems to be that one proposition, p, can justify another, h, only if p is known to be true (unlike Meyers and Stern, who demand only that p in fact be true).[5]

I think, though, that there are examples very much like Gettier's that do not rely on this allegedly false principle. To see this, let us first consider one example in the form in which Meyers and Stern discuss it, and then consider a slight modification of it.

Reprinted from the *Australasian Journal of Philosophy* 52 (1974): 68–69, by permission of the author and the editor. Copyright 1974, *Australasian Journal of Philosophy*.

Suppose Mr. Nogot tells Smith that he owns a Ford and even shows him a certificate to that effect. Suppose, further, that up till now Nogot has always been reliable and honest in his dealings with Smith. Let us call the conjunction of all this evidence *m*. Smith is thus justified in believing that Mr. Nogot who is in his office owns a Ford (*r*) and, consequently, is justified in believing that someone in his office owns a Ford (*h*).[6]

As it turns out, though, *m* and *h* are true but *r* is false. So, the Gettier example runs, Smith has a justified true belief in *h*, but he clearly does not know *h*.

What is supposed to justify *h* in this example is *r*. But since *r* is false, the example runs afoul of the disputed principle. Since *r* is false, it justifies nothing. Hence, if the principle is false, the counterexample fails.

We can alter the example slightly, however, so that what justifies *h* for Smith is true and he knows that it is. Suppose he deduces from *m* its existential generalization:

(*n*) There is someone in the office who told Smith that he owns a Ford and even showed him a certificate to that effect, and who up till now has always been reliable and honest in his dealings with Smith.

(*n*), we should note, is true and Smith knows that it is, since he has correctly deduced it from *m*, which he knows to be true. On the basis of *n* Smith believes *h*—someone in the office owns a Ford. Just as the Nogot evidence, *m*, justified *r*—Nogot owns a Ford—in the original example, *n* justifies *h* in this example. Thus Smith has a justified true belief in *h*, knows his evidence to be true, but still does not know *h*.

I conclude that even if a proposition can be justified for a person only if his evidence is true, or only if he knows it to be true, there are still counterexamples to the justified true belief analysis of knowledge of the Gettier sort. In the above example, Smith reasoned from the proposition *m*, which he knew to be true, to the proposition *n*, which he also knew, to the truth *h*; yet he still did not know *h*. So some examples, similar to Gettier's, do not "turn on the principle that someone can be justified in accepting a certain proposition . . . even though [his evidence] is false."[7]

Notes

1. *The Journal of Philosophy* 70 (March 22, 1973): 147–60.
2. Ibid., p. 147.
3. (1973).
4. Ibid., p.152.
5. Armstrong ultimately goes on to defend a rather different analysis.
6. Meyers and Stern, "Knowledge Without Paradox," p. 151.
7. Ibid., p. 147.

15   Knowledge and Falsity

ROBERT SHOPE

In attempting to disarm Gettier-type objections to the traditional analysis of knowledge, some philosophers have maintained that the putative counterexamples described in those objections attribute certain false beliefs to the agent in such a manner as to vitiate the force of the objections. Other philosophers have responded that no such false beliefs are involved in at least some of those examples, and that they constitute genuine counterexamples to the traditional analysis of knowledge as justified true belief. I shall assess this controversy and argue that the proper way to deal with Gettier-type examples is by prohibiting false propositions at certain places in what I shall call "justification-explaining chains."

For much of my discussion, I shall concentrate on the case of the clever reasoner, found in Keith Lehrer's *Knowledge*. It is a variant of the well-known example of Mr. Nogot. In the latter example, a teacher has among the pupils in his office Mr. Nogot and Mr. Havit. The teacher possesses no evidence suggesting that Mr. Havit owns a Ford, but he does possess evidence sufficient to justify his believing that Mr. Nogot owns a Ford: Mr. Nogot shows him papers saying he owns one, drives one in front of the teacher, has previously been reliable in his dealings with the teacher, and so forth. From his belief that Mr. Nogot owns a Ford, the teacher deduces that someone in the office owns a Ford. However, Mr. Nogot does not own one and has been shamming, whereas Mr. Havit actually does own a Ford. Thus, the teacher has justified true belief but not knowledge that someone in the office owns a Ford.

Here, the teacher does have a false belief, namely, that Mr. Nogot owns a Ford, which enters into his reasoning to his conclusion. Accordingly, some philosophers have sought to nullify the force of the example by maintaining that when one's belief is justified, it never crucially depends upon one's having false beliefs; for example, never depends upon one's using a false belief as a non-superfluous basis for reasoning to one's conclusion.

Reprinted from *Philosophical Studies* 36 (1979): 389-405, by permission of the author and the publisher. Copyright 1979, D. Reidel Publishing Company.

In response to this move, Lehrer introduces a variant of the Nogot case in which the teacher is a "clever reasoner" and is interested only in whether one of his students owns a Ferrari, without caring which student owns one. Thus,

> he might reason that, though his only evidence of a Ferrari owner among his students is what he knows about Mr. Nogot and a certain car [i.e., that Nogot claimed he owned a Ferrari, drove one in front of him, etc.], there is at least the possibility that someone else owns one, and, hence, it is safer to accept the more general statement that at least one person in his class owns a Ferrari than the quite specific claim that Mr. Nogot owns one. Hence, without concluding that Mr. Nogot owns a Ferrari, the teacher in question concludes that at least one person in his class owns a Ferrari. This conclusion is derived from a set of perfectly true statements about Mr. Nogot and the consideration that someone else in class may, for all he knows, own a Ferrari. But even this clever reasoner does not know that there is a single Ferrari owner among his students. [pp. 20–21]

In "How Do You Know?" (*American Philosophical Quarterly* 11 [1974]: 113–22), Ernest Sosa criticizes Lehrer's viewpoint by noting that whether I am justified in believing *H:* "Someone in my office [class] owns a Ford [Ferrari] on the basis of *E,* my evidence about Mr. Nogot's behavior "surely depends on whether I see a connection between *E* and *H,*" so that in the cases Lehrer describes, "you could make no connection between *E* and *H* except by way of a falsehood" (p.116). Thus, we might say that anyone so dull-witted as to infer *H* directly from *E* without believing in a connecting step, such as the intermediate conclusion that Mr. Nogot owns a Ford (Ferrari), can hardly be said to be justified in believing *H.* Sosa shows that his own analysis of knowing survives Lehrer's example once we treat the false belief that Mr. Nogot owns a Ford (Ferrari) as part of what putatively justifies the teacher in believing his conclusion (whether or not he actually reasons from that belief). For Sosa's analysis maintains that a purported justification fails to yield knowledge if it crucially depends upon a false belief.[1]

As support for his treatment of the Nogot example, Sosa cites a paper by Robert G. Meyers and Kenneth Stern "Knowledge without Paradox" (*Journal of Philosophy* 70 [1973]: 147–60). They maintain that whether the teacher, call him Smith, is justified in concluding *H* depends on

> how Smith views his evidence. Suppose, for instance, that Smith *is not* prepared to defend *H* on the basis of *R,* i.e., "Mr. Nogot who is in my office [class] owns a Ford [Ferrari]." Is it then plausible to hold that he is justified in believing that *H?* Clearly not; and most likely Smith would agree [p. 152].

But Lehrer can reply that when we are not dealing with a dull-witted Smith but with a teacher who is a clever reasoner, then the teacher is indeed prepared to defend his conclusion by citing a connection between *E* and *H.* But in citing it, he does not maintain that *R* is *true,* or rely on his *believing R*. Yet he does believe in a certain connection between E and H involving the *proposition R*.

Before assessing Lehrer's treatment of the case of the clever reasoner further, we may consider the possibility raised by Richard Feldman in "An Alleged Defect in Gettier Counterexamples" (Chapter 14, this volume). Feldman says that in the original example concerning Mr. Nogot, the teacher can relate E and H without involving R, simply by deducing from E its existential generalization:

> (*N*) There is someone in the office who told Smith that he owns a Ford and even showed him a certificate to that effect, and who up till now has always been reliable and honest in his dealings with Smith.

Feldman claims that Smith can use a belief in N as evidence for his claim that someone in the office owns a Ford, without using any false statement as part of his evidence for that conclusion.

It is important to see that Feldman has only shown that in this variation of the example no false belief forms a premise in the teacher's reasoning. But we should not confuse the process of *presenting* to oneself a justification for one's belief, or the process of reasoning through it, with the fact that the belief *is* justified.[2] Part of what makes a person's belief justified may be his believing true propositions which do not form part of his reasoning process. Accordingly, in his analysis of knowing, Sosa says that for every true proposition of the form, "S is justified in believing h," where h is not self-evident, we can "show what 'makes these propositions true' *via* epistemic principles," provided that the latter are combined with other truths of the form "S is justified in believing q," "S is justified in believing r," and so forth, and possibly with some propositions that do not attribute particular beliefs to S.[3] Thus, the question arises whether Feldman's teacher can *be* justified in believing H without also believing proposition M, which we may briefly express as follows: "The person mentioned in N who spoke to Smith is a person in the office who owns a Ford." It does not matter for Sosa whether the latter proposition enters into the teacher's reasoning to his conclusion. What matters is whether there is a set, *(a)*, of epistemic principles, and a set, *(b)*, of propositions, including ones describing the teacher as justified in believing various things (and perhaps including ones describing other epistemic or non-epistemic facts about the teacher), where *(a)* and *(b)* are jointly but not separately sufficient to entail that the teacher is justified in believing his conclusion, but where *(b)* does not describe the teacher as justified in believing M. Sosa's account indicates that if the attribution of belief in M is unavoidable, then the teacher does not know his final conclusion to be true—for his belief in M is false. Thus, until sets *(a)* and *(b)* are actually provided in an elaboration of Feldman's example, the case of the clever reasoner may present more of a challenge to philosophers who wish to dismiss Gettier-type examples by construing the persons described in those examples as holding false beliefs.

In order to understand how Lehrer can deal with the application of Sosa's views to the case of the clever reasoner, we may take note of the fact that when Sosa says that S is justified in believing p, Sosa means that S actually does believe p and is justified in that belief.[4] But when the clever reasoner reaches conclusion H': "Someone in the class owns a Ferrari," he does not believe R': "Mr. Nogot owns a Ferrari." Instead, he believes the following proposition:

(*C*) Someone in the class other than Mr. Nogot may, for all I know, own a Ferrari; moreover, evidence E is sufficient to justify any belief that I might have in R', *and the latter proposition does entail H'*.

Lehrer may maintain that the teacher's justified true belief in C is sufficient to make the teacher justified in believing H'. Notice that C only speaks of a belief in R' as one the teacher might have, without entailing that he does have it.

One challenge that can be raised to this suggestion is that the teacher is being irrational in failing to believe R' if he is already prepared to believe H'. Two points appear to be adequate to answer this objection. First, the question is whether the teacher is justified in believing H' in such a way as to know it to be true, not whether he is unjustified in failing to believe R'. A person does not have to be epistemically perfect regarding all his other epistemic attitudes in order to be justified in holding a given one. Second, Lehrer has described the clever reasoner as consciously considering the fact that he reduces his risk of believing something false by accepting the more general conclusion H' without also believing the more specific proposition R'.

We might think it psychologically implausible that someone could believe that general conclusion without believing the more specific statement, but it is worth recalling an example offered by Brian Skyrms in "The Explication of 'X knows that P' " (*Journal of Philosophy* 64 [1967]: 373–89), when he urged that the difficulties raised by the Gettier-type examples are genuine:

Suppose that a scientist has good evidence for a very general law (or theory represented as a conjunction of laws) T; that T entails a more specific law L; that the scientist, having made the appropriate derivation, knows that the entailment holds and by virtue of this fact knows that the evidence in question is good evidence for L; that he believes L on this basis; that the evidence in question is not direct evidence for L; that L is true and T is false [p. 378].

A scientist who is a clever reasoner may very well realize that he takes a greater risk of being wrong in believing T than in merely believing the more specific law *L*. It is psychologically possible and need not be irrational for him to believe the latter while suspending judgment on the former until further testing of it. This suggestion is even more plausible when there is already some further support for *L*, independent of *T*, but support which is not strong enough by itself to justify believing *L*.

Thus, it may be correct to regard Lehrer's case of the clever reasoner analogously, even though *R'* in that example is not so sweeping as a scientific theory. The point is that the teacher incurs greater risk of believing something false by believing both *R'* and *H'* than he does by believing just *H'*. Indeed, Lehrer may intend us to include as one conjunct of *C* the teacher's assessment of this risk, but for simplicity I have omitted this detail.[5]

A suggestive approach to the original case of Mr. Nogot and to the case of the clever reasoner appears in John H. Dreher's paper "Evidence and Justified Belief" (*Philosophical Studies* 25 [1974]: 435–39). Dreher presumes that the traditional analysis of inferential knowledge as justified true belief employs the phrase "justified belief" to mean believing on good evidence. He adds that this is a sense of the term "evidence" in which there can be no such thing as false evidence—or, to improve upon Dreher's wording, no such thing as a false proposition describing the evidence for something (cf. pp. 435–36). Thus, the false proposition *P*, "Mr. Nogot owns a Ford [Ferrari]" cannot be—or cannot describe—good evidence for proposition *Q*: "Someone in the office [class] owns a Ford [Ferrari]." Letting *F* be the evidence concerning Mr. Nogot's behavior, Dreher points out that the conjunction of *F* and *P* also cannot describe evidence for *Q*, since that conjunction is false. Thus, the only remaining candidate to describe evidence for *Q* is *F*. But, Dreher observes,

> if *F* is good evidence for *Q*, then *F* is good evidence for *Q* *only* because *F* is good evidence for *P* . . . and *F* does not "directly" support *Q* in the way in which facts sometimes support disjunctions without supporting either disjunct. [p. 437]

Dreher claims that the falsity of *P* prevents *F* from describing evidence for *Q*, even though the teacher, who does not know that *P* is false, may mistakenly think that *F* describes good evidence for *Q*. Dreher concludes that Gettier-type examples fail to be counterexamples to the traditional analysis of knowledge as justified true belief. For in such examples, the person lacks good evidence for what he believes and is not in the relevant sense justified in believing it.

Although this final conclusion may be too extreme, I believe that Dreher's approach contains a worthwhile insight. However, it is not clear from his remarks how to formulate a general requirement for a true proposition, *f*, to describe good evidence for another proposition, *q*, in rder to be able to deal with all Gettier-type cases. Let us consider a number of possibilities, ending with what I take to be the correct view.

(i) It would be too strong to require that there be no false proposition p, uch that f describes good evidence for q thanks to describing good vidence for p. Suppose that a scientist, who is looking at a measuring nstrument that he knows to be a generally reliable source of information bout a certain range of phenomena, realizes that f' is true: "The nstrument is showing reading r on its meter." This may provide him with vidence that a certain phenomenon is present. but since he can see that his phenomenon is not present, f' also allows him to know that q' is true: "The instrument is not in working order." Here, f' describes good vidence for q' because it describes evidence for a false proposition.

One might be dissatisfied with this example on the grounds that when a neasuring instrument is broken its readings no longer serve as evidence oncerning the range of phenomena that it normally measures. If this is o, then the following example is not subject to a similar response. Suppose that f' is true: "Mr. Spotter, who is a generally reliable observer egarding a certain range of phenomena, reports that he looked at a type of phenomenon within that range and observed proposition p'' to be true of that phenomenon." Suppose further that the report provides me with ome good evidence that p'' (whatever it may be) is true. However, because I am aware of other overwhelming evidence that p'' is false, I know q'' to be true: "Either Mr. Spotter did not look carefully or he did not pay special attention to what he saw." Thanks to the fact that his eport is some good evidence for what I know to be false, I know q'' to be rue. The mere fact that Mr. Spotter did not look carefully or with special ttention is not enough to make his report cease to be some good evidence n support of p''. For the range of phenomena about which he is a generally reliable observer may include many instances where he can ccurately report what occurs after a mere glance, while paying no more han ordinary attention to what is before him. Yet when his report does rr, q'' may provide me with the appropriate explanation of why I am in oossession of misleading evidence.

(ii) Someone might object that in the above example it is not *only* because I have some good evidence for p'' that I have good evidence for q''. For I also have some good evidence for q'' consisting in the fact that what Mr. Spotter claims to have seen did not occur. Here, no mention is made of his report being good evidence for p'' so I am not sure that this haracterization of the example is correct. But if it is, should we then take Dreher's general requirement to be that there is no false proposition, p, uch that part of the explanation of why f describes good evidence for q is he fact that f describes good evidence for p? This requirement is also too trong. For it is not satisfied by my knowledge that q''' is true: "Someone s providing me with good but misleading evidence that p'' is true."

(iii) It would be too strong to require that a full, correct explanation of why f describes good evidence for q can be given without mentioning any false proposition. For the false proposition p'' does need to be mentioned in order to give a full, correct explanation of why f' describes good evidence for q''.

(iv) If we require only that some correct statement (not necessarily a full, correct explanation) of why f describes good evidence for q can be given without mentioning any false proposition, then the requirement becomes useless. For one could propose that in the case of the clever reasoner, what makes the teacher's evidence good evidence for the proposition "Someone in the class owns a Ferrari" is that it is good evidence for some (unmentioned) proposition entailing that someone in the class owns a Ferrari. The requirement would not show why this is an improper claim.

(v) Perhaps it would be useful to require that a full, correct explanation of why f describes good evidence for q can be given without *asserting* any false proposition.[6] However, this alone will not handle a clever reasoner who refuses to accept the false proposition, $P:$ "Mr. Nogot owns a Ferrari," and who, under pressure, merely includes the following conjunct in his explanation:

(C') Proposition F (which describes Mr. Nogot's behavior) describes good evidence for proposition $Q:$ "Someone in the class owns a Ferrari," because F describes good evidence for P and P entails Q.

Notice that in asserting C' the clever reasoner does not assert the false proposition P. Even if he does thereby assert the proposition that F describes good evidence for $Q,$ and even if such an assertion is false, the point of the requirement was to show why the assertion is false, and this has not yet been done.

(vi) Thus, we might be led to the following version of the requirement. There is some correct explanation of why f describes good evidence for q that either (1) has the form "f describes good evidence for q because f describes good evidence for x and x entails q," where x is true; or (2) has the form "f describes good evidence for q because f describes good evidence for x and x describes good evidence for q," where x is true.

Unfortunately, there is a defect in the phrasing of (1). This may be illustrated by an example where x is the proposition "Someone in the class owns a Ferrari' and q the proposition "Either someone in the class owns a Ferrari or Brown is in Barcelona." Suppose the teacher claims that his evidence concerning Mr. Nogot's behavior is good evidence for q because it is good evidence for x and x entails q. Our requirement does not give a way of showing why this is an improper claim. For x is indeed true.

A similar defect occurs in (2). Let f' describe the fact that Mr. Listener receives from the generally reliable teacher a report of Mr. Nogot's behavior, and let x' be the proposition describing that behavior. If Mr. Listener claims to know q to be true, "Someone in the class owns a Ferrari," the wording of (2) does not show why it is improper to say that f' describes good evidence for q because f' describes good evidence for x' and x' describes good evidence for q.

(vii) We can avoid this type of difficulty and correctly deal with Gettier-type cases by appealing to what I shall call a *justification-explaining chain related to q*, defined as follows: It is an ordered set of propositions such that (a) the first member, m_1, is a true proposition of the form:

"f_1 is true, and that makes q justified,"

where f_1 describes something sufficient to make proposition q justified, (b) for any member, m_j, the successor of m_j is determined as follows: (i) there is no successor of m_j if and only if m_j is justified without anything making it justified and (ii) when something makes m_j justified then the successor of m_j is a true proposition of the form:

"f_{j+1} is true, and that makes m_j justified,"

where f_{j+1} describes something sufficient to make m_j justified, (c) each f_j is a proposition that is a disjunction of conjunctions or propositions that take any of the forms described below (allowing disjunctions and conjunctions to contain only one member):

(1) "p_2 describes evidence for p_1,"
(2) "p_2 is true, and p_2 entails p_1," where p_1 does not entail p_2,
(3) "p_i describes evidence for p_{i-1}, and p_{i-1} describes evidence for p_{i-2}, and . . . , p_3 describes evidence for p_2," where $3 \leq i \leq n$,
(4) "p_2 entails p_1," where p_1 does not entail p_2,
(5) a form described as in any of the above but with phrases of one or more of the following types substituting at one or more places in the description for the phrase "describes evidence for": "describes good evidence for," "describes evidence of such-and-such strength for," "describes something that justifies," "describes something that justifies to such-and-such a degree,"[7]
(6) any form other than one logically equivalent to a disjunction of conjunctions of propositions which take any of the above forms (allowing disjunctions and conjunctions to contain only one member),

and (d) for any one of $p_1, \ldots, p_n$ that is false, some member of the chain entails its falsity.

A justification-explaining chain is not to be confused with what might be called a justification-*making* chain, that is, a string of evidence leading up to q, or a succession of items each of which makes its successor justified and one of which finally makes q justified. For no member of a justification-*explaining* chain merely describes something that makes q justified or something that is a piece of evidence for q.

In order to see the importance of this difference, consider the form of the very first member of a justification-explaining chain in the case of the clever reasoner:

m_1: "f_1 is true, and that makes Q justified,"

where Q is the proposition "Someone in the class owns a Ferrari." It is only the first conjunct of m_1 that could describe the teacher's evidence for Q or a string of such evidence. The second conjunct of m_1 instead comments on an epistemic relation between f_1 and Q. Thanks to the second conjunct in m_1 and similar conjuncts in each member of a justification-explaining chain, a false proposition will eventually turn up in the remainder of the chain at a spot prohibited by the definition, and we shall be left with a mere pseudochain.

At least, this will happen if we attempt to construct a justification-explaining chain that is relevantly related to the teacher. There is indeed, *some* genuine justification-explaining chain not significantly connected with the teacher's epistemic situation. It is a chain that instead involves evidence possessed by Mr. Havit, and which allows Mr. Havit to know that Q is true. But the teacher does not grasp a suitable portion of *that* chain. One reason for this is that none of its members mention f_1 or the teacher's evidence. The teacher's believing Q is not justified through any connection with that chain.

Thus, Gettier-type examples may be dealt with by specifying the following necessary condition for S to have "justified factual knowledge" that q is true, that is, knowledge whose possession partly depends upon S's justifiably believing or accepting q:

(NC) If something makes proposition q justified then S's believing or accepting q is justified through its connection with a justification-explaining chain related to q.[8]

Developing a set of epistemic principles that specify how much of a justification-explaining chain must be within S's grasp when S has justified belief or justified acceptance is a project which I shall not embark upon here.[9] However, we are already able to understand why the standard Gettier-type examples fail to constitute instances of knowledge.

If, for example, one tried to describe a justification-explaining chain partly within the grasp of the clever reasoner, one would need to include in m_2, the successor of m_1, a conjunct, c, that describes something sufficient to justify the second conjunct in m_1. An unsatisfactory candidate for c is one that itself includes the following proposition of form (4), or an analogous one of form (5), as a conjunct: "That Mr. Nogot owns a

Ferrari entails that someone in the class owns a Ferrari." To include such a conjunct in c would be to render the chain a mere pseudochain by including a false proposition as p_2. In that case, necessary condition NC fails to be satisfied. For in this example—in contrast, say, to that of Mr. Spotter—it is not in the least plausible to suppose that some member of the chain entails that p_2 is indeed false.

Notice that this point holds whether or not the set of epistemic principles requires S *to believe* any of the conjuncts of m_2. The point is that the chain is not a *genuine* justification-explaining chain in this example, and so condition NC is not met. The useful insight that I have extracted from Dreher's approach is that in order to characterize non-basic knowledge so as to block Gettier-type examples, we must speak of the justification of the proposition that S believes and not merely of the justification of S's believing it.[10]

Alternatively, we might attempt to construct a justification-explaining chain in the case of the clever reasoner in a manner suggested by Feldman's example. Let N^* be the existential generalization of the teacher's evidence. The first member, m_1, of the putative justification-explaining chain might have the form "N^* is true, and that makes Q justified." In continuing to describe the chain, we would need to propose that something makes the second conjunct in m_1 justified, and would eventually be led to include as a conjunct of some successor of m_1 the statement Z: "N^* is true, N^* describes [good] evidence for P, and P entails Q," where P is a false proposition tantamount to the following: "The person mentioned in N^* who spoke to the teacher was a person in the class who owned the Ferrari of which he spoke." However, such a chain is a mere pseudochain because the second conjunct in Z is a proposition of form (1) (or (5)) with a prohibited false proposition in place of p_1, and the final conjunct a proposition of form (4) with a false proposition in place of p_2.[11]

One may grasp certain portions of a justification-explaining chain without having one's belief justified through its connection with such a chain. Consider the following variant of the Nogot example. One student in the class, Ms. Withit, happens to know that Mr. Nogot does not own an automobile. But she also knows that Mr. Nogot will go to any length in order to impress the teacher with his affluence and with his ability to keep up with the Havits. Ms. Withit not only witnesses Mr. Nogot's deceit of the teacher, but she, too, knows that Mr. Nogot has been otherwise reliable in his dealings with the teacher. It is apparent to Ms. Withit that the only plausible explanation of Mr. Nogot's extraordinary charade is that Mr. Havit must own a Ferrari and that Mr. Nogot has got wind of the fact, so that Mr. Nogot has been motivated to borrow or to steal a Ferrari and to fake the corresponding papers for this morning's performance, while presuming that the teacher will soon learn of Mr. Havit's ownership of a similar luxury. Perhaps this is enough to allow Ms. Withit to know Q to be true. It is at least enough for proposition Q to be justified in light of the information and reasoning utilized by Ms. Withit. If so, then we must admit that the corresponding justification-explaining chain includes the evidence, E, about Mr. Nogot's behavior that is possessed by the clever reasoner, and that E does occur in the putative justification-explaining chain which might be put forth in an attempt to support the teacher's acceptance of Q. Indeed, we might even begin spelling out both a genuine chain and such a pseudochain by offering as m_1 in each chain the following proposition: "E is true, and that makes Q justified." What must be emphasized, therefore, is that if we tried to explain why the teacher's belief in Q is justified, we could not merely say that the facts described in E justify his belief. We would need to maintain that they do so because they are good evidence for the proposition "Mr. Nogot owns a Ferrari." But at this point we part company with an account of what makes Ms. Withit justified in believing Q, and in appealing to such considerations we have actually gone outside anything included in a corresponding justification-explaining chain related to Q.[12]

It no longer matters for our purposes whether Dreher is correct in maintaining of Lehrer's examples that the teacher fails to be justified by the evidence in believing that someone owns the type of car in question. Although their view of such examples may be correct, the intuitions of other epistemologists disagree. We may simply note that if the teacher's belief is justified, it is nonetheless not justified through its connections with evidence mentioned in a justification-explaining chain related to the proposition which the teacher believes, nor is the proposition non-derivatively justified. On the present account, this is sufficient reason for denying that the clever reasoner possesses knowledge.[13]

I shall conclude by illustrating the way in which other familiar Gettier-type examples are dealt with by inclusion of condition *NC* in an analysis of factual knowledge.

In Roderick Chisholm's sheep example, S takes there to be a sheep in the field under conditions k which are such that, when a person does thus take there to be a sheep in the field, the person is justified in believing proposition Q_1: "There is a sheep in the field." On this occasion, the man has mistaken a dog for a sheep. However, unknown to him, a sheep is indeed at another spot in the field.[14] Let F_1 be the true proposition: "S takes there to be a sheep in the field in conditions k." When attempting to construct a justification-explaining chain related to Q_1 that is relevantly connected with S's belief, we might render member m_1 as follows: "F_1 is true, and that makes Q_1 justified." But in continuing the chain, we must describe something that makes m_1 a justified proposition. This requires us to describe something sufficient to make the second conjunct of m_1 justified. It is tempting to say that the second conjunct is justified because the truth of F_1 makes P_1 justified and P_1 entails Q_1, where P_1 is the proposition "The thing S takes to be a sheep in the field is a sheep in the field." But since P_1 is false, the definition of a justification-explaining chain prohibits such an explanation except when some member of the chain entails that P_1 is false, which cannot plausibly be maintained in this example.[15]

The only other approach that comes to mind is to forestall failure briefly *à la* Feldman and to deduce from F_1 its existential generalization N_1: "There is someone in conditions k who takes there to be a sheep in the field." Suppose that we continue to describe the chain by saying that the second conjunct of m_1 is justified in part by the state of affairs mentioned in a proposition such as the following:

> "F_1 is true, that makes N_1 justified, and N_1 describes (good) evidence for Q_1."

But a further member of the chain will, in turn, have to contain a conjunct explaining why the final conjunct in the above proposition is justified. There is no apparent way to explain this that is even initially plausible except by advancing a proposition such as the following:

(R)   "N_1 is true, that makes P'_1 justified, and P'_1 entails Q_1,"

where P'_1 is the proposition "The thing taken by someone in conditions k to be a sheep in the field is a sheep in the field" (or, alternatively, "Something taken by someone in conditions k to be a sheep in the field is a sheep in the field"). But P_1 is false, and any admission of this in the chain would clearly undercut the role of R in helping to explain why the second conjunct of m_1 is justified.[16]

Finally, consider Brian Skyrms' example of a pyromaniac who has often used Sure-Fire matches and who, just before striking a particular one, possesses evidence described by the true proposition F_3: "Sure-Fire matches have always and often lit for me when struck except when wet, and this match is a Sure-Fire and is dry." The pyromaniac, not thinking about any causal considerations, simply makes the "singular predictive inference" directly to conclusion Q_3: "This match will light now as I strike it." Unknown to the pyromaniac, this particular match has impurities that make it impossible to light through the friction of striking, but it nonetheless will light, thanks to an unsuspected, coincidental burst of rare Q-radiation. The pyromaniac has no false beliefs, but nonetheless fails to know a moment before striking that the match will light when he strikes it.[17]

Marshall Swain, in "Defeasibility: A Reply to R. B. Scott" (*Philosophical Studies* 29 [1976]: 425–28), maintains that if the pyromaniac's evidence is good enough to justify his believing Q_3, then it is also good enough to justify believing the following false generalization:

(S_1)   Any dry Sure-Fire match in this box will ignite when struck.

Swain points out that such matches will not light if there is no oxygen present (cf. pp. 426–27).

But the force of this observation is diminished by Swain's admission that the pyromaniac's justification for believing Q_3 is based on an analogy with previous instances, and "depends essentially on being justified in believing that this match is relevantly like the previously examined ones" (p. 427). The relevant similarity must include the circumstances surrounding ignition, and these will include the presence of oxygen, whether or not the pyromaniac is aware of it. So instead of being justified in believing the false S_1, the pyromaniac is actually justified in believing the following true, albeit vague, generalization:

(S_1')   Any Sure-Fire match in this box will ignite when struck in circumstances such as those surrounding the previous ignitions that were relevant to ignition.

To be sure, Swain lists other propositions that the pyromaniac is justified in believing which are indeed false:

(S_2)   This match is like previously struck Sure-Fire matches in all respects relevant to ignition.

(S_3)   This match has the same composition as previously struck Sure-Fire matches [cf. p. 427].

However, we can construct a slightly different version of the example in which the pyromaniac still fails to know that Q_3 is true, yet S_2 and S_3 are true. Suppose that, as luck would have it, the pyromaniac's past sample also contained an instance in which Q-radiation, unknown to him, was what ignited a defective match just like the present one in composition. Obviously, we cannot plausibly read S_2 and S_3 as entailing that all the matches struck previously had just one composition. The factory might have varied the composition of its well-made matches from time to time in response to variations in the supply of available manufacturing materials. So ignition may have been due on different occasions to rather different chemical processes even when it did occur because of striking.

I believe that a false proposition such as the following is nonetheless going to surface during any reasonably plausible attempt to construct a justification-explaining chain related to Q_3 which is connected with the pyromaniac's belief, even though the pyromaniac may not consider such a false proposition:

(S_4)   If there is a reason for the present match's lighting then, relative to the set of reasons (possibly varied) which there were for ignition of those Sure-Fire matches previously observed by the pyromaniac to light after striking, the reason for which the present match will light after striking is akin to one of those in the set that was not a reason for the lighting of the matches in an inductively insignificant portion of the sample.

Although I lack space to discuss the point at the length it deserves, the question of whether the present reason was one related to an inductively insignificant portion of the sample may depend, among other things, upon how many instances were in that portion and how varied the circumstances were surrounding the different instances in that portion.

This points to the way in which my account would deal with the modified pyromaniac example. Suppose we attempt to describe a justification-explaining chain related to Q_3 whose parts are relevantly connected with justification of the pyromaniac's belief in Q_3. We are prohibited from including the false S_4 as a conjunct in some f_j when we seek to give a fuller and fuller explanation of why the sample serves as (good) evidence for proposition Q_3. But no other way of constructing such a chain is apparent for this example.[18]

Notes

1. Consideration of the technical details of Sosa's paper is not necessary for the present discussion. I criticize his views at length in "Knowledge as Justified Belief in a True, Justified Proposition," and *The Analysis of Knowing,* chap. 3.

2. Cf. William Alston, "Two Types of Foundationalism," p. 175n. (Chapter 3 above.)

3. It may also involve propositions of the form "S is in a position to know that p is true." I again omit further consideration of technical details.

4. Sosa says that a proposition of the form "S is justified in believing p" is one type of "S-epistemic proposition," characterizing the latter as "a proposition concerning a certain other proposition (or certain other propositions) and either (i) to the effect that *it is (they are) believed by S* and how reasonably, or (ii) to the effect that S is in a position to know whether it is (they are) true, or (iii) some logical compound of propositions of types (i) and (ii)." (p. 122; cf. p. 120) (emphasis added) For Sosa's discussion of being in a position to know, see pp. 117–19.

5. David B. Annis says that Lehrer is in the ironic position of being unable to deal with the case of the clever reasoner by means of Lehrer's own analysis of knowledge. (See his review of *Knowledge, Philosophia* 6 [1976]: 209–13.) For appraisal of this charge and my own criticisms of Lehrer's analysis of knowledge, see Shope, *The Analysis of Knowing,* chap. 2.

6. Possibilities (i) and (v) were obliquely raised in a personal communication from Lehrer to Harman in which Lehrer suggested that we need to consider whether S would be able to completely justify his belief in q without appealing to any false statement or to any statement that could only be "shown to support" q by "reasoning through" a false statement. Cf. Gilbert Harman, "Lehrer on Knowledge" (*Journal of Philosophy* 63 [1966]: 245–46).

7. I presume that this list of substitute phrases is interpreted broadly enough to

cover the distinctions which philosophers often make between reasonable, acceptable, and evident propositions.

8. I shall not attempt to decide here whether there is any proposition that is justified although nothing makes it justified. If there is no such proposition, even in the case of basic knowledge, then we may omit the second conjunct of the antecedent in *NC*, as well as clause (i) in the definition of a justification-explaining chain.

9. Some facts that are needed to make proposition q justified may not be known or believed by S when S's believing q is nonetheless justified. For example, a young child may be justified in believing that a particular object is before him even though he does not yet have the concept of "taking oneself to be seeing" an object. Again, a description of the conditions of perception may go beyond the child's concepts by speaking of the normality of his perceptual equipment. For further discussion of the justification of propositions and beliefs, see "Knowledge as Justified Belief in a True, Justified Proposition." For an indication of how varied the factors are that bear on whether a person's belief is justified, see Adam Morton, *A Guide Through the Theory of Knowledge*, p. 51; Jeffrey Olen, "Is Undefeated Justified True Belief Knowledge?," *Analysis* 37 [1976]: pp. 150-52; and Ernest Sosa, "How Do You Know?", pp. 116–19.

I assume that condition *NC* is concerned with a belief's being justified in relation to epistemic goals, rather than say, moral or religious goals. For a rationale linking the concept of a justification-explaining chain to the search for epistemic goals by an epistemic community see "Knowledge as Justified Belief in a True, Justified Proposition."

10. Some might argue that Lehrer should resist the criticism of Sosa, Meyers, and Stern, and should refuse to interpolate any connection in S's mind between F and Q; indeed, Lehrer's reply to Pailthorp notes that one might try to explain why the second conjunct of m_1 is justified as follows: "Q has a (certain) high probability on evidence F and that makes the proposition 'The truth of F makes Q justified' itself justified." (Cf. "The Fourth Condition of Knowledge: A Defense" in *Review of Metaphysics* 23 [1970]: 126–27). But such an explanation cannot be included in a genuine justification-explaining chain because it is false. As Lehrer eventually pointed out (cf. *Knowledge*, 144-45), following H. E. Kyburg, Jr. (cf. *Probability and the Logic of Rational Belief* [Middleton, 1961], p. 197), high probability is not sufficient for justification.

11. Similarly, if Z has the form "N^* is true, N^* describes good evidence for P, and P entails Q," then it is a conjunction of propositions of forms (6), (5) and (4) with a false proposition in place of p_1 in the proposition of form (5) and in place of p_2 in the proposition of form (4).

12. An analogous point can be made if we treat the Withit example in a manner similar to Feldman's version of the Nogot example.

13. Michael Williams hints at an approach somewhat similar to an appeal to justification-explaining chains ("Inference, Justification, and the Analysis of Knowledge"). Williams says that we might try ruling out false propositions in "what a person would (or perhaps ought to) say if questions of justification were pressed." (p. 263) However, the clever reasoner would not assert the proposition that Mr. Nogot owns a Ferrari as a "conclusion" about Mr. Nogot (cf. p. 262). Moreover, children might not be expected to spell out as many portions of a justification-explaining chain as adults in a similar situation. (cf. n. 9)

14. Cf. *Theory of Knowledge*, 2nd ed., p. 105.

15. Chisholm mentions the relevance of a proposition similar to P_1 (cf. ibid., p. 111). For criticism of Chisholm's own solution to the Gettier problem, see Shope, *The Analysis of Knowing*, chap. 4.

16. That is, P_1' is false provided that nobody else is presently taking there to be a sheep in the field. Otherwise, S's reasons for lacking knowledge would be similar to those in the case of Ms. Withit.

17. *Op. cit.*, pp. 382–83.

18. The present discussion has concentrated on the use of *NC* to deal with Gettier-type examples. In order to provide an illuminating account of justified factual knowledge, the concept of a proposition's being justified, which is utilized in *NC*, must be explained in relation to the acceptability of the proposition to an epistemic community. This will allow us to deal with the "social aspects" of knowledge (cf. "Knowledge as Justified Belief in a True, Justified Proposition," and *The Analysis of Knowing*, chap. 7).

A Bibliography on Empirical Knowledge

PAUL K. MOSER

For a listing of additional works on empirical knowledge, the reader should consult the bibliography by Nancy Kelsik in *Justification and Knowledge*, ed. G. S. Pappas (Dordrecht: D. Reidel, 1979), pp. 183–211; the bibliography by Robert Shope in *The Analysis of Knowing* (Princeton: Princeton University Press, 1983), pp. 239–49; and the bibliography by Frederick Schmitt in *Naturalizing Epistemology*, ed. H. Kornblith (Cambridge: MIT Press, 1985), pp. 269–99.

General Works

Ackermann, Robert. *Belief and Knowledge*. Garden City: Doubleday, 1972.

Alston, William P. "Meta-Ethics and Meta-Epistemology." Pp. 275–97 in *Values and Morals*, ed. A. I. Goldman and J. Kim. Dordrecht: D. Reidel, 1978.

———. "Level-Confusions in Epistemology." Pp. 135–50 in *Midwest Studies in Philosophy, Vol. 5: Studies in Epistemology*, ed. P. French, T. E. Uehling, and H. K. Wettstein. Minneapolis: University of Minnesota Press, 1980.

———. "Concepts of Epistemic Justification." *The Monist* 68 (1985): 57–89. Also Chapter 1, this volume.

———. "Epistemic Circularity." Forthcoming in *Philosophy & Phenomenological Research*.

Armstrong, David M. *Belief, Truth, and Knowledge*. Cambridge: Cambridge University Press, 1973.

Aune, Bruce. *Knowledge, Mind, and Nature*. New York: Random House, 1967.

———. "Epistemic Justification." *Philosophical Studies* 40 (1981): 419–29.

Ayer, A. J. *The Problem of Knowledge*. Baltimore: Penguin Books, 1956; London: Macmillan & Co.

Bonjour, Laurence. *The Structure of Empirical Knowledge*. Cambridge: Harvard University Press, 1985.

Butchvarov, Panayot. *The Concept of Knowledge*. Evanston, Ill: Northwestern University Press, 1970.

Canfield, John, and Franklin Donnell, eds. *Readings in the Theory of Knowledge*. New York: Appleton-Century-Crofts, 1964.

Chisholm, Roderick M. *Perceiving: A Philosophical Study*. Ithaca: Cornell University Press, 1957.

————. *Theory of Knowledge.* 1st ed. Englewood Cliffs, N.J.: Prentice-Hall, 1966. 2nd ed. 1977.

————. *The Foundations of Knowing.* Minneapolis: University of Minnesota Press, 1982.

Chisholm, Roderick, and Robert Swartz, eds. *Empirical Knowledge.* Englewood Cliffs, N.J.: Prentice-Hall, 1973.

Cornman, James W. *Perception, Common Sense, and Science.* New Haven: Yale University Press, 1975.

Dancy, Jonathan. *An Introduction to Contemporary Epistemology.* Oxford: Basil Blackwell, 1985.

Danto, Arthur. *Analytical Philosophy of Knowledge.* Cambridge: Cambridge University Press, 1968.

Dicker, Georges. *Perceptual Knowledge.* Dordrecht: D. Reidel, 1980.

Dretske, Fred I. *Seeing and Knowing.* Chicago: University of Chicago Press, 1969.

Feldman, Richard, and Earl Conee. "Evidentialism." *Philosophical Studies* 48 (1985): 15–34.

French, Peter, T. E. Uehling, and H. K. Wettstein, eds. *Midwest Studies in Philosophy, Vol. 5: Studies in Epistemology.* Minneapolis: University of Minnesota Press, 1980.

Fumerton, Richard A. *Metaphysical and Epistemological Problems of Perception.* Lincoln: University of Nebraska Press, 1985.

Ginet, Carl. *Knowledge, Perception, and Memory.* Dordrecht: D. Reidel, 1975.

————. "The Justification of Belief: A Primer." In *Knowledge and Mind,* ed. C. Ginet and S. Shoemaker. New York: Oxford University Press, 1983.

Goldman, Alvin I. *Epistemology and Cognition.* Cambridge: Harvard University Press, 1986.

Haack, Susan. "Theories of Knowledge: An Analytic Framework." *Proceedings of the Aristotelian Society* 83 (1983): 143–57.

Hamlyn, D. W. *The Theory of Knowledge.* Garden City: Doubleday, 1971.

Harman, Gilbert. *Change in View.* Cambridge: MIT Press, 1986.

Hill, Thomas. *Contemporary Theories of Knowledge.* New York: Macmillan, 1961.

Hintikka, Jaakko. *Knowledge and Belief.* Ithaca: Cornell University Press, 1962.

Lehrer, Keith. *Knowledge.* Oxford: Oxford University Press, 1974.

Lewis, C. I. *An Analysis of Knowledge and Valuation.* LaSalle, Ill.: Open Court, 1946.

Malcolm, Norman. *Knowledge and Certainty: Essays and Lectures.* Ithaca: Cornell University Press, 1963.

McGinn, Colin. "The Concept of Knowledge." Pp. 529–54 in *Midwest Studies in Philosophy, Vol. 9,* ed. P. French, T. E. Uehling and H. Wettstein. Minneapolis: University of Minnesota Press, 1984.

Morton, Adam. *A Guide Through the Theory of Knowledge.* Encino, Calif.: Dickenson, 1977.

Moser, Paul K. *Empirical Justification.* Dordrecht: D. Reidel, 1985.

Moser, Paul K., and Arnold VanderNat, eds. *Human Knowledge: Classical and Contemporary Approaches.* New York: Oxford University Press, 1986 (forthcoming).

Nagel, Ernest, and Richard Brandt, eds. *Meaning and Knowledge.* New York: Harcourt, Brace & World, 1965.

O'Connor, D. J., and Brian Carr. *Introduction to the Theory of Knowledge.* Minneapolis: University of Minnesota Press, 1982.

Pappas, G. S., ed. *Justification and Knowledge.* Dordrecht: D. Reidel, 1979.

Pappas, G. S., and Marshall Swain, eds. *Essays on Knowledge and Justification.* Ithaca: Cornell University Press, 1978.

Pollock, John L. *Knowledge and Justification.* Princeton: Princeton University Press, 1974.

——. *Contemporary Theories of Knowledge.* Totowa, N.J.: Rowman & Littlefield (forthcoming).

——. "Epistemic Norms." *Synthese* (in press).

Quine, W. V., and J. S. Ullian, *The Web of Belief.* New York: Random House, 1970. 2nd ed. 1978.

Roth, Michael, and Leon Galis, eds. *Knowing: Essays in the Analysis of Knowledge.* New York: Random House, 1970.

Russell, Bertrand. *Human Knowledge: Its Scope and Limits.* New York: Simon & Schuster, 1948; London: Allen and Unwin.

Schlesinger, George N. *The Range of Epistemic Logic.* Atlantic Highlands, N.J.: Humanities Press, 1985.

Shope, Robert. *The Analysis of Knowing.* Princeton: Princeton University Press, 1983.

Sosa, Ernest. "Epistemology Today: A Perspective in Retrospect." *Philosophical Studies* 40 (1981): 309–32.

——. "Presuppositions of Empirical Knowledge." *Philosophical Papers* (1986) (in press).

Stalnaker, Robert C. *Inquiry.* Cambridge: MIT Press, 1984.

Swain, Marshall. *Reasons and Knowledge.* Ithaca: Cornell University Press, 1981.

Will, Frederick. *Induction and Justification.* Ithaca: Cornell University Press, 1973.

Wolgast, Elizabeth. *Paradoxes of Knowledge.* Ithaca: Cornell University Press, 1978.

Woozley, A. D. *Theory of Knowledge.* London: Hutchinson, 1949.

Epistemic Foundationalism

Almeder, Robert F. "Basic Knowledge and Justification." *The Canadian Journal of Philosophy* 13 (1983): 115–28.

Alston, William P. "Varieties of Privileged Access." *American Philosophical Quarterly* 8 (1971): 223–41.

——. "Has Foundationalism Been Refuted?" *Philosophical Studies* 29 (1976): 287–305.

——. "Self-Warrant: A Neglected Form of Privileged Access." *American Philosophical Quarterly* 13 (1976): 257–72.

——. "Two Types of Foundationalism." *Journal of Philosophy* 73 (1976): 165–85. Also Chapter 3, this volume.

——. "Some Remarks on Chisholm's Epistemology." *Nous* 14 (1980): 565–86.

——. "What's Wrong With Immediate Knowledge?" *Synthese* 55 (1983): 73–95.

————. "Plantinga's Religious Epistemology." Pp. 287–309 in *Alvin Plantinga*, ed. J. E. Tomberlin and P. van Inwagen. Dordrecht: D. Reidel, 1985.

Annis, David B. "Epistemic Foundationalism." *Philosophical Studies* 31 (1977): 345–52.

Armstrong, David M. *Belief, Truth, and Knowledge*. Cambridge: Cambridge University Press, 1973.

Audi, Robert. "Psychological Foundationalism." *The Monist* 62 (1978): 592–610.

————. "Foundationalism, Epistemic Dependence, and Defeasibility." *Synthese* 55 (1983): 119–39.

Ayer, A. J. *The Foundations of Empirical Knowledge*. New York: Macmillan, 1940.

————. "Basic Propositions." Pp. 60–74 in *Philosophical Analysis*, ed. M. Black. Englewood Cliffs, N.J.: Prentice-Hall, 1950. Reprinted in Ayer, *Philosophical Essays* (London: Macmillan, 1965).

Bonjour, Laurence. "Can Empirical Knowledge Have a Foundation?" *American Philosophical Quarterly* 15 (1978): 1–13. Also Chapter 4, this volume.

————. "Externalist Theories of Empirical Knowledge." Pp. 53–74 in *Midwest Studies in Philosophy, Vol. 5: Studies in Epistemology*, ed. P. French, T. E. Uehling, and H. K. Wettstein. Minneapolis: University of Minnesota Press, 1980.

Chisholm, Roderick. *Theory of Knowledge*. 1st ed. Englewood Cliffs, NJ: Prentice-Hall, 1966. 2nd ed. 1977, esp. chaps. 2 and 4.

————. "On the Nature of Empirical Evidence." Pp. 253–78 in *Essays on Knowledge and Justification*, ed. G. S. Pappas and M. Swain. Ithaca: Cornell University Press, 1978.

————. "The Directly Evident." Pp. 115–27 in *Justification and Knowledge*, ed. G. S. Pappas. Dordrecht: D. Reidel, 1979.

————. "Theory of Knowledge in America." Pp. 109–96 in Chisholm, *The Foundations of Knowing*. Minneapolis: University of Minnesota Press, 1982.

————. "A Version of Foundationalism." Pp. 3–32 in Chisholm, *The Foundations of Knowing*.

Churchland, Paul M. Chapter 2 in *Scientific Realism and the Plasticity of Mind*. Cambridge: Cambridge University Press, 1979.

Cornman, James W. "Foundational versus Nonfoundational Theories of Empirical Justification." *American Philosophical Quarterly* 14 (1977): 287–97. Reprinted in *Essays on Knowledge and Justification*, ed. G. S. Pappas and M. Swain. Ithaca: Cornell University Press, 1978.

————. "On Acceptability Without Certainty." *Journal of Philosophy* 74 (1977): 29–47.

————. "On the Certainty of Reports about What Is Given." *Nous* 12 (1978): 93–118.

————. "On Justifying Non-Basic Statements by Basic-Reports." Pp. 129–49 in *Justification and Knowledge*, ed. G. S. Pappas. Dordrecht: D. Reidel, 1979.

————. *Skepticism, Justification, and Explanation*. Dordrecht: D. Reidel, 1980.

Dancy, Jonathan. *An Introduction to Contemporary Epistemology*, chapters 4 and 5. Oxford: Basil Blackwell, 1985.

Fumerton, Richard A. *Metaphysical and Epistemological Problems of Perception*, chapter 2, Lincoln: University of Nebraska Press, 1985.

Goldman, Alan H. "Appearing Statements and Epistemological Foundations." *Metaphilosophy* 10 (1979): 227–46.

————. "Epistemic Foundationalism and the Replaceability of Ordinary Language." *Journal of Philosophy* 79 (1982): 136–54.

Heidelberger, Herbert. "Chisholm's Epistemic Principles." *Nous* 3 (1969): 73–82.

Heil, John. "Foundationalism and Epistemic Rationality." *Philosophical Studies* 42 (1982): 179–88.

Kekes, John. "An Argument Against Foundationalism." *Philosophia* 12 (1983): 273–81.

Kornblith, Hilary. "Beyond Foundationalism and the Coherence Theory." *The Journal of Philosophy* 72 (1980): 597–612. Reprinted in *Naturalizing Epistemology,* ed. H. Kornblith. Cambridge: MIT Press, 1985.

Kvanvig, Jonathan. "What Is Wrong With Minimal Foundationalism?" *Erkenntnis* 21 (1984): 175–87.

Lewis, C. I. *Mind and the World Order.* New York: Charles Scribner's Sons, 1929.

————. *An Analysis of Knowledge and Valuation,* chapters 7 and 8. LaSalle, Ill.: Open Court, 1946.

————. "The Given Element in Empirical Knowledge." *The Philosophical Review* 61 (1952): 168–75.

Moser, Paul K. "A Defense of Epistemic Intuitionism." *Metaphilosophy* 15 (1984): 196–209.

————. "Does Foundationalism Rest on a Mistake?" *Conceptus: Zeitschrift fur Philosophie* 19 (1986) (forthcoming).

————. *Empirical Justification,* chapters 4 and 5. Dordrecht: D. Reidel, 1985.

————. "Whither Infinite Regresses of Justification?" *The Southern Journal of Philosophy* 23 (1985): 65–74.

————. "Ascending from Empirical Foundations." Forthcoming in *Synthese* 68 (1986).

Pastin, Mark. "Lewis' Radical Foundationalism." *Nous* 9 (1975): 407–20.

————. "Modest Foundationalism and Self-Warrant." Pp. 141–49 in *American Philosophical Quarterly Monograph Series, No. 9: Studies in Epistemology,* ed. N. Rescher. Oxford: Basil Blackwell, 1975. Reprinted in *Essays on Knowledge and Justification,* ed. G. S. Pappas and M. Swain. Ithaca: Cornell University Press, 1978.

Pollock, John L. *Knowledge and Justification,* chapter 2. Princeton: Princeton University Press, 1974.

————. "A Plethora of Epistemological Theories." Pp. 93–113 in *Justification and Knowledge,* ed. G. S. Pappas. Dordrecht: D. Reidel, 1979.

Quinton, Anthony. "The Foundations of Knowledge." Pp. 55–86 in *British Analytic Philosophy,* ed. Bernard Williams and Alan Montefiore. London: Routledge & Kegan Paul, 1966. Reprinted in Chisholm and Swartz, eds., *Empirical Knowledge.* Englewood Cliffs: Prentice-Hall, 1973.

————. *The Nature of Things.* London: Routledge & Kegan Paul, 1973.

Russell, Bertrand. "On Verification." *Proceedings of the Aristotelian Society* 38 (1937–38): 1–15.

————. *An Inquiry into Meaning and Truth,* chapters 9 and 10. New York: W. W. Norton, 1940.

————. *Human Knowledge: Its Scope and Limits.* New York: Simon & Schuster, 1948.

Scheffler, Israel. *Science and Subjectivity.* Chapters 2 and 5. New York: Bobbs-Merrill, 1967; 2d ed., Indianapolis: Hackett, 1982.

Sellars, Wilfrid. "Does Empirical Knowledge Have a Foundation?" in "Empiricism and the Philosophy of Mind." Pp. 253–329 in *Minnesota Studies in the Philosophy of Science,* Vol. 1, ed. H. Feigl and M. Scriven. Minneapolis: University of Minnesota Press, 1956. Reprinted in Sellars, *Science, Perception, and Reality.*

―――. *Science, Perception, and Reality.* London: Routledge & Kegan Paul, 1963.

Schatz, David. "Foundationalism, Coherentism, and the Levels Gambit." *Synthese* 55 (1983): 97–118.

Sosa, Ernest. "The Foundations of Foundationalism." *Nous* 14 (1980); 547–64.

―――. "The Raft and the Pyramid: Coherence versus Foundations in the Theory of Knowledge." Pp. 3–25 in *Midwest Studies in Philosophy, Vol. 5: Studies in Epistemology,* ed. P. French, T. Uehling, and H. Wettstein. Minneapolis: University of Minnesota Press, 1980. Also Chapter 6, this volume.

Strawson, Peter F. "Does Knowledge Have Foundations? Pp. 99–110 in *Teorema, Mono. 1: Conocimiento y Creencia.* Universidad de Valencia, 1974.

Swain, Marshall. "Cornman's Theory of Justification." *Philosophical Studies* 41 (1982): 129–48.

Van Cleve, James. "Foundationalism, Epistemic Principles, and the Cartesian Circle." *The Philosophical Review* 88 (1979): 55–91.

―――. "Epistemic Supervenience and the Circle of Belief." *The Monist* 68 (1985): 90–104.

Epistemic Coherentism

Airaksinen, Timo. "On Nonfoundationalistic Theories of Epistemic Justification." *The Southern Journal of Philosophy* 19 (1981): 403–12.

Blanshard, Brand. *The Nature of Thought,* Vol. 2. London: Allen & Unwin, 1939.

Bonjour, Laurence. *The Structure of Empirical Knowledge.* Cambridge: Harvard University Press, 1985.

―――. "The Coherence Theory of Empirical Knowledge." *Philosophical Studies* 30 (1976): 281–312. Also Chapter 5, this volume.

Dancy, Jonathan. "On Coherence Theories of Justification: Can an Empiricist be a Coherentist?" *American Philosophical Quarterly* 21 (1984): 359–65.

―――. *An Introduction to Contemporary Epistemology.* Oxford: Basil Blackwell, 1985.

Davidson, Donald. "A Coherence Theory of Truth and Knowledge." Pp. 423–38 in *Kant oder Hegel,* ed. Dieter Henrich. Stuttgart: Klett-Cotta, 1983.

Firth, Roderick. "Coherence, Certainty, and Epistemic Priority." *The Journal of Philosophy* 61 (1964): 545–57. Reprinted in R. M. Chisholm and Robert Swartz, eds., *Empirical Knowledge.* Englewood Cliffs: Prentice-Hall, 1973.

Harman, Gilbert. "Knowledge, Inference, and Explanation." *American Philosophical Quarterly* 5 (1968): 164–73.

―――. "Knowledge, Reasons, and Causes." *The Journal of Philosophy* 67 (1970): 841–55.

―――. *Thought.* Princeton: Princeton University Press, 1973. Chapter 8 reprinted as Chapter 12, this volume.

Lehrer, Keith. "Justification, Explanation, and Induction." Pp. 100–133 in *Induction, Acceptance, and Rational Belief,* ed. M. Swain. Dordrecht: D. Reidel, 1970.

———. *Knowledge*. Oxford: Oxford University Press, 1974.
———. "The Knowledge Cycle." *Nous* 11 (1977): 17–26.
———. "Self-Profile." Pp. 3–104 in *Keith Lehrer*, ed. R. J. Bogdan. Dordrecht: D. Reidel, 1981.
———. "Knowledge, Truth, and Ontology." Pp. 201–11 in *Language and Ontology: Proceedings of the 6th International Wittgenstein Symposium*, ed. W. Leinfellner, E. Kraemer, and J. Schank. Vienna: Holder-Pichler-Tempsky, 1982.
Lehrer, Keith, and Stewart Cohen. "Justification, Truth, and Coherence." *Synthese* 55 (1983): 191–208.
Lemos, Noah. "Coherence and Epistemic Priority." *Philosophical Studies* 41 (1982): 229–316.
Moser, Paul K. "On Negative Coherentism and Subjective Justification." *The Southern Journal of Philosophy* 22 (1984): 83–90.
———. *Empirical Justification*, chapter 3. Dordrecht: D. Reidel, 1985.
———. "Epistemic Coherentism and the Isolation Objection." *Grazer Philosophische Studien* (forthcoming).
Pastin, Mark. "Social and Anti-Social Justification: A Study of Lehrer's Epistemology." Pp. 205–22 in *Keith Lehrer*, ed. R. J. Bogdan. Dordrecht: D. Reidel, 1981.
Reichenbach, Hans. *Experience and Prediction*. Chicago: University of Chicago Press, 1938.
Rescher, Nicholas. *The Coherence Theory of Truth*. Oxford: Clarendon Press, 1973.
———. "Foundationalism, Coherentism, and the Idea of Cognitive Systematization." *The Journal of Philosophy* 71 (1974): 695–708.
———. *Cognitive Systematization*. Oxford: Basil Blackwell, 1979.
———. "Blanshard and the Coherence Theory of Truth." Pp. 574–88 in *The Philosophy of Brand Blanshard*, ed. P. Schilpp. LaSalle, Ill.: Open Court, 1980.
———. "Truth as Ideal Coherence." *The Review of Metaphysics* 38 (1985): 795–806.
Sellars, Wilfrid. "Givenness and Explanatory Coherence." *The Journal of Philosophy* 70 (1973): 612–24.
———. "Epistemic Principles. Pp. 332–48 in *Action, Knowledge, and Reality: Critical Studies in Honor of Wilfrid Sellars*, ed. H.-N. Casteñeda. Indianapolis: Bobbs-Merrill, 1975.
———. "More on Givenness and Explanatory Coherence." Pp. 169–81 in *Justification and Knowledge*, ed. G. S. Pappas. Dordrecht: D. Reidel, 1979.
Sosa, Ernest. "Circular Coherence and Absurd Foundations." In *Truth and Interpretation*, ed. E. Lepore. Oxford: Basil Blackwell, 1986.
———. "The Coherence of Virtue and the Virtue of Coherence: Justification in Epistemology." *Synthese* 64 (1985): 3–28.
Tibbetts, Paul. "The Weighted Coherence Theory of Rationality and Justification." *Philosophy of the Social Sciences* 10 (1980): 259–72.

Epistemic Contextualism

Airaksinen, Timo. "Contextualism: A New Theory of Epistemic Justification." *Philosophia* 12 (1982): 35–70.

Annis, David B. "A Contextualist Theory of Epistemic Justification." *American Philosophical Quarterly* 15 (1978): 213–19. Also Chapter 9, this volume.
———. "The Social and Cultural Component of Epistemic Justification: A Reply." *Philosophia* 12 (1982): 51–55.
Morawetz, Thomas. *Wittgenstein and Knowledge.* Amherst: University of Massachusetts Press, 1978.
Moser, Paul K. *Empirical Justification,* chapter 2. Dordrecht: D. Reidel, 1985.
Rorty, Richard. "From Epistemology to Hermeneutics." In *Acta Philosophica Fennica, Vol. 30: The Logic and Epistemology of Scientific Change,* ed. I. Niiniluoto and R. Tuomela. Amsterdam: North-Holland Publishing Co., 1978.
———. *Philosophy and the Mirror of Nature,* chapter 7. Princeton: Princeton University Press, 1979.
Shiner, Roger. "Wittgenstein and the Foundations of Knowledge." *Proceedings of the Aristotelian Society* 78 (1977–78): 103–24.
Sosa, Ernest. "On Groundless Belief." *Synthese* 43 (1979): 453–60.
Williams, Michael. *Groundless Belief.* Oxford: Basil Blackwell, 1977.
———. "Coherence, Justification, and Truth." *The Review of Metaphysics* 34 (1980): 243–72.
Wittgenstein, Ludwig. *On Certainty,* ed. G. E. M. Anscombe and G. H. von Wright. Oxford: Basil Blackwell, 1969.

Epistemic Reliabilism

Armstrong, David M. *Belief, Truth, and Knowledge.* Cambridge: Cambridge University Press, 1973.
———. "Self-Profile." Pp. 30–37 in *D. M. Armstrong,* ed. R. J. Bogdan. Dordrecht: D. Reidel, 1984.
Audi, Robert. "Defeated Knowledge, Reliability, and Justification." Pp. 75–95 in *Midwest Studies in Philosophy, Vol. 5: Studies in Epistemology,* ed. P. French et al. Minneapolis: University of Minnesota Press, 1980.
———. "Justification, Truth, and Reliability" (unpublished).
Bach, Kent. "A Rationale for Reliabilism." *The Monist* 68 (1985): 246–63.
Bonjour, Laurence. "Externalist Theories of Empirical Knowledge." Pp. 53–75 in *Midwest Studies in Philosophy, Vol. 5: Studies in Epistemology,* ed. P. French et al. Minneapolis: University of Minnesota Press, 1980.
Cohen, Stewart. "Justification and Truth." *Philosophical Studies* 46 (1984): 279–95.
Dretske, Fred I. "Conclusive Reasons." *The Australasian Journal of Philosophy* 49 (1971): 1–22. Reprinted in *Essays on Knowledge and Justification,* ed. G. S. Pappas and M. Swain. Ithaca: Cornell University Press, 1978.
———. *Knowledge and the Flow of Information.* Cambridge: MIT Press, 1981.
———. "The Pragmatic Dimension of Knowledge." *Philosophical Studies* 40 (1981): 363–78.
———. "Precis of *Knowledge and the Flow of Information.*" *The Behavioral and Brain Sciences* 6 (1983): 55–63.
Feldman, Richard. "Reliability and Justification." *The Monist* 68 (1985): 159–74.
———. "Schmitt on Reliability, Objectivity, and Justification." *The Australasian Journal of Philosophy* 63 (1985): 354–60.
Feldman, Richard, and Earl Conee. "Evidentialism." *Philosophical Studies* 48 (1985): 15–4.

Firth, Roderick. "Epistemic Merit, Intrinsic and Instrumental." *Proceedings and Addresses of the American Philosophical Association* 55 (1981): 5–23.

Foley, Richard. "What's Wrong with Reliabilism?" *The Monist* 68 (1985): 188–202.

Friedman, Michael. "Truth and Confirmation." *The Journal of Philosophy* 76 (1979): 361–82. Reprinted in *Naturalizing Epistemology,* ed. H. Kornblith. Cambridge: MIT Press, 1985.

Ginet, Carl. *"Contra* Reliabilism." *The Monist* 68 (1985): 175–87.

Goldman, Alvin I. "Discrimination and Perceptual Knowledge." *The Journal of Philosophy* 73 (1976): 771–91. Reprinted in *Essays on Knowledge and Justification,* ed. G. S. Pappas and M. Swain. Ithaca: Cornell University Press, 1978.

———. "What Is Justified Belief?" Pp. 1–23 in *Justification and Knowledge,* ed. G. S. Pappas. Dordrecht: D. Reidel, 1979. Also Chapter 7, this volume.

———. "The Internalist Conception of Justification." Pp. 27–52 in *Midwest Studies in Philosophy, Vol. 5: Studies in Epistemology,* ed. by P. French et al. Minneapolis: University of Minnesota Press, 1980.

———. *Epistemology and Cognition,* chapter 5. Cambridge: Harvard University Press, 1986.

Heil, John. "Reliability and Epistemic Merit." *The Australasian Journal of Philosophy* 62 (1984): 327–38.

Kapitan, Tomis. "Reliability and Indirect Justification." *The Monist* 68 (1985): 277–87.

Kornblith, Hilary. "Beyond Foundationalism and the Coherence Theory." *The Journal of Philosophy* 72 (1980): 597–612.

———. "The Psychological Turn." *The Australasian Journal of Philosophy* 60 (1982): 238–53.

———. "Justified Belief and Epistemically Responsible Action." *The Philosophical Review* 92 (1983): 33–48.

———. "Ever Since Descartes." *The Monist* 68 (1985): 264–76.

Luper-Foy, Steven. "The Reliabilist Theory of Rational Belief." *The Monist* 68 (1985): 203–25.

Lycan, William G. "Armstrong's Theory of Knowing." Pp. 139-60 in *D. M. Armstrong,* ed. R. J. Bogdan. Dordrecht: D. Reidel, 1984.

Moser, Paul K. *Empirical Justification,* chapter 4 and Appendix. Dordrecht: D. Reidel, 1985.

———. "Knowledge Without Evidence." *Philosophia* 15 (1985): 109–16.

Nozick, Robert. *Philosophical Explanations,* chapter 3. Cambridge: Harvard University Press, 1981.

Pappas, George S. "Non-Inferential Knowledge." *Philosophia* 12 (1982): 81–98.

Pastin, Mark. "Knowledge and Reliability: A Critical Study of D. M. Armstrong's *Belief, Truth, and Knowledge." Metaphilosophy* 9 (1978): 150–62.

———. "The Multi-perspectival Theory of Knowledge." Pp. 97–111 in *Midwest Studies in Philosophy, Vol. 5: Studies in Epistemology,* ed. P. French, T. Uehling, and H. Wettstein. Minneapolis: University of Minnesota Press, 1980.

Pollock, John. "Reliability and Justified Belief." *The Canadian Journal of Philosophy* 14 (1984): 103–14. Also Chapter 8, this volume.

Schmitt, Frederick F. "Justification as Reliable Indication or Reliable Process." *Philosophical Studies* 40 (1981): 409–17.

———. "Knowledge, Justification, and Reliability." *Synthese* 55 (1983): 209–29.

———. "Reliability, Objectivity, and the Background of Justification." *The Australasian Journal of Philosophy* 62 (1984): 1–15.

————. "Knowledge as Tracking." *Topoi* 4 (1985): 73–80.

Shatz, David. "Reliability and Relevant Alternatives." *Philosophical Studies* 39 (1981): 393–408.

Shope, Robert K. "Cognitive Abilities, Conditionals, and Knowledge: A Response to Nozick." *The Journal of Philosophy* 81 (1984): 29–47.

————. *The Analysis of Knowing,* chap. 5. Princeton: Princeton University Press, 1983.

Sosa, Ernest. "Knowledge and Intellectual Virtue." *The Monist* 68 (1985): 226–45.

————. "Epistemic Justification and Intellectual Virtue." *Topics in Philosophy* (1986) (forthcoming).

Swain, Marshall. "Justification and the Basis of Belief." Pp. 25–49 in *Justification and Knowledge,* ed. G. S. Pappas. Dordrecht: D. Reidel, 1979.

————. "Justification and Reliable Belief." *Philosophical Studies* 40 (1981): 389–407.

————. *Reasons and Knowledge*, chapter 4. Ithaca: Cornell University Press, 1981.

————. "Justification, Reasons, and Reliability." *Synthese* 64 (1985): 69–92.

Van Cleve, James. "Reliability, Justification, and the Problem of Induction." Pp. 555–67 in *Midwest Studies in Philosophy, Vol. 9,* ed. P. French, T. Uehling, and H. Wettstein. Minneapolis: University of Minnesota Press, 1984.

Naturalized Epistemology

Bogen, James. "Traditional Epistemology and Naturalistic Replies to Its Skeptical Critics." *Synthese* 64 (1985): 195–223.

Boyd, Richard. "Scientific Realism and Naturalistic Epistemology." In *Philosophy of Science Assoc. Proceedings* 80 (1982), Vol. 2. East Lansing, Mich.: Philosophy of Science Association.

Dancy, Jonathan. *An Introduction to Contemporary Epistemology,* chapter 15. Oxford: Basil Blackwell, 1985.

Duran, Jane. "Descriptive Epistemology." *Metaphilosophy* 15 (1984): 185–95.

Goldman, Alvin I. "Epistemics: The Regulative Theory of Cognition." *The Journal of Philosophy* 75 (1978): 509–23. Reprinted in *Naturalizing Epistemology,* ed. H. Kornblith. Cambridge: MIT Press, 1985.

————. "Epistemology and the Psychology of Belief." *The Monist* 61 (1978): 525–35.

————. "Varieties of Cognitive Appraisal." *Nous* 13 (1979): 23–38.

————. "Epistemology and the Theory of Problem Solving." *Synthese* 55 (1983): 21–48.

————. "The Relation between Epistemology and Psychology." *Synthese* 64 (1985): 29–68.

Haack, Susan. "The Relevance of Psychology to Epistemology." *Metaphilosophy* 6 (1975): 161–76.

Kornblith, Hilary. "The Psychological Turn." *The Australasian Journal of Philosophy* 60 (1982): 238–53.

————. "Introduction: What Is Naturalistic Epistemology?" Pp. 1–13 in *Naturalizing Epistemology,* ed. H. Kornblith. Cambridge: MIT Press, 1985.

Lycan, William G. "Epistemic Value." *Synthese* 64 (1985): 137–64.

Putnam, Hilary. "Why Reason Can't Be Naturalized." Pp. 229–47 in Putnam, *Realism and Reason: Philosophical Papers, Vol. 3*. Cambridge: Cambridge University Press, 1983.

Quine, W. V. "Epistemology Naturalized." Pp. 68–90 in Quine, *Ontological Relativity and Other Essays*. New York: Columbia University Press, 1969. Also Chapter 10, this volume.

———. "The Nature of Natural Knowledge." Pp. 67–81 in *Mind and Language: Wolfson College Lectures*, ed. S. Guttenplan. Oxford: Oxford University Press, 1975.

Rorty, Richard. *Philosophy and the Mirror of Nature*, chapter 5. Princeton: Princeton University Press, 1979.

Roth, Paul. "Siegel on Naturalized Epistemology and Natural Science." *Philosophy of Science* 50 (1983): 482–93.

Siegel, Harvey. "Justification, Discovery, and the Naturalizing of Epistemology." *Philosophy of Science* 47 (1980): 297–321.

———. "Empirical Psychology, Naturalized Epistemology, and First Philosophy." *Philosophy of Science* 51 (1984): 667–76.

Sosa, Ernest. "Nature Unmirrored, Epistemology Naturalized." *Synthese* 55 (1983): 49-72.

Stroud, Barry. *The Significance of Philosophical Scepticism*, chapter 6. Oxford: Clarendon Press, 1984.

———. "The Significance of Naturalized Epistemology." Pp. 455–71 in *Midwest Studies in Philosophy, Vol. 6: Analytic Philosophy*, ed. P. French, T. Uehling, and H. Wettstein. Minneapolis: University of Minnesota Press, 1981. Reprinted in *Naturalizing Epistemology*, ed. H. Kornblith. Cambridge: MIT Press, 1985.

Swain, Marshall. "Epistemics and Epistemology." *The Journal of Philosophy* 75 (1978): 523–25.

The Gettier Problem

Audi, Robert. "Defeated Knowledge, Reliability, and Justification." Pp. 75–95 in *Midwest Studies in Philosophy, Vol. 5: Studies in Epistemology*, ed. P. French, T. Uehling, and H. Wettstein. Minneapolis: University of Minnesota Press, 1980.

Chisholm, Roderick M. "Knowledge as Justified True Belief." Pp. 43–49 in Chisholm, *The Foundations of Knowing*. Minneapolis: University of Minnesota Press, 1982. Also Chapter 13, this volume.

Cohen, Stewart. "Defeasibility and Background Beliefs." *Philosophical Studies* 39 (1981): 263–74.

Dancy, Jonathan. *An Introduction to Contemporary Epistemology*, chapter 2. Oxford: Basil Blackwell, 1985.

Dretske, Fred I. "Conclusive Reasons." *The Australasian Journal of Philosophy* 49 (1971): 1–22.

Feldman, Richard. "An Alleged Defect in Gettier Counter-Examples." *The Australasian Journal of Philosophy* 52 (1974): 68–69. Also Chapter 14, this volume.

Gettier, Edmund. "Is Justified True Belief Knowledge?" *Analysis* 23 (1963): 121–23. Also Chapter 11, this volume.

Goldman, Alvin. "A Causal Theory of Knowing." *The Journal of Philosophy* 64 (1967): 357–72. Reprinted in *Essays on Knowledge and Justification*, ed. G. S. Pappas and M. Swain. Ithaca: Cornell University Press, 1978.

———. "Discrimination and Perceptual Knowledge." *The Journal of Philosophy* 73 (1976): 771–91. Reprinted in *Essays on Knowledge and Justification*.

Harman, Gilbert. "Knowledge, Inference, and Explanation." *American Philosophical Quarterly* 5 (1968): 164–73.

———. "Knowledge, Reasons, and Causes." *The Journal of Philosophy* 67 (1970): 841–55.

———. *Thought,* chapters 7-9. Princeton: Princeton University Press, 1973. Chapter 8 reprinted as Chapter 12, this volume.

———. "Reasoning and Evidence One Does Not Possess." Pp. 163–82 in *Midwest Studies in Philosophy, Vol. 5: Studies in Epistemology*, ed. P. French, T. Uehling, and H. Wettstein. Minneapolis: University of Minnesota Press, 1980.

Kaplan, Mark. "It's Not What You Know That Counts." *The Journal of Philosophy* 82 (1985): 350–63.

Klein, Peter D. "A Proposed Definition of Propositional Knowledge." *The Journal of Philosophy* 68 (1971): 471–82.

———. "Knowledge, Causality, and Defeasibility." *The Journal of Philosophy* 73 (1976): 792–812.

———. "Misleading Evidence and the Restoration of Justification." *Philosophical Studies* 37 (1980): 81–89.

———. "Real Knowledge." *Synthese* 55 (1983): 143–64.

Lehrer, Keith. *Knowledge,* chapter 9. Oxford: Oxford University Press, 1974.

———. "The Gettier Problem and the Analysis of Knowledge." Pp. 65–78 in *Justification and Knowledge*, ed. G. S. Pappas. Dordrecht: D. Reidel, 1979.

———. "Self-Profile." Pp. 75–96 in *Keith Lehrer*, ed. R. J. Bogdan. Dordrecht: D. Reidel, 1981.

Moser, Paul K. "Epistemic Explanation and the Gettier Problem" (forthcoming).

Roth, Michael D., and Leon Galis, eds. *Knowing: Essays in the Analysis of Knowledge*. New York: Random House, 1970.

Shope, Robert K. "Knowledge as Justified Belief in a True, Justified Proposition." *Philosophy Research Archives* 5 (1979): 1–36.

———. "Knowledge and Falsity." *Philosophical Studies* 36 (1979): 389–405. Also Chapter 15, this volume.

———. *The Analysis of Knowing*. Princeton: Princeton University Press, 1983.

Slaght, Ralph. "Is Justified True Belief Knowledge?: A Selective Critical Survey of Recent Work." *Philosophy Research Archives* 3 (1977): 1–135.

Sosa, Ernest. "How Do You Know?" *American Philosophical Quarterly* 11 (1974): 113–22. Reprinted in *Essays on Knowledge and Justification*, ed. G. S. Pappas and M. Swain. Ithaca: Cornell University Press, 1978.

———. "Epistemic Presupposition." Pp. 79–92 in *Justification and Knowledge*, ed. G. S. Pappas. Dordrecht: D. Reidel, 1979.

Swain, Marshall. "Knowledge, Causality and Justification." *The Journal of Philosophy* 69 (1972): 291–300. Reprinted in *Essays on Knowledge and Justification*, ed. G. S. Pappas and M. Swain. Ithaca: Cornell University Press, 1978.

———. "Epistemic Defeasibility." *American Philosophical Quarterly* 11 (1974): 15–25. Reprinted in *Essays on Knowledge and Justification*.

———. "Reasons, Causes, and Knowledge." *The Journal of Philosophy* 75 (1978): 229–49.

———. *Reasons and Knowledge*. Ithaca: Cornell University Press, 1981.

Thalberg, Irving. "In Defense of Justified True Belief." *The Journal of Philosophy* 66 (1969), 794–803.

Williams, Michael. "Inference, Justification, and the Analysis of Knowledge." *The Journal of Philosophy* 75 (1978): 249–63.

Epistemological Skepticism

Brueckner, A. L. "Skepticism and Epistemic Closure." *Philosophical Topics* 13 (1985): 89–117.

Chisholm, Roderick M. "The Problem of the Criterion." Pp. 61–75 in Chisholm, *The Foundations of Knowing*. Minneapolis: University of Minnesota Press, 1982.

Cornman, James W. *Skepticism, Justification, and Explanation*. Dordrecht: D. Reidel, 1980.

Dancy, Jonathan. *An Introduction to Contemporary Epistemology*, chapter 1. Oxford: Basil Blackwell, 1985.

Foley, Richard. "Review of Peter Klein's *Certainty: A Refutation of Scepticism*." *Philosophy & Phenomenological Research* 44 (1984).

Hilpinen, Risto. "Skepticism and Justification." *Synthese* 55 (1983): 165–74.

Johnson, Oliver. *Skepticism and Cognitivism*. Berkeley: University of California Press, 1978.

———. "Ignorance and Irrationality: A Study in Contemporary Scepticism." *Philosophy Research Archives* 5 (1979): 368–417.

Klein, Peter D. *Certainty: A Refutation of Scepticism*. Minneapolis: University of Minnesota Press, 1981.

———. "Real Knowledge." *Synthese* 55 (1983): 143–64.

Lehrer, Keith. "Why Not Scepticism?" *The Philosophical Forum* 2 (1971): 283–98. Reprinted in *Essays on Knowledge and Justification*, ed. G. Pappas and M. Swain. Ithaca: Cornell University Press, 1978.

———. *Knowledge*, chapter 10. Oxford: Oxford University Press, 1974.

———. "The Problem of Knowledge and Skepticism." Chapter 2 in James Cornman, Keith Lehrer, and George Pappas, *Philosophical Problems and Arguments: An Introduction*. 3d ed. New York: Macmillan, 1982.

Luper-Foy, Steven. "What Skeptics Don't Know Refutes Them." *The Pacific Philosophical Quarterly* 65 (1985): 86–96.

Luper-Foy, Steven, ed. *The Possibility of Knowledge: Nozick and his Critics*. Totowa, N.J.: Rowman & Littlefield (forthcoming).

Moser, Paul K. "Justified Doubt Without Certainty." *Pacific Philosophical Quarterly* 65 (1984): 97–104.

Naess, Arne. *Skepticism*. London: Routledge & Kegan Paul, 1969.

Nozick, Robert. *Philosophical Explanations*, chapter 3. Cambridge: Harvard University Press, 1981.

Oakley, I. T. "An Argument for Skepticism Concerning Justified Belief." *American Philosophical Quarterly* 13 (1976): 221–28.

O'Connor, D. J., and Brian Carr. *Introduction to the Theory of Knowledge*, chapter 1. Minneapolis: University of Minnesota Press, 1982.

Odegard, Douglas. "Chisholm's Approach to Scepticism." *Metaphilosophy* 12 (1981): 7–12.

———. *Knowledge and Skepticism*. Totowa, N.J.: Rowman & Littlefield, 1982.

Pappas, George. "Some Forms of Epistemological Scepticism." In *Essays on Knowledge and Justification*, pp. 309–16. Edited by G. Pappas and M. Swain. Ithaca: Cornell University Press, 1978.

Rescher, Nicholas. *Scepticism: A Critical Reappraisal*. Oxford: Basil Blackwell, 1979.

Slote, Michael. *Reason and Scepticism*. New York: Humanities Press, 1970.

Sosa, Ernest. "Nozick vs. the Skeptic." In *The Possibility of Knowledge: Nozick and His Critics*, ed. S. Luper-Foy. Totowa, N.J.: Rowman & Littlefield (forthcoming).

Strawson, Peter F. *Skepticism and Naturalism*. New York: Columbia University Press, 1985.

Stroud, Barry. "The Significance of Scepticism." In *Transcendental Arguments and Science*, ed. P. Bieri, R. Horstmann, and L. Krüger. Dordrecht: D. Reidel, 1979.

———. *The Significance of Philosophical Scepticism*. Oxford: Clarendon Press, 1984.

———. "Skepticism and the Possibility of Knowledge." *The Journal of Philosophy* 81 (1984): 545–51.

Unger, Peter. "Two Types of Scepticism." *Philosophical Studies* 25 (1974): 77–96.

———. *Ignorance*. Oxford: Clarendon Press, 1976.

———. "A Defense of Skepticism." *The Philosophical Review* 80 (1971): 198–218. Reprinted in *Essays on Knowledge and Justification*, ed. G. Pappas and M. Swain. Ithaca: Cornell University Press, 1978.

Vinci, Thomas. Critical Notice of Peter Klein's *Certainty: A Refutation of Scepticism*. *The Canadian Journal of Philosophy* 14 (1984): 125–45.

Watkins, John. *Science and Scepticism*. Princeton: Princeton University Press, 1984.

Wittgenstein, Ludwig. *On Certainty*. Edited by G. E. M. Anscombe and G. H. von Wright. Oxford: Basil Blackwell, 1969.

Woods, Michael. "Scepticism and Natural Knowledge." *Proceedings of the Aristotelian Society* 54 (1980): 231–48.

Yourgrau, Palle. "Knowledge and Relevant Alternatives." *Synthese* 55 (1983): 175–90.

Index